1945

The World We Fought For

1945

The World We Fought For

ROBERT KEE

LITTLE, BROWN AND COMPANY

Boston   Toronto

Library of Congress Catalog Card No. 85-50327
First American Edition

Maps by Patrick Leeson

Printed and bound in Great Britain

'This new year of 1945 can be the greatest year of achievement in human history . . . 1945 can and must see the substantial beginning of the Organisation of World Peace. This Organisation must be the fulfilment of the promise for which men have died and fought in this war . . .'

> President Roosevelt,
> *State of the Union Message,*
> *Washington, 6 January 1945*

'There is a spirit abroad in Europe which is finer and braver than anything that tired continent has known for centuries and which cannot be withstood. You can, if you like, think of it in terms of politics, but it is broader and more generous than any dogma. It is a confident will of whole peoples who have known the utmost humiliation and suffering and have triumphed over it, to build their own life once and for all. I like best to think of it as millions – literally millions – of people, young in heart whatever their age, completely masters of themselves, looking only forward and liking what they see . . .

'There is a marvellous opportunity before us – and all that is required from Britain, America and the USSR is imagination . . .'

> Major Frank Thompson,
> *fighting with Bulgarian partisans,*
> *executed by Bulgarian Fascists,*
> *June, 1944.*

'The Allies took up arms in defence of Poland's integrity, and to-day they seek a division of Poland in order to conclude the conflict . . . If such is to-day's reality, what will to-morrow's reality be?'

> *Osservatore Romano,*
> *18 December 1944*

'Another great war, especially an ideological war, fought as it would be not only on frontiers but in the heart of every land with weapons far more destructive than men have yet wielded will spell doom perhaps for many centuries of such civilisation as we have been able to erect since history began to be written. It is that peril which . . . we have laboured and are striving sincerely and faithfully to ward off . . .'

> Winston Churchill,
> *House of Commons,*
> *15 December 1944*

For Georgie, Alexander and Sarah

Contents

Acknowledgements

The sources for every detail in this narrative are to be found in the files for 1945 of the following newspapers and weeklies:

in Britain, *The Times*, the *Manchester Guardian*, the *Sunday Times*, the *Daily Telegraph*, the *News Chronicle*, the *Daily Express*, the *Daily Mirror*, the *Daily Herald*, the *Listener*, the *New Statesman and Nation* and *The Economist;*

in the United States, the *New York Times*, the *Washington Post*, the *New York Herald Tribune*, the *Chicago Herald Tribune* and the *San Francisco Chronicle;*

in France, *Le Figaro, Le Monde, Franc-Tireur, Le Populaire, Combat* and *L'Humanité.*

I am grateful to all the proprietors, editors and journalists of that time who left such vivid material in the public domain.

My thanks are also due for help and encouragement to Gill Coleridge, Ray Roberts, Christopher Sinclair-Stevenson, Jonathan Hill and to the courteous and efficient staffs of the London Library and the British Library Newspaper Library at Colindale. A tribute as well as thanks are due to Topsy Levan for professional assistance far beyond her customary typing skill which was in itself indispensable.

A Chronology of The Second World War

1939

March
31   British Government's pledge to aid Poland 'at once . . . with all the support in their power' if Poland attacked by Germany.

August
23   Nazi–Soviet Pact signed in Moscow.

September
1   Germany invades Poland at dawn.
3   Great Britain declares war on Germany at 11 am; France declares war on Germany at 5 pm.
4–5   Rapid German advance across Poland continues.
9   Germans reach Warsaw.
10   British Expeditionary Force begins to arrive in France.
13   German advance continues everywhere in Poland, though Warsaw still holds out.
17   Soviet Union invades Poland.
27   Warsaw surrenders.
28   Soviet Union and Germany partition Poland.

October
6   Peace offer from Hitler, based on German victory in Poland, rejected by Britain and France.
16   First German air raid on British Isles (Firth of Forth); a few Naval casualties.

November
4   Congress amends United States Neutrality Act to advantage of Britain and France.
13   First bombs on British soil (Shetlands); rabbit killed.
30   Soviet Union invades Finland.

December

9   First British soldier of World War II killed in action.

13 Battle of River Plate.

17 German battleship *Graf Spee* scuttled off Montevideo.

1940

January

Rationing introduced in Britain.

March

12 Finland signs peace with Soviet Union.

16 First British civilian killed by German bomb in Orkney.

April

9   Germany invades Denmark and Norway.

14 British forces land in Norway.

May

9   First German bombs on British mainland, near Canterbury.

10 Germany invades Holland, Belgium and Luxemburg. British troops enter Belgium. Chamberlain resigns. Churchill becomes Prime Minister.

15 Germans break through in the Ardennes; French army in difficulties. Holland surrenders.

24 First air raid by Luftwaffe on British town (Middlesbrough).

28 Belgium surrenders. Evacuation from Dunkirk begins.

June

3   Dunkirk evacuation complete. Over 330,000 British and Allied troops withdrawn.

Norway surrenders.

10 Italy declares war on Britain and France.

14 Germans enter Paris.

16–17 Marshal Pétain forms French Government and asks for armistice terms from Germany. Rest of British Expeditionary Force evacuated from France.

June

22 France signs armistice with Germany.

24 France signs armistice with Italy.

28 General de Gaulle recognised by British Government as leader of Free French.

30 Germans occupy Channel Islands.

July
3   British attack French Navy at Oran and Mers-el-Kebir.
5   Marshal Pétain's Government at Vichy breaks off relations with Britain.
8   Attempted attack by British on French Navy at Dakar.

August
8   Battle of Britain begins.
24   First Luftwaffe raid on Central London.
26   First all-night raid on London.

September
      Battle of Britain won.
27   Japan joins Rome–Berlin Axis.

October
28   Italy invades Greece.
29   British troops land in Greece.

November
14   Coventry air raid.

December
9   British start successful offensive against Italians in Western Desert.
29   City of London set on fire in heavy German night raid.

1941

January
10   Soviet Union renews pact with Germany.
19–30 British and Australians advance further in Western Desert.

February
6   Benghazi in Western Desert captured by British.

March
11   President Roosevelt signs Lend-Lease Bill.
27   Pro-German Government in Yugoslavia overturned.

April
3   British evacuate Benghazi; retreat starts.
6   Germans invade Greece and Yugoslavia.
10   British troops fighting in Greece.
13   Germans occupy Belgrade. Russo–Japanese neutrality pact signed.

| 26 | British and Australian troops in further retreat in Western Desert. |
| 27 | Germans enter Athens. |

May
2	Allied troops evacuate Greece.
10	Hess lands in Scotland.
	Heavy air raid on London.
19–31	Battle for Crete; British, Australian and New Zealand troops evacuate.

June
| 22 | Germans attack Russia. |

July
| 12 | Anglo–Russian treaty signed. |

August
| 11 | Churchill and Roosevelt on board USS *Augusta* agree Atlantic Charter. |

September–October
| | German advance in Russia; before Moscow (Oct. 5th), take Kharkov (Oct. 24th). |

November
| 18 | British start new offensive in Libya. |

December
7	British declares war on Finland, Hungary and Rumania. Japanese attack on US Fleet at Pearl Harbor.
8	Britain and US declare war on Japan. Japanese invade Malaya.
9	Japanese invade Philippines.
10	HMS *Prince of Wales* and HMS *Repulse* sunk off Malaya. Japanese take US base Guam.
11	Germany and Italy declare war on United States.
14	British report Japanese in Burma.
16	Germans retreating before Moscow.
17	Japanese invade N. Borneo.
24	British retake Benghazi in Libya (Siege of Tobruk raised on 9th).

1942

January

21   German counter-offensive in Libya.

23   Japanese land in Solomon Islands.

29   Germans and Italians re-take Benghazi.

February

11–12   German battleships *Scharnhorst, Gneisenau* and *Prince Eugen* escape from Brest.

15   British in Singapore surrender to Japanese.

27–28   Battle of Java Sea. Heavy Allied losses.

March

1   Russians launch offensive in Kersch Peninsula.

8   Japanese take Rangoon.

April

10   Japanese take Bataan (Philippines taken by June).

18   First US air attack on Japanese mainland.

25   German raid on Bath, reprisal for RAF bombing (other 'cultural' raids on Exeter, Norwich).

May

1   British evacuate Mandalay and start retreat from Japanese into India.

4–8   Battle of Coral Sea. Japanese convoy hit.
Japanese on Corregidor (Philippines).

16   Germans take Kersch in Russia.

26   Big German and Italian offensive in Libya.

31   Japanese midget submarines attempt raid on Sydney Harbour.

June

3–6   Battle of Midway Island: US victory over Japanese navy.

12–21   Japanese on Aleutian Islands.

13   After tank battles in Western Desert British retreat (Tobruk taken 21st).

24   Germans 50 miles across Egyptian frontier.

July

1   Germans reach El Alamein in Egypt. Germans take Sevastopol in Crimea.

27   Germans take Rostov.

August

5–31   Germans advancing in Russia; cross River Don on 24th; start
       Leningrad offensive on 28th.
7   Americans land on Guadalcanal.
9   Naval Battle of Savo Island: heavy allied losses.
18   Montgomery in command of Eighth Army.
19   Dieppe raid.
23–25 Naval/Air battle E. Solomons: Japanese broke off.

September

1   Fierce fighting round Stalingrad.
12   Japanese within 40 miles of Port Moresby, New Guinea.
23   Russian counter-offensive at Stalingrad.

October

23   Battle of El Alamein begins.

November

3   Germans and Italians retreating in Egypt.
6–15   Battle of Guadalcanal: US victory: heavy losses both sides.
8   US and British forces land in French North Africa.
11   Germans enter unoccupied zone of Vichy France and send
       troops to Tunisia.
12   Fierce fighting at Stalingrad.
13–19 British advancing in Libya; Tobruk and Benghazi retaken.
27   French fleet scuttled in Toulon as Germans enter.

December

       Fighting in Stalingrad.

1943

January

14   Roosevelt and Churchill meet at Casablanca. 'Unconditional
       surrender' decided on.
18   Siege of Leningrad raised.
25   Red Army takes Voronezh.
31   Field-Marshal Von Paulus and 16 other German Generals
       surrender at Stalingrad.

February

8–16   Red Army successes (Kursk, Krasnodar, Rostov, Voroshilov-
       grad and Kharkov retaken).

March

1–3   Pacific battle of Bismarck Sea: Japanese convoy destroyed.

3–15 Russians retake Rzhev and Vyasma but evacuate Kharkov
      again.

21   Eighth Army attacks on Mareth Line. Red Army takes Byel-
      gorod.

April

7–30 Allied offensive in Northern Tunisia

May

11   Americans on Aleutian Islands.

13   Germans surrender in Tunisia.

June

11–12 Italian Mediterranean islands Pantelleria and Lampedusa
      surrender.

July

5   New German offensive in Russia.

10   Allies invade Sicily.

12   Red Army counter-attack in Russia.

25   Mussolini resigns and is arrested (later rescued by German
      parachute troops).

August

2   End of eight days' intensive bombing of Hamburg.

4–5   Russians retake Orël and Bielgorod.

17   Allied conquest of Sicily completed.

23   Russians retake Kharkov.

25   Mountbatten Supreme Allied Commander S. E. Asia.

(August–December   American progress in Pacific: landings on Solo-
      mon Islands, New Guinea, New Georgia, Gilbert Islands.)

September

3   Italian armistice.

8   Italy surrenders.

9   Allies land at Salerno.

16–25 Russians retake Novorossisk, Briansk and Smolensk.

October

1   Allies occupy Naples.

7   Russians cross River Dnieper.

13   Italy declares war on Germany,

25   Russians retake Dnepropetrovsk.

November

4   Eighth Army and Fifth Army link up in Italy.

6   Russians retake Kiev.

22-26   Cairo Conference (Churchill and Roosevelt).

28   Teheran Conference (Churchill, Roosevelt and Stalin).

December

24   Major Russian offensive west of Kiev.

1944

January

4   Battle begins for Cassino in Italy.

8   Russians retake Kirovograd.

16   Eisenhower appointed C-in-C Allied Expeditionary Force, Europe.

22   Allied landings at Anzio south of Rome.

(January–March   British progress in Burma

January–August   American and Australian progress in New Guinea)

February

3   German offensive against Anzio beachhead.

8–22   Russian successes: Nikopol, Staraya Russa and Krivoi Rog retaken.

15   Allies bomb Cassino monastery.

March

4–10   Big Russian offensive in Ukraine.

6   First big US Army Air Force attack on Berlin.

22   Japanese invade India (driven out by 17th August).

31   Russians enter Rumania.

April

10–18   Russian successes in Crimea (Odessa, Simferopol, Tarnopol and Balaclava retaken.

16   British retake Imphal (India) from Japanese.

May

9   Sevastopol retaken.

June

4   Allies occupy Rome.

6   D-Day. Allied invasion of Normandy.

13   First V1 – Flying Bomb – attacks on Britain.

19–20   Battle of Philippine Sea: Allied victory over Japanese

| 23 | Russians start offensive on Central Front. |
| 27 | Americans liberate Cherbourg. |

July
9	British and Canadian troops capture Caen.
12–14	Big Russian advances in Baltic.
18	British and Canadians break through south-east of Caen in Normandy.
20	Failure of plot against Hitler after bomb planted by Count von Staufenberg fails to kill him.
21	Americans land on Guam (Japanese resistance ends 9 Aug.).
23–26	Russians advancing in Poland; Lublin and Lvov taken.
24	Americans land on Marianas Islands.
27	Americans break through west of St Lô in Normandy.

August
1	Warsaw rising.
12	Germans in retreat from Normandy.
15	Allies land in southern France.
25	Paris liberated. Rumania declares war on Germany.
25–31	Russians advance in Rumania; Bucharest entered 31st.

September
2	Eighth Army breaks through Gothic Line in Italy.
3	Brussels liberated.
4	Finnish armistice with Russia.
5	Russia declares war on Bulgaria.
8	First German V-2 rocket attack on England (landing in Chiswick).
9	War between Russia and Bulgaria ends.
11	First crossing of German frontier by US troops, north of Trier.
13	Allies sign armistice with Rumania.
17	British First Airborne Division landings at Arnhem, Nijmegen and Eindhoven (withdrawn from Arnhem 25–26 September).
19	Americans take Brest.
22	Canadians take Boulogne. Russians take Tallinn (Estonia). British take Rimini.
30	Calais surrenders.

October
4	Allied forces land in Greece.
9–10	Churchill visits Moscow with Eden for talks with Stalin.
14	British enter Athens.
18	Russians enter East Prussia.

19	Americans land in Philippines (Leyte): Japanese ships destroyed in naval battles.
20	Russians and Tito's Partisans liberate Belgrade.
21	Germans surrender Aachen.
23	General de Gaulle recognised by Allies as Provisional Government of France.
28	Allies sign armistice with Bulgaria.

November

22	French take Mulhouse; Americans take Metz.
24	Allies take Strasbourg.
28	Port of Antwerp open.
28–29	First American night air attack on Tokyo.

December

16	Germans start counter-offensive in the Ardennes.
17	Montgomery placed in command American First and Ninth Armies and British Second and Canadian First Armies.
22–23	Germans within four miles of River Meuse.
26	Surrounded American troops in Bastogne relieved.
30	Hungary declares war on Germany.
31	Rochefort in Ardennes retaken by Allies.

1945

January

4	British take Akyab, chief Japanese base in Arakan.
9	Americans land on Luzon (Philippines).
11	Laroche (Ardennes) recaptured.
12	Start of Russian offensive.
17	Russians enter Warsaw.
19	Russians enter Lodz, Cracow.
20–31	Russians take Tannenberg, Bromberg, Gleiwitz in Silesia, Memel and enter Pomerania and Brandenberg.

February

4	Americans enter Manila: Yalta Conference (4–12).
13	Dresden raid.
19	Americans land on Iwo Jima (Japanese resistance ends 17th March).

March

4   Americans in full control of Manila.

7   Americans find undestroyed bridge across Rhine at Remagen, establish bridgehead on east bank.

11   German bridgehead west of Rhine at Wesel finally eliminated.

17   Koblenz taken.

18   Very heavy daylight air-raid on Berlin.

20   British retake Mandalay (Burma).

23   Allies under Montgomery cross Rhine.

27   Last V2 falls on London – at Orpington.

28   Russians take Gdynia. Last air-raid warning in London.

29   Americans take Mannheim.

30   Russians take Danzig and Kustrin.

April

1   Germans surrounded in Ruhr. Americans invade Okinawa (Japanese resistance ends 21st June).

4   Russians take Bratislava. French take Karlsruhe.

5   Russia ends Neutrality Pact with Japan.

9   Russians take Königsberg. Allied offensive opens in Italy.

10   Buchenwald overrun.

10–11 Hanover, Essen taken.

12   Death of President Roosevelt.

13   Russians take Vienna.

16   Belsen overrun. New Russian offensive West and South-West of Berlin.

20   Americans take Nuremberg.

25   San Francisco Conference.

29   Dachau overrun.

May

1   Death of Hitler.

2   Berlin surrenders to Russians. British and Russians meet on Baltic.

3   British take Hamburg; re-take Rangoon (Burma).

4   All German forces in Holland, North-West Germany and Denmark surrender.

5   Rising in Prague.

7   Unconditional surrender of all German forces to Britain, Russia and United States at Rheims, to come into force one minute after midnight on 9th May.

8   VE Day; surrender confirmed by Keitel in Berlin.

9   Prague liberated. Channel Islands liberated.

xxv

June
10 Australians in N. Borneo.
26 UN Charter signed.

July
5   MacArthur completes liberation of Philippines. Polling Day in British General Election.
14 US warships bombard Japan.
16 Potsdam Conference.
26 British General Election results declared. Potsdam ultimatum to Japan.

August
2   Potsdam conference ends.
5   Atomic bomb dropped on Hiroshima.
8   Russia declares war on Japan.
9   Atomic bomb dropped on Nagasaki. Russians cross Manchurian border.
10 Japanese offer to surrender broadcast from Tokyo.
11 Allied reply.
14 Japan accepts Allied terms.
15 VJ Day.

Introduction

The purpose of this book is to give some idea of what it was like, in Britain and the United States, to live through the last months of the Second World War. It is a narrative of the events of that time written for anyone who may be curious about what happened then or who, some forty years later, may have partly forgotten.

My method has been to relay the picture which a reader of British and American newspapers and listeners to radio broadcasts might have received as the year unfolded. This conveys one minor, but I think valuable aspect of history, namely the look of events before later events turned them into history. Newspapers, for all their obvious limitations, often preserve details and emphases which can otherwise disappear in the sweep of later overall assessment.

Since this contemporary view is being read forty years later, there is another element at work: the inescapable knowledge of what happened subsequently. This is intended to give another dimension between the lines.

If the book has a theme it is that of any writer: the confused nature of human beings and their qualities and, in particular, the frequent gap between their aspirations and their achievements. The victors in this war, as can be seen here, aspired to something higher than the victory they achieved, namely: the prevention of a Third World War. We do not yet know if, in that, they have been successful.

London 1985

Chapter One

'Have you received the document of unconditional surrender? Are you prepared to sign it and execute its provisions?'

The British Air Chief Marshal Tedder, Deputy Supreme Commander in Europe under General Eisenhower, put the question. The Chief of the German High Command, Field-Marshal Keitel, fixed a monocle into his left eye and held up the document.

'Ja. In Ordnung.'

The scene was a room in a technical school in the Russian-occupied east Berlin suburb of Karlshorst, one of the very few buildings still left standing there. It was three-quarters of an hour before midnight (British Summer Time) on the 8th of May, 1945.

Keitel took the glove off his right hand and signed his confirmation of the surrender of all German armed forces which had been agreed at Rheims the day before.

Tedder and Marshal Zhukov of the Red Army, who had been sitting beside him, also signed. Keitel's tall aide, Oberst-Leutnant Karl Brehm, was in tears. Keitel tried to cheer him up. 'You can make a fortune after the war writing a book about this: "With Keitel in the Russian Camp".'

With his military medals Keitel was wearing the National Socialist Golden Party emblem. In the opinion of those present he was keen to demonstrate both his Prussian and his National Socialist identity.

The Germans left the room, and the table on which the surrender document had been signed was immediately spread with a great banquet in Russian style. This lasted until after 4 o'clock in the morning. Speeches were made.

'When these men left this room,' said Andrei Vishinsky, Soviet Vice-Commissar, 'Germany was torn from the pages of history, but we shall never forget and we shall never forgive.'

Tedder said 'Despite all the trouble the enemy took, trying to divide us and trying to start arguments between us, we have got to Berlin together. May we be allies in victory as well as in war and win that victory which matters more than anything.'

I

The war against Germany was technically to end three-quarters of an hour after Keitel's signature, at one minute after midnight (British Summer Time) on May 9th. But all day long on May 8th (officially proclaimed VE – Victory in Europe – Day in the west) great crowds in London and New York had already been celebrating the end in Europe of the Second World War. Moscow was still waiting.

Keitel's confirmation of the identical surrender signed the day before at Rheims had, like the surrenders of individual German army groups of the preceding days, been made simultaneously to Britain, Russia and the United States. Although it was only to come into force at a minute after midnight on May 9th, at once, in the west, in Churchill's words, 'the cease-fire began to be sounded all along the fronts.' This accounted for the official proclamation of VE Day on May 8th. In the east, however, the Germans continued hourly to take advantage of their technical right to go on fighting against the Red Army, hoping to be made prisoners of the western Allies rather than of the Russians.

The Russians did not announce the completed surrender until after it had officially come into force on the night of May 8th to 9th. The next day, even though some Germans still continued to fight in Czechoslovakia, the people of Moscow celebrated too. They were wildly enthusiastic and ready to share their joy. A *Manchester Guardian* correspondent there wrote that never before had the Soviet people shown their whole-hearted appreciation of Allied help so freely and emphatically. Anyone who looked like a foreigner in Moscow was kissed, hugged and generally fêted. A junior official at the British Embassy was called upon to make a speech by the crowd outside that building and loudly applauded. A British woman journalist on the staff of the paper *British Ally*, out walking with her dog, was chaired, with her dog, all the way back to her hotel. Americans leaving the same hotel were eagerly pounced on and asked to make speeches.

A British staff-sergeant in uniform was seized on by a crowd of women and girls in the street and tossed high into the air with cries of '*Pobeda! Pobeda!*' ('Victory! Victory'!). He lost his hat in the process but, being asked for a song, responded gallantly with *Tipperary*. Later he and others in British uniform taught the Moscow crowds to sing 'Pack up your troubles in your old kit bag.'

Such feelings were of course fully reciprocated. King George VI himself sent messages to both Stalin and President Kalinin, speaking of the new friendship which had been forged between the British and Soviet peoples by the war, and trusting that 'Our wartime comradeship in arms will be followed by ever-closer understanding and

Confirmation of the Rheims surrender in Berlin on May 8th, 1945; Air Chief Marshal
Tedder and Marshal Zhukov
'May we be allies in Victory as well as in war . . .'

co-operation between our two peoples in the years of peace which will follow.'

In London too the scene had been a joyful one, and traditionally British. There was a certain programmed reaction for this sort of occasion in both Britain and the United States – crowds thronging Piccadilly Circus and Times Square, cries for the King outside Buckingham Palace, snow-storms of ticker-tape in Broadway. A pattern of celebration set by the Armistice after the First World War, twenty-six years before, had passed into folk-lore. The models were duly followed now, but in both countries a different mood appropriate to the time was noted by observers.

Bonfires had been lit in both the East End and West End of London on the night of the 7th, and in anticipation of what was expected of them, thousands of soldiers, sailors and airmen with their girls in paper hats had then gathered in Piccadilly to a great bursting of balloons and whirring of rattles.

On the day itself it was reported that there was none of the almost savage plunging into revelry which had marked the more sudden Armistice of 1918. There was little drunkenness and still less aggressive horse-play. The characteristic scene in London, wrote the *Manchester Guardian*, was of little groups of people singing or dancing in the middle of a crowded pavement, molesting nobody, happily absorbed in enjoying themselves. Thousands of family parties drifted along the streets. The paper noticed a particularly large number of parties made up of girls without a man, singing with linked arms: ATS, WAAF, Land Girls and typists. No doubt, it said, uniformed service had produced in many girls a group spirit and a new feeling of their value and independence as women. Quite apart from which the civilian girls had been earning good money which was a contributory cause to their independence.

A. J. Cummings of the *News Chronicle* also noticed a decent orderly spirit in the midst of the general elation. There was self-discipline among the flags and rattles and many-coloured caps.

The crowds were not really noisy, he said, there were just little pools of noise, among the young soldiers on leave, arm-in-arm with their girls. What was being expressed was a conscious sense of release from strain, rather than triumphant exaltation.

But there was enough special quality of joy to send another *News Chronicle* reporter into rhapsodies. 'There has never,' he wrote, 'been a scene to equal this in London, perhaps in the whole world.'

What particularly moved him was the sight of the great crowds who waited for hours in the sun, laughing and picnicking on the grass in the parks around Buckingham Palace. Such crowds had begun to collect

4

'Pobeda, pobeda'; Moscow on May 9th

outside the Palace the day before but with no positive reward. On the 8th of May itself it was different. The balcony of the Palace on which the King and Queen were expected to appear was draped in crimson and gold. And the crowds waited for the Royal Family to emerge through a window which was still seen to be made of the brown boarding and mica which had served as protection against the V-bombs. At 3 o'clock the crowds listened to the voice of Churchill broadcast through loud-speakers, officially telling them of the end of the war against Germany. He paid tribute to 'our heroic Russian comrades, whose prowess in the field has been one of the grand contributions to the general victory.' It was a short and largely factual broadcast without rhetoric, and heard thoughtfully, concluding, as it did, with a sombre reminder:

'We may allow ourselves a brief period of rejoicing, but let us not forget for a moment the toil and efforts that lie ahead. Japan, with all her treachery and greed, remains unsubdued . . .'

It was a note he was to repeat over and over again in the short, often impromptu speeches he made that day, a timely reminder to a people who, even before the victory over Germany, had often found the Pacific war remote. His broadcast had been from the War Cabinet room in Whitehall and when he left there to drive down Whitehall to Parliament Square and the House of Commons he sat perched on the roof of his open car, puffing a cigar and giving the V-sign to the crowds massed on the pavements.

Inside the Chamber, as he appeared behind the Speaker's chair, the packed House rose and broke into ecstatic cheers with wild waving of Order Papers.

Churchill simply repeated the words of his broadcast and added a special tribute to the House of Commons itself which, he said, had 'proved itself the strongest foundation for waging war that has ever been seen in the whole of our long history.' He thanked everyone in the House, wherever they might sit, 'for the way in which the liveliness of Parliamentary institutions has been maintained under the fire of the enemy.' The House then adjourned to the nearby church of St Margaret's, Westminster to give 'humble and reverent thanks to Almighty God for our deliverance from the threat of German domination.' It was noted that during the service Churchill followed with pleasure the words of the 124th Psalm: 'Even as a bird out of the fowler's net escapes away, so is our soul set free.'

Meanwhile, outside the Palace the crowds had been rewarded by the appearance over and over again of the King, in the uniform of Admiral of the Fleet, the Queen in a love-in-the-mist blue frock and a blue halo hat, Princess Elizabeth in her ATS uniform and Princess Margaret in a

Moscow by night; London by day

blue dress slightly darker than that of the Queen. There had been wild cheers and waves and attempts to sing the National Anthem which faltered into 'For he's a jolly good fellow.' In one of the intervals between their appearances the crowd became aware of Churchill's car making its way through them into the Palace. Tears were seen on his cheeks as he drove through. Then, at about half-past five, the Royal Family appeared again and Churchill with them.

He did not wave. He had no cigar and he gave no V-sign. He simply stood there with his head slightly lowered and then made one deep, all-embracing bow to the crowd. As the cheering broke out again and again, the King and Queen and the Princesses waved and blew kisses to the people below.

That evening in Whitehall, with crowds crushed shoulder to shoulder round the fountains in Trafalgar Square while soldiers and sailors played a barrel-organ further up outside the National Gallery with crowds dancing round them to 'Knees Up, Mother Brown', Churchill addressed the crowd directly. 'God bless you all,' he said. 'This is your victory – the victory of the cause of freedom in every land. In all our long history we have never seen a greater day than this.'

In New York, in a curious way, they had seen the day twice. An Associated Press correspondent had broken the official embargo on the story of the surrender at Rheims and from mid-morning on 7th May, close of day in Britain, crowds had started gathering in Times Square, New York, wildly jubilant in the traditional manner, tooting horns among the falling ticker-tape, while the news swept through the city with what the *New York Times* called 'gale velocity'.

'Men and women, utter strangers,' wrote Meyer Berger of that paper, 'shouted it to one another singly and in groups. Housewives screamed it from their windows. Clerks and typists shrilled it from their skyscrapers. Rivercraft east and west took it up with sirens and whistle-blasts. Cabbies pounded it out on their horns . . . men and women ran from homes, hotels and from subways, many unable to decide best how to express their joy.'

A particular feature of the celebration in the garment areas of the city between 30th and 40th Streets was the casting into street canyons not just of scraps of paper, ledgers, playing-cards, stationery, streamers, and ticker-tape but also of bale upon bale of textiles. Silks, woollens, and prints were turning and twisting in the thin morning sunlight. At 35th and 7th Avenue an entire bolt of shining white cloth spun through the air. It bellied in the wind like an enormous sail, curled and writhed and finally twisted itself on an electric sign. 6th, 7th and 8th Streets and Broadway were eight to ten inches deep in multi-coloured fabrics. Parked cars and cabs became draped in it. Men and women tore it from

London garden, VE Day; 'happily absorbed in enjoying themselves . . .'

their hats and from their shoulders. There was dancing, singing and drinking in the streets.

The only thing that gradually began to dampen enthusiasm was the absence of any official confirmation that this was in fact VE Day and that the war was over. And then at 3 o'clock there came through the loud-speakers in the streets a rather desperate appeal from Mayor La Guardia. He implored 'all who have thoughtlessly left their jobs to return to work, and I want to beg them again that having taken time off, not to do it again. Just remain on your jobs as a tribute to the men who have won the war in Europe and as a token of support to the men who are fighting and dying at this moment in the Pacific.'

A hush fell on the soldiers, sailors and bobby-soxers in Times Square as they looked sheepishly at one another and the crowd slowly began to disintegrate. At 5 o'clock the electric sign on the *New York Times* office announced from London that VE Day would be tomorrow.

Tomorrow came, but was inevitably something of an anti-climax even in New York. Rain washed out the morning, but in the evening merry-making crowds duly reassembled, the majority of them soldiers and sailors with their girls, and traffic in streets from the Lower Fifties to the Lower Forties was brought to a standstill except for the move-ment of police patrol cars. Some people who appeared masquerading as Hitler or Mussolini were tactfully escorted out of the crowds by the police.

Apart from the inevitable anti-climax – in itself a double one since the Associated Press had inaccurately reported the breaking-out of peace a fortnight before – there was a general awareness that those celebrating with the traditional enthusiasm of New Year's Eve or Election Night represented only one strand in the nation's feeling. The sense of thanksgiving was essentially a quiet one. Even the crowds in Times Square were shouting: 'Two down and one to go. On to Tokyo!'

Nor was New York itself particularly representative of the rest of the United States. Clifton Utley, reporting from Chicago said there were scarcely more than normal crowds on the streets there, though in Madison Street there was for a time a snake-dance of very young high school boys and girls, chanting: 'On to Japan!' An editorial in the *Indianapolis Star* was headed: 'Onward to VP [Victory in the Pacific] Day' and another in the *Milwaukee Journal* 'We thank God and press on'. Churches were full and the broadcast of the official news by President Truman achieved a rating of 64.1% of all adult listeners, a record in radio history. But he too sounded the same warning note, together with thankfulness: '. . . The victory won in the West must now be won in the

Dancing in Fleet Street . . . and the morning after: a war still to be won

East. The whole world must be cleared of the evil from which half the world has been freed.' Deeper still in people's minds on both sides of the Atlantic was another solemn and awesome thought. It was expressed in King George VI's broadcast which was also relayed, together with the full hour's BBC victory programme, to the United States.

'There is great comfort,' said the King, 'In the thought that the years of darkness and danger in which the children of our country have grown up are over, and please God, for ever. We shall have failed, and the blood of our dearest will have flowed in vain, if the victory which they died to win does not lead to a lasting peace, founded on justice and good will. To that, then, let us turn our thoughts on this day of just triumph and proud sorrow; and then take up our work again, resolved as a people to do nothing unworthy of those who died for us and to make the world such a world as they would have desired, for their children, and for ours.'

The conference which had been meeting for the past fortnight in San Francisco to work out the charter of a United Nations Organisation to safeguard such a lasting peace, merely paused for two minutes of silent thanksgiving and then continued its work normally as did all factories engaged on war production. Reports of the routine proliferations of ticker-tape read strangely beside notices in the same newspapers to the effect that: 'Victory in the Pacific calls for more supplies – more waste-paper . . . speed victory, cheer up wounded veterans. Ask about the V-V Waste Paper programme.' (But in fact ticker-tape was collected for that cause by street cleaners.) 'We must adjust our minds to continuing sacrifices on the home front,' wrote the *New York Times* in an editorial. 'Food shortages are certain to be present for a considerable time to come. It will be frivolous to complain. The use of gasolene in the Pacific theater is prodigious. It will be needed on a larger scale than ever. There can be no joy-riding here. The casualty lists will grow longer.'

And yet something prodigious in the history of mankind had happened. As another *New York Times* editorial on the same day put it: 'The greatest threat that has ever been directed against modern civilisation exists no longer.'

Or, as the *Manchester Guardian* wrote, '. . . We dare not forget that war still rages over one quarter of the globe, that British, Americans and Chinese are being wounded or killed every hour of the day and that many of the men who have won this victory in Europe will have again to screw their courage to the sticking-point and risk their lives in the Far East. Yet . . . it remains a moment of immense deliverance. . . . We have solved nothing. We are no nearer the Golden Age. But at

The biggest cheer of all; Buckingham Palace, May 8th

least we have stopped the onrush of evil. We have won the right to hope.'

It had not been possible to say anything like that only a few months before when the year opened.

It's official; the end of hostilities in Europe, one minute after midnight, May 9th

Chapter Two

There had been then, everywhere, what the English poet W. H. Auden sitting in one of the dives of 52nd Street, New York, had scented at the very start on the 1st September 1939: 'the unmentionable odour of death.'

From Northern Norway where the Germans as they retreated drove the population from their homes – slaughtering even the reindeer they depended on for food – to the lagoons north east of Ravenna where a Canadian Army Corps groped forward through the marshes to contact Italian partisans, from the Atlantic coast where encircled but undefeated German garrisons faced groups of the French Resistance sometimes so ill-equipped they had no boots, to the Vistula where Russian armies were poised for a new offensive which they hoped would finish off the war, from Jugoslavia and the shores of Greece through Burma to the China seas, men were killing each other on a scale never known before. Whereas, in the month in which Auden sat in his 52nd Street dive, a British Prime Minister had pledged that Britain would never use bombs to terrorise civilians, now two or three thousand aircraft a day were being despatched over Germany and doing exactly that. Even in southern England, long since delivered from the worst of German air raids, civilians were being killed at an average rate of more than ten a day by V2 rockets. And as the German 'New Order', giving way before the confused triumph of liberation, began to yield up its terrible secrets in France, Belgium and Poland, people read at their breakfast tables of men and women hung by the wrists until they died, or gassed like vermin, or placed naked in water-filled barrels in sub-zero temperatures to freeze to death or just shot one by one in the back of the neck and pushed forward down cellar steps to slump in heaps.

Death itself was of course quite mentionable. Casualty lists appeared regularly in the newspapers; and the dead were often numbered meticulously: 238,880 British killed and missing up to December 1944 – 362,742 from the whole Commonwealth, 208,917 Americans and 1,911,300 Germans. (It was difficult to be accurate about the total of Russian dead, even to the nearest million, and figures for the Chinese

NUMBER SEVEN

"Yes, you will have to fight as hard as your brothers, my boy, and maybe fight harder."

and Japanese were equally imprecise.) None of these figures included those for the great battle raging at the beginning of the year in the Ardennes where the Americans and British had just succeeded, at least temporarily, in halting a strong surprise offensive which the Germans had launched nine days before Christmas. There the German dead were found piled-up like logs in the snowy forests. Elsewhere, on one relatively insignificant day in the first week of January 1945, the communiqués listed 401 Japanese dead (and 5 captured) on the Philippines island of Leyte; '600 bodies of German officers and men' in the grounds of a textile factory in Budapest; and 'more than 300 Germans and Ustashi dead' and '35 Gestapo men killed' in Jugoslavia. Even in the liberated concentration camps, it was found that the degrading methods by which prisoners had been sent to their deaths were catalogued with bureaucratic precision. The actual odour of death itself, the sweet, corrupt and corrupting stench of the reality, was of course confined to those places where the horrors occurred. It was this that made it possible to take a quite reasoned, everyday approach to what was going on, to take death, at a certain distance, really quite easily for granted.

'For the holy love of God let's listen to the dead,' cried the US army newspaper *Stars and Stripes*, 'let's learn from the living.' The London weekly *The Economist* wrote: 'The year is opening gloomily for the Allies.' Commentators on both sides of the Atlantic echoed its depressing tone. 'We are entering a New Year that a great many people would like to have over and done with,' wrote the *New York Times*. 'A considerable part of it is not going to be happy for any sensitive person . . .' And the London *Daily Telegraph* wrote on the 1st January of 'shadows on this New Year's Day all the darker for being unexpected.'

The paper was referring principally to the great military shock which the American First Army had received from the Ardennes offensive in the previous fortnight. This had burst a hole some thirty miles wide and fifty miles deep in the western front from which Americans, British and French had previously been advancing slowly but steadily and hoping to move into Germany. The American columnist Dorothy Thompson wrote that the German offensive had 'astonished the world.' And it was only on New Year's Day that it could first be seen to have been halted at least for the time being, by the recapture of the Belgian town of Rochefort at the tip of the great bulge in the Allied line.

The attack had for the time being robbed the British and Americans of both strategic and tactical initiative in the west. In the east the Russians, though conducting a localised offensive on the eastern borders of Czechoslovakia and fighting savage street-battles for Budapest against strong German counter-attacks, had elsewhere hardly moved from the line of the Vistula and the borders of East Prussia, to which their last great offensive had brought them in the summer of 1944. The greater part of Poland, for whom Britain and France had gone to war five years earlier, was still occupied by the Germans. And although a New Year message broadcast by Moscow to the Red Army declared that positions had been taken up for the final onslaught on Germany and that 'in 1945 the whole might of the formidable Soviet arms will be flung at the enemy', the American columnist Drew Pearson said it was no secret that US military men were bitterly disappointed at the Russian delay.

In Italy, up which the Allies had been doggedly making their way since the summer of 1943, and where the Germans were still able to mount successful local counter-attacks, the British Commander-in-Chief, Field Marshal Alexander had recently stated that there was little hope of driving the enemy from the Po valley before the spring. That campaign's original objective of striking up into Germany from the south seemed more remote than ever. And although in the Far East the Japanese were now on the defensive with the British Fourteenth Army advancing in Burma towards Mandalay and the American General Macarthur back in part of the Philippines, the size of the task still to be accomplished against Japan, and the earlier Anglo-American agreement to give the war against Germany a certain priority, meant that it was the outlook in Europe that dominated minds at the New Year. There had even been a significant revival of German submarine activity with Allied merchant shipping losses greater than for a long time as the U-boats, using newly-developed technical devices, penetrated further than before into areas of shipping close inshore.

There was also another quite different cause for alarm.

The American commentator, Raymond Gram Swing, broadcasting from London for the BBC said: 'We are going through the most serious crisis of the war.' He was not, however, referring primarily to military or naval matters. What he was above all worried about was a rift which had developed among the Allies, involving particularly an estrangement between Britain and the United States.

Chapter Three

That a touchiness rooted in historical traditional was often ready to pervade Anglo-American relations at some level had been demonstrated the previous November by an otherwise utterly trivial matter more properly of concern, if at all, to a newspaper's literary pages, though the *Washington Post* had made of it a leading article. Noel Coward, describing a visit to some American wounded in his Middle-East Diary had written of the 'magnificent fighting men' of Texas and Arizona, but had continued that he was less impressed by 'some of the mournful little Brooklyn boys living there amid the alien corn with nothing worse than a bullet-wound in the leg or a fractured arm.' The *Washington Post*, describing him as 'a sort of unpaid propagandist for the British interest,' said that it really seemed as if the time had come 'for our British friends to put Mr Coward on the official payroll, to give him a fat salary just to keep quiet and to keep himself out of print. It would be wrong to say that he is too clever for his own good since his personal fortune has proved that he makes a very good thing indeed out of his cleverness, but it might be accurate to say that he is much too clever for the good of his country.' Similar hypersensitivity now affected more serious differences.

The political situation in countries in Western Europe newly cleared of the Germans was one in which both Britain and the United States, whose first consideration had been simply to get the Germans out, found themselves suddenly on unfamiliar and uncertain ground. A policy had been agreed by which liberated countries should be democratically free to choose whatever Government they wanted, while the winning of the war remained the chief objective. What caused trouble was that the Americans, now playing the greatest international rôle in their history, seemed more concerned than the British about the ideological part of this formula. There had been mounting criticism in the press and elsewhere in the United States of British actions in Belgium, Italy and, above all, Greece.

Elections in liberated countries, obviously, could not be held until the war was won. Provisional arrangements had been made for co-operation between exiled Governments and the Resistance movements. But such arrangements often fitted awkwardly into the complex social and political scene in countries suddenly released from German occupation. Men whose reality had been for years to endure hardship and risk torture and death in a fight, for the highest of patriotic motives, against the whole fabric of their society, now felt that they rather than those from exile who had been no part of such reality had the principal right to determine what the new reality and the new society should be like. To themselves, they had acquired an almost mystical right to responsibility. To have to watch those who had not shared their experience taking charge of events as a matter of course often seemed an affront.

Two features made this delicate situation particularly difficult to deal with. One was the Communist Party – a significant section of the Resistance everywhere – with its well-organised and rationally conceived political ambition for power. The other was the economic disorder which followed liberation. In the words of the London weekly *Economist*, the Occupation had provided 'an air of stability and normality to the material existence of the great mass of peaceful and non-political citizens who shunned the hazards of active resistance.' Where previously there had been a structure, however undesirable, there was now a vacuum.

For many observers it was the need to harness the energy of the Resistance to constructive purposes that seemed to present the major problem. The *New York Times* reporter Anne O'Hare McCormick wrote that most of the Resistance were only nominal Communists, '. . . but unless they are fed, clothed, given work to do and a sense of responsibility, they will certainly become militant anti's, either Communist or Fascist. More than lines on the map, these aggrieved and bewildered youths will make the future pattern of Europe. In dealing with them the Allied Powers are dealing with the future, so far with singular lack of understanding, vision or political sense.'

Only in France had the transition to a new political order been achieved without undue embarrassment, though economic conditions, particularly in Paris were desperate, with severe shortages of food and fuel. This relative success in France was partly due to a certain mystically relevant quality of his own which General de Gaulle had brought with him across the Channel, though even he had difficulty in keeping within bounds the Resistance Movement's thirst for vengeance against collaborators and often quite petty officials of the Vichy régime. Three Resistance officers had to be sentenced, early in January, to long terms of imprisonment for killing at Maubeuge two judicially reprieved collaborators, in order to quieten a lynch mob outside the gaol.

In Belgium no member of the returning exile Government had brought with him anything like General de Gaulle's authority and prestige. A political crisis had developed there by the middle of November 1944 over the disarming and disbandment of left-wing resistance units. Two Communist members of the Government and the Minister for the Resistance resigned and large crowds of demonstrators appeared in the streets of Brussels carrying red flags and hammer and sickle insignia, and singing the Internationale. Arms were not carried openly but the bulge of revolvers and occasionally even the shapes of ill-concealed rifles were discernible under coats and tunics. 'A bas Pierlot!' [the Prime Minister] came the cries: 'Pierlot assassin!' Pierlot's resignation was demanded, together with the formation of a new democratic government, the punishment of collaborators and more food and coal.

Major-General Erskine, the British Allied Deputy Supreme Commander in Belgium had said his troops would intervene on behalf of the Belgian Government if the order to the Resistance to disarm were disobeyed. Some of the crowd broke through to the Government buildings and there were casualties among them when the police fired. On the 29th November a National Day of Protest was called against the Pierlot Government, together with a General Strike. Columns of demonstrators began advancing on Brussels from different parts of the country and steel-helmeted British troops moved out to disarm them. In Brussels itself British tanks protectively surrounded the Chamber of Deputies within which the Pierlot government succeeded in obtaining special powers by a democratic vote of 116 to 12. The situation was momentarily de-fused by this and by the continued physical and moral support of General Erskine and the British army.

An instinctive American inclination to detect in all this a display of British imperialism was effectively countered by Churchill in the House of Commons when he drew attention to the fact that General Erskine was acting under the orders of his Supreme Commander, the American General Eisenhower. But the incidents caused some heart-searching in the States and a columnist in the *Washington Post* wrote: 'It is certainly most unfortunate that the Pierlot régime found itself compelled to depend on Allied intervention to keep under government control Communists and other leftish elements of the Belgian Resistance. It is not the Allies' official policy to impose any Government on the peoples liberated from the Nazi yoke . . .' This principle of non-intervention, he maintained, had to be emphasised over and over again; otherwise it was morally impossible to insist that the Soviet armies should respect the same principle.

The British did not escape so unscathed from American criticism in their next intervention which followed only a few days later. They were to incur a rebuke from the State Department itself.

In that part of Italy which had been occupied or 'liberated' by the Allies, the Allied Control Commission had transferred political authority to a coalition Italian Government headed by Signor Bonomi, a Premier of the pre-Fascist era whose Cabinet now included leaders of all the main democratic parties – de Gasperi (Christian Democrats), Nenni (Socialists) and Togliatti (Communists). At the end of November, Bonomi had appointed as his Foreign Minister the veteran anti-Fascist Count Sforza, a man who had spent twenty years in exile as an opponent of Mussolini, principally in the United States. Italy was still technically a monarchy, awaiting a referendum on that institution in the future, and Sforza's republican views were well-known. It was generally accepted that in pursuance of these he had intrigued against the Badoglio Government, which had replaced Mussolini after the armistice, and that his hostility to Badoglio contradicted an earlier pledge he had given Churchill to co-operate with it. But Sforza was on good terms with Bonomi. Now the British diplomatic representative in Italy (who had recently assumed the status of Ambassador as a gesture of British recognition to the dignity of the new Italian democracy) made it clear to the Italian Government that Britain regarded Sforza as politically unreliable and undesirable as Foreign Minister. A deputation of Italian Ministers, including de Gasperi and Togliatti, called on the Ambassador to try and make him reverse this view, but failed. Bonomi's new Italian Government had no alternative but to bow before what amounted to a British veto.

The exercise of this veto had caused dismay in the United States where Sforza was highly regarded and nonetheless so for his republican views. The dismay was compounded by an ill-judged performance by Anthony Eden, the British Foreign Secretary, in the House of Commons, in which he appeared to confuse Sforza's hostility to the Badoglio Government with a totally unfounded accusation of intrigue against the Bonomi Government. Count Sforza, said Eden, was 'not a man that gives us confidence' and when Aneurin Bevan said that Britain was manifesting the same reactionary attitude as it had done in Belgium, Eden replied, somewhat inconsequentially, that there was no parallel since Belgium had been an ally and Italy our enemy. Another Labour Member called out that Sforza had been fighting Mussolini when Eden had been supporting him. Eden replied sarcastically that since Sforza had been in the United States throughout that period he must have found the battle very hard.

American newspapers were already voicing strong expressions of unease. A leading article in the *Washington Post* spoke of the increasing 'bewilderment of Americans concerning Allied policy in Italy. . . . Most Americans,' the *Post* continued, 'will feel Eden should have been more specific in his accusations, thereby exhibiting what the Declaration of Independence calls "a decent respect for the opinions of mankind".' The next day a columnist in the paper said that the real reason for the veto against Sforza was that he had manifested too much independence, and the article went on to express fundamental mistrust of British political attitudes. 'The British Government's anti-fascism,' it said, 'is of much later origin than Sforza's and its roots are pragmatic rather than ideological. Great Britain has never opposed Fascism as such (witness British policy towards Franco) . . .'

The State Department itself issued a pronouncement saying that the US Government 'has not in any way imparted to the Italian Government that there would be any opposition on its part to Count Sforza. Since Italy is an area of combined responsibility we have reaffirmed to both the British and the Italian Governments that we expect the Italians to work out their problems of government along democratic lines without influence from outside.'

The rebuff to Britain was unequivocal, if restrained. Edward Stettinius, US Secretary of State, refused to make any further comment at his Press Conference. But other Americans were less diplomatic. The columnist Marquis Childs wrote: 'Winston Churchill and the clique around him want to believe that you can put a little paint and a little varnish on the old order and prop it up in place again. It won't prop.' 'British policy in Italy today,' wrote the *Washington Post*, 'and the same is true everywhere in the Mediterranean, is to see that Governments are established which are willing to do Britain's bidding. . . . The rôle which Britain is playing in Greece differs only in degree but not in kind from the rôle she is playing in Italy.'

Events at that moment occurring in Greece were, for Americans, as well as for a sizeable liberal opposition in Britain herself, rapidly substantiating this view. There had been no democracy in Greece since the dictatorship established by General Metaxas under the King in 1936. The Government restored by the Allies after the German withdrawal was a royal one though committed under its Premier, Papandreou, to a democratic system. It met difficulties at once on its return to Athens when the powerful left-wing and largely Communist units (ELAS) of the Resistance's political Popular Front (EAM) refused, in spite of an earlier agreement, to disarm when ordered to do so. Their reason was that right-wing elements were not being disbanded as the agreement also stipulated. ELAS converged in strength on Athens itself.

On the 4th December 1944 in Athens the Greek police fired on a

24

crowd shouting 'Democracy!' and protesting against the disarming order on ELAS. The police were acting under the orders of a Government which had full British support, and British Sherman tanks and armoured cars were out in the streets though they did not themselves fire that day. Fifteen demonstrators were reported killed and 148 wounded.

Inevitably the British tanks themselves were soon in action. Three days after the trouble had begun it was unofficially estimated that 171 people had been killed in Athens and 395 wounded.

In the United States many saw these events as further evidence of British imperialism once again sinisterly at work. A letter-writer to the *San Francisco Chronicle* complained that 'American boys spilled their blood in Europe to protect the mighty Empire.' And the *Chicago Herald Tribune*, long a critic of Britain, did not now spare the American President. 'Mr Roosevelt's fine purpose,' it wrote, 'at least since 1937, has been to preserve the British Empire. Now that the end has been achieved, and at very high cost to us, the State Department discovers that Britain is stepping out on her own to dominate as much of the world as she can, and this apparently amazes the State Department.'

As British support for the beleaguered Government in Greece hardened, with RAF Wellingtons and rocket-firing Spitfires and British naval guns intervening in the fight against the ELAS forces trying to take control of Athe.., American voices became more strident still. 'No more shameful pages of history can be written,' declared a letter-writer to the *Washington Post*. '. . . The British people are losing their friends and the loyalty and gratitude of the nations they freed because the British Government is a government of reaction . . .'

'Something very like a crisis exists beneath the surface in the relations between the Allies who are fighting this war,' wrote Marquis Childs, 'and there is no use in trying to conceal it with cheerful statements that all is well. . . . It is for the post-war future that this present crisis bodes ill. I believe that most Americans who think about these things are deeply troubled about the turn of events in Occupied Europe.' He said that people all over the United States and not just in Washington were asking: 'Isn't it just the same kind of game of power politics that they are playing over there? Are things really so very much different from what they were in 1938 and 1939? . . . A profound doubt is beginning to assail millions of Americans. We do remember the Atlantic Charter and the Four Freedoms. While it may be, as I think it was, a war for our survival, to most of us it was more than that . . .'

Another rebuke, though tactfully implied rather than stated, now came from the State Department. Churchill had said in the House of Commons that it was for Greeks to decide whether they wanted a

25

Monarchy or a Republic, and whether they wanted a Rightist or Leftist form of government. Secretary of State Stettinius now commented pointedly that he was in full agreement with this. But when asked if he also endorsed that part of Churchill's statement which said that if necessary the British army would be used to prevent the creation of a Communist dictatorship, Stettinius declined to comment further. He equally refused to amplify his remarks when asked if he condoned the use of British tanks and 'planes against ELAS.

Churchill himself maintained: 'Democracy is not a harlot to be picked up in the street by a man with a tommy-gun.' *

Americans had also for some time had further cause for criticism of the British in an area that was even more difficult, for it involved relations with the third member of the Grand Alliance: Soviet Russia. In the House of Commons debate Churchill had once again made clear, as he had done before, that he was in favour of redrawing the eastern frontiers of Poland in such a way as to admit Russian claims to all territories east of the former Curzon Line (i.e. virtually those which they had occupied in September 1939); compensation would be given to Poland from German territories in the west. Senator Brooks of Illinois had already expressed US anxiety succinctly. 'The American people,' he said, 'did not send their sons abroad to fight and die for the safety of Great Britain nor to fight and die for the triumph and extension of Russian influence. The cream of America has been de-spatched to fight and die for American safety primarily and for the safety and welfare of humanity.'

Churchill's support for Russia's claim to a large area of eastern Poland put the US State Department in a quandary. Hitherto it had evaded the issue, saying the United States' approach was that the matter of frontiers should be settled after the war. As Barnet Nover of the *Washington Post* wrote, it was maintaining 'a prayerful silence, hoping like Mr Micawber that something would turn up . . .' He went on: 'Since the Polish problem could not be ignored at any meeting of the Big Three, Churchill's stand means that President Roosevelt would either have to accept the Anglo-Russian thesis on this question or, by rejecting it, increase the pressure on Allied unity . . . This is the sorry pass to which the *mañana* complex in our European relations have brought us. The chickens of indecision are coming home to roost.'

At his next press conference, Secretary of State Stettinius merely said

*Defending British policy in Belgium against a charge from Aneurin Bevan that British intervention there was unwarranted because there had been no threat to democracy Churchill had replied: 'I should have thought it was hardly possible to state the opposite of the truth with more precision.'

that he could not make any comment on Churchill's Polish remarks but promised to give a statement 'soon' on United States policy with respect to British and Russian moves in Europe. He did however make the announcement that there would be a Big Three meeting in the latter part of January, 1945 or early February.

Critics of both Britain and the Roosevelt Administration were in full cry. Senator Taft of Ohio said, 'It looks like the end of the Atlantic Charter and the return of power politics.' Senator Reynolds, a Democrat from North Carolina, said it was disheartening to find Churchill 'acquiescing in the dismemberment of a people for whom he advised going to war.' There were demands in Congress for a US statement on Poland that would make the Administration's position clear, and Representative Barry, a Democrat from New York, urged the State Department to 'inform Churchill that Poland is an ally and not an enemy nation, and that we Americans haven't suffered more than half a million casualties to divide Europe between Great Britain and Russia.' Representative O'Toole, another Democrat from New York, said that he had written to both Churchill and Stalin saying that recent political events 'portend an early renewal of this war,' a view which was shared by an unnamed diplomat who had just commented to the columnist Marquis Childs: 'We are racing just as hard as we can for a Third World War. It will come in ten or fifteen years.'

Voices increasingly bitter against Britain joined the chorus. Representative Gavin from Pensacola complained of Churchill's being apparently 'content to let us throw thousands of our boys into action to carry on the fight, hundreds of whom are liquidated every day.' And he had said this even before the start of the German Ardennes offensive, the brunt of which was soon being borne by the Americans. Senator Brooks talked of America sending her sons to push Germany back while both Britain and Russia were 'engaging in a race for the future balance of power on the European continent.'

The United States had just drafted men between the ages of 26 and 38. Senator Wheeler, a Democrat from Montana, declared: 'It is hard for me to understand why we, with the biggest army in the world, should find it necessary to draft more men when we have four times as many in the war as the British.'

Meanwhile Stettinius issued his promised declaration of the State Department's view on Poland. This hedged carefully between criticism of Britain and any positive ideological commitment of its own. The first part said that the United States stood 'unequivocally for a strong, free and independent Polish State with the untrammeled right of the Polish people to order their internal existence as they see fit.' But it went on to say that it had consistently been the United States Government's policy

27

that questions relating to boundaries should be left in abeyance until after the war. However, the United States would have no objection to a mutual agreement on the future frontiers of Poland reached by those United Nations directly concerned, since this would make an essential contribution to the prosecution of the war against the common enemy. If, as a result of such agreement, the Government of the people of Poland were to decide that it would be in the interests of the Polish State to transfer national groups, the United States Government, in co-operation with other Governments would assist Poland insofar as practicable in such transfers. The statement concluded: 'The United States Government continues to adhere to its traditional policy of declining guarantees for any specific frontiers.'

Senator Johnson, a Democrat from Colorado, commented understandably: 'This language is all very bewildering and confusing. The fault must be mine.' The *Chicago Herald Tribune* commented: 'There is nothing in this record of power politics which should astonish anyone who knows how Europe has been run for at least half a dozen centuries. The only people who should be astonished are those who were so naive as to believe that the world after the war would be organised in accordance with the principle of self-determination laid down in the Atlantic Charter . . .'

The *Chicago Herald Tribune* correspondent in Washington even reported that there was a disposition in some quarters there to ascribe the American reverses in the Ardennes to 'the preoccupation of Great Britain and Russia with their manoeuvrings in European power politics.' And the *Washington Post* itself reported that it would be foolish to deny a flare-up of isolationist sentiment in the United States in recent weeks.

Even the most sober voices were alarmed at the general drift of events. The former Under-Secretary of State, Sumner Welles wrote in the *Washington Post*: 'As the year 1945 dawns, the American people face a future which seems less certain than at any moment since the war began. At the very time when our armed forces are making their greatest sacrifice to speed the final victory, the objectives for which they fought seem less assured then they did three years ago. There has become evident a wide and growing rift in the basic political understanding between the three major Allies. Unless the rift is restored no lasting peace settlements can be concluded.'

Other voices were less tactful. A letter in the *San Francisco Chronicle* claimed how 'yesterday in her dark hour England whimpered for aid against the arrogant. Today, the winning of her last battle made certain by the blood and wealth of America, England is arrogant.' Had the US, this letter argued, gone all out to destroy Japan first, and let Russia and

England be bled weak against the German military might, America today would be 'pounding Japan into the dust, enhancing its prestige to overshadow that of Russia and England. Had America this rightful present, she would not today be merely a bewildered partner in making half of Europe safe for Communism and the other half safe for British Imperialism.'

The rising tone of American criticism had been incurring increasing resentment in Britain. The London correspondent of the *New York Times*, Raymond Daniell, reported a whole series of articles in the British press comparing United States' efforts in the war unfavourably with Britain's – 'oblique digs in Uncle Sam's ribs,' he called them, 'in reprisal for the current vogue of twisting the lion's tail in the United States.' The British press and people, he said, were 'behaving like a misunderstood husband. . . . They are in a mood to cast aside old family ties to woo the Soviet Union seriously, regardless of any jealous outcries from Washington. The British people and Government are "fed up" as they say here, with being lectured on the moralities of European politics.' And the year ended with a broadside from Britain all the more remarkable for coming from an organ of the press long noted for its willingness to understand the US point of view and to explain this where necessary to the British people.

'With every outburst of righteous indignation in America,' wrote *The Economist*, 'the ordinary Englishman gets one degree more cynical about America's real intentions of active collaboration, and one degree more ready to believe that the only reliable helping hand is in Soviet Russia. This is the popular, the instinctive reaction. . . . The effect of each of these recurrent spasms of Anglophobia is to raise, each time more seriously, the question of the extent to which British policy can safely be shaped in reliance upon American collaboration. Just how much British safety can be gambled on American goodwill?'

The *Yorkshire Post*, pleased that someone had at last spoken out on behalf of Britain 'in the face of bitter and often unfair criticism of British policy,' commented: 'We do not mind being lectured by Americans within reason (since this is an old American custom), but we want to know how far we can rely on them in future for the maintenance of peace and world trade for the good of all.'

The fear was that American commitment to responsibility for the post-war peace would fail as it had failed after the First World War when, for all President Wilson's 14 Points, Congress had refused to ratify the Peace Treaty and the US had never become a member of the League of Nations.

As one of the earliest *Times*'s leading articles of the year had put it: 'The real question at issue in Europe is not whether politics there, as everywhere else, will be governed by considerations of power, but whether American power will be one of the effective and permanent factors governing them.' And the *Yorkshire Post*'s article was headed: 'Will America Kindly Say?'

President Roosevelt gave a press conference that same day. He skilfully evaded any direct comment on *The Economist*'s article by saying that he had not seen it. He admitted that there were differences of attitude among the Allies – some important, some unimportant – but wondered whether it was really desirable to talk about such things out loud. On the general question of principles about which the Allies might or might not be divided, he reiterated a standpoint he had taken up before, namely that the Atlantic Charter with its delineation of the Four Freedoms and in particular the right of all peoples to choose the form of government under which they lived, was to be regarded as a statement of the ideal like the Ten Commandments, rather than of something that was easily attainable.

There did however emerge from this press conference further hope of an event in the future which might defuse the growing tension at the highest level. The President had earlier that day told Senator Berkeley and other Congress leaders that he was hoping to meet Churchill and Stalin some time 'soon'. Asked at the press conference what 'soon' meant, Roosevelt with characteristic playfulness, merely replied that if you examined the words 'soon' or 'anon' they would be found to have approximately the same meaning.

Thus 1945 which most Allied commentators thought, in spite of setbacks, would bring ultimate victory over Germany, revealed from the start the first serious heart-searchings since 1939 over the aims for which the war was being fought. Recognition, as a result of the Ardennes offensive that the fight was going to be much harder than had at one time been expected, merely compounded the sense of moral disturbance.

A correspondent from Virginia wrote to the *Washington Post* on the last day of the old year to say that he had spent Christmas Day 'thinking of our soldier boys . . . thinking of their discouragement now that they know that they are not fighting for freedom and liberty of peoples as they were told they were. Knowing that this World War Two is but a campaign, as was World War One, in the shifting of nations, in the building of empires and will settle nothing of any duration. . . . The foundation of World War Three is laid,' he concluded, 'with England the best-hated nation in Europe.'

The *New York Times* made a brave attempt to put the new unease into perspective and to examine difficulties between the Allies with a sense of proportion. Because, it said, of the prospect of a unilateral settlement in Poland, the fact of British 'interference' in Greece, the British rejection of an Italian Foreign Minister whom the Italians had chosen for themselves, and 'because half of the British Press has lost for the moment its sense of proportion and its temper, because misery, want, unemployment still dominate large parts of Europe as aftermaths of a still-unfinished war, because nations stirred to their very depths by years of hardship and torture and humiliation do not settle down as quickly as we wish . . . civilian voices are beginning to be heard on our side of the Atlantic, proclaiming mournfully that all is lost.' This, the paper argued, was not so.

'We went to war,' it continued, 'to defend ourselves against aggression. We did not tell our boys when they were drafted that they were being taken from their schools and farms and workshops to maintain a particular frontier in Europe or Asia, or to draw a better frontier in its place. We went to war because two savage enemies had made war on us. It is preposterous to say,' concluded the *New York Times*, 'that by winning the war, regardless of anything that may come afterward, we shall not have accomplished a great and good purpose, commensurate with whatever cost it may entail. We shall have preserved our independence as a nation. We shall have kept our friends and helped to keep our friends alive. We shall have served a world in which democracy can live and breathe. We shall have turned back the greatest threat that has ever arisen to the spiritual and moral values of western civilisation. All is not lost when this is true.'

All the same, the immediate outlook was dispiriting. 'Anglo-American relations,' commented the *Manchester Guardian* with some understatement, 'seem rather unhappy just now.' 'Military victory when it comes,' wrote the London *News Chronicle*, 'may be followed not by co-operation but by sharp inter-allied tension.' 'We are in a fine mess,' said the American columnist Dorothy Thompson.

But the BBC's American commentator Raymond Gram Swing thought it preferable that such differences should appear now 'rather than that we should conceal our differences and have them disillusion us and the world at the end of the war. Now, we can work under the pressure of war, under the pressure of the need of allies, and under the still greater pressure: the challenge of knowing that men must still die by the tens of thousands.'

The real danger of course, which such a comment seemed to disregard, was that the very need to find agreement under this pressure of war might result in mere cosmetic agreement all the more likely to disintegrate in peace.

Chapter Four

Some of the tens of thousands still to die must have been among the crowds who welcomed the New Year with traditional revelry on New Year's Eve in Times Square, New York and Piccadilly Circus, London. New York police reckoned that three-quarters of a million people turned out in the dank fog and soaking rain of Times Square. There they witnessed the restoration of a small traditional ceremony in abeyance since the United States entered the war in December, 1941. The lighted globe on the top of the Times Tower which had then been switched off was aglow once again so that on the stroke of midnight it could be lowered, as every year between 1908 and 1941, to be replaced by the New Year flashing out boldly into the night: now, 1945. This was seen as a measure of confidence that the globe could henceforth remain lit until victory and peace were achieved, and cheers and screams and roars from the crowd greeted the simple transformation scene.

Nevertheless journalists noted that for all the large sums of money being spent in New York movies, theatres, night-clubs and restaurants, and the determination to have a good time 'written on the faces of the hurrying throng,' it was a 'reasonably subdued crowd of merrymakers,' and that they welcomed the New Year 'hopefully but warily.' Robert Waithman, in an American Diary for the London *News Chronicle* wrote: 'This New Year's Eve in America is rowdy and uneasy. The reckless noises almost cover up the common anxiety; almost but not quite . . .' War casualties, he pointed out, were higher than at any time in American history, and were going to continue.

There were harder times ahead for American civilians too, with a butter shortage looming, a need to cut sugar consumption and the possibility of clothes-rationing. A system of rationing shoes was in fact already in force, allowing three pairs a year, but a rumour that the effectiveness of the ration 'stamp' was about to be reduced had led to a recent rush of panic-buying. Moreover, the Office of Price Administration had just announced rationing for a number of foods hitherto points-free. Canned or bottled fruits, vegetables, all beef, as well as top grades of lamb, veal, pork, ham and bacon were now rationed together with butter, margarine and cheese. American civilians were going to have to put up with less food in the next three months than at any time since the beginning of the war. Hardship was not to be excessive. They were in fact eating seven per cent more food of all kinds than they had averaged between the years 1935 and 1939. It was just that under the shock of the Ardennes disaster and other disappointments, a number of basic assumptions about the invulnerability of the American way of life seemed suddenly in question.

'The blunt truth is,' wrote Walter Lippmann, 'that all of us – and I know of no exceptions – have underestimated the power of our enemies. We have allowed ourselves to see things as we wished to see them, and not as they are. Now we must see them as they are, and find in the truth not comfort and ease but steadfastness and resolution.'

The United States Government now showed resolution by an Order banning all horse-racing in the United States from January 3rd until further notice. Previous records for the amount of money spent on betting were at once beaten day after day at Tropical Park, Miami and at Fair Ground, New Orleans, as the deadline approached. John Lardner, the syndicated columnist, wrote that he didn't think James Byrnes, the War Mobilisation Director, realised what a cultural gap he was creating by his decree. Lardner said that his own personal experience of the twenty million-odd people who bet on horses in the States was that seventeen and a half million of them talked and thought of nothing but horses and betting; the other two and a half million talked about horses and the weather. 'The plight of the latter,' he wrote, 'will not be completely cruel. . . . There will be an ample and uninterrupted supply of weather for some time to come.' But he was worried about the others, even though there was consolation from the continued racing in Cuba and Mexico.

Further cultural setbacks of this nature were not anticipated. Such sports as professional football and baseball, wrote the *New York Times*, were 'safe for the time being from any outright Order suspending them during the war.' It was possible, though, that the closing of the race-tracks would be followed by a curtailment of passenger train services in the United States. The Director of the Office of Defence Transportation declared that 'needless passenger movement is getting to the point where it is embarrassing the war effort.'

In Britain, where train passengers had for years been told to ask themselves whether their journey was really necessary, horse-racing remained sacrosanct. But in all other respects Britons were suffering from much more severe wartime deprivations than Americans, as the Washington columnist Drew Pearson pointed out to a public whose Congressmen and newspapers had come to look at their cousinly ally with less than cousinly feelings. A planned use of British civilian clothing coupons, wrote Pearson in the *Washington Post*, entitled a man to buy one suit every two and a half years, one shirt every nine months, one pair of socks every five months, and a pair of shoes a year. A woman could buy a dress every nine months, a piece of underclothing every four months, a nightgown every four years and a pair of stockings every two and a half months. Further limitations on consumer goods included one kettle every three and a half years, and one knife, fork and spoon every five years, while virtually no basic petrol ration was available.

What Pearson did not say was that in the city of Leeds specifically, but also in many other big cities in Britain, the black market, for a number of people, removed much of the austerity from the nominal regulations.

'You can buy almost anything you like in the Leeds black market,' wrote a *News Chronicle* reporter, and he cited suit lengths up to £8, silk stockings at £2 a pair and whisky at £4 a bottle. The *Yorkshire Evening News* reported that those who travelled the country extensively said unhesitatingly that what was going on in Leeds was 'going on in every other city in this land.' The Deputy Chairman of the Leeds Watch Committee said that in Manchester and Liverpool you could even buy shipments before they were landed. The Board of Trade said they brought a thousand prosecutions annually and sent a larger number of 'cautionary letters.'

Similarly, although food rationing in Britain was much stricter than in America, acceptable ways round the system were not unavailable. A poem by Allan M. Laing in the first *New Statesman* of the year, entitled 'A Grace for Black Market Turkey' was in the form of a parody of a well-known Church of England hymn:

> Let us with a knowing wink,
> Praise the Lord for food and drink,
>   Who His choicest gifts doth send
>   Unto them with cash to spend.
>
>   · · · · · ·
>
> Praise Him Who, with broadest mind,
> Saved us all from being fined;
>   Who, by giving us thick skin
>   Spared us consciousness of sin.

The passing of a little extra cash now and again for the occasional delicacy – if only a few extra eggs – was in fact hardly considered black market at all. The serious black market was for those with contacts as

The Alliance: good individual relations, but 'the American people did not send their sons abroad to fight and die for the safety of Great Britain.' Baseball at Harrow

well as plenty of money, and was thus by definition out of the reach of many people for most of the time.

There was no way round other hardships. German rockets were still falling on south-east and even occasionally north-east England, killing people in churches, hospitals, houses, pubs and cinemas. 367 people had been killed and 847 injured in December and the numbers were to be higher for January.

In the United States there was no more than a fairly remote possibility of any such experience. It was true that the C-in-C of the US Atlantic Fleet had just said that some buzz-bomb attempt against New York or other east coast cities was quite likely within thirty to sixty days, either from some of the three hundred U-boats in the Atlantic or from long-range 'planes, but he did not envisage any very serious consequences.

'They might,' he said, 'try to hit the Empire State building to cause panic. They may kill a few people and cause some damage. But they won't be able to launch more than ten to twelve rocket-bomb attacks.'

So far the most direct attention Americans had received on their own soil from the Germans had been from eight Nazi saboteurs, who had been caught in 1942 – six of them being subsequently executed. But then on New Year's Day 1945 came the news that two Nazi spies had recently landed by rubber boat from a German submarine which had entered Frenchman's Bay on the coast of Maine. One of the landed spies was a discharged US merchant seaman who spoke without a trace of foreign accent, unlike the other, a former German Telefunken employee in South America. Both were well-equipped with dollars and forged papers but both were arrested through the combined vigilance of a small New Hampshire boy and the FBI before they could assemble short-wave radio sets to any purpose. But again the relatively favoured position of the United States on the home front was what the incident stressed. And a certain innocence was emphasised by the comment from the Director of the FBI itself, J. Edgar Hoover, who said that a great many persons seemed to think that the war was over, but this and 'certain other matters' would dispel that idea.

Perhaps because people in Britain had over the years become acclimatised to greater hardships and worse setbacks than Americans, and because habit had enabled them to evolve a readier sense of practical and moral compromise with both, they appeared to confront the difficulties of the New Year with greater equanimity. In any case no journalist remarked on anything but frenzied jollity among the thousands of British and American servicemen and their girls who danced round a boarded-up Eros statue in Piccadilly Circus as the New Year approached, or linked arms to form long crocodiles singing and yelling down Coventry Street to Leicester Square, only reluctantly breaking to let cars and taxis pass. For the first time since 1939 a dimmed-out version of street lighting was permitted. Just before midnight GIs stopped their 'Yippees' to shine their torches on the Guinness clock which had been neon-lit before the war. The singing and shouting was hushed for the last minute of the old year. Then the first stroke of the New Year was greeted with an outburst of cheering and the singing of *Auld Lang Syne*, and the dancing continued. It was a sober if joyful crowd with only a few whisky bottles discernible. The *News Chronicle* described it as 'the craziest, warmest, most turbulent New Year welcome of the war,' with crowds singing *Roll Out The Barrel* and *Yankee Doodle* and dancing *Ring-a-Ring-o'-Roses* around white-helmeted US military police. As the *Chronicle*'s man in the States was to report, though some quarters said that Anglo-American relations had dropped to their lowest level in living memory, 'this does not seem so at individual level.'

At one individual level indeed it was possible to number the successes. The magazine *Good Housekeeping* and the Office of War Information in London estimated that in 1944 there had been between 12,000 and 15,000 marriages between GI's and English girls. For the benefit of the latter they issued a *Bride's Guide to the USA*. This began with the sensible advice: 'Change your pronunciation if it causes misunderstanding, otherwise don't.' It warned the brides that American humour was sometimes different from English and had to be taken calmly. The 'kidding', it said, was not all that easy to get used to, but you had to learn to take it. 'Dress your smartest,' it enjoined, 'for your first interview with the in-laws, and remember that, except in the smallest villages, lipstick is expected.' It warned of the likely differences in behaviour of spectators at a ball game from those at a cricket match, and also emphasised an important difference in attitudes to children between Britain and the United States. In the United States children were expected to do better than their fathers, while in Britain the ideal had in the past often been for children to tread in their fathers' footsteps.

The Guide might also have prepared the GI brides, but did not do so, for the greater prevailing sensitivity in the States to the issues and difficulties of war by contrast with the more resigned acceptance of problems in Britain. But the greater comforts of the society into which they were moving amply compensated for its more febrile wartime mood.

Above all what the GI brides were leaving behind was shabbiness.

'Shabbiness,' wrote the *Manchester Guardian* in a survey of London life, 'has descended deeply upon us. Much of London is still plaster-faced, so without paint that it looks dingier than other cities. Scarcity of cosmetics and corsets and good stockings affects the appearance of our hard-working women, and the upper middle-class West Londoner who used to be quoted as an exemplar in male dress has at last settled deep into shabby and ill-mended costume and his pre-war wardrobe fails and fades. . . . In the bitter Christmas weather many girls went without stockings. At night now there is more light to reveal our shabbiness. In December here the lights went sufficiently on for one to see the cab on the opposite side of the street and now motor-car lamps are legally unmasked.'

It was the shabbiness perhaps which encouraged a certain introvert preoccupation with difficulties which, though significant in contrast with those imposed on Americans at home, were petty beside what had to be endured at the time in almost every country of the European continent. In Holland, four-fifths of which was still under German occupation, food for the civilian population was down to 700 calories a day and even in Allied Paris there was a desperate shortage of potatoes and flour. In Britain bread was still unrationed. Nevertheless here the minutiae of war-time regulations commanded permanently serious attention.

It was announced at the beginning of January that in planning clothing for school-children in the coming term, it would not be possible to draw in advance on the coupons which were to become valid on the 1st of February. Further information disclosed however that the quality and quantity of boys' woollen underwear was slowly improving, and a fairly good supply of blazers could be expected by April, but so much labour had been switched into the manufacture of demobilisation suits for the end of the war that tailored overcoats and suits for boys could now take up to three or four months.

A comforting domestic concession was announced on the first day of the year. Furniture removals by road were to be allowed to take place up to a distance of 120 miles instead of the previous sixty. This was 'to relieve hardship to the public'. On the other hand, before the first week of the year was out, the Minister of Agriculture announced that milk would have to continue to be rationed until 1949, and the Ministry of Fuel and Power was issuing warnings that in the prevailing freezing weather (which provided some compensation for skaters in London parks), there was an extremely heavy strain on gas and electricity services and the public were asked to be careful in their use of them, particularly between 8 and 10 o'clock in the morning. In Paris, where except in military offices almost no central heating any longer functioned and people huddled indoors in overcoats, they were lucky to have electricity for their fires for a few hours during the course of the day.

The pattern of crime in Britain inevitably reflected the nature of the times. It was not that the criminals often turned out to be soldiers, either British or American. (Two early domestic murders of the year – those of a London taxi-driver with a cleft chin and of a land-owning former diplomat – were the work of GI's, and a soldier burglar of the Wiltshire regiment was given three years for striking an 84-year-old woman in the course of his crime.) But the quality of the crimes themselves was often a product of wartime conditions. Thus a gang of three well-dressed girls were operating in Piccadilly Circus to relieve US servicemen of their relatively lavish pay, usually between the hours of 11.30 p.m. and 1 a.m. Their technique was for one of the girls to approach the GI and talk to him while the two others came up from behind and pinnioned his arms, enabling her to seize his wallet. In Hornsey there was an outbreak of stealing toys from children in the street because there was such a ready sale for second-hand toys of all kinds. The practice was for the thief to prowl about suburban streets until he saw an unaccompanied child holding a toy. He would then stop the child and pretend to admire it, making off with the toy when it was handed over for inspection. Other thieves were simply snatching toys from children's hands or from perambulators parked outside shops.

The black market gave rise to many convictions, not only of major operators but of many minor ones too for the receiving of often quite mundane goods, the shortage of which in the shops made their un-authorised retail a profitable business. Thus when 21,912 lipsticks were stolen from Cyclax, Limited, a street trader was fined £20 for receiving nine dozen of them marked five shillings each, which he was selling for three shillings and sixpence. Against the bigger operators a major campaign had been announced for 1945.

One particular war-conditioned crime had, however, lately receded in incidence. The three hundred or so rate-subsidised British Restaurants still in service in the London area, providing over a quarter of a million meals a week, now suffered much less from the petty pilfering of crockery and cutlery to which they had been subjected during the air raids. People then who had lost their homes had regularly come to this source of civic benefit to replace the cups and knives, forks and spoons which had disappeared under the rubble.

A different type of special wartime 'crime' was in the news in the first week of the year. 127 workers at the Walker-on-Tyne Naval Shipyards who had gone on strike there while employed under the Essential Works Order, were fined ten pounds each with ten shillings costs and fourteen days to pay for doing so.

They refused to pay, declaring that they would continue to stay out since it was their right as trades unionists to do so, and the eminent lawyer, Sir Patrick Hastings, was briefed to represent one of them in a test-case.

Individual refusal to work could be dealt with more summarily. A twenty-year-old girl artist of West Brompton, Pamela Lorden, was sentenced in January to six weeks' imprisonment without the option of a fine for failure to comply with a Ministry of Labour direction to attend for interview at Fulham Road Institution as a cleaner.

Less easy to get at were the 20,000 building workers out of a total of 130,000 at work on bomb damage repairs, who by the 3rd January had still failed to turn up for work after the Christmas holidays. The borough of Camberwell alone had 600 absentees on that day. These men, too, were employed under the Essential Works Order and their absence was badly holding up repairs to London's war damage. It was revealed on the first day of January that the number of working days lost in strikes in the previous year had been over three and a half million, the worst figure for over ten years. The greater number of them had been lost in the coal industry: 2,466,000.

*

A political truce between the three main parties had existed in Britain since the summer of 1940 and voices were raised from time to time for the ending of it. *The Daily Telegraph*, in its New Year's Day leader, censured these, saying 'how irrelevant were their shrill cries' beside the news from the Ardennes.

'Perhaps,' the paper went on, 'there will be a wider and fuller admission that the last quarter of an hour before victory must be as unrelaxed as the time spent under the menace of defeat.'

By the terms of the political truce, when a by-election occurred the candidate of the party which had previously held the seat was un-opposed by the previously unsuccessful parties in that constituency. Three by-elections were pending in January and the truce was to continue; but in one of the constituencies, Chelmsford, the seat was to be fought by a new left-wing party, Common Wealth which had already acquired three Members of Parliament by playing no part in the truce. This very phenomenon was itself an indication that beneath the surface of the political truce forces for social change were not quite still; Blake's 'Jerusalem' had been adopted as the national anthem of 5,835 Women's Institutes with their 288,300 members. *Picture Post* commented that 'it expresses the members' resolve to work for a better Britain' or as the poem itself had it, 'to build Jerusalem in England's green and pleasant land.'

Welfare from the cradle to the grave? Women's Institute calling for the New Jerusalem

It was nearly ten years since there had been a general Election in Britain, by far the longest gap in her democratic history. The prospect of the end of the war, however tantalisingly delayed, brought with it the certainty of a General Election soon afterwards.

Chapter Five

For the time being, however, political minds in Britain were still largely preoccupied with matters outside the country. There was, for instance, the question of whether the official policy for Germany of 'unconditional surrender' was in fact the right one or whether it would simply make the Germans fight harder. There was also the more general question of what to do with the Germans after the war. Above all there were those problems in the liberated countries which were causing the awkward relations between Britain and America, particularly the problems in Greece.

This subject could arouse just as bitter emotional criticism of British policy in the British press and in Parliament as it did in the United States. The Common Wealth candidate in the Chelmsford by-election announced that he was going to make British policy in Greece his main election issue. A letter in the first issue of *Picture Post* for the year ran, 'In time to come we shall no doubt, tell the German people that they should have stopped the evil committed in their name. If we, the British people in much easier circumstances, cannot stop the evil committed in our name in Greece, we lose any right to cast one pebble.'

A leader in *The Times* on 5th January, looking at political developments there while British forces continued to fight the left-wing resistance units of ELAS in and around Athens, found few grounds for hope. The awkward issue of the monarchy had, it was true, been eased by a visit to Athens by Churchill and Eden, and the appointment of a Regent, Archbishop Damaskinos, until a decision could be taken on the King's return. The Cabinet under Papandreou had been replaced by one headed by the long-exiled and Republican-minded though authoritarian General Plastiras. But the new Government also made demands that ELAS should disarm and withdraw from Athens, and these were again rejected by ELAS on the grounds that this Government too refused to disarm its own right-wing brigades and the police and gendarmerie, which, ELAS maintained, were largely riddled with Fascists and former collaborators. *The Times* itself thought the Plastiras Cabinet insufficiently representative.

British forces had been gradually, though bloodily, gaining the upper hand. On a single day in the previous week they had killed 300 ELAS men and taken 800 prisoners. They had just recaptured the main power station and were working to restore electricity to Athens.

'A British victory,' wrote *The Times*, 'which no doubt can be ultimately assured, will offer no solution . . .'

The tone of the article was little different from one appearing in the *New Satesman* that week entitled 'Still Shooting Our Friends'. We were killing, it argued, some of the most spirited of our Allies.

'While fresh troops are landing in Piraeus we are postponing any hope of quickly driving the Germans out of north Italy, Rhodes and Crete . . . with every shot we fire on this sacred battle-ground against Greek friends, we make it harder for any of our Allies whether in France, America or the Balkans, to trust or respect us.'

But a letter from a British soldier then in Greece, honestly enough printed in the same issue, denied that ELAS had seriously fought guerilla warfare against the Germans.

'That is the first mistake some of our foolish and misinformed MP's are making. Instead, they hoarded arms of all types, some of which were sent by us, and, of course, when the time came, refused to hand them in. The reason, of course, being that they had used them to terrorise the population and needed them for their *coup d'état* which they started at the beginning of December. They are a small minority, but very well organised, and have succeeded in holding down large areas by purely gangster and terrorist methods. . . . There seems to be some doubt about British action here, at home, but there is none on the spot; the alternative would have been to stand by and see unparalleled massacre.'

The Times and both the Liberal papers, the *Manchester Guardian* and the *New Chronicle*, continued to take the *New Statesman*'s view. But the *News Chronicle* too was honest enough to report that when on 5th January ELAS resistance virtually ceased in Athens and their units withdrew to the hills, there were cheering and deliriously happy crowds thronging the streets of northern Athens, enjoying unrestricted movement for the first time for a month. 'The British master-plan to squeeze out the rebels with a minimum of destruction has been an unqualified success,' wrote its correspondent. On the 12th January a truce was signed by the British General Scobie and representatives of ELAS. For some days previously however ELAS had been taking several thousand civilian hostages away with them.

Meanwhile, fighting more relevant to the defeat of Germany had been in full swing in the Ardennes in one of the bloodiest battles of the war.

*

44

Fighting in Athens; British troops shooting their friends

An ELAS casualty

Rundstedt's troops though checked, continued stubborn resistance against American attempts to squeeze from north and south the great bulge in the Allied line. It was thought that they might well still prove capable of a new initiative. The British, already jolted out of complacent feelings that the war was approaching its end, and inspired by the American defence and relief of Bastogne, a communications centre surrounded in the salient, learned at the beginning of the year, after a censorship delay, of some involvement of their own in the fighting, though the Americans bore the brunt of it throughout. At the moment of the most extreme penetration of the German advance, on Christmas Eve, when spearhead Panzers were racing for the bridgehead town of Dinant on the Meuse and had come within four miles of it, British armour had managed to reach Dinant twenty-four hours ahead of them and had fanned out in front of the river to strengthen the American defence just in time. It was now learned too that part of the British Second Army, diverted south from Holland, was helping the Americans batter against the northern perimeter of the bulge, while two American armies hammered similarly from the south, principally at the indentation they had already made for the relief of Bastogne.

It was at Bastogne that the American Brigadier-General McAuliffe of the 101st Airborne Division had sent an already famous reply to the German Commander's surrender demand. He told how this had come about to the BBC on January 3rd.

'When we got it we thought it was the funniest thing we ever heard. I just laughed and said, 'Nuts', but the German Major who brought it wanted a formal answer; so I decided – well, I'd just say "Nuts", so I had it written out: "QUOTE, TO THE GERMAN COMMANDER: NUTS. SIGNED; THE AMERICAN COMMANDER UN-QUOTE". . . . With the kind of troops I had, a Commander can do anything.'

The reply, which plainly displeased the Germans, was almost as much a source of dismay to the Agence France Presse who, looking around for a way to translate it, finally arrived at: '*Vous n'êtes que de vieilles noix.*'

Now from Bastogne the Americans were hoping to meet the American and British forces driving towards them from the north and thus turn Rundstedt's bulge into a pocket within which a substantial proportion of his forces would be trapped.

But as late as the 2nd January, the London *Times* Military Correspondent found it difficult to decide even whether the Germans were withdrawing to a shorter line or concentrating for a renewed offensive. German leadership, he said, had always excelled in bulge tactics and the enemy might still be hoping to make more out of the present

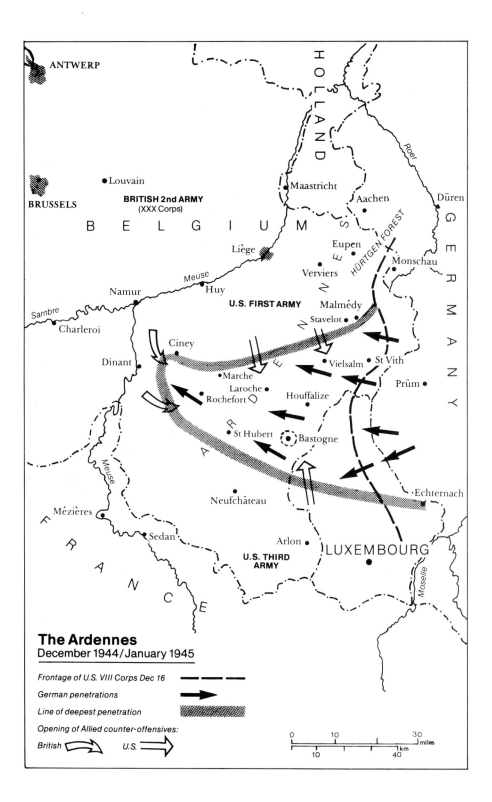

ANTWERP

BRUSSELS

Louvain

HOLLAND

Maastricht

Aachen

Düren

BRITISH 2nd ARMY
(XXX Corps)

B E L G I U M

Roer

G
E
R
M
A
N
Y

Liège

Eupen

Monschau

HÜRTGEN FOREST

Verviers

Meuse

Namur

Huy

U.S. FIRST ARMY

Malmédy

Stavelot

St Vith

Sambre

Charleroi

Ciney

Marche

Vielsalm

Prüm

Dinant

Laroche

Houffalize

Rochefort

St Hubert

Bastogne

A
R
D
E
N
N
E
S

Meuse

Neufchâteau

Échternach

Mézières

Sedan

Arlon

LUXEMBOURG

U.S. THIRD
ARMY

Moselle

F
R
A
N
C
E

The Ardennes
December 1944/January 1945

Frontage of U.S. VIII Corps Dec 16

German penetrations

Line of deepest penetration

Opening of Allied counter-offensives:

British   U.S.

0   10   30
                              miles
                        km
      10   40

situation. The change, he thought, was likely to come soon; 'With both sides sparring for position as they are, he would be a bold man who would prophesy what form it will take. We have not yet regained the initiative, though our prospects of doing so look better.'

And even two days later he was writing of the German tank counter-attacks against General Patton's thrusts around Bastogne, 'Whether these are delaying actions or cover further offensive intentions by the enemy cannot yet be judged, but it is clear enough that there is still plenty of fight left in him.'

The American Secretary for War in Washington, Henry Stimson, issued the warning that Rundstedt was 'keeping enough troops in the area for another punch to be possible.'

The continued German capability for further offensive in the west was shown by a number of new strong diversionary attacks which they now launched many miles south of the bulge, in the Saar basin, in the Wissembourg gap and in the northern Vosges. In the Saar, German forces attacking on a 70-mile front pushed back the US Seventh Army some fifteen miles at times in a few days from places which had taken months to gain.

That German war production too had maintained a remarkable resilience under the continual bombing was also revealed by the Ardennes offensive, in which the Germans made use of an improved mark of Tiger tank and their new Me 262 twin-engined jet fighter. On New Year's Day itself the Germans had taken the Allies by surprise in the air with a mass attack on airfields behind the lines at low level, putting more aircraft into the air in the West on that day than at any other time since 1940. The quality of the German flying had been erratic and their own losses were considerable but it was clear from reports that came through the censorship that Allied losses, too, had not been negligible. Hanson Baldwin of the *New York Times* wrote that the attack had caught some airfields by a surprise comparable with that enjoyed by the Germans at the beginning of the Ardennes offensive, and added that Allied losses were 'by no means light.'

The real shock of this air attack, like that of the Ardennes offensive itself, was to the complacency of Allied morale. Alan Moorehead, the *Daily Express* correspondent in Brussels, had looked out of his window that New Year's morning and having become used to seeing nothing but Allied aircraft fly past was amazed to see half a dozen Messerschmitts come dashing past the cathedral and the Gare du Nord at ground level, apparently making for the airfield. There had been no air raid warning and no anti-aircraft fire. He reported that some Allied medium bombers had been caught on the ground by machine-gun bullets and cannon-fire. Few bombs had been used. Some of the

German aircraft flew into the ground. The Allies finally claimed 364 German aircraft destroyed – the greatest loss to the Luftwaffe, it was said, since the war began.

Not only the strength of German resistance but appalling weather made the fighting in the Bulge particularly desperate. Apart from the difficulties this created on the ground, it at times deprived the Allies of their air superiority by preventing all flying. All war correspondents stressed the constant flurries of snow, the iron-hard frozen ground and the sub-zero temperatures.

Robert Barr of the BBC talked to a sergeant just back with a patrol that had been out crawling on their stomachs through the snow and hiding in snowdrifts for ten to fifteen minutes at a time. Their clothes – the sergeant had on three sweaters, two scarves and a stocking cap pulled down over his ears – had been frozen stiff when they got back and they were thawing them out over a stove. Out in the street he pointed out the route his patrol had taken. 'The woods over there,' he said – and Barr felt he could almost throw a snowball into them from where he stood – 'are thick with Germans.' They were dug into foxholes with branches of pine trees over them for camouflage and warmth.

Christopher Buckley of *The Daily Telegraph* wrote that 'the curtain of snow descending upon the Ardennes battlefield adds to the eeriness of the operations. The patrols who feel their way forward along forest roads seeking contact with enemy rear-guards find their visibility has abruptly decreased. . . . Sooner or later they will stumble upon a road-block – six or eight broad tree-trunks piled across the road. Somewhere behind the road-block, concealed among the trees there may be, there probably will be, a tank capable of blowing any armoured car into pieces. . . . And somewhere close up to the barrier of felled trees are two inconspicuous little slit trenches. An infantryman might stumble right on to them before he realised that each contained a German sniper.'

Cornelius Ryan, also of the *Telegraph*, described something of the weight of the Allied counter-offensive: 'The whole 200 square miles at the nose of Runstedt's offensive is just one slithering mass of shells; they pour in from all sides in one continuous stream.' The German divisions were so tightly packed there, he said, that one US artillery section had fired as many as 18,000 shells in six hours. 'In nearly every forest that the Americans have reached around the Bulge,' continued Ryan, 'they have found piles of German dead. In one covering only a small area, 700 . . . in another copse, 300.'

S. L. Solon of the *News Chronicle* also described the great weight of destruction to which the Germans had been subjected in the slowly-narrowing waist of the salient. 'The destruction of equipment,' he wrote, 'is on a tremendous scale. The dead lie in grey heaps on frost- and snow-covered fields.' But the Germans alive in the west of the salient whom the Allies were trying to cut off were fighting furiously.

The Ardennes fighting of this first week of the year could be summed up by saying that though it had seen Rundstedt's salient further reduced and the Germans suffering heavy losses, there had been no disaster to them. In fact in spite of immense pressure from south and north little success had yet been met in trying to close the salient's waist. General Patton thrusting from the south towards Houffalize to try and cut one of the two main east-west supply roads, had had no more success than the Americans and British trying to cut off the other road that ran through Laroche. The only place where any sizeable number of German tanks had been cut off so far in the whole battle had been at the apex of the salient round Rochefort.

While the Allies, relieved that they had contained Rundstedt, still wondered what he might be capable of next, veiled recriminations had of course already been voiced about the way in which they had been taken by surprise before Christmas, particularly when they had had complete air superiority. Such recriminations inevitably floated, however tactfully, in the direction of the Supreme Allied Commander, General Eisenhower. No one suggested that he was actually to blame but on the 5th January, A. J. Cummings writing in the *News Chronicle* suggested that, though very popular, Eisenhower did perhaps have too many administrative problems on his hands and that the British General Montgomery should be his deputy.

'If he is not to be chosen,' he went on, 'some changes of method and personnel are obviously essential in the Allied military brains trust in the west. The main battle has only just begun, the crisis is not past.'

The following day it was revealed that Montgomery had in fact been in command of both the American and British armies on the northern perimeter of the bulge for many days as they fought their way forward through the heavy snowstorms in visibility of less than a hundred yards or so among the wooded hills.

That his success there was by no means yet definite, in spite of a three-mile advance and some 1,300 prisoners, was confirmed by the *News Chronicle* reporter Stanley Baron who wrote rather more pessimistically than some of his colleagues: 'In this wearisome world of white through which the battle now rages, there are no developments yet to justify expectations on our side either of a big haul of prisoners or a great tale of damage.'

Montgomery himself, however, was not a man to underrate his own success. He gave a press conference on Sunday, 7th January.

'The battle has been most interesting,' he said, 'I think possibly one

The Ardennes: some of the bloodiest fighting of the war. A knocked-out American tank;
German prisoners taken back under guard

of the most interesting and tricky battles I have ever handled. . . . The first thing to be done was to "head off" the enemy from the tender spots and vital places. Having done that successfully, the next thing was to "see him off" – that is to rope him in and make quite certain that he could not get to places he wanted. . . . He was "headed off" and then "seen off". He is now being "written off".'

Uninhibited, it seemed, about giving the impression that this 'writing-off' was largely due to his own generalship, he was careful also to distribute praise all round. Of his enemy he said 'I used to think that Rommel was good, but my opinion is that Rundstedt would have hit him for six. Rundstedt is the best German General I have come across in this war. He is very good. He knows his stuff.'

And then, since after all it had been American armies under their own Generals who had borne the brunt of the battle, he awarded them his seal of approval too. 'Rundstedt,' he said, 'was really beaten by the good fighting qualities of the American soldier . . . I want to take this opportunity to pay a public tribute to him. He is a brave fighting man, steady under fire and with the tenacity in battle which stamps the first-class soldier . . . I have now formed a very great affection and admiration for the American soldier . . .'

Montgomery's professional ability ensured that he would not have spoken out as he did, had he not felt his confidence justified. Thus by the second week of the New Year it could be safely assumed that the actual danger from the Rundstedt offensive was over. Whether or not the Germans would suffer a major disaster similar to that which they had experienced in the Falaise gap in Normandy in August was, however, still in doubt.

Two days after Montgomery's press conference, with tank battles raging among the swirling snow-storms, there were still no signs of a major German withdrawal. And another twenty-four hours later *The Times* correspondent was writing: 'Over a white countryside, as difficult for fighting as it is beautiful, the business of writing-off the enemy in the Ardennes remains a grim and arduous task.'

There could be no doubt that the salient was shrinking, though villagers in the Ardennes were themselves far from sure that the Germans would not be back again. Four days later when a new American attack opened on the northern part of the Bulge, it became clear that Rundstedt was likely to succeed in withdrawing the greater part of his surviving forces. The Germans were withdrawing, wrote *The Times*, but it was 'not a picture of our men moving in easily behind them'; the enemy were fighting stiff rearguard actions.

They also continued to be capable of offensive actions elsewhere. One of their diversionary attacks to take pressure off the Bulge had

From *Punch*: Shutting the Doors on the Bulge

crossed the Rhine near Strasbourg and when in the second week of the year those French civilians who had immediately fled in panic returned, it was not long before they were wondering whether they had been right to do so. For on the 10th January Strasbourg found itself threatened from two sides, from the new bridgehead twelve miles to the north, and by an attack from the Colmar pocket west of the Rhine from which the Germans had not yet been driven. *The Times* reported from Paris 'increased uneasiness about the position of Strasbourg and the Alsatian plain.' Two days later the *News Chronicle* announced: 'The German threat in the Strasbourg area looms with increasing urgency.' It was not to go away so easily.

On the morning of January 16th American armies driving from opposite sides of the Bulge met in Houffalize. This did indeed mean at last the virtual 'writing-off' of the deep salient which the Germans had thrust into the Ardennes a month before. '. . . The episode of the 1944 German invasion of the Ardennes is virtually finished,' wrote *The Times*.

However, Rundstedt's more or less successfully ordered withdrawal of his troops meant that some of them at least were now available for use further south. And the extraordinary continuing resilience and tenacity of German military strength was manifested in further successes in the Strasbourg area. 'Strasbourg: Serious Turn' was a *Manchester Guardian* headline as late as January 20th. The German forces in the Wissembourg Gap had succeeded in linking up with the bridgehead north of the city. There was now, according to the paper, a formidable increase 'in the striking force which the enemy can use in an attempt to drive to the west.' The threat to Strasbourg (the loss of which would be a severe further political blow to Allied morale) was now 'unquestionably much more grave.'

Particularly alarmed by the prospects in Alsace were of course its French inhabitants who had given a rapturous welcome to the liberating Allies on their arrival and now found themselves faced with the likelihood of German vengeance.

But within days the danger had receded. The relief was partly due to American and French attacks on the Colmar pocket to the south of Strasbourg which began to make decisive progress. In the northern bridgehead too the Germans, though fighting stubbornly, were forced onto the defensive. But the real cause lay in something other than the pressure of the Western Allies.

'The end of German hopes in Alsace,' was a *Manchester Guardian* headline of February 3rd.

Such hopes had been wrecked by events of far greater magnitude elsewhere. For the last ten days of January, Allied air attacks in the west had concentrated against a continuous flow of German rail traffic moving away from the western front altogether towards the East.

On the 12th January after a thunderous barrage by hundreds of Red Army guns, Russian troops and armour launched at last what the Germans described as 'the greatest attack of all time' on the Vistula. It was this offensive which finally put paid to any possible further German successes in the west and indeed, by the end of January, was utterly to transform the course of the war in Europe in the Allies' favour.

Chapter Six

Even before the start of the Russian offensive, minds on both sides of the Atlantic had been turning increasingly towards thoughts of an eventual peace.

When the year opened it had been difficult to assess rationally exactly when the war in Europe was likely to end. Over-confident predictions made even after the failure of the attempted breakthrough at Arnhem in the autumn of 1944 had been rendered embarrassingly wrong by the Ardennes offensive. That the Allies could have no doubt of final victory seemed obvious, though this very obviousness lent exasperation to the equally obvious realisation that victory was not to be immediate. Probably the most generally held view of the way the war was going as it entered its seventh calendar year had been voiced by Churchill in a New Year message he sent to the Danish Resistance.

'I cannot promise you,' he said, 'that the end is near; but I can say that the Nazi beast is cornered and that its destruction is inevitable. . . . The wounds inflicted by the armed might of the Grand Alliance are mortal.' And he added that the gallant efforts of the Resistance Movements throughout Europe had played their part with the armies, navies and air forces of the United Nations in bringing this about.

(His message received appropriate acknowledgement the very next day when eighty armed members of the Danish Resistance stormed and wrecked the Torotor wireless factory at Charlottenlund, Copenhagen which had been manufacturing the 'magic eye' steering mechanism for V2's. Armed with machine-pistols and rifles and a 20-mm automatic gun they destroyed the pillbox at the entrance, overpowered the guards – some of whom were killed – and wrecked the factory without loss to themselves.)

President Roosevelt in his State of the Union message of the 6th January, struck the same sort of cautiously confident note as Churchill. But the shock of the Ardennes offensive led him to lay greater emphasis on the caution. 'We have no question of the ultimate victory,' he said. 'We have no question of the cost. Our losses will be heavy. . . . We must never make the mistake of assuming that the Germans are beaten until the last Nazi has surrendered.'

There was a defensive note altogether in some of this Inaugural Speech to the 79th Congress which would have struck anyone without knowledge of recent disappointments as surprising. Roosevelt's election victory the previous November had been an amazing achievement. Campaigning as an internationalist, he had been elected President of the United States for a fourth term, on a record poll of fifty million voters. In the elections for Congress, isolationists like Senator Nye of North Dakota and Representative Hamilton Fish of New York had been rejected. Commentators agreed that the election showed conclusively the nation's determination to take part in some post-war international peace-keeping organisation such as had already been sketched-out at a conference at Dumbarton Oaks near Washington in 1944. However, the *New York Times* in a leader on the 3rd January added: 'Only two months have passed since this decision was made, but already the climate of opinion has changed.'

Since the election, American disappointment with British policy in Italy and Greece and what seemed like its cynical attitude to Poland, had been aggravated by the reminder from the Ardennes of what the European war was costing America in lives while much of the war against Japan was still to be fought. This had again brought out many of the querulous doubts on which isolationism traditionally thrived. Senator Reynolds, a Democrat from North Carolina, one of the few isolationists returned to Congress in November, now proudly proclaimed that he was 'more of an isolationist and America-firster than ever before.'

Roosevelt, while on the defensive, made no concessions to such views.

'Always,' he said, 'from the very day we were attacked, it was right militarily as well as morally to reject the arguments of those short-sighted people who would have had us throw Britain and Russia to the Nazi wolves and concentrate against the Japanese.'

The decision to concentrate ground and air forces against Germany rather than Japan was based on the reasoning that Germany was better able to turn her conquests into further ability to wage war. Roosevelt stressed the need for far greater efforts on the part of the United States to carry the war through to final victory. The sharply-rising needs of war production were, he said, being seriously hampered by manpower shortages. He again urged, as he had done before, that Congress should enact a measure for the 'total mobilisation of all our human resources for the prosecution of the war.' He wanted a National War Service law which would enable the four million men then classified medically as 4F to be used 'in whatever capacity is best for the war effort.'

And he turned his mind towards the eventual peace.

'It is,' he said, 'not only a common danger which unites us but a common hope. Ours is an association not of governments but of peoples – and the peoples' hope is peace . . . a peace that is durable and secure. . . . In the future world the misuse of power, as implied in the term "power politics", must not be a controlling factor in international relations. That is the heart of the principle to which we have subscribed.'

It was as if by subscribing to the principle, the principle was established. He conceded that power was a factor in world politics but said that in a democratic world this power would have to be linked with responsibility and justify itself 'within the framework of the general good'.

'In our disillusionment after the last war,' he went on, 'we preferred international anarchy to international co-operation with nations which did not see and think exactly as we did. . . . We must not let that happen again or we shall follow the same tragic road again – the road to a third World War.'

There was some open recognition of realities: 'The nearer we come to vanquishing our enemies the more we inevitably become conscious of differences among the victors . . . I should not be frank if I did not admit concern about many situations – the Greek and Polish for example . . .'

But that was all. The situations were not faced up to. It was as if, somehow, to say that the problems were difficult was all that was really required for their solution.

The Dumbarton Oaks blue-print for a new world peace organisation had involved a Security Council able to take military action if necessary where a threat to peace had occurred. But the all-important question of the method by which countries who were members of this Security Council were to vote had had to be left open as 'still under consideration.' Roosevelt seemed content to cite Dumbarton Oaks as a reason in itself to hope that future discussions would succeed in developing a democratic and fully-integrated world security system; '. . . The aroused conscience of humanity will not permit failure in this supreme endeavor.'

At least after this State of the Union message there could be no doubt of Roosevelt's personal determination to commit the United States to a profound sense of responsibility for the post-war world. However, those who understood the power of Congress to reject anything, including treaties, to which the President might try to commit it, knew that Presidential commitment in itself was not enough. The crucial question, after the President's speech was how the Republican opposition would react.

A foreign policy debate was announced in the Senate for Wednesday,

January 10th and Joseph Harsch talked on the BBC of the isolationist newspapers licking their lips in anticipation and prophesying that their isolationist spokesmen in the Senate would have a field-day at the President's expense. 'But,' as he reported, 'it was not an isolationist field-day; it turned out to be what some future historian may choose to label the "black Wednesday of American isolationism".'

The debate was opened by Senator Arthur Vandenberg, the Republican Party's leader in the Senate, who in the past had been, as Harsch put it, 'rather quietly in the middle on Foreign Policy issues', though some people thought him inclined to isolationism. He now delivered an eloquent and deeply-felt speech which while committing himself and the United States no less unequivocally than Roosevelt to post-war responsibility for the peace, did so with a remarkably sharper edge of realism than the President. He began by saying that this was one of those critical moments in the life of every nation which called for 'the straightest, the plainest and the most courageous thinking of which we are capable. . . . It is not only desperately important to America. It is important to the world. It is important not only to this generation which lives in blood. It is important to future generations if they shall live in peace.'

The clash of rival foreign interests, he said, which had motivated wars for countless centuries, was 'not likely suddenly to surrender to some simple man-made formula, no matter how nobly meditated. . . . We not only have two wars to win. We also have yet to achieve such a peace as will justify this appalling cost. Here again an even more difficult unity is indispensable, otherwise we shall look back upon a futile, sanguinary shambles and – God save the mark! – we shall be able to look forward only to the curse of World War number three.'

He showed more preparedness than Roosevelt to face some of the specific issues which made the reality rather than the aspiration of peace-time unity difficult, and he criticised the United States Government for not having made its position sufficiently clear on a number of these issues simply from fear of contributing to international dissension.

'It cannot be denied,' he said, 'that citizens, in increasing numbers, are crying, "What are we fighting for?"'

The first thing to assert was '. . . that we have not lowered our sights . . . that the smell of victory is not an anaesthetic which puts our earlier zeals to sleep.' And he re-stated those earlier zeals in terms of the Atlantic Charter which, for all Roosevelt's more recent attempts to equate it with the purely aspirational quality of the Ten Commandments, had been communicated to Congress in a signed document by Roosevelt himself on August 21st, 1941 and had been embedded in a

59

joint resolution of all the United Nations on the 1st January, 1942. 'We still propose,' he went on, 'that none of the United Nations shall "seek aggrandisement, territorial or otherwise".... We still propose, outside the Axis, that "there shall be no territorial changes which do not accord with the freely-expressed wishes of the people concerned".... Similarly we still propose to "respect the right of all peoples to choose the form of Government under which they will live.... These basic pledges cannot now be dismissed as a mere nautical nimbus [a reference to the fact that the Charter was first devised personally by Roosevelt and Churchill aboard a battleship on the high seas].... They march with our armies, they sail with our fleets. They fly with our eagles. They sleep with our martyred dead.'

He swiftly put old-fashioned isolationism behind him. World War Two, he said, had 'put the gory science of mass murder into new and sinister perspective.... If World War number three ever unhappily arrives, it will open new laboratories of death too horrible to contemplate. I propose to do everything within my power to keep those laboratories closed for keeps.'

He said that an idealism unshared by other nations was a plain menace which could not be underwritten in the post-war world. It was impractical to expect countries to act on any other final motives than self-interest. The real question was: where did self-interest lie? And he boldly seized on the most difficult example of all the problems facing the United Nations.

'Russia's unilateral plan,' he said, 'appears to contemplate the engulfment, directly or indirectly, of a surrounding circle of buffer States, contrary to our conception of what we were fighting for in respect to the rights of small nations and a just peace.'

Russia's announced reason for this was her insistent purpose never again to be at the mercy of another Germany tyranny, and Senator Vandenberg saw that as a perfectly understandable reason. But what better suited the Russian self-interest in the long term: 'A cordon of unwillingly-controlled or partitioned States, thus affronting the opinions of mankind, as a means of post-war protection against a renaissance of German aggression? Or to win the priceless asset of world confidence ... by embracing the alternative; namely, full and whole-hearted co-operation with and reliance on a vital international organisation in which all of us shall honourably participate to guarantee that Axis aggression shall never rise again?'

Suddenly Senator Vandenberg too could make it all seem simple. 'Fear of reborn German aggression in years to come is at the base of most of our contemporary frictions.... America has this self-interest in permanently and conclusively and effectively disarming Germany and

Japan. It is simply unthinkable that America or any other member of the United Nations would allow this Axis calamity to reproduce itself again.'

He proposed an immediate hard and fast treaty between the major Allies for joint military action on behalf of collective security in the peremptory use of force, if needed, to keep Germany and Japan permanently demilitarised. The US President as Commander-in-Chief should have the right to initiate such action instantly without the need to consult Congress.

On this assumption that the threat of renewed aggression by Germany and Japan was the major post-war problem, all present problems could be unravelled. Unilateral decisions taken out of present military necessity could be accepted as only temporary: they would be subject to final revision in the objective light of the post-war peace organisation which would implement this treaty.

Though the isolationist press immediately repudiated Senator Vandenberg for his betrayal of their cause, his speech was generally accepted as having an historic ring. Speaking as he did for the majority of the Republican Party, the Senator's important immediate contribution was immensely to strengthen President Roosevelt's hand at the forthcoming meeting of himself, Churchill and Stalin. Of this meeting it was still only known that it was to be held somewhere, soon. But on it were now increasingly focused the world's hopes for the future.

In the meantime, leaving aside the immediate major consideration of how and when the war in Europe would be finally won, it was possible to develop some cautious optimism about how the prospects for peace were shaping.

In Greece the truce signed between ELAS forces on the 12th January to come into force at midnight on the 14th had held.

Chapter Seven

Quite apart from the successful conclusion of the truce in Greece, the whole nature of the British intervention there had begun to take on a more acceptable complexion. Only a week before ELAS withdrew from Athens and the Piraeus, many Liberals in Britain had been saying that it was the British Government who should withdraw.

"The fighting in Greece must be stopped,' F. Seymour Cocks, a Labour MP had said at Nottingham on 7th January, 'and our troops should be withdrawn to barracks. . . . A blow has been struck at democracy which people will never forget.'

The Times had declared that there should be no settlement in Greece and no workable Greek Government except with the co-operation and acceptance of that National Liberation Front which ELAS represented. And the *Daily Herald* leader-writer said there could be no doubt that *The Times* spoke for liberal opinion in the country on the subject.

But some hard realities were beginning to penetrate liberal opinion. It was not only serving members of the British forces who were painting a less than classically idealistic democratic portrait of ELAS. The correspondent of the *Herald* itself reported from Athens on 7th January a sworn statement from a Greek priest about hostages, including women, whom he had seen being taken daily by ELAS through Chani Kamboli towards Thebes. He described them as half-naked and bare-footed and said that those who could not walk were being killed in the most inhuman way. The Regent, Archbishop Damaskinos, a man whom Churchill described as 'with his headgear, towering up morally as well as physically above the chaotic scene,' also reported with some anguish what was going on:

'Withdrawing northwards, the other side is carrying thousands of hostages of all ages and both sexes, regardless of the condition of their health, to submit them to unheard-of brutalities in the name of liberty.'

Soon the *Daily Herald* leader-writer himself was changing his tune with, on 10th January, some counsel to the men of ELAS to 'beware of assuming that liberal opinion in Britain and other countries is prepared automatically to endorse their every decision and action.'

It was in the House of Commons on 18th January that the first really coherent picture of what had been happening in Greece was revealed by Churchill. Although, obviously, it could be said to be a partial account since he was defending British policy, yet, substantiated as it was by remarkably detailed evidence of atrocities, it seemed to confirm that ELAS was hardly the liberal democratic force many liberal democrats had assumed. The opposition to British policy suddenly looked much less plausible than a few weeks before. Even Aneurin Bevan, normally a reliable irritant to Churchill in the absence of any official Opposition, confined himself to some less than usually effective interruptions.

Churchill began by saying that never in his wartime experience had he known a British Government to be so maligned and its motives so traduced by the press.

'How,' he asked, 'can we wonder, still less how can we complain of the attitude of hostile or indifferent newspapers in the United States when we have in this country witnessed such a melancholy exhibition as that provided by some of our most time-honoured and responsible journals –' (at this obvious reference to *The Times* there were loud and prolonged cheers) 'and others to which such epithets would hardly apply.' He reminded the House that Britain had gone into Greece on the invitation of a Greek Government in which all parties, including the Communists, were then represented. Since the Germans had left, the principle preoccupation of the small British force that had arrived had been to distribute food, clothing and supplies, a process which involved scattering our troops over a wide area on the coast and at small points inland. The result of this intervention had been that before the outbreak in Athens took place, Greece had been made safe from hunger.

Troop dispositions made for this purpose however had obviously paid little attention to military necessity. Churchill admitted that he had underrated the power of the Communist-directed ELAS. 'I must admit,' he said maliciously, 'that I judged them on their form against the Germans.' He was reproached for this insinuation by one Labour Member with cries of, 'It is not true; it is a slander on the Greeks.'

Churchill replied that from having studied the record with great pains and patience in recent weeks he had undoubtedly come to the conclusion that 'the ELAS armed bands at any rate for the last two years played very little part against the Germans.' They were not to be regarded in the same class as the French or Belgian Maquis or the Italian Partisans. They had kept the arms which we had given them for use against the Germans principally in order to be able to strike in a *coup d'état* when the Germans left and 'make Greece a Communist State with the totalitarian liquidation of all opponents.'

Churchill then recounted the series of painful events which had

63

involved the British forces in open warfare with them – in the course of this happening on the word 'Trotskyists' instead of 'Communists', this, he said, having 'the advantage of being equally hated in Russia'. By the skin of our teeth, he concluded, we had saved the day and with the truce that was now in force there was a hope that the Greek people including EAM or what was left of it and ELAS would be able to talk over their future successfully under the guidance of Archbishop Damaskinos in peace and normal tranquillity.

Fuller details of how ELAS treated their hostages and political opponents continued to emerge. The British Ambassador in Athens, Mr Rex Leeper, had sent a long despatch from which Churchill quoted.

'Ever since the Germans left,' it ran, 'the small but well-armed Communist Party has been practising a reign of terror all over the country. Nobody can estimate the number of people killed or arrested before the revolt in Athens actually began, but when the truth can be told there will be a terrible story to tell. When the fighting began in Athens the brutalities increased rapidly. Men, women and children were murdered here in large numbers and thousands of hostages were taken and dragged along the roads and many left to die.'

There followed some accounts of personal experiences. A Lieutenant Colonel Morrow, of the King's Royal Rifles, had cross-questioned a large number of escaped or otherwise returned hostages at a field dressing station. On Christmas Day a column of them had been collected by ELAS in a suburb north of Athens and after being relieved of their footwear and many of their overcoats were forced to march for days in the dead of winter along mountain roads covered with snow. Every day some died of exhaustion and others were executed. They were left entirely to their own resources for food but the inhabitants in the villages from whom they begged were mostly too terrorised to do more than look on in impotent sympathy. Occasionally they could buy a half-loaf of bread from their ELAS guards at exorbitant prices. However, it seemed inadvisable to reveal possession of money because one woman discovered to have some was deprived of it and shot on the excuse that she had been working for the British. A few fortunate stragglers from this column had been picked up in the last stages of exhaustion, their bare feet in ribbons. Hitherto those no longer able to walk had been executed; but the guards here had been in a hurry and received warning that British armed patrols were on their tail.

'Tell me the old, old story!' cried Willie Gallacher, the one Communist Member of the House. Churchill replied: 'You not only have the pleasure of having it told to you but of reading it in the documents.'

Leeper's dispatch told the story of another column of 800 hostages of whom about 200 had died within ten days. The total number seized, he

Victims of ELAS; a British TUC delegation 'filled with horror'

said, ran into thousands and included many reputable men and women well-known to the Greek public. A great many survivors had by now returned to Athens to tell the tale.

A grisly tale of another sort was told by a Captain R. F. G. Blackler, of the Royal Artillery who, at Peristeri, an Athens suburb, having been informed that a great many hostages had been executed by ELAS and buried in ditches on the outskirts, proceeded to the places where exhumation of bodies had begun and interrogated the cemetery guardian. The latter said that batches of fifteen to twenty hostages had been brought to the north-east corner of the cemetery every day by ELAS and murdered. Their bodies were buried in some disused trenches. Captain Blackler had examined the trenches which extended over some 200 yards and were now filled with earth though trial diggings had uncovered bodies along most of its length. Farther north were more trenches and pits which, according to the cemetery guardian, also contained bodies of hostages who had been executed there. This man estimated that in all some 1,200 to 1,500 people had been executed, mostly with knives or axes. Captain Blackler said that this testimony was borne out by his own examination of partially exhumed bodies which had deep wounds in the back of the head or neck. He said that apparently these hostages had been taken in Athens during the early days of the fighting and were systematically exterminated until the ELAS withdrawal.

There was of course some hope that after the truce such barbarities might be less frequent. But one report from the Greek Red Cross at Salonika described how between 1 p.m. and 2 p.m. on January 16th – two days after the truce – thirty-one ill civilians, of whom seventeen to twenty were dying, were seized by ELAS from the municipal hospital there, loaded on to bullock-carts in their pyjamas – some wearing only pyjama trousers – and taken off to Verroia.

The British Ambassador commented: 'Greek Communists have not only imitated the Germans in taking hostages. They have, and still are, treating them with the ruthless brutality of the Gestapo.' This hideous imitative factor was something on which the *News Chronicle* journalist, Gerald Barry, commented in the *News Chronicle* after interviewing prominent men on the left wing coalition (EAM) side.

'The shootings and the taking of hostages,' he said, 'are now admitted by responsible EAM-ites themselves, from Siantos [their leader] downwards, to have been unpardonable. They explain them but do not attempt to excuse them. . . . Something has happened in Greece, something common in varying degree to every occupied country in Europe. The Nazis have taught the down-trodden people of Europe a terrible lesson. The outbreak of savagery in Greece – and the excesses have not all been confined to one side – is the pattern of Nazi technique observed by tortured minds and reproduced in circumstances of extreme tension.'

Two British soldiers of the Royal Engineers taken prisoner by ELAS while working a pumping station inland as they had been doing for months, had managed to escape from a column of hostages on January 11th and reported that stragglers were shot where they fell. They described the attitude of the ELAS guards to both military and civil prisoners as 'throughout severe and brutal in the extreme.' In the light of such facts, *The Times* which had so noticeably lent its support to critics of British policy when EAM and ELAS had been held up as symbols of the progressive democratic forces in Europe, now partially retreated.

'It was perhaps inevitable,' it commented, 'that the direction of the National Liberation Front should have fallen for the time being into the hands of extremists, because of the accumulated mistrust between Left and Right in Greece and the undoubted, if unfounded apprehension of a reaction with British aid. Those extremists must now recognise that the undemocratic imposition of their own radical settlement is neither tolerable nor acceptable. The grievous ill they have done by their excesses to Greek freedom and reform and to the unity of progressive forces can already be glimpsed. . . . That the cruel disorders of the Civil War have discredited those who were chiefly responsible for starting it, and that punishment for proved crimes will rightly be demanded can be assumed . . .'

The cruel disorder continued. A telegram from the British Consul-General in Salonika dated 27th January reported that the Bishop of Kassandra, who had occupied the See for 37 years, said that ELAS were committing many murders of leading inhabitants in Khalkithiki and that corpses without heads were a common sight. He added that people were now ninety-five per cent against ELAS and would exterminate them if only they had arms. Another message from the Consul-General of the same date reported the Bishop of Xanthi as saying that ELAS was still arresting people daily in large numbers, stripping them of their shoes and most of their clothing and marching them almost naked to the monastery at Zaborba where they were dying of cold and hunger. He said that 500 prisoners had been murdered by an ELAS regiment largely recruited from Bulgarians, six of whom boasted openly of killing 145 prisoners between them. The Bishop of Xanthi too added that the sentiments of the ordinary people were now almost unanimous against ELAS.

Clement Attlee, the Labour leader and Deputy Prime Minister, a man of impeccable humanitarian socialist credentials, chided critics of the Government's Greek policy in the House of Commons. He denied that the Greek Government was a Government of the Right. Almost all its members had been in revolt against the dictatorship, many had been exiled and put in prison. In Greece there had been a forcible attempt by a minority to seize power. Some people who called themselves Left were not believers in democratic methods. It was up to Britain to see that power was not monopolised by the people to whom she had previously given arms.

Another Democratic Socialist, Sir Walter Citrine, Secretary-General of the Trades Union Congress left a few days later with a TUC delegation including representatives of the National Union of Railwaymen, of the Dyers and Bleachers and of the Boot and Shoe Operatives to examine the situation in Greece in person. It did not take long to come to certain conclusions. At a lunch given for him by the Greek Confederation of Labour on the day after its arrival, Sir Walter Citrine declared that it was 'utterly impossible for the British Government to discontinue its responsibilities' in Greece. He had spent that morning interviewing the widows of 41 out of 114 trades unionists who had been murdered by ELAS – 'Red Fascists' he was to call them in his eventual report. The day before he had seen nearly 300 bodies at Peristeri, and had said on the spot: 'I am filled with horror at what I have seen. It was necessary for me to come here to see the naked truth – naked as most of the bodies lying here.'

He had also met 500 Paratroopers of the British Second Independent Paratroop Brigade who had been in Greece since October 14th. From them he heard many stories about ELAS which again were hardly compatible with the idealistic image which ELAS had managed to procure for itself in Britain. He found among the British troops 'great and universal resentment' at what they considered to have been the one-sided and unfair manner in which recent events had been presented to the British public. He heard from them how when they had been pursuing the Germans they had often met ELAS units coming in the opposite direction. ELAS apparently had done little actual fighting, as distinct from carrying out sabotage, against the Germans. Their principal concern had been to seize power and annihilate internal opposition. The troops were unanimously of the opinion that if Britain had not acted as she had done there would have been a wholesale massacre in Athens. The ELAS troops were, the delegation was told by the Paratroopers, 'the dirtiest fighters' they had ever encountered.

A few days later, in fulfilment of the terms of the truce, ELAS returned 1003 British Army and RAF prisoners to Athens. *The Times* special correspondent reported them as being in 'good shape', apart from 50 who were sick. They had made, he said, an excellent recovery from the harassing treatment they had received. They had been given little food and had been made to march long distances in bad weather, deprived of boots. 'The ten to whom your correspondent talked expressed the deepest hatred and detestation of ELAS, not so much because of the treatment they had received, but because of the atrocities which ELAS had carried out against their civilian hostages – some of which they had seen, others heard about.' According to the report of these returned prisoners-of-war there was no doubt that ELAS by their savage excesses had lost a great part of that sympathy which many ordinary people had felt for them when the Civil War first began on December 3rd, the point at which they had achieved virtually complete domination of EAM, a coalition in which they had all always been the dominating influence.

With the return of the prisoners and of at least some of the hostages, and above all with a wider appreciation of prevailing political realities in Greece, the problems for the Allies there began to seem less acute. This impression of settlement was to be confirmed, at least for the immediate future, for Greece itself when an agreement was eventually signed at Varkiza on February 12th between the Greek Government and representatives of the Central Committee of EAM.

By this agreement the Government guaranteed to secure democracy and, 'the suppression of any illiberal law', the restitution of full Trades Union liberties and to lift the prevailing martial law. There were to be free elections and a plebiscite on the monarchy within the year. The Civil Service and all police and security services were to undergo a special purge of collaborators. There was to be a leniently framed amnesty to cover all political crimes committed since the start of the fighting on December 3rd, 1944 though this was to exclude common law crimes 'which were not absolutely necessary to the achievement of the political crime concerned'. Those who did not receive the amnesty could not be prosecuted for the excepted offences after six months in the Athens area, or in the rest of Greece, after the end of 1945. All remaining hostages taken by ELAS were to be set at liberty at once. ELAS itself was to be immediately demobilised and disarmed.

It was a settlement which, while offering some compromise over the sternest demands for vengeance and indeed natural justice, also offered a reasonable prospect for democracy. It rested principally on the exercise of that superior force for which the British Government had been so vilified at home and abroad. 237 British soldiers had been killed in the course of the five weeks' fighting, more than in the entire operation in which they had liberated the country from the Germans.

*

The political barometer in another country where liberation had at one time contained problems of a delicate and, for the Grand Alliance, potentially dangerous nature also now seemed set relatively fair. In Yugoslavia, where at one time the internecine rivalry of two separate Resistance Movements – that of the royal General Mihailovitch's Chetniks and the Communist Partisans of Josep Broz Tito – had presented a political difficulty for the Allies, the problem had been largely resolved as long ago as 1943 when on military considerations, Churchill had decided to back Tito as the most effective force fighting the Germans there. Mihailovitch's Chetniks had thereafter tended to look for support against the Partisans elsewhere, and since the only alternative source lay in the Occupation Forces themselves, they had been led into a series of local accommodations, principally at first with the occupying Italians. Even King Peter, in exile in London, in whose name Mihailovitch purported to be acting, found it necessary to repudiate his General and form a Government under a Doctor Subasitch with instructions to collaborate with Tito's National Liberation Movement. Subasitch had gone to Yugoslavia to see Tito and as a result a new royal Government had been formed in London of six Ministers including two who were representatives of Tito himself.

In November 1944 after another visit by Subasitch to Tito a new agreement between the two was reached and signed on December 7th. This was astutely worded to incorporate aspirations of both royalists and Communists.

'In compliance with the principle of the continuity of the Yugoslav State,' it ran, '. . . and the clearly-expressed will of all Yugoslav nations, demonstrated by their four years' struggle for a new, independent and federative State, built upon the principles of democracy, we desire and make every effort for the people's will to be respected at every step and by everybody . . .'

King Peter was not to return until the people had pronounced on whether he should or not and 'in his absence the Royal Power shall be wielded by a Regency Council.' Tito had agreed that this Regency Council should be appointed by 'a constitutional act of the King' in agreement with Tito as President of the National Committee of Liberation of Yugoslavia and Subasitch as Prime Minister of the Royal Government. The Regency Council were to take their oath to the King, while the Government were to take their oath to the people. An agreed extended Tito-Subasitch Government was to be formed and to continue in being until elections could be held for a Constituent Assembly under a law which would 'guarantee complete freedom of elections, freedom of assembly and speech, liberty of the press, franchise for all and a secret ballot.' Until then the Anti-Fascist Council of the National

Liberation Movement of Yugoslavia would wield the legislative power in the country.

The agreement received, understandably, the seal of approval by Britain, the United States and Russia. (Subasitch had paid a special visit to Moscow to have the agreement endorsed by Molotov.) The fear of Britain and the United States had been at one time – as it was still the fear of King Peter – that Tito, most powerful of all Resistance leaders, with the most effective unified Resistance Movement of any German-occupied country, being a Moscow-trained Communist, would use his power to turn Yugoslavia into a Communist dictatorship. Even the *Manchester Guardian* noted that although Marshal Tito had publicly disowned any intention of introducing Communism permanently into Yugoslavia, 'it is known that there are very extreme elements among his followers, and it is from this that the fear of a Communist Dictatorship arises.'

The Tito-Subasitch agreement was designed to set at rest the minds of any such doubters. The new Government actually stated that it would 'publish a declaration proclaiming the fundamental principles of the democratic liberties and guaranteeing their application. Personal freedom, freedom from fear, freedom of worship, liberty of conscience, freedom of speech, liberty of the press, freedom of assembly and association will be specially emphasised and guaranteed; and, in the same way, the rights of property and private initiative.'

This then, on paper, was to be the new Yugoslavia in federal form which Marshal Tito had brought into being. No good democrat could complain of anything here except possibly that in the circumstances the signature to it of a Moscow-trained Communist like Tito was almost too good to be true. No one however suggested as much, except, by implication, King Peter himself.

The King in fact had still not endorsed the agreement in the second week of January and was reported to be discussing it with his advisers. The *Manchester Guardian* thought that he had been receiving advice from extremists to disown the agreement and to dismiss Subasitch, but thought it hardly likely that he would risk doing so. On the 10th January King Peter paid a visit to Eden and Churchill and the next day he issued a statement giving the agreement only qualified approval, and stating objections both to the suggested form of Regency and to the concentration of legislative power in the interim before elections in the hands of the Anti-Fascist Council of the National Liberation Movement. 'This,' he said, 'suggests a transfer of power in Yugoslavia to a single political group.'

It was made clear at once that this statement had not been drawn up in consultation with the British Government, but that King Peter had decided to issue it before going to see Churchill and Eden. The British Government in fact approved the agreement and had tried to prevent King Peter from issuing the statement. The *Manchester Guardian* commented that 'it was only fair to say' that his doubts about the Anti-Fascist National Liberation Movement's domination by the Communist Party were arguable but that by his peremptory issuing of this statement on the advice of the right-wing against the advice of the British Government he had 'dangerously narrowed his chances of having his views considered.' In a leading article the paper reminded him that minor monarchs in exile had clipped wings '. . . . It is said that the King wants to prevent his country becoming a Communist State; he is going the right way to ensure it.'

There followed demonstrations against the King in Belgrade throughout the night of Saturday, January 13th and into Sunday morning. Crowds marched through the streets carrying placards declaring: 'We don't want the King. We want Tito. Down with the destroyers of our unity!'

Within days the King was to make things much worse for himself by dismissing Subasitch from office for not making the agreement with Tito regally and democratically more watertight. The King did this even though Tito had actually reiterated to him on January 20th his desire to continue to deal 'in a democratic and constitutional way only through the Royal Government.'

Tito now allowed himself to express understandable annoyance in Yugoslavia. 'These are not honest politics but machinations aimed at creating confusion and civil war,' he declared with some plausibility.

But a strange constitutional situation was now disclosed in this clipped-wing Monarchy. For it was by no means clear that Subasitch intended to accept his dismissal, and Churchill in the House of Commons said that if King Peter's endorsement to the agreement could not be obtained, then he would simply be presumed to have given it in order to enable Subasitch to travel to Yugoslavia and together with Marshal Tito, put it into force.

In the end, and auspiciously on what was thought to be the eve of the anticipated Big Three meeting between Roosevelt, Churchill and Stalin, the King gave in. He withdrew his dismissal of Subasitch and a face-saving formula was devised by which the Tito-Subasitch agreement was to be put into effect while 'endeavouring in this to take account of the observations' which the King had made in his statement of 11th January. He accepted the notion of the Regency Council. It was thought that Tito could have no objection to this and indeed his representative in London, General Velebit expressed his approval. It was, as *The Times* said, 'a virtual settlement' of the problem and a leader in the paper expressed relief at the end of a situation 'which could have embarrassed the major Allied Powers.' The way was now clear for Subasitch to go to Yugoslavia with the members of his Royal Government and co-operate with Tito. In theory at least it seemed as harmonious a blend of technically irreconcilable forces as the most idealistic of President Roosevelt's speechwriters could have wished for.

There was in any case a general feeling of reassurance attached to the image of Marshal Tito in Britain. Churchill, in a Debate in the House of Commons on January 18th had referred to him as 'one of my best friends'. Some days later readers could turn for further reassurance to an article by Philip Jordan in *Picture Post*. Jordan had been a *News Chronicle* war correspondent in Yugoslavia with Tito. He now wrote of him, 'It would be more correct to speak of the common-sense method of the Government which he leads, rather than to infer that he is a Dictator, for, if those who have visited Yugoslavia in this war, and have had the privilege of his acquaintance, know anything for certain, they know that he is no more Dictator of Yugoslavia than Winston Churchill is Dictator of Britain. If any reliable measure of power were available, it might well show that Churchill is a freer agent than Tito . . .'

Jordan added that to suppose that Tito 'imposes his will on both his Cabinet and his country by threat of armed force is either to misread or . . . distort, possibly unwittingly, the situation as it now exists.'

Only one serious problem now remained to disturb the outward facing equanimity of the Grand Alliance: that of Poland. Resolution of this would have to await the applied wisdom of Roosevelt, Churchill and Stalin at their forthcoming meeting. The world in the meantime watched the full power of the Russian winter offensive unfolding in the East.

Chapter Eight

New Year's Eve in Moscow had seen, according to the *New York Times*, the greatest demonstration of gaiety since the war had started. There was much dancing and singing and the leading hotels opened long-closed special ballrooms where American-style dance-bands played until 5.30 a.m. Five hundred guests at the Hotel Metropole ate an eight-course turkey banquet. It was the first New Year's Eve since 1941 on which there had been no German invaders except prisoners on Russian soil.

Alexander Werth, reporting for the BBC from Moscow described the prevailing mood there in the first days of 1945. For some time, he said, the war had seemed very far away (the last great Russian offensive had ended on the Vistula in August) but the fighting now going on round Budapest was stirring people's imagination into a renewed war-consciousness. And what particularly fuelled that imagination was the sense that the final stage of a war of which people were so weary was at last at hand. All the New Year resolutions, said Werth, were to the effect that the war must end in 1945, and a poor view was taken of any prophecies that it would draw out into 1946.

Hardships among the Russian population were fewer than during the first and second terrible years of war but housing was still very bad, particularly in Moscow where there had been an abnormal influx of population. Clothing and most elementary household goods were really short, though a word borrowed from Moscow thieves' jargon, 'blat' – which meant 'influence and wire-pulling' – sometimes alleviated the worst of the shortages. There was a good deal of juvenile delinquency, with so many children whose fathers were dead or at the front, and whose mothers were working all day in factories.

'But,' wrote Werth, 'despite all the petty and unpleasant and painful problems which are squarely faced, there is throughout the country an immense feeling of pride and confidence in the future. . . . There is a fearful amount of work ahead. But people will tackle this work joyfully – though on one condition only – that everything is done now to assure that Europe is a peaceful continent for at least fifty or a hundred years.'

The Germans reported the start of the new offensive on the Vistula at

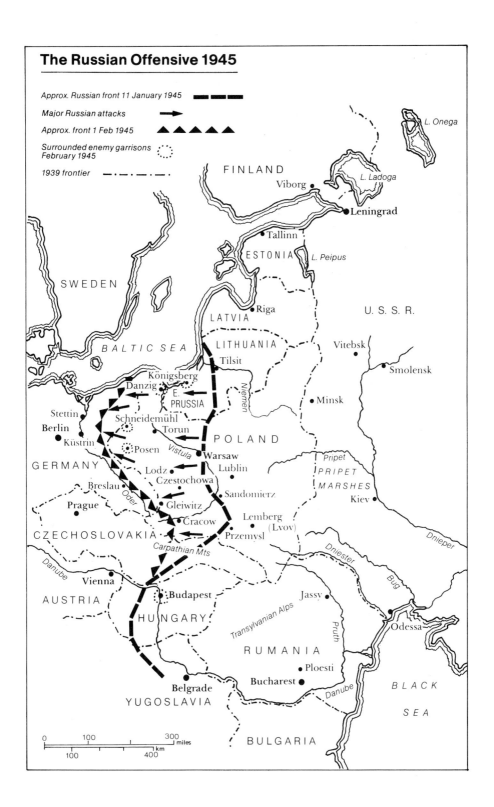

The Russian Offensive 1945

Approx. Russian front 11 January 1945

Major Russian attacks

Approx. front 1 Feb 1945

Surrounded enemy garrisons
February 1945

1939 frontier

L. Onega

FINLAND

Viborg

L. Ladoga

Leningrad

Tallinn

ESTONIA

L. Peipus

SWEDEN

Riga

LATVIA

U. S. S. R.

BALTIC SEA

LITHUANIA

Vitebsk

Tilsit

Smolensk

Königsberg

Danzig

E.
PRUSSIA

Niemen

Minsk

Stettin

Schneidemühl

Torun

Berlin

POLAND

Küstrin

Posen

Vistula

Warsaw

Pripet

GERMANY

Lodz

Lublin

PRIPET

Czestochowa

MARSHES

Breslau

Oder

Sandomierz

Kiev

Prague

Gleiwitz

CZECHOSLOVAKIA

Cracow

Lemberg
(Lvov)

Dnieper

Przemysl

Dniester

Carpathian Mts

Bug

Danube

Vienna

Budapest

Jassy

AUSTRIA

HUNGARY

Transylvanian Alps

Pruth

Odessa

RUMANIA

Ploesti

BLACK

Belgrade

Bucharest

SEA

YUGOSLAVIA

Danube

| 0 | 100 | | 300 | miles |
| 100 | | | 400 | km |

BULGARIA

10 a.m. on Friday, 12th January. But the Russians had always made a habit on such occasions of saying nothing until there was a development to report. On 13th January in a special Order of the Day, Marshal Stalin announced that striking out from the bridgehead over the Vistula which they had held since last summer at Sandomierz, divisions of the Red Army under Marshal Koniev had broken through the German positions to a depth of 25 miles. Long columns of German prisoners were being marched back to the Russian rear, many of them still bleeding from nose and ears as a result of the terrific blast effect of the Soviet artillery barrage. In two days the whole Eastern front was ablaze on a 600-mile stretch from East Prussia to the Carpathians, with 2,000,000 Russians and 1,500,000 Germans locked in a swift and terrible combat unprecedented in military history. 'The Red Army is heading for Berlin,' wrote Ilya Ehrenberg in *Pravda*. 'In Berlin we shall be.'

In the first few hours of the offensive German radio had been stressing the power and scope of the German defensive positions in the east: '. . . bunkers, mine-fields and defence works which, staggered in depth, extend far to the rear. The German soldiers' resistance should prove too hard a nut for the Bolsheviks, and may result in their breaking their teeth.'

The Soviet paper *Red Star* said that veterans who had fought from the Volga to the Vistula gazed in amazement at the destruction wrought by the artillery in the intricately prepared German defence. A war reporter with Marshal Rokossovsky's forces gave an account of the Russian assault after the barrage: 'The men on my sector went over the top with the rest at 11 o'clock. There were very few Germans still alive in the first two lines. Hand-to-hand engagements in the third and fourth lines continued until 2 in the afternoon. The place was a warren of trenches combined with permanent defences. Every country house and farm was an island of resistance.' He described how the Soviet troops on some sectors had to fight their way over 45 lines of trenches, working out roughly at about one trench every quarter of a mile. But, he added: 'Cities and villages in the depth of the breach are intact, so swift were the manoeuvres that gave them into our hands.'

The Russian tanks in their white winter camouflage were indeed surging forward round German strong-points in wide enveloping movements, leaving whole garrisons surrounded to fight on in towns, villages and even isolated houses in the countryside. Peasant cottages built of thick logs provided ready-made wooden forts from which, as well as from great country mansions, the Germans put up fierce resistance. But they were crushed, as *Pravda* put it, 'by the lava-like torrent of the Red Army.'

The German radio was soon describing how police, Volkssturm (Home Guard) and even 14-year-old boys 'in the clothes in which a few hours ago they were in school' were being flung into the gaps to fight in the front line.

Armies under Marshal Zhukov burst through German defences north and south of Warsaw, while Rokossovsky struck into East Prussia. By the 17th January Warsaw itself had been captured – 'the capital of our ally Poland,' as Stalin described it in his Order of the Day. Moscow guns fired salvoes for three hours in celebration of the Warsaw victory and of the capture of Czestochowa by Marshal Koniev who was now within fourteen miles of the German border. The next day he was across it and into Silesia – an industrial and mining zone of Germany, second only in importance to the Ruhr. On the 19th January Stalin's Order of the Day announced that the Red Army was 30 miles inside East Prussia. By January 23rd, only eleven days after the start of the whole offensive the Red Army was on the Oder itself.

'On the barricades of the Reich,' declared one German radio commentator, 'we view the situation with realistic seriousness. These hours will tell whether we are to go down in a red inferno.' The principal German military commentator, General Dittmar, described the issue as being 'balanced on a razor's edge'.

The pace and sweep of the Russian advance surpassed anything expected by their Allies or feared by the Germans and was astonishing the world. The *Manchester Guardian* wrote that it had changed the face of the war. 'Only a week ago the people of Europe were resigned to a long and dour struggle. Now all is changed.' The *New York Times* agreed that the whole military situation had been dramatically transformed. Its military correspondent Hanson Baldwin said that the offensive transcended in strategic importance anything that was happening in Western Europe or indeed the Philippines – whither General Macarthur had returned as he always said he would. 'A weight,' wrote Hanson, 'has been lifted from the minds of those who direct our strategy.'

He reminded his readers however that the Russian successes could not and should not be taken as meaning the solution – except on a unilateral basis – of the political problems that plagued Europe. And the political aspect of the Russian military triumph was in the London *Daily Herald* leader-writer's mind when he wrote, of the forthcoming Big Three conference: 'Now or never is the time for co-ordinating the political aims, as at previous conferences military aims were co-ordinated. Past conferences have ensured the winning of the war. The next will ensure the making of the peace.'

The BBC weekly paper *The Listener* wrote of 'a sufficiency of real problems whose solution must be sought, and sought quickly, if we are all to make the most of our opportunities. Indeed, the number of such problems is bound to increase as the disintegration of Germany draws nearer. For this reason we take great comfort, not only in this present offensive which may bring the end nearer, but also in the prospect of an early meeting of the principal Powers on the Allied side. Readiness to meet the successful outcome of the great battles now on foot is second only in importance to success in the field.'

The political situation in countries liberated by the Russians had so far, with one exception, provided on the whole less public embarrassment to the Alliance than that in the liberated countries of the West. As the Red Army had moved remorselessly forward towards or over the frontiers of former enemy countries such as Finland, Hungary, Bulgaria and Rumania, elements of the existing régimes in these countries – and in the case of Finland the democratic Government itself – sensing an approaching German defeat within their own domains, had taken what steps they could to seek accommodation with the advancing Russians. Governments which could at first claim at least partial continuity with the previous establishment sought and obtained armistices. Thus although the regions cleared of the Germans were, except in Finland, entirely dependent for stability on the Red Army and the local Communists whom the Russians inevitably favoured, there was nowhere any immediate challenge to the new order of things. For the time being this could be seen to rest on the sort of consent to which there is no alternative.

Only in Poland, where the Germans had allowed no sort of local government, was there a highly delicate situation. Half of the country had been liberated by the Red Army but it was that part largely claimed by the Soviet Union in any case, indeed forcibly occupied by it at the time of the Nazi-Soviet Pact in 1939. In these territories the Soviet Union had now installed at Lublin a Moscow-trained Communist committee which it recognised as the Provisional Government of Poland.

This move was a source of considerable, if discreet embarrassment to Britain and America, who continued to recognise the pre-war régime exiled since 1939 in London as the Provisional Polish Government. Moreover, it was these London Poles whom the Polish Resistance (the Home Army) continuing to fight the Germans in the still-occupied area of Poland, also recognised as their legitimate Government. They regarded the pro-Russian Lublin Committee with mistrust, and in turn were themselves, together with the London Government, reviled by Lublin as Fascists. But although this situation was awkward for the Big Three Alliance, its full difficulties only now began to emerge into the open as the Russians moved into those parts of Poland still occupied by the Germans, the free territorial integrity of which they were pledged to recognise.

In Russia, crowds listened nightly to the triumphant Orders of the Day blared through loud-speakers at Moscow street corners, and waited for the guns to boom and the yellow, green and red rockets to race up into the night sky above the snow-covered streets. But here too, in addition to satisfaction that full justice was being meted-out to the Germans at last, there were thoughts about the future.

In his speech on the anniversary of the October Revolution at the end of 1944, Stalin had emphasised what, to Russian minds, was the first consideration for the peace. The alliance of Soviet Russia, Great Britain and the United States was based not on 'accidental, ephemeral motives, but on vitally important lasting interests.' He had no doubt that the Alliance would stand up to the concluding stage of the war and dwelt on the importance of the scheme first sketched-out at the Dumbarton Oaks Conference near Washington in September 1944 for some sort of international peace-keeping organisation.

'The activities of this international organisation,' said Stalin, '. . . will be effective if the great Powers which have borne the brunt of the war against Germany continue to act in the spirit of unanimity and concord. They will not be effective if this indispensable condition is violated.'

He made it clear, as Senator Vandenberg was to do, that he saw the principal problem for the future as a new German menace after Germany's ultimate recovery from defeat. And now as the three main lines of the Russian advance – towards Danzig, Berlin and Dresden – 'thrust,' as the *New Statesman* put it, 'into Germany's vitals,' *Pravda* reiterated the underlying Russian concern to which these victories were to put an end:

'If we are determined to be in Berlin, it is because we owe our children a real peace and not an *ersatz* peace, which the Germans would like to palm off onto us. That will never happen. Our people cannot be expected to build new towns and new houses if they know people in Germany are already quietly manufacturing new weapons of war, new V2's or 3's or 20's, and that the executioners of Maidanek are designing even bigger and better concentration camps.'

But the apparently unceasing day by day triumph of the Russian advance momentarily swept aside long-term thoughts. In Moscow the question, 'How far to Berlin?' had almost replaced the normal greeting. Zhukov's tanks were, by the 26th January, within a hundred miles of the capital and on the last day of the month reported to be within 45 miles of it. In Silesia, Koniev had captured Gleiwitz and had reached Breslau. Russian airmen described the advance as looking, from the air, like a huge octopus weaving long tentacles among the Silesian towns and villages. *The Times* called the offensive 'a masterpiece of the art of war.' It was, said Lord Addison in the House of Lords: 'Perhaps the greatest co-ordinated military attack in history.' In less than three weeks the Russians advancing on an enormous front had covered 225 miles.

'No praise can be too great for the Russian achievement,' wrote the *Sunday Times*. 'We in Great Britain take off our hats to the Russian people.'

Soviet war reporters described the devastation as the German scorched earth policy in Silesia scarred the countryside and sent great palls of smoke up from the towns and villages. In the fields German troops machine-gunned the cattle before joining the long columns retreating to the west. One reporter described the roads littered with smashed German equipment and piles of household goods abandoned by the refugees. He said the Russian spearheads were continually finding trains intact with wagons loaded to the roof with supplies. 'But,' he went on, 'although every German civilian has fled there are still occupiers in the smashed towns and villages. They can be seen wandering through the smoke, turning over the wreckage and snatching something here and something there. They are the former Polish slaves of the German burghers and farmers, seeking the forsaken garments of their masters before they start their own long trek home in zero temperatures to Poland.'

It was not only the cattle whom the Germans were machine gunning. When the Russians liberated Lodz they found the remains of a weaving-mill at Radogoszczi which the Germans had used as a prison. Before leaving, they had set fire to it with all the Polish prisoners inside. Those who tried to escape from the smoke and flames were mown down by machine-guns. Similar evidence of what the German 'New Order' had meant for those on whom it had been imposed was to be found everywhere. An English reporter, Iris Morley, had been shown a small concentration camp at Klooga near Talinn in Estonia. It consisted, she said, of some big white houses 'rather like a girls' school at Folkestone' and standing in very pleasant country. Inside one of these houses she found the bodies of some 700 people whom the Germans had machine-gunned before leaving. Still living in the house next door were 40 prisoners who had somehow escaped. She asked them if it were not terrible for them to have to go on living there, even for a few days until the official investigation was completed. They replied, 'But why? The food is wonderful now. It's like living in a first class hotel.'

'You see,' she wrote, 'it didn't matter any more that they had only to look out of the window to see the bodies of people they had known and lived with rotting in the rain. That's what happens to you after a year or two of torture interrupted by murder. You don't die of horror: you accept it.'

She was then taken into the woods where the Germans had killed the remaining 2,300 prisoners; 'They had cut platforms of logs, shot one layer of people, then piled more logs and so on until the layers were twelve deep, and then tried to burn them.' Empty beer- and mineral water-bottles were still lying about the place, left there by the SS after their day's work. As Iris Morley walked away from the scene a woman survivor said to her: 'You think you are talking to a human being, don't you? I look like one and sound like one – but you see, I am not a human being any more.'

Some of the milder horrors of war were now being experienced by Germans themselves. Columns of lorries crammed with refugees and their luggage were now rolling through the streets of the battered capital from one station to another. There were no men among them, only women and children – 'Wide-eyed,' wrote a Swedish reporter, 'they looked out from under their caps at the ruined streets of Berlin, which they were obviously seeing for the first time.' The German radio itself talked of millions of refugees in columns, some between 30 and 40 miles long, trekking west, away from the advancing Red Army. 'Only a limited percentage of refugees,' said the radio, 'die on the way.'

After the first few days of the offensive the German radio comments had adopted a fairly realistic tone. 'Penetrations' were admitted and the failure to stem the advance was explained by the need for time in which to build new defensive fronts further back. An apocalyptic note was allowed to enter broadcasts. For example: 'Germany's destiny is about to be decided. There is no going back, no side stepping, no quarter. Only one thing is left – struggle.' A broadcast to the German forces on January 20th emphasised the tactical considerations in a retreat: 'A defender who has to husband his forces cannot assign his strategic reserves immediately to a particular sector. It would be useless to throw in reserves haphazardly. The attacker must halt sooner or later to regroup and at this moment the defender must take counter-measures.'

But there were no immediate signs that any such counter-measures were being effectively taken. What was continually emphasised was a determination to stand fast even where it was impossible to do so. In Silesia the German radio on January 27th said; 'Every yard will be defended to the last.' In East Prussia: 'Every yard of soil is being contested with unheard-of bitterness.' In Danzig: 'Every man capable of bearing arms is bound in duty to resist with all his strength.'

There was little attempt to conceal from the German population as a whole that the situation was extremely serious. Hans Fritzsche, broad-casting on 27th January began with the words: 'The war communiqués of the last few days have filled many a German heart with deepest anxiety.' He reminded the Germans of how both British and Russian peoples had stood firm in their adversity and exhorted them to show the same spirit while a new front was being organised. 'Every German soldier and every Volkssturm man fighting the Bolshevik flood at some point of the enormous penetration is today imbued with the realisation that it depends on him where and how this front is to be formed.'

Goebbels himself was striking a note of near-Wagnerian doom: 'If Germany succumbs the whole of Europe including Britain will be thrown into disaster,' he wrote in *Das Reich* at the beginning of February. He went on: 'One would think that the peoples of Europe who fear and hate Bolshevism would hasten to our aid. But no – the German people stand almost deserted. It is difficult to imagine a more moving tragedy.'

Statements made by General Franco in sunnier times may well have been coming to mind. 'If there were one moment of danger,' Franco had said at Seville early in 1942, 'if the road to Berlin were to be opened, it would not be one division of Spanish volunteers who would go; a million men would offer themselves.' Three months later Franco's Foreign Secretary, Suñer, had declaimed: 'If the great German bulwark were not able to contain the tremendous Russian peril, Spain would not help with 15,000 but a million men.'

Since then, however, General Franco had for the second time changed his attitude to the war. In 1940 he had switched from neutrality to non-belligerency, and in July 1941 had asserted that the Allies had lost. Early in 1944 he had prudently switched back from non-belligerency to strict neutrality. The Germans were now unlikely to obtain any help from that quarter.

For the world at large, there were now just two questions to ask about the offensive, and they were inter-related. First, could the Germans manage to regroup and form any sort of front at all? And secondly, could the Russians manage to maintain the impetus of their advance with their supply-lines obviously now considerably stretched?

As the *New Statesman* put it: 'Dare Zhukov go all out for Berlin until he knows where and in what strength he may have to expect a German counter-attack?'

On the 30th January the *Manchester Guardian* reported from Moscow that there were indications that the Russians needed a breather. They had been fighting without a halt for 17 days, their lines of communication were greatly extended while those of the Germans had become shorter. The German High Command had had time to remove reserves from the interior of Germany including the western front and to form some sort of line along the Oder. Before risking the final plunge the Red Armies needed a certain degree of re-grouping. They had to mop-up the considerable German pockets left behind and to reinforce their spearheads with more armour and infantry. They could then gather strength for the final assault on Berlin. Between the Oder and Berlin lay 100 miles of ideal country for tank warfare – very flat with only a small population and little woodland. The chief obstacle was the Oder itself which at the key point of Küstrin was between 150 and 200 yards wide – that, and the unknown quantity of the strength of Germany's spirit of resistance. The Reich Labour Minister, Dr Robert Ley, proclaimed on the 29th January: 'We shall fight before Berlin, for Berlin and behind Berlin.'

The military correspondent of *The Times* on the 1st February thought it highly significant that, according to the Germans, Zhukov was bringing infantry into Brandenburg. The Russians were certainly going to meet opposition before they reached Berlin and it might be heavy opposition. Though there was no doubt that Zhukov's offensive would rank with any of the great exploitations of victory in military history, anything might happen in the near future and it seemed probable that the Germans had by this time collected enough troops to make a real fight for their capital. The Russians knew that they could not take on such a battle with armour alone and their problem was to transport and supply their infantry, whom Soviet correspondents described as 'racing on in captured lorries.' The trouble was, as *The Times* pointed out, that once an army stopped and sat down it was always a considerable business to get it moving again.

On top of these considerations came news of a sudden thaw to slow the Russian advance. Water released from the Carpathians into the Silesian plains swelled the Oder, shifting pontoons. Floating ice smashed bridges and Russian sappers had to struggle with the elements on dark, rainy nights while German counter-attacks increased.

As the world speculated about the possibility of a major German counter-attack and the moment of its launching, the stream of women and children in carts and on foot poured through Berlin from east to west, and the Volkssturm and civilians erected barricades in the capital and waited for the worst. A German military spokesman emphasised that Berlin would indeed be a highly defensible fortress as its ruins and innumerable skeletons of burnt-out vehicles proved plentiful and excellent material with which such barricades could be constructed. Red Air Force men flying over Berlin described an uncanny stillness in the east of the city with trams standing motionless on the tracks, their roofs covered in thick white snow while none of the factory chimneys were smoking. Only in the west of the city was there the constant stream of cars, carts and pedestrians moving out.

In the interval between the slowing-down of the offensive and whatever stage was to come next, the Russians looked back on the last three weeks with what Alexander Werth in Moscow described as 'immense pride' and 'deep moral satisfaction'. They had the feeling that after the terrible hardships they had endured and the terrible initial failures of the war, the people, the army and the régime had all justified themselves. And, said Werth, thinking of the future, 'Russia's wartime achievement fills people with confidence that if so stupendous an organisation as that required for the present offensive could be made to work like clockwork, then there is bound to be enough talent for organisation in this country to restore the country's economy and built up prosperity in minimum time.'

Chapter Nine

An all important question now seemed to be: how strong was German morale? And if strong, what was the basis of its strength?

A BBC correspondent who in the autumn of 1944 had talked to thirty German prisoners just out of the battle line had found that 29 of them believed that Germany was beaten and only one that she could still win. Talking to a similar number captured in the Ardennes on January 4th he found that they divided fifty-fifty on the same issue. A 'high British authority' told A. J. Cummings of the *News Chronicle* that 'the soldiers of the Wehrmacht are fighting with a passion of ferocity that few of us believed any longer to be possible. In defence of their Fatherland they appear to have captured something of the spirit of Britain in 1940.'

The strength and quality of German morale was now clearly going to be a decisive factor in determining the course and duration of the war. With the Ardennes offensive over and 'the greatest attack of all time' on Germany's eastern front, what was the effect on that morale likely to be?

The situation in the west gave no immediate grounds for despair. The most ambitious hope for the Ardennes offensive had clearly been that by striking across the Meuse and eventually capturing Antwerp, it would divide the British and American armies rather as the offensive of 1940 had divided the British and French. Nothing like that had happened for all the early success. But Rundstedt's more or less successful control of his later defensive action within the salient meant that it could be presented in a light that was by no means defeatist. A review of the situation on the German radio as early as January 13th, the day after the great Russian offensive opened, declared:

'The main strategic purpose of the German thrust into Belgium has now been fulfilled: it caused a postponement – the extent of which cannot yet be gauged – of Eisenhower's offensive plans for this year.'

Whatever the original purpose might have been this was a not unreasonable assessment. It was possible to reason further that if the Allies could be kept out of Germany they would eventually be forced by exhaustion to talk terms of peace. This was certainly the view of a

German paratroop Colonel just captured in the Ardennes. Though bitter about the incompetence by which his 900 men had been dispersed over a wide area and subsequently easily rounded-up, he was, nevertheless confident that Germany would win the war. But his notion of victory was qualified. 'The war,' he said, 'will result in a stalemate.'

As for civilian morale, pronouncements on the German radio and in the newspapers were not, in a totalitarian state, necessarily the evidence they purported to be. But such pronouncements were not necessarily unrepresentative either. Even totalitarian propaganda has to be tailored to some extent to what is acceptable and thus itself reflects something of what those for whom it is intended really think. Goebbels, the supreme propagandist of the Third Reich, could plausibly confirm the 'Britain 1940' syndrome when he broadcast on January 5th to a people suffering daily and nightly bombardment by thousands of aircraft:

'How proud we must be today, and our children will be, to belong to his nation! There is none more heroic under the sun . . . anyone who has the honour of a share in leading this nation cannot but regard his service as a divine service. Let them offer us America's treasures on golden salvers; we want only to be Germans. The world will one day no longer be able to withhold its admiration. Our virtues stamp us as the earth's first nation and thus render us quite invincible.'

It was in the personality of Hitler himself that Goebbels found an almost mystical justification for such confidence. But Hitler's own voice had not been heard since the attempt on his life on July 20th.

There had for some time been a feeling in the west that the power of Hitler himself had been partially eclipsed in Germany, and that his place had largely been taken by Himmler and Goebbels who were manipulating the Führer's image. This impression had received encouragement from Hitler's own long silence and especially from his failure to deliver the traditional speech which had always been his custom on the anniversary of the Munich Putsch of 1923, November 9th.

Three days after that date, a statement, said to have been written by Hitler, had in fact been read out by Himmler on the radio. In this the Führer had pleaded his need to pay constant attention to the affairs of the nation as the reason for his inability to speak for himself. 'Work does not allow me to leave headquarters even for a few days,' ran the message. '. . . As long as I am alive Germany will not suffer the fate of European States flooded by Bolshevism.' It seemed curious that not even a short personal recording had been possible in those headquarters, and speculation immediately centred on his state of health.

According to the *Washington Post* Hitler's mysterious silence had

From *Punch*: 'His Servant's Voice'; Himmler in control?

deluged London with reports that he was dead, sick, seriously ill or suffering from nervous disorders. The latest rumour was that he had had to have a throat operation performed by an Austrian surgeon but, since this came from German sources it was thought only to be a convenient covering-up of his failure to speak on such an important occasion. The London *Daily Express* reported that 'authoritative quarters' believed that he had been seriously injured in the bombing of the 20th July. The *Daily Mail* on its front page voiced the opinion of a British psychologist, William Brown, to the effect that 'the Führer may now be approaching the final phase of his mental sickness.' It noted that Hitler had been silent longer than at any time since his rise to power in 1933.

In the middle of December, 1944, to coincide with the Ardennes offensive Himmler had again made a broadcast, once more encouraging those who wished to think that he had in some way eclipsed Hitler. What he had to say was a useful pointer to what those in charge of German morale then thought could most successfully sustain it. 'The worst is now over,' Himmler declared. 'We have succeeded in holding and pinning down the enemy both in the east and the west. We have had to take some heavy blows ourselves in the course of the fighting but I happen to know the situation is still worse in the enemy camp. It is just a question of staying for the distance.'

By the problems of the 'enemy camp' Himmler had seemed to be referring to differences between the Allies, and Goebbels certainly seized on these, particularly in the case of Britain's embarrassment in Greece.

'What did I tell you?' he cried, ignoring the fact that the Russians, unlike the Americans, had not criticised the action against the Communists there and seemed to be allowing Greece to be a British sphere of influence. 'Against the coolly scheming Stalin, Churchill hasn't got the ghost of a chance. . . . The anti-Reich coalition is breaking up before our eyes . . .'

At the same time the German radio was playing much Beethoven and Brahms and broadcasting the work of Goethe and Schiller to foster the notion of German culture under siege. The Führer's own alleged confidence had been reaffirmed when another message from him was read on the anniversary of the Strength Through Joy organisation by Robert Ley, the Nazi in charge of the Workers' Front. 'When this fateful struggle has come to a successful end,' ran Hitler's message, 'we will continue to build the socialistic structure of the Reich.'

Then on the 1st January, more than six months after Hitler's voice had last been heard, he did indeed speak to the nation in person. Inevitably in Britain and America almost as much attention was paid to the manner of his delivery, and the various interpretations of his physical and mental state to which this gave rise, as to the content. And though there were those who wondered whether it was really Hitler in person speaking or some double, the consensus was that it was the Führer himself.

Interest in the physical phenomenon seemed to arouse some contradictory conclusions. Both the London and the *New York Times* said that Hitler spoke much faster than usual, while Frederick Laws, the radio critic of the *News Chronicle* said that his speech was slower. He also said it was 'less emotional' and *The Times* at least agreed that he had spoken without shouting – 'without rhetorical pauses' added the *New York Times*. Laws noted that he seemed to lack the stimulus of an audience to orchestrate him with applause and that he did not seem good at the fireside chat. It was generally agreed that the speech was a recording, partly because of the sound quality – it seemed to come from a large empty room – but also because Hitler at one point referred to 'the end of this year' (meaning the old one) whereas in fact the speech was broadcast after midnight on January 1st, German time. Some thought it was not just one recording but a patchwork of old recordings, but Frederick Laws ridiculed this as 'rubbish'.

Hitler began as if there were indeed some need to explain his long silence: 'Only the turn of the year causes me to speak to you today. . . . The present time has demanded more than speeches from me . . .'

His theme was that while in the past year Germany's enemies had confidently been predicting victory for themselves, it continued to evade them as it had done year after year throughout the war and would continue to do so.

'With the certainty of a sleepwalker,' he said, 'one called August 1944 the month of unconditional surrender and prophesied, shortly after that, a joint meeting of the leading statesmen in Berlin before Christmas. A short while ago the new date was January, then March 1945. Now it is declared more carefully, as these two months are rapidly coming nearer, that it was to be August. In June they will surely again talk about the winter of 1946, except that the war will in fact end in the meantime and not by German capitulation – this will never come – but by German victory.'

It was obvious, he went on, that Germany's enemies neither knew the German people nor the meaning of the National Socialist State, which could never be replaced either by Bolshevism or by 'democratic-plutocratic ideology'.

'I should like to state once more . . . that this nation, this State and its leading men are unshakeable in their will and unswerving in their fanatical determination to fight this war to a successful conclusion in all circumstances – if it means taking in our stride all the reverses which fickle fate may impose on us . . . we are resolved to go to the extreme. The world must know that this State will, therefore, never capitulate. The German Reich of today – like all great States of the past – may on its way be exposed to reverses, but it will never be deflected from this road. The world must know that the present leaders of this State share the sorrow and suffering of its people but will never capitulate on account of suffering and sorrow; that on the contrary it is resolved to meet every crisis with still greater effort, to make up by increased working zeal for what has been lost by tardiness.'

He contrasted the lack of war aims among the Allies – except for the Jews, who simply wanted to destroy and enslave the German people – with the Germans' own clear knowledge of what they were fighting for:

'. . . The preservation of the German man and woman . . . our Fatherland . . . our 2,000-year old civilisation . . . for, as they intend to exterminate our people, they are already trying this out during the war by means hitherto unknown to civilised mankind. . . . However, like the Phoenix from the ashes so first of all from the ruins of our towns German determination has risen in spite of all. It has taken possession not only of millions of soldiers but also of millions of workers, female workers, or women and even of children. The suffering inflicted on these millions individually is immeasurable, but equally immeasurable is the greatness of their bearing. When one day this time of trial has come to an end every German will be boundlessly proud to declare himself a member of such a nation. One day the time will come in which the violation of culture practised by our enemies will continue to burn in our memory and will be felt as a disgrace by themselves.'

After praising what had already been achieved by rejection of what he called 'the bourgeois social order' and by recognition of the truth that 'the liberal age is a thing of the past,' he praised the 'unprecedented achievements of the German workers in German factories.

'Thus, whatever our enemies smashed was rebuilt with superhuman industry and unparalleled heroism and this will continue until one day our enemies' undertaking comes to an end. The German spirit and German determination will enforce this. This, my racial comrades, will one day go down in history as the miracle of the twentieth century.'

He concluded with a promise to the Almighty that Greater Germany would fulfil its duty 'in the firm belief that the hour will strike when victory will ultimately come to him who is most worthy of it, the Greater German Reich.'

Strength through Will was the secular message. For many Germans, much that had been hidden from view in the workings of the National Socialist State had always been transcended by faith in the power and personality of the Führer. Presumably the same semi-mystical confidence could now help dispel the obscurities of the military situation. The speech was a strange mixture of steeled aspiration, courage and suppressed hysteria. But read with awareness of the German fighting spirit in the field and of the resilience of German war production for all the continuous bombing, it made clear at least that whatever the Allies might be fighting for, the Germans felt themselves still to be fighting for something too. The *New York Times*, while writing of the speech's 'urgent desperation' commented that 'the Allies will also have to take note of the fanatical defiance in it' and added that the latest German offensive in the west had shown that Hitler's boasts were by no means empty.

If the Allies wanted to know what was likely to lie ahead for them in the European war it would indeed have been more useful to ponder the speech's fanaticism than to speculate about the circumstances in which it was delivered or the physical condition of the man who delivered it. But it was a tribute to the Führer's continued ability to cast a spell that he could exercise even for his enemies, on however superficial a level, some of the elusive fascination of myth. Even the *New York Times* had said that the most important thing about the speech was its demonstration that Hitler was still alive. Two days later William Hickey of the London *Daily Express* was still playing what he called 'Britain's familiar guessing-game', 'What is the matter with Hitler?' A nurse who had done her training in an ear, nose and throat hospital had told him that, while the voice was indeed unmistakably Hitler's, 'this monotone is peculiar to people who are stone-deaf.' Hickey merely commented that this suggested that the bomb which it was known had injured Hitler in some way on the 20th July had been more powerful than previously realised.

In fact an authentic account of Hitler's physical and psychological condition was available, and the *Manchester Guardian* and other papers were soon to avail themselves of it, publishing an interview with a Hungarian General, Janos Vörös. The General had spent many hours with Hitler in his headquarters in East Prussia when sent there in September by Admiral Horthy to try and get agreement to Hungary's withdrawal from the war. Though Hitler had then shown severe signs of strain it seemed that he had been neither deafened nor in any other way seriously injured by the explosion of the 20th July. His face was, however, puffy and unhealthy and his voice was hoarse. Vörös said that his mental condition seemed to have deteriorated since he had last seen him in May, 1944. 'Plainly he was sick in mind and body,' he said. This judgement might well have been retrospectively exaggerated for the visit had been a failure and Vörös had since himself thrown in his lot with the Hungarian Government installed by the Russians. But what seemed significant for the future was the manner in which the Führer had dismissed Hungary's request to be allowed to secede from the Axis out of hand. 'Now we are all sitting in one boat in a dreadful storm,' he had said. 'He who jumps overboard – man or nation – will surely drown. It is possible that the boat will capsize, but it is likely that it will reach land. To the last man, to the last drop of blood I will defend the Fatherland.'

His voice had risen almost to a shriek as he said this. It was the nearest he had come, said Vörös, to predicting ultimate success for his cause. The thought of millions of lives being poured out in a useless sacrifice for the monstrous entity of the Nazi party had appalled the Hungarian. Yet all the indications were that this was exactly what was in store for Europe in the coming year. In the same week as Hitler's New Year's Day broadcast an appeal was made over the German radio to the German people by Himmler, Goebbels, Bormann (the Führer's Deputy) and Funk (the economic chief of the Reich). It ran as follows:

'The united effort of three world Powers has not succeeded in forcing us to our knees. . . . The homeland, in spite of the enemy's bomb-terror, has proved itself worthy of the heroism of its soldiers. The whole of the German people has followed the call for the prosecution of the war without compromise. Hundreds of thousands of women and girls have replaced able men and thus made it possible to create numerous new Divisions of Volkgrenadiers. . . . For those in training we urgently need clothing and equipment. In the name of the Führer we call on you German men, women and German youth for a people's sacrifice.'

The announcement went on to say that between the 7th and 28th of January there were to be collections of uniforms and parts of the uniforms of the Party, the Wehrmacht, the Police, the Fire Brigade, the postal services, as well as shoes, boots, collapsible tents, blankets, rucksacks, cooking utensils, steel helmets, spades. Clothing and knitting materials of all kinds were also to be collected. 'Each citizen,' concluded the appeal, 'must give everything which he does not absolutely require. Give everything that you can spare to the fighting front.'

As the *Manchester Guardian* had written in a leader after Hitler's speech, the riddle of his health or whereabouts was 'irrelevant.' Considering the few cards left in Nazi hands, it commented, it would be difficult to imagine a more effective speech. What he had said was that Germans were fighting for the preservation of their nation and for the future of their children. 'It is the only appeal that Hitler has left. We may find that it would have been more politic, if less frank, to have been more restrained in the open discussion of our plans for settling Germany.'

The last picture; Hitler leaves the Bunker to decorate young German soldiers

'Unconditional surrender' had long been the term used unequivocally by the three major Allies. It had first been proclaimed at the Casablanca conference early in 1943 by President Roosevelt, had been re-affirmed by Roosevelt, Churchill and Stalin at the Teheran conference at the end of 1943, and now in the middle of January 1945 was to be further re-affirmed by Winston Churchill in the House of Commons. There had been questions about the wisdom of the policy from time to time. Might it not frighten the Germans into a more stubborn resistance than they would otherwise have offered?

Churchill, on January 16th was, as before, at least prepared to acknowledge the existence of such a question. But he posed it with a typically mischievous slant. 'What, for instance,' he asked, 'should be our attitude towards the terrible foe with whom we are grappling? Should it be unconditional surrender, or should we make some accommodation with them for a negotiated peace, leaving them free to re-gather their strength for a renewal of the struggle after a few uneasy years?'

There were other ways to put the question. The doubt which lay in the minds of people like the writer of the *Manchester Guardian* leader centred on whether 'unconditional surrender' might not necessarily prolong suffering and the shedding of blood. Even if the Nazi leadership were themselves unlikely ever to consider terms, it could unnecessarily encourage the German people's tenacity by giving them no alternative but to stand with the leadership. Churchill implicitly acknowledged this possibility when he continued: 'But the President of the United States and I, in your name, have repeatedly declared that the enforcement of unconditional surrender upon the enemy in no way relieves the victorious Powers of their obligations to humanity or of their duties as civilised and Christian nations. I read somewhere that when the ancient Athenians, on one occasion, overpowered a tribe in the Peloponnese which had wrought them great injury by base and treacherous means, and when they had the hostile army herded on the beach, naked for slaughter, they forgave them and set them free, and they said this was not done because they were men; it was done because of the nature of Man. Similarly in this temper we may now say to our foes: "We demand unconditional surrender, but you well know how strict are the moral limits within which our action is confined. We are no extirpators of nations, or butchers of peoples. We make no bargain with you. We accord you nothing as a right. Abandon your resistance unconditionally. We remain bound by our customs and our nature."'

He went on to point out that several countries had already unconditionally surrendered to the various Allies.

'Take Finland, take Italy: their peoples have not all been massacred and enslaved. On the contrary, so far as Italy is concerned, there are moments when one has almost wondered whether it was they who had unconditionally surrendered to us, or whether we were about to surrender unconditionally to them.'

The sally raised laughter in the House, but considering the widespread social distress which then prevailed in many parts of Italy did not particularly contribute to serious acceptance of his theme.

He concluded, 'This, at least, I can say on behalf of the United Nations to Germany: "If you surrender now, nothing that you will have to endure after the war will be comparable to what you are otherwise going to suffer during the year 1945." Peace, though based on unconditional surrender, will bring to Germany and Japan an immense immediate amelioration of the suffering and agony which now lies before them. We, the Allies, are no monsters, but faithful men trying to carry forward the light of the world, trying to raise from the bloody welter and confusion in which mankind is now plunged a structure of peace, of freedom, of justice, and of law, which system shall be an abiding and everlasting shelter for all. That is how I venture to set before the House today the grave issue called "unconditional surrender"'.

There were to be criticisms of other parts of Churchill's speech that day but no one found fault with this statement or suggested that by holding out some less harsh formula, the 'suffering and agony' which now lay ahead, not only for Germany and Japan but also, at least in terms of life and injury, for the Allies, might be reduced. The whole question was in any case academic. Unity between the three Allies was, as Churchill had said earlier in his speech, the overriding concern, indispensable to the winning of the war. For the Russians, who since 12th January had so dramatically altered the war's course, 'unconditional surrender' was the only acceptable price for the suffering they themselves had endured.

'We have not come to liberate the Hitlerites from Hitler,' wrote the Russian journalist Ilya Ehrenberg. 'We have come to liberate ourselves and the whole world from an aggressive Germany.'

But confronted by this continued demand for unconditional surrender, how did German morale, to which Hitler had lent his own mystical substance in the less menacing circumstances of January 1st, adapt now to the sweeping Russian advance which by the end of the month had so starkly transformed the outlook for Germany?

Strength, it seemed, could continue to be drawn from the very seriousness of the situation. New battle lines began to emerge as the Russian impetus slowed. The fighting spirit of those German army units encircled and left behind made it easier to feel that one day the tide might turn. Moscow itself cited, for instance, the encircled garrison at Torun as an example of the obstinacy with which such pockets were fighting. The remnants of several divisions which had withdrawn there after their defeat in the Vistula valley were isolated in the town and the old fortress – several thousand men in all. The Russians had to bring up heavy guns to shatter the tough walls of the forts and only when these had done their work or bundles of grenades had been thrust into the embrasures did the half-crazed defenders emerge. Here and there they emerged still fighting, to be cut down in the open by machine-gun fire.

Though large numbers of prisoners had been taken in the offensive as a whole, there had been nothing comparable with the collapse of fighting morale among the French armies in 1940 or the Russian armies in 1941 before similar lightning armoured penetration of a broad front. Moscow itself was warning that fierce battles lay ahead. 'Hitlerite Germany,' *Pravda* had said in a leader broadcast on January 20th, 'precariously balancing on the edge of the precipice will resist with the ferocity of despair . . .'

Certainly a fanatical spirit was being invoked. When a member of Goebbels' Propaganda Ministry, Dr Werner Nauman, had flown into Posen as it waited to take the full onslaught of the Russian advance, he had told a meeting there that few would live to see the glorious and proud moment of German victory. It was likely that the majority of them would be killed so that their children and great-grandchildren might live in a Nazi-run Germany. At the same time other German broadcasts gave a cooler and more rational insight into the seeming disasters. 'Considering this momentum,' said a Home Front broadcast on January 20th, 'it is inevitable that local measures cannot suffice to check the enemy's further advance. Here fresh forces must be brought up from the extreme rear. Until these measures can begin to take effect, the defenders on the spot must improvise.'

What, of course, this commentator failed to mention was that a significant part of Germany's strategic reserves had already been committed to the Ardennes offensive and seriously depleted there. The official interpretation of that offensive now was simply that it had prevented a simultaneous attack in the west to coincide with the attack from the East. 'We can now have some safety in our rear,' as one commentator put it.

Forster, the Danzig Gauleiter, who broadcast on January 27th reminding the Germans of the steadfastness shown by the British and Russian peoples in their own gravest perils, equally disregarded the effect of the Ardennes offensive on the strategic reserves. 'We know,' he went on, 'that so far we are offering only an improvised opposition to the enemy advancing towards us from the east but behind us stands the organisation which is preparing the new front.' Goebbels wrote in *Das Reich*: 'In East Prussia the situation is improving. In Silesia, the Russian onslaught is losing its punch. In Hungary, Budapest will soon be free. The Atlantic is infested with U-boats. The German Air Force will return. Like a storm, the decisive battle is slowly approaching and it will bring to Germany a thousand years of supremacy in Europe.'

Behind all this, as ever, lay the unfathomable power of the Führer's personality. A broadcast to Slovakia on January 23rd told how 'the greatest dreamer, Adolf Hitler, has become the Reich's greatest realist. The lonely leader of Nordic man is communing with his God.'

On the twelfth anniversary of Hitler's accession to power, on the 30th of January, he communed once again with his own people. Twelve years before, Goebbels had written in his diary on this day: 'The Führer has moved into the Chancellor's Palace. . . . It is like a dream come true.'

It was necessary to convey now that it had not become a nightmare.

This was the shortest speech Hitler had ever given on this anniversary – sixteen minutes in length. He spoke, according to *The Times*, more quietly than usual but more vigorously than at the beginning of the month. He spoke of a 'gruesome fate exterminating men in their tens and hundreds of thousands'. But the message of ultimate triumph over such a fate by will and faith was the same. '. . . By dint of utmost exertions, and in spite of all setbacks and all our grim trials, we shall ward it off and master it. That this should even be possible is only because since 1933 the German people has undergone an inner metamorphosis. If it had been the Germany of the Versailles Treaty, Germany would long since have been swept away by the storm-tide from Asia.'

His theme was simple but again near-mystical: National Socialism had triumphed in Germany and therefore the continuity of that triumph could not be broken. The people's natural power of resistance, which neither Jewry 'for all its machinations' nor the bourgeoisie could undermine had been brought to its fullest strength by National Socialism.

'. . . Our nation's power of resistance has increased so tremendously since January 30th, 1933 that it is now beyond compare with earlier times. By maintaining this inner strength of resistance we have the safest guarantee of final victory. . . . That National Socialism was able to arouse and harbour this spirit in our German people is its greatest achievement. One day, when the bells of peace ring out at the close of this tremendous world drama, it will be seen what the German nation owes to this spiritual rebirth – nothing less than its existence on earth.'

The indestructibility of National Socialism and of the German people were thus made identical. The equation served a neat double purpose. The high morale of National Socialism alone ensured survival, thus only National Socialism would survive.

The Führer allowed himself one contemptuous glance at the alternative. Referring to arguments among the Allies over unconditional surrender he said that Allied statesmen who had been outlining Germany's fate had recently been taken to task by their newspapers which urged them to show more cunning and to make promises. 'Pay no attention to any Wilsonian-like promises from the democracies,' he said. (A reference to President Wilson's unredeemed Fourteen Points at the end of World War One.) 'They themselves are no longer able ever to honour such an obligation. It is like one sheep assuring another sheep that it would protect it against a tiger. I repeat my prophecy of former days: not only will Great Britain be incapable of taming Bolshevism. Her own development must necessarily be more and more that of a body infected with this wasting disease. The democracies will not be able to rid themselves of the evil spirits called by them from the steppes of Asia.'

If such reasoning seemed to suggest that the future, if only an infected one, lay with Great Britain rather than the Reich, the Führer immediately dismissed such an inference by returning to his main theme: 'Germany will never suffer that fate. So much is guaranteed by the victory we gained at home twelve years ago.'

And he concluded by concentrating on that personal focus around which National Socialism had always revolved.

'Today, however, I should like to leave you in no doubt about one thing: in the teeth of a hostile world I chose my way at a time when I was an unknown. I went on still unknown, until I reached that final success. But it was alleged that I was dead. Always my death was longed-for. Yet in the end I came out on top . . . I can only be absolved from my duty by Him who called me to it. On July 20th when a bomb exploded within a few feet of me it was within the power of providence to kill me and put an end to my life's work. The fact that on that day the Almighty protected me I regard as a confirmation of the mission entrusted to me. . . . In the end Almighty God will not abandon the man who throughout his life wanted nothing but to preserve his people from a fate which they did not deserve. . . . In this hour I appeal to the whole German people, and above all to my old comrades and to all soldiers, to arm themselves with an even greater and tougher spirit of resistance until the day when we, as we did once before, shall place on our cenotaph a wreath with ribbons bearing the inscription: "Yours are the laurels in spite of everything." I expect every German to do his duty to the last. I want them to bear every sacrifice that is and will be demanded of them.

I expect every fit German to stake his life and body in battle. I expect the sick and the infirm to work to the last ounce of their strength. I expect the urban populations to forge the weapons for this struggle. I expect the peasants to provide bread for the soldiers and workers in this struggle and to cut their own needs to the bone. I expect all women and girls to continue to support the struggle with utmost fanaticism. I appeal with particular confidence to German youth. . . . However grave the crisis it will be mastered in the end by our unshakeable will, by our readiness for sacrifice, and by our power. We shall overcome this calamity. Once again victory will go, not to the Asiatic steppes, but to Europe and at its head the nation which for fifteen hundred years has been Europe's foremost power against the east and will remain so, our Greater German Reich, the German nation.'

'He had nothing to say,' wrote *The Times*, 'that could bring comfort to his hearers in the presence of visible doom . . .'

Such a judgement was true in one sense but ignored other senses to which, by definition, the editor of *The Times* in London was not attuned. It was the very presence of 'visible doom' on which National Socialism was counting to produce a miracle. Of course it was also aware that there were Germans who doubted its miracle-producing properties. But the very possibility of any opposition to the National Socialist ideal was itself used to inspire and strengthen the National Socialist resolve.

The SS newspaper, the *Schwarze Korps* had, a few days before Hitler's speech, attacked those Germans who said that they had not wanted the war and that therefore they should not be held responsible for it by the Allies. 'These people,' it said with some truth, 'who now claim that they are disinterested, enjoyed the favourable results of National Socialism. They took part in the so-called assimilation of Jewish properties and in the economic development of the Reich. Every German will suffer the same fate in the event of defeat.' And two days after Hitler's speech Goebbels writing in *Das Reich* had said: 'It is just before zero hour. Let no coward think that in this hour of peril he can get away with placing his life above the life of Germany or that he has the right to accuse our leaders.'

Such a national mood purveyed daily through newspapers and radio to which the German people had long dutifully attended, was re-inforced by commentaries from spokesmen often thought more detached from the official party line than the leaders. General Dittmar, whose commentaries ranged even more objectively over the military situation than the German High Command's reasonably honest reports, himself seemed to lend the sanction of reason to fanaticism.

'Action,' he said in the first week of February, 'is always better than the dull suffering to which we are to be condemned. It would be better

99

even if it were of no avail, for although it would lead to a horrible end, passivity would lead to an endless horror.'

Goebbels supplied the poetry. 'The horsemen of the Apocalypse,' he cried, 'are fouling our land. Your leaders know that your sufferings are as nothing to what lies in store if we abandon the fight and confide ourselves to the magnanimity of a foe who knows no mercy, who is drunk in his thirst for vengeance. We must drain the cup of war to its bitter dregs, yet keep our heads, if we are to hold on until that moment when the danger, having reached its culmination, becomes visible to all. We will then come out the victors.'

In the light of all this a sober assessment of the future came from Eisenhower's headquarters in Brussels – where, with the Russians only 45 miles from Berlin, a common greeting was said to be 'How are the Russians doing?' SHAEF announced that the hope that the Germans might surrender, if and when the Red Army reached Berlin, was discouraged by all known facts of the Nazi régime's intentions and the morale of the German soldiers and people. Although, it said, obvious doom now faced the Third Reich it seemed likely that a painful and bloody struggle would still be needed on both eastern and western fronts before its leaders and many of its soldiers and civilians could be made to succumb to it.

In the meantime preparations had to be made for the day when that would happen.

There were unmistakable signs that the meeting between the Big Three leaders of the Grand Alliance was at last about to take place. The *New York Times* correspondent in London reported that President Roosevelt's special advisor, Harry Hopkins, had been there, though his visit had passed almost unnoticed. Similarly, he reported, the absence of both Churchill and Eden from the capital was not being remarked upon publicly. Cairo radio said that the conference had already started but had not said where. The meeting was to be, said the *New York Times*, 'a kind of preliminary peace conference.' 'The three statesmen,' wrote Anne O'Hare McCormick in that paper, 'have come together to deal with victory. The decisions they have to make are difficult and inexorable. The decisions the President has to make on behalf of the United States are perhaps the most momentous in our history. What will they be?'

Chapter Ten

There was a solemn awareness that the shaping of the post-war world was about to begin. There was also an increasingly realistic attitude towards those awkward problems with which the Big Three would have to concern themselves. In an important Foreign Affairs debate in the United States Senate on the 15th of January the voice of realism had spoken through the person of Senator Burton K. Wheeler, a Democrat from Montana.

Although a supporter of Roosevelt's domestic policy, Wheeler had long been an astringent critic of his foreign policy or rather of what he considered to be the lack of it. Quite apart from now branding 'unconditional surrender' as 'a brutal and asinine slogan' he daringly described the tentative plans for a post-war World Security Organisation outlined at Dumbarton Oaks as 'a plan to underwrite tyranny'. His theme was that the war was developing into a struggle for a new balance of power. Despite, he said, many proclamations of democratic ideals on the part of the Allies, there was no real unity between on the one hand Britain and Russia who were attempting to create their own spheres of influence in a new balance of power, and on the other the American people who were still hoping to justify the sacrifices of the war by achieving a fair and lasting peace. The so-called unity among the Big Three, said the Senator, was merely the result of 'an international shotgun wedding'. Instead of supporting the principles of disarmament, sovereignty, human freedom and non-intervention in the internal affairs of other nations, the Allies were now making military and political decisions which violated all these principles. Moral degeneration had set in.

The Senator specifically charged the Russians with 'seeking to sovietise Poland' and said that in the course of the alleged Russian liberation a large part of the Polish underground had either been liquidated or thrown into concentration camps. 'Under the present armistice terms now being forced upon the countries of Eastern Europe one by one,' he said, 'thousands upon thousands more human beings are being subjected to the terms of a ruthless conqueror.'

He had been speaking for more than two hours when another Democratic Senator, Claud Pepper from Florida, jumped up and protested that the Soviet Union had for years pleaded the need for a collective security system but the United States had ignored this and now that they were on the point of creating some kind of international system with the other major nations, Senator Wheeler was casting doubt on their intentions and even speaking as if he did not want the United States to press on to Berlin or Tokyo or create an international security system at all.

Senator Wheeler replied at once that he did not want a negotiated peace. But Senator Pepper had effectively exposed him. For, thus forced to make clear what exactly it was that he did want, or rather how exactly what he wanted was to be achieved, his own brand of austere realism began to blur almost as mistily as the idealism of President Roosevelt. Wheeler said he certainly wanted to see Japan crushed and the Axis military might destroyed and held down; but all nations must adopt a universal Bill of Rights, and a United Nations Political Council must immediately be created to provide for democratic settlement in harmony with the principles of the Atlantic Charter of territorial questions in Europe. He did not say how this was to be achieved either with or without the Russians' consent. He merely affirmed that there must be a pledge by the United Nations to support free plebiscites under international supervision in the liberated countries, and that a United States of Europe was the only way in which peace could be secured on the Continent.

As the *New York Times* commentator, Arthur Knock, remarked: 'Senator Wheeler balked at endorsing the alternatives implied by his criticism.' He did not say that the United States should have declined to aid or receive the aid of Russia in the war against Germany, or that the United States should have rejected the assistance of Great Britain in the war against Japan. In Knock's view the only truly realistic approach made so far to the thorny problems of the post-war peace was that of Senator Vandenberg who had seen the watertight prevention of any post-war German aggression as 'at the heart of the immediate problem which bedevils our Allied relationship.'

This conviction that it was the re-emergence of aggressive German nationalism which was the fundamental menace to the peace of the post-war world was widely held. It was the enemies of today who were seen primarily as the potential enemies of tomorrow. 'Our primary war aim,' wrote Anne O'Hare McCormick in the *New York Times*, 'is to disarm Germany and Japan and keep them disarmed in order to prevent that "third war" that prophets of despair are already conjuring up.'

President Roosevelt's Special Adviser Harry Hopkins had written in the *American Magazine*: 'We must accept . . . that the earth is not civilised enough to make worldwide disarmament practical for peace-loving nations. . . . When this war ends we must immediately prepare to defend ourselves, particularly to make sure that our enemies realise that if they dare to strike again they will lose again. I have no doubt that powerful forces in Germany and Japan are preparing even now for their next attempt to conquer us. We will try to keep them impotent, but only a permanent army of occupation would be able to keep them from re-arming eventually.' He foresaw a need to be wary of 'fifth columns and sheep's clothing enemies' preparing to attack, who would attempt to convince the Allies that they were lovers of peace, interested only in becoming good friends and customers.

In Britain, too, Sir Stafford Cripps, the Minister of Aircraft Production, while insisting that the Allies should treat the Germans as brothers and with friendship once peace was restored, also insisted 'upon taking measures to protect and comfort our other European brothers upon whom you [the Germans] and your leaders have inflicted such untold suffering.' He told a meeting of Baptists he addressed in London, 'The whole of the younger generation in Germany and many of the older ones too have been imbued with a fanatical materialistic nationalism that is very strong and deep-seated. The end of the war will not destroy that spirit in the Nazis. They will continue working to avenge their defeat.'

All such warnings were accompanied by fearful projections of what a Third World War would be like. 'A new range of fears has been created in the world,' said Cripps and went on to speak of 'the fear of the new weapons, each more ghastly and terrible than the last, each carrying its destruction farther and farther into the territories of other nations. . . . No one,' he added, 'knows – or even can – the climax of the terrors of this unending exhibition of human ingenuity or how frightful will be the weapons of another war if it should come . . .'

Harry Hopkins' warning against a renewed German menace had made exactly the same point. 'We don't know,' he had said, 'what new weapons will be developed. Robot bombs, armies landed from the air and from submarines, enormous bombing 'planes and perhaps gas will be among the devices that might be used in an attempt to defeat us quickly if we are not prepared. Before such an attack, attempts will be made to cause us to become careless and complacent.'

Herbert Morrison, the British Home Secretary, addressing a Labour meeting in Manchester, gave a similarly sombre warning. World War Three, he said, would involve the use of 'new and terrible' aerial projectiles.

'This warfare,' he went on, 'is going to develop to a greater intensity, a greater precision as the scientist masters it, and soldiers know more and more about it. New methods of defence, adequate, safe and instantaneous may be evolved, but they have not been evolved yet. You may get a war before we know anything about it. . . . If you get World War Three it might mean the end of the human race – and if we haven't got the guts to stop it we deserve such an end.'

This precarious feeling about the nature of any future war, whether brought about by the Germans, Japanese or from any other source, gave a particular urgency to the immediate task of the Big Three. Their final conference of the war was, so rumour ran by 4th February, already taking place somewhere on the Black Sea.

Chapter Eleven

A leading article in the London *Daily Herald* on the eve of the Black Sea conference said it had now become clear to all thoughtful people that the downfall of Hitler, unconditional surrender and the liberation of occupied territories would not end the crisis through which mankind was struggling. 'We face the possibility that the boons for which our men are still fighting and dying will be snatched from us. This gloomy picture need not be realised. It will not be realised if the leaders of the United Nations apply themselves with sufficient vigour to the problems of political and economic collaboration. But the moment is now, it cannot be any further postponed. . . . A mere agreement to agree,' it added, 'will not satisfy the hopes of the people.'

The American poetess Edna St Vincent Millay had, in January, published a poem which expressed her own urgent concern:

> 'This was a war for freedom, so we thought it;
> And so we fought it,
> You knew this, all of you,
> You promised us a new
> World – a decent one this time,
> A world a man might live in without shame.
> How is it going forward, this great enterprise, this plot
> To outwit Evil – Are the blueprints done?
> And may we see them? No? Why not?
>
> The time is not yet ripe, you state.
>
> We say: "The time is ripening fast, the time will rot
> At the core, too late
> For harmony, the proper moment past."'

The London *Times* echoed her in its own fashion: 'Now the time is ripe – indeed the need is urgent – to set about preparing the progress for peace.'

There was no shortage of other voices, particularly in parts of the United States press and Congress to suggest urgency and apprehension. But the *New York Times* giving level expression to such anxieties, offered reassurance.

'In certain quarters in this country,' it wrote, 'as well as in Britain there does seem to be a touch of apprehension. It is as though some observers desired Russia to be strong enough to ensure an Allied victory but not quite as strong as she actually is.'

It pointed out that curiously these were usually the same people who only a few months before had been fearful that the Russian armies might halt on some prearranged line and there negotiate a truce which would release German soldiers for the western front.

'Surely,' went on the paper, 'all the United Nations have an interest in an enduring peace. The Russian system, though greatly different from our own, rests on an expressed ideal of the welfare of the common man. Nor need we doubt in the least that Marshal Stalin and his associates honestly plan, once they have made their frontiers secure according to the view of security, to build up living standards in Russia in an atmosphere of international peace. They have roused their people to unparalleled exertions and sacrifices to defend what even the Communists have called "Holy Russia". They might not be able to rouse them to an imperialistic war even if they desired to do so. The final measure of their success would be more for the average Russian to eat, or for him to wear, better housing, a better life. . . . If these are their objectives we can welcome their co-operation after victory as we have rejoiced in it in the days of battle. We have common ground with them in the march on Berlin. We must find common ground in the march of all mankind towards goodwill and peace.'

But what if common ground were not to be found? A letter to the paper from a New York businessman insisted that the issue was not to be fudged. The United States, he said, had gone into the war to establish the ideal of world-wide freedoms and any world organisation into which it entered would have to make this the first and foremost consideration.

There were many other voices. Some assured the American people that there were no grounds for Russian and American dissension at all. Representative Augustus W. Benel, who had replaced the isolationist Hamilton Fish in Congress at the election, speaking at a Brooklyn American-Soviet Friendship meeting, said of the two great countries:

'They have no common frontier, neither wants anything the other has except by way of exchange in the open market, and there is no history of past victories, defeats or injustices to embitter the peoples of the two countries against each other . . .'

And he went on to give an explanation of what might sometimes seem like Russian intransigence:

'. . . Our papers carry frequent utterances about the probability of war between the two countries. . . . Naturally enough an attitude of this sort on this side of the Pacific brings a reaction in like vein from writers in the Soviet press who seem equally unaware of the necessity of temperate speech.'

C. L. Sulzberger in the *New York Times Magazine* found grounds for qualified optimism. It was, he said, 'foolish to dismiss the fact that great mutual distrust for the USSR still existed among many minds in the United States, Britain and France, vis-à-vis the Soviet Union and vice versa.' But in the past three years there had been much progress towards removing that distrust, though more had to be done. 'It would be ridiculous to suppose that victory would eliminate many pressing international problems which become clearer weekly, and mutual anxieties concerning the juxtaposition of these mysteries and invisible things called spheres. Firm hands and cool heads all round are necessary to solve such puzzles.'

In Britain, Lord Templewood, once Sir Samuel Hoare and at the beginning of the war a member of Neville Chamberlain's Government, was among those who found it difficult to disguise his misgivings. In a speech in the House of Lords he said that in regard to the Big Three Conference he agreed with a previous speaker, Lord Addison, about 'the magnificent achievements of our Russian allies during the last few weeks.' But he was also, he said, somewhat disturbed about 'certain recent developments'. Under their eyes there had gradually been taking shape the new pattern of Europe. It was very different from the pattern some of them had contemplated two or three years before. It was differing in certain material respects from the principles of the Atlantic Charter . . .

An example of what he was talking about had been taking place in Bulgaria, where certain features in the political situation appeared disturbing. For although the Russians were not intervening openly in political matters there, the fact that the Red Army was in occupation seemed to be giving the local Communists the right to do what they liked in the country, virtually unchallenged. In theory the Russian attitude was impeccable. In Moscow in October 1944, Molotov had told the United States Armistice Commission: 'Bulgaria will remain a democratic country and we will not interfere in her internal affairs. Bulgaria will remain with her democratic government and her present order and will govern herself in the manner she may decide.' However, the reality seemed to be developing differently.

The *New York Times* correspondent, Joseph Levy who had just spent six weeks in the country reported early in January 1945: 'The people of Bulgaria are disappointed and feel that they are being cheated by the

Allies. The average Bulgar believed the promises made over the Allied radio from London, Moscow and New York that when his country was liberated from the Germans he too would be liberated and eventually enjoy President Roosevelt's Four Freedoms. . . . But, instead, he feels Bulgaria today, four months after liberation from the Nazi yoke, is subjected to a Bulgarian dictatorial régime as unbearable and distasteful to the vast majority of Bulgars as was the former Nazi-inspired Fascist Government.'

There were four major parties in the so-called Bulgarian 'Fatherland Front' Government – the Agrarian, Zveno, Socialist and Communist parties. And although the Communists only represented, it was reckoned, some two per cent of the people of Bulgaria, it was their party which had borne the brunt of the fighting against the Nazis. Although, at the liberation, the partisans had been welcomed down from the mountains as heroes and behaved as such for a short period afterwards, they had soon come under the political control of the Party organisation which was far superior to that of any of the other political parties in the government. The forty-six-year-old veteran woman Communist, Tsola Dragoytchova, Secretary of the National Committee of the Fatherland Front in Sofia had almost unlimited power and was the real ruler of the country.

Levy reported that a virtual reign of terror prevailed in Bulgaria and that ordinary civil rights were almost non-existent. Such elementary democratic principles as free speech and free press criticism were taboo. He was convinced that the vast majority of the people in the country were ardently hoping for early Allied action to establish a democratic régime.

There had, he said, been at least two incidents in which the Red Army itself had intervened specifically to overrule the nominal democracy in favour of the Communist Party. When the new Bulgarian Cabinet passed a Decree permitting those officers who had not been strongly pro-German before the coup d'état of September 1944 to be reinstated in the army, General Birksoff, the Russian Commander of the Army of Occupation, had annulled the Decree on the grounds that it contravened that article of the Armistice Agreement which said that the new Bulgaria must do away with fascist elements. Again, when the Communist Party had wanted the leader of the Agrarian Party dismissed from his post because they found him difficult to work with, the occupation authorities had intervened and dismissed him.

Levy also reported that the Russians were treating the British and American officials in Bulgaria with great suspicion and some contempt. The British were regarded as the more suspect, the Americans as relatively harmless nuisances who had to be tolerated. Movement was restricted, even for members of the Allied Armistice Commission. The head of the British section of that Commission, and the head of the American section, two Major-Generals, had been physically prevented from going to lunch with the Bulgarian Commander-in-Chief because the Red Army said that his residence was outside the area within which they were permitted to circulate. The Bulgars were understandably said to be perplexed by all this. They saw the Russians driving around in American jeeps and American trucks provided under Lend-Lease and, witnessing the disregard with which the Allies who had provided them were treated, were puzzled. They may well have wondered whether in these circumstances the United States was likely to be able to establish that democracy for which, within their latest instalment of tyranny, Bulgaria was still yearning.

But the political fate of the Bulgars was unlikely in the long run to seem of sufficient significance to the Western Allies to be allowed seriously to disturb the already delicate atmosphere of the Crimean Conference. Acceptable resolution of another potentially awkward matter – the difficulty in Yugoslavia between the Communist Liberation Front under Tito and the Royal Yugoslav Government in London – had fortunately been reached by the Tito-Subasitch agreement just as the conference opened. Poland, though, was an issue of far greater significance and concern than either.

After all, it was to help save Poland that Britain had entered the war in the first place in September 1939. The fact that the Russians had then had a Treaty of Friendship with Nazi Germany and indeed had soon implemented this by occupying that part of sovereign Polish territory which had not been occupied by the Germans, made the present and future destiny of the country an issue of the most awkward sensitivity. Recent events had made it more awkwardly sensitive still.

The distinguished *News Chronicle* correspondent Vernon Bartlett had rightly discerned on the first day of 1945 that Poland would probably become the most striking example of the new tendency to divide Europe into zones of influence between the major Allied powers. The United States Republican representative for Wisconsin, Congressman Alvin E. Konski, spoke more bluntly. In the light of Churchill's recent commitment in the House of Commons to the Curzon Line frontier demanded by the Russians, Konski said that Poland, 'a gallant ally', had been 'sold down the river'. He called on Roosevelt to withdraw American troops from Europe unless the United Nations could agree on what they were fighting for there.

The last sovereign Polish Government had been in London since reassembling there after its flight through Rumania in 1939 and continued flight from Paris in 1940. Although, since 1941, it had been a member of the same Alliance as the Russians, relations between it and the Soviet Union had been broken off in 1943 following the discovery by the advancing Germans of the bodies of many thousands of Polish officers who had been shot and buried at Katyn. The Russians maintained that the murders had been committed by the Germans. The Germans invited a neutral commission to investigate the site. The Polish Government in London lent its support to such a proposal. The Russians withdrew recognition from them.

The Polish underground Home Army, owing allegiance to the London Government had consistently carried out sabotage and other activity against the Germans in occupied Poland. They had in 1943 and the early part of 1944 fought many pitched battles with German units and destroyed many trains. When the Russian summer offensive opened in that year this Polish Home Army received orders from London to co-operate with the attacking Russians and had helped the Red Army liberate cities such as Vilna and Lvov. In August 1944 when the Red Army arrived at the gates of Warsaw itself and began to enter Praga, the Warsaw suburb on the eastern bank of the Vistula, the Home Army had, again on orders from London, risen in the city itself.

For 63 days under their General Bor-Komorowski they had fought desperately but in vain against the Germans while the Russians, also meeting fierce German resistance had been unable – or, some said, unwilling – to get across the Vistula to help them. When Bor-Komorowski's men finally surrendered, a certain feeling that the Russians had been content to watch this annihilation of patriotic 'bourgeois' Polish elements politically opposed to Communism further aggravated the historic mistrust of Russia felt by many Poles in London and elsewhere.

A surviving combatant of the Warsaw Rising had arrived in London only a few days before the Crimean Conference opened. He and his wife had avoided being taken prisoner after the surrender by joining the columns of civilians being evacuated by the Germans to an internment camp from which they had subsequently managed to escape. (It was as well they did, for the death-rate in this camp was to be very high.) He was a Lieutenant Jan Novak of the Polish Home Army, a man of 30 who had married his wife in Warsaw on September 7th when, he said, 'We thought we had only a few more days to live.' He described the sixty-three days of fighting against the Germans in the city as 'a Hell you cannot even imagine.'

He said that when the Rising began on the 1st August 1944 the sound of a great battle on the east bank of the Vistula could be plainly heard, but that on the 2nd August about 8 o'clock in the evening there was 'a sudden complete and terrible silence' and the Russian air force appeared to cease its activity altogether. It was not until the second week of September that the battle there started up again and the Russians captured the suburb of Praga. The Poles, who were still masters of the west bank of the Vistula in one sector, could see Russian tanks and soldiers on the east bank. 'We could not understand why they did not cross,' said Novak.

When the Russians took the Praga telephone and wireless communications centre the Russians acknowledged messages received from the Poles but themselves sent no answers. On the day of the surrender itself Bor-Komorowski had sent the Red Army Marshal Rokossovsky a message to the effect that he could not hold out any longer unless help were to come very soon and he asked how soon it might be before it could be expected. He said he needed a reply within twenty-four hours. There was no reply. By the time Novak gave this account in London, of course, Warsaw had been recaptured by the Red Army in its January offensive but Novak had concluded his account by saying, 'After what has happened the Polish people are terribly afraid of what is coming.'

After the liberation of the town of Lublin, east of the Vistula, in the 1944 offensive, the Russians had set up the Polish National Committee formed from loyal members of the Polish Communist Party in Moscow. It was headed by hitherto largely unknown names – Bierut, Gomulka and Osubka-Morawski. Recognition of them as a Government caused embarrassment within the Alliance, whose other members continued to recognise the London Poles as the legitimate Polish Government.

An attempt had been made in the preceding months to achieve some sort of political *modus vivendi* between the London and Lublin Poles which would have avoided exposure of such an embarrassing rift. The Pole who had been Prime Minister of the London Government for the greater part of 1944, Mikolajczyk, had striven hard to avoid a breach and had gone to Moscow in July with the good wishes of the British Government to try to prevent one.

The chief point at issue had been the Russian demand for an immediate approval of the Curzon Line as the country's eastern frontier (with compensation to be sought from former German territories in the west) and the Russian wish to bring about a new legal basis for Polish sovereignty in a government to be composed of representatives both of the London and Lublin Poles. Mikolajczyk eventually agreed to try and work out some compromise with his London colleagues but on returning to London after a second visit to Moscow was unable to convince them that they should accept the new frontiers. Faced by his failure to find any basis for reconciliation between London and Lublin, he resigned and on 30th November 1944 a new London Government was formed, headed by the old Socialist Arciszewski as Prime Minister, who himself had only escaped from Poland in the summer. There were soon two rival Polish Governments, one on Polish soil backed by the physical presence of the Red Army, and two Polish Prime Ministers, Osubka-Morawski assuming that rôle in Poland, with Bierut as the Provisional Government's Chairman.

They proceeded to attack each other in the most vitriolic terms. Replying to the Lublin Committee announcement of the 31st December that it now constituted the legal sovereign Provisional Government of Poland the London Polish Government declared that in the parts of Poland now cleared of German occupation there existed neither freedom of speech nor of assembly.

'. . . The Polish nation,' it said, 'has no means of expressing its will and manifesting its disapproval of this new act of lawlessness on the part of the Lublin Committee. . . . The Polish nation will never recognise any authority of any totalitarian form imposed on Polish national territory and will not cease to stand for the genuine independence of Poland . . .' It insisted that after clearing all Polish territory of German occupation and the evacuation of all foreign troops from Poland, the Polish people should be able in free and democratic elections to choose the political system they wanted for their country and to elect a government in accordance with their own wills.

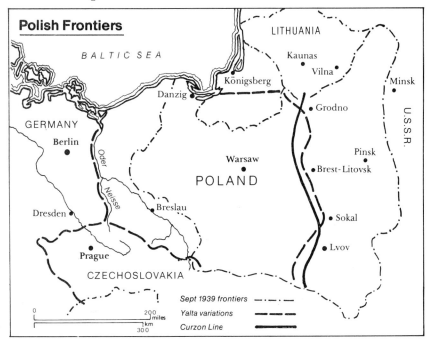

On paper there was, as the Russians saw it, nothing for any Pole to worry about. Ilya Ehrenberg himself put it on paper, in *Pravda*: 'Far be it from us to wish to force our ideas upon others. . . . Nowhere does the Red Army meddle in the affairs of other peoples.'

But few Poles found it easy to accept such assurances. As Lieutenant Novak said when he arrived in London at the end of the month: 'If the Devil could help the Polish people at this moment they would help him. But they do not think these people can help.'

The implacable hostility of the Lublin Poles for those in London, of whatever political complexion, was made clear when Bierut violently attacked Mikolajczyk even though Mikolajczyk himself had been attacking the London Premier Arcisewski for his intransigence and lack of flexibility. Mikolajczyk, said Bierut, was 'an impostor' and an 'enemy of the State'. The Lublin Premier Osubka-Morawski branded Mikolajczyk as a 'willing tool of reactionaries' and stated emphatically that the Provisional Government would 'stamp out' all possible opposition encouraged by the so-called Government in London. This touched on the particularly sensitive area of the underground Polish Home Army, which still took its orders from London. The Lublin and indeed the Red Army's attitude to this patriotic underground was what it had appeared to be at the time of the Warsaw rising and indeed Osubka-Morawski now specifically condemned that event as 'a provocative rising which considerably aided the Germans.' His attitude was that the only acceptable military instrument with which the Germans were to be attacked was the Red Army or those newly-organised Polish units within the framework of the Red Army which were under the control of the Lublin Government. He labelled the London-organised resistance as 'traitors, bandits, incorrigible malefactors and brawlers', and strangely adopting the terminology of the German occupiers accused it of inspiring 'terrorist' activities in liberated Poland. Mikolajczyk, he said, had done nothing to separate himself from this reactionary campaign against Polish democracy and he added, 'In such circumstances I assess negatively any chances of agreement.'

The new Polish Army organised by Lublin under the control of the Soviet Union was already said to consist of 30,000 officers and some 200,000 men either at the front or in training. Some of these paraded down the main street of Lublin early in January for an hour, riding in American Lend-Lease Studebaker and Chevrolet ten-wheeled trucks, while the President Bierut and the Prime Minister, Osubka-Morawski took the salute. Others had been stationed in the Warsaw suburb of Praga and took part in the great Russian offensive which eventually seized the capital on 18th January. Shortly before this triumph they had been visited there by a party of western correspondents who were given luncheon by the Commander of the new First Polish Army, Lieutenant-General Stanislaus Poplawski. He talked to them in the farm cottage which was his headquarters. 'Our soldiers,' he said, 'fight alongside the Red Army, but they always feel that the Americans and the British are behind them also.'

President Roosevelt had awarded him the DSC in 1943 with a citation in English and Russian, and he told the correspondents how deeply moved he had been to receive this. 'I wish for President Roosevelt,' he added, 'many years of life and successful work for democracy.'

The capture of Warsaw, its entry by uniformed Polish units fighting together with the Red Army and the immediate installation there of the 'Provisional Government' from Lublin of course added significantly to that Government's standing and prestige, though everyone knew that its real strength derived from Moscow. The comment of the London Poles on this great event scarcely bothered to be enigmatic. The Socialist Prime Minister Arciszewski took advantage of the occasion to recall, while noting 'the expulsion of German invaders from the ruins of our capital,' the cry which Warsaw Radio broadcast at the end of the 63-day struggle in 1944: 'We are fighting for freedom, we are fighting for the right to be free.'

'At this moment,' added Arciszewski, 'these words embody, as then, what Poland asks of the world.'

This, then, was the intricate problem of Poland which Churchill, Roosevelt and Stalin had now to try and resolve to their mutual agreement at their conference in the Crimea. In some ways the situation provided a mirror-image of what had been happening in the course of the liberation of German-occupied countries in western Europe. The 'reactionary' Polish underground of the Home Army, resisting the invitation of the official liberators to give up their arms and enrol under the official auspices of the new establishment were the counterparts of the 'Communists' of Belgium and Greece. And a similar confusion about the rights and wrongs of the issue bothered some honest democrats. In the United States the American-Polish Labour Council, which claimed to represent over half a million Americans of Polish origin and was affiliated to the big Labour Unions, openly backed the Lublin Government, hoping that 'our Government will find a way towards cordial co-operation with Soviet-recognised régimes.' It maintained that the overwhelming majority of the people in the liberated areas were giving support to Lublin. The people, it said, were practising democracy; trades unions were being established; churches and schools were open. Addressing the Lublin Government and the Russians the Council concluded: 'We have no doubt of your friendship for the aspirations of the Polish people to build a strong, independent and democratic Poland.'

In Britain the democratic Left – surprisingly perhaps after its Greek performance – was more sceptical. When the Lublin Committee had declared itself the first Provisional Government of liberated Poland, a leader in the Labour *Daily Herald* had called it 'not a surprise but our sombre expectations do not make the fact any more agreeable. . . . All the available evidence suggests that the Polish Government in London has commanded the allegiance of the majority of Poles. It is contemptible to denounce them as Fascists.'

Michael Foot, in his column in the *Daily Herald* on the 5th January wrote, '. . . In the main it is true that despite the obvious deficiencies of the Polish Government [in London] the Polish underground with its record of heroism second to none has preferred to take its orders from London rather than Moscow or Lublin. This is the first conclusion that makes it impossible for Socialists to hail the Lublin Committee as the heaven-sent saviours of their country. The Lublin Committee is much more of a clique than the men in London who speak in the name of the Polish Socialist Party and the Polish Peasant Party and who started organising opposition to the Germans in 1940.'

Foot said he was opposed to the Curzon Line frontier and subsequent compensation to Poland from German territories in the west. It would be unjust to the eight million Germans who happened to live there to expel them. He went on to develop his own brand of the international wishful thinking required if the Alliance were successfully to complete its immediate primary purpose of winning the war. Asking rhetorically whether a view such as his of the Lublin Poles might not involve us in a fatal quarrel with the Soviet Union, he replied that this was by no means necessarily so. True friendship with the Soviet Union did not mean that we had to accept every policy she supported as all-wise or all-sufficient. The Soviet Union could be pardoned for reposing faith in their own strength. They had been given 'good grounds both before and after Munich for fearing a capitalist plot against their country.'

'Our business,' he went on, 'is to convince the rulers and people of Russia that they may repose faith also in our strength, the strength of the Labour movement to govern the country. There is little hope for future peace in a drawing of strategic frontiers, mass transfers and private bargains between the Soviet Union and an opportunist ruling class in Britain. There is more hope both for peace and the proper development of world Socialism in the co-operation and exchange of views and doctrines, even if some of these doctrines differ, between the Soviet Union and a Socialist Government in Britain.'

But although a number of Labour Party politicians held prominent posts as Ministers in the British Government, there was not yet in any way a Socialist Government in Britain; Churchill, who had stopped off at Malta on his way to the Black Sea for preliminary consultations with Roosevelt, had to face the problem in more realistic terms.

There was some sign of hardening realism in official American circles. In Rome after his short visit to London and while on the way to the Black Sea himself, Harry Hopkins, Roosevelt's special representative, had given a press conference. At it, he said that he had rather changed his mind on his original view that the war should be successfully concluded before political problems were discussed and settled. It was contrary to American interests that any liberated country should adopt or continue to have a totalitarian Government in any form, regardless of the tag that might be put on it. He added that America might well swing back to isolationism if the peace were not based on the ideals for which the war had been fought.

The problem for realists was how to focus the ideals of the western democracies and those of Russia into a single vision. Some thought that it was exactly the attempt to do that which constituted the real danger. Harry Hopkins, reading the copy of the *New York Times* report of his Rome statement, could have found a letter in the paper from a reader much disgusted by what he had seen there recently about Bulgaria. For all the idealism of the Atlantic Charter, he wrote, 'those who are less befuddled by a foggy or groggy idealism see . . . a clear outline of Russia's determination to transform her temporary sphere of influence into a springboard for yet greater accomplishments. The sooner the masks of insincerity drop the better it will be for the world.'

Chapter Twelve

A last minute attempt, before the Conference, to combine some flexibility with a realistic attitude to Russia now came from an unexpected quarter. The London Poles said they were ready to divest themselves of some of their sovereignty on certain terms. They delivered simultaneously to the Foreign Office in London and the State Department in Washington a memorandum designed to help the great powers bring about a resumption of Polish-Russian negotiations 'on a basis of lasting and friendly co-operation'. The one condition they laid down was that any final solution of the Polish-Soviet problem should be based on international right and that vital Polish questions were not to be settled without consultation with the Polish Government. Within this framework they were ready to accept the setting-up of an Inter-Allied Military Commission in Poland to carry on the administration of Polish territory until free elections could be held. They merely stipulated that these elections should not be held until the millions of Poles now abroad – in prison camps, concentration and labour camps as well as in Polish fighting units in the west – had been able to return to Poland; also that the elections should not take place in the presence of any troops on Polish soil other than those belonging to the Inter-Allied Commission. But the Allies were about to deal with such matters on their own level and the memorandum received no reply.

Nothing was officially heard of the Conference until the afternoon of February 7th. Then it was announced that a meeting of Churchill, Stalin and Roosevelt, together with their Foreign Secretaries and Chiefs of Staff, taking place in the area of the Black Sea, had already reached agreement for joint military operations in the final phase of the war against Nazi Germany, and was now considering the problems of a secure peace, including the earliest possible establishment of an organisation to maintain it. The London correspondent of the *New York Times* reported that this first official announcement was generally taken as being a forecast of blows against Germany in the west soon to equal those which for the past four weeks had been so successfully striking her from the east.

The news of the Conference came as a surprise to most Russians, who did not even know that Stalin was absent from the Kremlin. Indeed, the Soviet Union had been chosen as the site largely because Stalin alone of the three leaders was personally involved in the conduct of military operations and did not want to leave the country. As late as January, Teheran, as in 1943, had been tipped as the most probable location. A further advantage of the Black Sea, it was thought by some, was that it would be easily accessible to any German delegation which might wish to come and sue for peace. There had been some rumours that that might happen if the Conference went on long enough.

In Moscow, Russians expressed delight about the complete agreement reached on joint military operations. There had in recent weeks been some tendency there, both in the press and in private conversation, to wonder why the Anglo-American allies did not put on their own big offensive to match the Red Army's in the east. But if, to the Russians, it was the military aspect of joint deliberations that seemed the most significant, the emphasis of expectation in Washington was slightly different. It was reported from there that Senators were growing impatient with the lack of more substantive news. The *New York Times* meanwhile continued to stress the meeting's widest possible significance, saying that it '. . . may well be the most fateful meeting of our times. . . . The shape of the forthcoming peace and the security and well-being of Europe and the Atlantic world may depend on how successful they are.'

Then on the 12th February it was announced that the meeting was over. It had been held in the fifty-room white granite Summer Palace of the former Czar Nicholas II at Yalta, a Black Sea resort in which many buildings had been badly damaged at the time of the German advance into the Crimea and on which repairs had been completed only a few weeks before. The backdrop of low mountains sloping down to the sea through cypress woodlands, vineyards, mulberries, figs, olives, pomegranates and tobacco plantations provided something of an idyllic setting for a conference trying to settle the peace of the world. The full communiqué (which revealed that it had been going on for a week, having started on February 4th) listed the results under nine headings.

The first of these expressed satisfaction 'from every point of view' at a 'closer co-ordination of the military effort of the three Allies than ever before.' The closer working partnership would result in a shortening of the war. The section concluded:

'Nazi Germany is doomed. The German people will only make the cost of their defeat heavier to themselves by attempting to continue a hopeless resistance.'

The second heading dealt with the occupation and control of Ger-

Yalta: Stalin and Churchill

Yalta: Roosevelt and Molotov

many. Germany was to be divided into three separate zones of occupation – one for each of the three Powers, and France was to be invited, 'if she should so desire,' to take a fourth. Determination was expressed 'to disarm and disband all German armed forces; break up for all time the German General Staff . . . ; remove or destroy all German military equipment; eliminate or control the German industry that could be used for military production; bring all war criminals to justice and swift punishment . . .' And this section concluded: 'It is not our purpose to destroy the people of Germany, but only when Nazism and militarism have been extirpated will there be hope for a decent life for Germans and a place for them in the comity of nations.'

Under the third section heading it was announced that Germany would have to pay reparations by way of compensation for the damage in kind she had wrought 'to the greatest extent possible'.

The fourth heading dealt with a Conference of the United Nations, called to meet at San Francisco on the 25th April 1945 to prepare the charter for the international organisation to maintain peace and security which had been outlined at Dumbarton Oaks. The problem of the voting procedures unresolved then was now, it was announced, resolved; details of the agreement would be made public after consultation with China and France.

The fifth heading, 'Declaration on Liberated Europe', contained nothing of which the most sensitive or suspicious conscience could complain, except possibly that all worries seemed to have disappeared too easily. The main principle of the Atlantic Charter was reiterated – the right of all peoples to choose the form of government under which they were to live, and assurance was given of the 'restoration of sovereign rights and self-government to those peoples who had been forcibly deprived of them by the aggressor nations.' The three Governments' one purpose was to concert their policies in order to assist the peoples of Europe 'to solve by democratic means their pressing political and economic problems.' They would jointly assist the liberated peoples 'to form interim governmental authorities broadly representative of all democratic elements in the population and pledged to the earliest possible establishment through free elections of Governments responsive to the will of the people; and to facilitate where necessary the holding of such elections.'

The sixth heading spelt out these pledges with particular reference to Poland. It began: 'We came to the Crimea Conference resolved to settle our differences about Poland.' A common desire was reaffirmed to 'see established a strong, free, independent and democratic Poland.' The need was recognised for a new Polish Provisional Government of National Unity: 'The Provisional Government which is now functioning in Poland should be reorganised on a broader democratic basis with the inclusion of democratic leaders from Poland itself and from Poles abroad.' Such a Government was to be 'pledged to the holding of free and unfettered elections as soon as possible on the basis of universal suffrage and the secret ballot.' There was only one thing about all this which a cynic might regard as odd. Inasmuch as a Polish Government was recognised at present, it was the former Lublin Committee, albeit with a need for democratic broadening. The London Polish Government, which was after all the only one recognised by both the United States and Britain received no mention at all except by implication as 'Poles abroad'.

As to the question of frontiers, the eastern frontier of Poland was, as had been expected, to follow the Curzon Line 'with digressions from it in some regions of five to eight kilometres in favour of Poland.' Poland was to receive 'substantial accessions of territory in the north and west.'

The remaining three headings of the communiqué concerned themselves with the approval of the recent Tito-Subasitch agreement in Yugoslavia, the establishment of permanent machinery for the Foreign Secretaries and of the three Powers to consult each other regularly every three or four months, and a final peroration reaffirming the common determination of the three Powers 'to maintain and strengthen in the peace to come that unity of purpose and action which has made victory possible and certain for the United Nations in this war.' This was described as 'a sacred obligation which our Governments owe to our peoples and to the people of the world.'

The Yalta communiqué was received with what the London *Times'* diplomatic correspondent described as 'unbounded satisfaction' in almost all quarters of the Allied world. *The Times* drew particular attention to the proposals for the settlement of the Polish question which, it said, were 'regarded as one of the greatest achievements of the Conference.' Its leading article spoke of a successful conclusion to a great event in history which demonstrated 'complete mutual confidence and unanimity of counsel.' It added: 'The world will seize at once upon the hope which it offers that the greatest of all stumbling-blocks to inter-Allied understanding is rolled away by the unanimity reached between the three Great Powers upon the future of Poland.'

The British left-wing weekly *The New Statesman* equally declared that 'perhaps the best work the Big Three did at Yalta . . . lies in their proposals for a Polish settlement.' While disappointed that the communiqué had not put more emphasis on the economic problems of Europe, the *New Statesman* applauded the fact that the Big Three had 'resolved not to quarrel, but to reach sensible compromises on political difficulties.'

The *Manchester Guardian* wrote: 'It can be said of this document . . . that the more it is studied the better it looks.' The paper's political correspondent said that it had produced an excellent impression at Westminster where it had acted like a stimulant after so much disenchantment in the recent past over such matters as Greece and the unharmonious relations between the Great Powers. 'The Crimean Declaration,' he went on, 'has blown away these distressing vapours at a stroke. Not only is it better in every detail than anyone had expected, but it furnishes such a convincing demonstration that the three Great Powers are not, after all, falling apart. . . . Members are unfeignedly glad to recognise that such fears as they had that Russia might be pressing too strongly her own solutions in the East, regardless of the larger interest, have no substance.'

In Moscow the results of the Conference were greeted everywhere with the warmest and most whole-hearted approval and satisfaction. Moscow Radio, broadcasting on the 17th February, described the communiqué as a 'world historical document, determining the fate of mankind for many decades to come.' As part of his appraisal the Russian commentator concluded on a specific note which attracted no special attention in the west:

'Britain represents democracy of one historic type,' he said, 'the USA another type, and the USSR yet another. . . . The peoples of liberated Europe have the possibility of creating democratic institutions according to their own choice. They can take as an example any form of democracy . . .'

In France, in spite of a strong sense of injured pride that General de Gaulle had not been invited to the Conference, great satisfaction was expressed at the terms of the agreement.

In South Africa, the Nationalist leader Malan attacked Yalta as a betrayal of the Atlantic Charter and pleaded for Germany as a bulwark in Europe against the flood of Bolshevism. General Smuts deplored what he called Malan's use of 'one of the great moments of history' for making petty political propaganda. He said that there was 'a new light shining', and himself quoted to the Union Parliament the words of the Moscow paper *Izvestia*: 'This is the greatest political event of modern times.'

In the United States, the 12th February – the day on which the Yalta communiqué was issued – was the day on which Americans were celebrating the birthday of Abraham Lincoln. At the 59th annual traditional Republican Lincoln Day dinner the former Republican President Hoover rose before a thousand Republicans and proclaimed the Yalta agreement to be '. . . a strong foundation on which to rebuild the world. If the agreements, promises and ideals which are expressed shall be carried out,' he said, 'it will open a great hope to the world. . . . It is fitting that it should have been issued to the world on the birthday of Abraham Lincoln.' The Republican Governor Thomas Dewey said in a message to the diners that 'The Conference just concluded would mean a real contribution to a future peace.' Alistair Cooke, commenting for the BBC on American reactions spoke of a mood of deep, almost religious gratitude at the results of the meeting.

The Yalta decisions were condemned from only two quarters. One, obviously, was the enemy, principally Germany. The German radio said that they constituted 'a mass murder plan, the total destruction of German industry, the mass deportation of the people by the Bolshevists;' and the German News Agency described it as 'the biggest political murder attempt of all time.'

The other quarter presented a more serious threat to Allied well-being. That Government of Poland which was recognised by Great Britain and the United States though not by Russia at once attacked mercilessly, and without any shadow of respect for the prevarications of its powerful allies, the veneer of resolution with which the communiqué had covered the Polish problem. A formal statement reminded the Allies of the memorandum delivered on the eve of Yalta with the London Polish Government's own proposals for easing the tension, and their emphasis that nothing could be undertaken without the authorisation of the Polish Government. The Yalta decisions had been taken not only without the authorisation of the Polish Government but also without even its knowledge of what was taking place. This, the London Poles maintained, constituted a contradiction of the elementary principles which bound the Allies and a violation of the letter and spirit of the Atlantic Charter which laid down the right of every nation to defend its own interests.

As for the decisions themselves, they could not be recognised by the Polish Government and could not be regarded as binding on the Polish nation. The severance of the eastern part of the national territory constituted a fifth partition of Poland, now accomplished by her Allies instead of as formerly by her enemies. The so-called Provisional Polish Government of National Unity merely legalised Soviet interference in Poland's national affairs. As long as the only troops on Polish soil were Soviet troops such a Government would not safeguard the unfettered right of free expression to the Polish nation, even in the presence of British and American diplomats. The Polish London Government repeated its preparedness to discuss changes based on its memorandum and asserted in conclusion that it was the sole legal and generally recognised Government of Poland, which for five and a half years had directed the struggle of the Polish State and nation against the Axis countries, both through the underground movement in the homeland and through the Polish armed forces abroad.

Appeals were immediately issued to those Polish forces by the London Government to maintain their fighting spirit in spite of 'the heavy blow which the Polish cause has suffered'. It urged them to 'keep peace, dignity and solidarity as well as to maintain the brotherhood in arms with the soldiers of Great Britain, Canada, the United States and France.' Lieutenant-General Anders, Commander of the Second Polish Corps, issued a similar call to his men to maintain discipline and dignity 'during this tragic moment for Poland and our nation.' The Socialist Prime Minister Arciszewski, making a personal protest of his own against what the Allies had done, made a pertinent point when he reminded people that he was himself no remote emigré but had been a leader of the underground in Poland for five years. His Deputy Prime Minister had also spent the greater part of the war fighting the Germans in the Polish underground.

All this was acutely embarrassing for the Allies, particularly the British Foreign Office situated in the same capital as the protesting Poles, who were in fact the only Polish authority they recognised. Blame for the embarrassment was however laid squarely at the door of the Poles themselves. *The Times* reported that 'in British official circles it is regretted that more mature consideration was not given to the matter' by the London Poles. It was thought improbable that the former London Prime Minister Stanislav Mikolayczyk would go along with Arciszewski's statement. Twenty-four hours after the Polish protest the British Government had still made no response to it but *The Times* diplomatic correspondent again stressed that 'regret is widespread that more time was not given for reflection' by the Polish Government.

In the United States too the only sharp protest at first was from certain American-Polish organisations, though their objections were soon to be taken up and developed by isolationist newspapers moving against the grain of general approval of the Yalta Agreement.

Chapter Thirteen

Opening a three-day Debate on Yalta in the House of Commons on February 27th, Churchill declared that the Conference had 'faced realities and difficulties in so exceptional a manner that the results constitute an Act of State on which Parliament should formally express its opinion.' His first task was to deal with a relatively subsidiary matter, the absence of France from the Conference, and he introduced this with a statement which, though cheered by the House, had a curiously old-fashioned ring in the brave new world Yalta was being deemed to inaugurate. 'The first principle of British policy in Western Europe,' he said, to prove that France was not being belittled, 'is a strong France and a strong French army.'

But, he went on, nations bearing the main brunt and burden of the war had a right to meet as and when they thought necessary in order effectively to discharge their duties in the common cause. There were in any case plenty of decisions taken at Yalta to satisfy the French: the invitation to take over a Zone of Occupation in Germany, for instance, and a place on the Allied Control Commission in Germany after unconditional surrender, together with an important rôle for her in the coming San Francisco Conference on April 25th. (That none of this, however, was adequate balm for French pride had been shown when General de Gaulle found himself 'too busy' to fly south to the Mediterranean to meet Roosevelt on the President's return from Yalta to the States.)

On the subject of the international organisation to be founded at San Francisco, Churchill had little to say at the moment because the newly agreed voting procedure had first to be discussed with France and China. But he did stress that the new organisation must take into account the special responsibility of the Great Powers and be framed so as not to compromise their capacity for effective action if called for at short notice. 'At the same time,' he added, 'the world organisation cannot be based upon a dictatorship of the Great Powers. It is their duty to serve the world and not to rule it.' He trusted that the voting procedure agreed at Yalta would meet these two essential points. The new organisation, he said, would be far stronger than the former League of Nations and he referred to it as 'this strongly-armed body that we look to to prevent wars of aggression or the preparation of such wars and to enable disputes between States, both great and small, to be adjusted by peaceful and lawful means. . . . We may have good hopes, and more than hopes – a resolute determination – that it will shield humanity from a third renewal of its agonies.'

He next referred to the Allies' unanimous resolution that Germany should be totally disarmed, that Nazism and militarism in Germany should be destroyed and war criminals justly and swiftly punished. All German industry capable of military production was to be eliminated or controlled. But he stressed that the German people would not be left without the necessary means of subsistence. 'Our policy is not revenge. It is to take such measures as may be necessary to secure the future peace and safety of the world. There will be a place, one day, for Germans in the comity of nations, but only when all traces of Nazism and militarism have been effectively and finally exterminated.' A few minutes later he went on, 'I now come to the most difficult and agitating part of the statement which I have to make to the House – the question of Poland.'

There were two issues, the frontiers of Poland and the freedom of Poland, and he made it clear that the freedom, independence, integrity and sovereignty of Poland had always seemed to the Government more important than the actual frontiers. He had never concealed from the House that personally he thought the Russian claim to the Curzon Line – first advanced to the Allies in November 1943 at the Teheran Conference – was just and right and if he championed this frontier for Russia now it was not because he bowed to force but because he thought it was the fairest division of territory that could be made in the circumstances. At Yalta, Stalin himself had made a number of minor alterations to the Curzon Line, all in favour of Poland; and there were to be substantial accessions of territory for Poland in the north and west from former German lands greater in size than the territory to the east of the Curzon Line. Quite apart from the historic and natural justice of these arrangements, Churchill stressed the great service which the Russians had rendered Poland by freeing it in a little more than three weeks from 'the awful cruelty and oppression under which the Poles were writhing.' As many as three and a half million Polish Jews alone were said to have been slaughtered, and it was certain that enormous numbers had perished in one of the most horrifying acts of cruelty, 'probably the most horrifying act of cruelty, which has ever darkened the passage of Man on the earth.'

Summing-up on the matter of frontiers he said: 'I have rarely seen a case in this House which I could commend with more confidence to the good sense of Members of all sides. But,' he went on, 'even more important than the frontiers of Poland, within the limits now disclosed, is the freedom of Poland.' There were loud cheers at this. 'The home of the Poles,' he said, 'is settled. Are they to be masters in their own house? . . . Is their sovereignty and their independence to be untrammelled, or are they to become a mere projection of the Soviet State, forced against their will by an armed minority to adopt a Communist or totalitarian system?'

The fact that he posed such questions so bluntly seemed to indicate some anxiety in Churchill's own mind. This was, as he himself said, 'a touchstone far more sensitive and vital than the drawing of frontier lines.' To answer his own questions he could really only fall back on what he called 'the most solemn declarations' made by Stalin that the sovereign independence of Poland would be maintained, adding that in due course the new world organisation would assume some measure of responsibility for this. 'The Poles,' he concluded, 'have their future in their own hands, with the single limitation that they must honestly follow in harmony with their Allies a policy friendly to Russia.'

The actual 'free, unfettered democratic elections' promised by the Yalta agreement, would, said Churchill, have to wait of course until after the war had been won – or, as he put it, 'while the war is on we give help to anyone who can kill a Hun' (here there was laughter followed by cheers).

Lord Dunglass, the Conservative Member for Lanark,* interrupted to ask for something a little more specific on the matter of elections. Churchill did no more than reaffirm that free unfettered elections were what the new Polish Government was pledged to and were a responsibility which His Majesty's Government themselves had assumed. And as if to forestall criticism on another point, he added that nothing in the agreement affected the continued recognition by His Majesty's Government of the Polish Government in London.

Again, he himself voiced a number of pertinent questions as if doubts had indeed occurred to his own mind. 'How,' he asked, 'will phrases like "free and unfettered elections on the basis of universal suffrage and secret ballot" be interpreted? Will the new Government be properly constituted, with a fair representation of the Polish people. . . . Will the elections be free and unfettered? Will the candidates of all democratic parties be able to present themselves to the electors and to conduct their campaigns? What are democratic parties? People always take different views . . .'

*Many years later, as Sir Alec Douglas-Home, to be Prime Minister and later still as Lord Home, Foreign Secretary.

127

In the long run there was repeatedly only one sanction for the pledges of Yalta which Churchill or anyone else could advance as surety for their trustworthiness, and if that could not be accepted then the outlook was bleak indeed. As Churchill succinctly expressed it: 'The impression I brought back from the Crimea and from all my other contacts is that Marshal Stalin and the Soviet leaders wish to live in honourable friendship and equality with the western democracies. I feel also that their word is their bond. I know of no other Government which stands to its obligations even in its own despite more solidly than the Russian Soviet Government. I decline absolutely to embark on a discussion about Russian good faith. It is quite evident that these matters touch the whole future of the world. Sombre indeed would be the fortunes of mankind if some awful schism arose between the western democracies and the Russian Soviet Union, if all future world organisation were rent asunder and if a new cataclysm of inconceivable violence destroyed all that is left of the treasures and liberties of mankind.' Cheers followed each of his references to the Soviet Government's good faith.

All agreed that Churchill's exposition of the Yalta decisions – and indeed other aspects of the international situation on which he touched, including Italy, Turkey, Saudi Arabia, Syria and the Lebanon and Greece – was a masterpiece of considered utterance. None could doubt him when in his conclusion he admitted that in the whole war he had never felt so grave a responsibility as he had done at Yalta. He ended: 'I am sure that a fairer choice is open to mankind than they have known in recorded ages. The lights burn brighter and shine more broadly than before. Let us walk forward together.'

There were, however, still doubts in the air and these were given expression. Arthur Greenwood, replying for the Labour Party on the question of Poland, said he did not wish to exacerbate the situation but 'it was foreign to the principles of British justice for the fate of a nation to be decided in its absence and behind its back.' There were loud cheers at this. Greenwood said he held no brief for the Polish Government, but he did not think that it had been too well treated by His Majesty's Government. He thought that it had made mistakes and had told his Polish friends so. But admitting all that, it was a really cardinal sin for three great powers, one of which had an interest we had not got, in the absence of a people whose lives were being bartered away, to determine the future of any country.

Dunglass now returned to the issue. He said that it would be comfortable to believe that relationships between men were always governed by reason, but the reality of history was that the governing principle was power. There was world concern for post-war Europe over the differences between Russia and Poland because it was a test case in the relationship between a great power wielding great military might and her smaller and weaker neighbour. No country had earned a greater right to independence than Poland, and no country had been given more pledges in treaty and declaration and thus, in its weakness, a greater claim upon the magnanimity of its friends. Their hearts would need to be of stone if they were not moved by these considerations. While accepting the territorial settlement as inevitable on the basis of Russian power, Dunglass could not accept the Prime Minister's view that this was also an act of justice. He believed, he said, 'most profoundly that it is an essential British interest that we should be seen to preserve our moral standards in international behaviour.' As to the elections, he asked himself similar questions to those which Churchill had been asking. What was to be the machinery which would ensure the free elections? With such questions unanswered he said he was himself unable to decide how to vote in this Debate.

Captain Graham, the Conservative Member for the Wirral, spoke equally realistically. He said that it was a mortal reflection that the Empire which stood alone in 1940 against the embattled might of triumphant Germany, could not now, when she had mighty Allies by her side, stand up for juster treatment for our first and martyred ally in this war. If that were so, let us at least comport ourselves with dignity and honour and not pretend that something which was unjust was in reality quite right.

When the Debate was resumed the next day some Conservatives of a similar mind moved an Amendment to the Motion seeking approval of the Yalta decisions. This Amendment ran: 'But, remembering that Great Britain took up arms in a war of which the immediate cause was the defence of Poland against German aggression and in which the overriding motive was the prevention of the domination by a strong nation of its weaker neighbours, [this House] regrets the decision to transfer to another Power the territory of an ally contrary to treaty and to Article 2 of the Atlantic Charter, and furthermore regrets the failure to ensure to those nations which have been liberated from German oppression the full right to choose their own Government free from influence of any other Power.'

The mover of the Amendment Maurice Petherick, the member for Penryn and Falmouth, referred to the 'terrible situation' with which Britain was now faced as a result of Yalta, and said that he would not now be feeling so critical if only the Prime Minister had come back and had said: 'Well, I've done my best to argue with Russia. I cannot admit that they are right, and all I can admit is that they are in occupation in the country; they are our strong ally, and one on whom we are going to depend for the future; therefore I have done my best.' But what the

Prime Minister had done was to come back and say that the settlement was a fair and just one. 'After the complete and utter crushing of Germany as a military power,' said Mr Petherick, 'what is to come next? Is there to be another power acting in a similar fashion and growing up in the world?'

On the Government side, Harold Nicolson, the National Labour member for Leicester West went further even than Churchill in advancing that proposition of faith on which the argument for Yalta ultimately rested. Citing Stalin's refusal to criticise in any way our conduct of affairs in Greece he concluded that 'Marshal Stalin has demonstrated that he is about the most reliable man in Europe.' Emanuel Shinwell, Labour Member for Seaham, said that while not wanting to exacerbate feeling in the Debate he could not refrain from pointing out that the names of those who sponsored the Amendment were reminiscent of the Chamberlain era, of the Anglo-German Fellowship and the Friends of Franco era and many other questionable episodes of the past. It appeared to him that Honourable Members were much more concerned with hostility towards Soviet Russia than they were to promote the best interests of the Poles. And he too fell back on the only position there was to fall back upon: the good faith of Marshal Stalin and his Foreign Minister Molotov. What, he asked, was the good of talking about an alliance with Soviet Russia and then questioning her good faith? 'Our future in Europe is closely bound up with Soviet Russia. It is important that we should accept the good faith of Marshal Stalin, accept his word tested and tried out. Then if we discovered on some future occasion that we had been let down let us complain of it. Do not let us complain in advance. . . . The Yalta declarations . . . were the first definite step towards an enduring peace.'

Eden, the Foreign Secretary, replying for the Government on the Debate on the Amendment, having argued at some length the historical case for the Curzon Line frontier in the east, stated honestly the all-important consideration of continued Allied unity. 'If any life is to be restored to Europe,' he said, 'if it is to be saved from anarchy and chaos, it can only be by the three Great Powers working together.' He said that the foreign policy of Britain had for centuries been based on the determination that no one country should dominate Europe and he believed that no one country was ever going to do so. Some Members, in talking about Poland, not only had Poland in mind but the fear that Russia, flushed with the magnificent triumph of her armies, was dreaming dreams of European domination. Eden pointed out that that was, of course the constant theme of German propaganda today just as it had been their theme before the war. 'Make no mistake,' he said, 'the moment this fighting ceases Germany will be out on the old theme of

130

propaganda again. She will again try to play us off against Russia, and Russia against America and ourselves. She will play on all that pity, which she knows so well how to do. The whole orchestra of German self-pity will work up again to *fortissimo*. Let us be very careful that we do not fall victims to that.'

And, again with honesty, he concluded by saying that Churchill knew perfectly well that these matters were by no means wholly resolved. 'We are in the midst of this business. We are not through it. We have many difficult stages to fulfil. Neither my Rt Honourable friend nor I can give any undertaking what our measures of success may be. But unless Honourable Members feel that we should not try, and I cannot believe that they do, I would ask them to give us the encouragement to go forward.'

The Amendment was lost by 396 votes to 25 – a Government majority of 371.

The next day the main Government Motion to approve the Yalta decisions was passed by what *The Times* called 'the extraordinary vote' of 413 to nil – the only opponents being the two tellers for the Opposition from the Independent Labour Party.

25 Conservatives abstained, most of them the same people who had voted for the Amendment. One of those abstaining was a junior member of the Government, the Parliamentary Secretary to the Ministry of Town and Country Planning, H. G. Strauss who now resigned, writing to Churchill that he had considered carefully all that he and Eden had said in the debate but that he found it 'impossible to approve of the treatment of the Polish people by the Crimean Conference'. Churchill's reply was that in the circumstances it was 'an appropriate and becoming course' for Strauss to take. He added: 'I earnestly hope that events will convince you, since our words have not succeeded, that the true and real freedom of the Polish Parliament is an essential part of the cause for which His Majesty's Government are striving.'

The Times, in a leader on the eve of the debate had been more positive. 'All the evidence suggests,' it wrote, 'that what Marshal Stalin desires to see in Warsaw is not a puppet Government acting under Russian orders but a friendly Government which, fully conscious of the supreme importance of Russian-Polish accord, will frame its own independent policies in that context.'

Roosevelt on his return to Washington made his own statement to Congress about the decisions at Yalta, beginning on a personal note by saying that he returned from the seven thousand mile trip to the White House refreshed and inspired: 'The Roosevelts are not, as you may suspect, averse to travel; we thrive on it.'

Reiterating the twin purpose of the conference, to bring about the defeat of Germany with the greatest possible speed and the smallest possible loss of men, and to build the foundations for a lasting peace among the nations of the world, he said that, on the last score, 'a tremendous stride' had been made. Though Hitler had been hoping for some crack in the wall of Allied unity and his propaganda machine had been working on this objective for months, he had failed. 'Never before have the Allies been more closely united, not only in their war aims but in their peace aims; and they are determined to continue to be united with each other, and with all peace-loving nations, so that the ideal of lasting world peace will become a reality.'

Once again, the threat to lasting peace, even after peace had arrived, was still seen as coming potentially from Germany. Roosevelt stressed that unconditional surrender did not mean the destruction or enslavement of the German people as the Nazi leaders were insisting. At the same time it must mean the end not only of Nazism with all its barbaric laws and institutions, and the 'speedy and just – and severe' punishment of Nazi war criminals, but also the complete disarmament of Germany and the destruction of German militarism and military equipment and the end of its production of armaments.

'Our objective in handling Germany is simple: it is to secure the peace of the future world. Too much experience has shown that that objective is impossible if Germany is allowed to retain any ability to wage aggressive war.' He himself had seen the effects of German militaristic savagery at Sevastopol and Yalta itself. 'I know that there is not enough room on earth for both German militarism and Christian decency.'

On the question of the new international peace-keeping organisation, he looked forward to the San Francisco Conference on April 25th, where he hoped the charter could be established for an organisation which would preserve the peace of the world and permanently outlaw the forces of aggression.

On Poland he expressed very full satisfaction that the best possible arrangement had been reached both with regard to frontiers and a new government. At this point, however, when reading his speech he looked up and said: 'I did not agree with all of it by any means. It did not go as far as I wanted in certain areas. But all British and Russian desires were not satisfied.' He went on to say he was convinced that they had the most hopeful agreement possible for a free, independent and prosperous Polish State, with the new Provisional Government pledged to a free election as soon as possible on the basis of universal suffrage and a secret ballot.

And, unlike the Yalta document itself, he mentioned Japan. He said that combined British and American staffs at Yalta had made their plans to increase the attack against Japan and the Japanese warlords could know that they were not being overlooked. It was, he said, 'still a tough, long road to Tokyo. The defeat of Germany will not mean the end of the war against Japan. On the contrary, America must be prepared for a long and costly struggle in the Pacific. But the unconditional surrender of Japan is as essential as the defeat of Germany, if our plans for world peace are to succeed.'

Roosevelt concluded by saying that the statesmen of the world must not fail American fighting men as they failed them after the First World War. 'We cannot fail them again and expect the world again to survive. . . . The Crimean conference . . . spells the end of a system of unilateral action and exclusive alliances and spheres of influences and balances of power and all the other expedients which have been tried for centuries – and have failed. . . . I am confident that the Congress and the American people will accept the results of this conference as the beginnings of a permanent structure of peace upon which we can begin to build, under God, that better world in which our children and grandchildren – yours and mine, the children and grandchildren of the whole world – must live.'

The American correspondent of the BBC, Joseph Harsch, had reported even before Roosevelt's speech that there was almost no further discussion of the Yalta decisions as early as the second week after their announcement. It was true that isolationists now in the political wilderness as far as their traditional faith was concerned, switched their attack on United States foreign policy from criticism of its involvement at all in European affairs to criticism of the way in which, in the course of that involvement, it allowed the Russians to get the better of it. Senator Wheeler of Montana had described the conference as 'a great victory for Stalin and Russian imperialism'. And in Congress after Roosevelt had addressed it the Republican Representative Knutson of Minnesota described the President's speech as 'a studied attempt to sell a bill of goods without opening the wrapper'. Also, predictably, some Polish-American organisations were hostile. Representative Konski, a Republican from Wisconsin where many Polish-Americans lived, expressed the bitterness they felt when he said of Roosevelt's report: 'He talked about a free and independent Poland. One hundred and thirty thousand Polish boys cannot even go home without being sent to Siberia.'

But although such objections often caught attention abroad they were in no sense representative of general opinion in the United States, either in Congress or in the country. As Joseph Harsch put it, the country accepted the Crimean decisions, 'accepted the steps which lead from them and the aims which lie ahead, at the foot of the Golden

Bridge in San Francisco on April 25th . . . beyond the point of acute public controversy.'

Roosevelt himself gave signally generous recognition to the consensus by appointing a bi-partisan delegation to San Francisco, and in a goodwill gesture to the combination of old guard Republicans and Southern Democrats in Congress, he had not nominated a single New Deal Democrat.

This post-Yalta consensus at the end of February 1945 reflected a new sense of relaxation and optimism in the United States, very different from that disillusionment which had prevailed only two months before at the time of the British-American differences and the Ardennes offensive. Of course this new confidence and the wish to give Yalta the benefit of any doubt owed much to the great Russian offensive which had suddenly brought the prospect of early victory so much nearer since those bleak days of December and early January.

At the same time, ironically, new measures to intensify the American war effort, largely inspired by recent inadequacies, were now hitting the American public. A Bill to make some 600,000 men between the ages of 18 and 45 either fight or work in a war industry or essential civilian services had just gone through Congress and though it still had a long way to go before becoming law it was an indication of the extent to which American war production had been suffering from a labour shortage. Desertion of jobs and absenteeism had for some time been recognised as a serious problem. A shortage of Boeing bombers at one point had been traced to the fact that at the main factory in Washington there had been a hundred per cent turnover in its labour force in one year; for every two hundred men trained for a special job, one hundred had left within a matter of months for easier, more congenial or more rewarding occupations.

In an attempt to curb absenteeism a Government Decree now struck at the American way of night-life. All places of entertainment had to close at midnight. And in spite of a last-minute attempt by Mayor La Guardia of New York (where most of the nightclubs were) to get the curfew extended to one o'clock in the morning, the measure went ahead and as Alistair Cooke reported, 'the unfamiliar cry of "Time, gentlemen, please!" was called all over the United States.' The intention was not only to discourage absenteeism from factories on the morning after, and cut down the amount of labour employed in non-essential industries such as entertainment, but also to save coal, of which there was a shortage due to the demands on transport for the war effort.

With the prospect of an end to the war in Europe once again in sight, it was inevitable that not only would the new 'Work or Fight' Bill be fought politically with some tactical persistence but also that the midnight curfew should cause resentment. Some business firms were already making arrangements for the eventual victory celebrations, and certain States had passed a law forbidding the sale of alcohol for twenty-four hours after the announcement of victory.

But of course there was another victory to be won as well as that over Germany. For the United States in particular, victory over Japan was going to involve a long, bitter and bloody struggle of which only the very first stages were now in progress.

Chapter Fourteen

With two wars of quite different characters to fight in two such widely-separated areas of the world as Europe and the Pacific, the Western Allies had a problem of priorities to add to their difficulty with formidable enemies in each.

At the beginning of the war with Japan, in December 1941, and the first six months of 1942, they had been totally and at times desperately on the defensive in the Pacific, while developing resources with which both to help the Russians with supplies and eventually move to an offensive against Germany in Europe. By June 1942 the Japanese had, with the exception of a few coastal areas of China and the southern part of New Guinea, conquered all territory in the Pacific west of Midway Island and north of Australia, including the Philippines. They were in possession of all British imperial territory east of India.

In June 1942 the Japanese had experienced their first setback from the Americans at the naval battle of Midway. Thereafter the Americans, first by landings at Bougainville and Guadalcanal in the Solomon Islands, and then in 1943 with a series of leaps from one Pacific island to another, had extended the scale of their recovery into a full strategic offensive. Often leaving isolated Japanese pockets behind, intact but neutralised, they moved gradually back after much bloody fighting through the Solomons, New Guinea and other islands of the Pacific towards the Philippines, winning further battles at sea against the Japanese navy, and realising a growing supremacy in air power. In October 1944 General Macarthur was back in the Philippines which he had been forced to leave in March 1942, and by the beginning of 1945 the Americans were safely in command of the two Philippine islands of Leyte and Mindoro, keys to the central island of Luzon and the capital, Manila. On the mainland of Asia the British 14th Army had driven the Japanese from the frontier of India and were pushing from Northern Burma towards the key town of Mandalay, which commanded the entrances to the central Burma plain, with the port of Rangoon beyond.

Only in China was the situation less satisfactory. The Japanese had

136

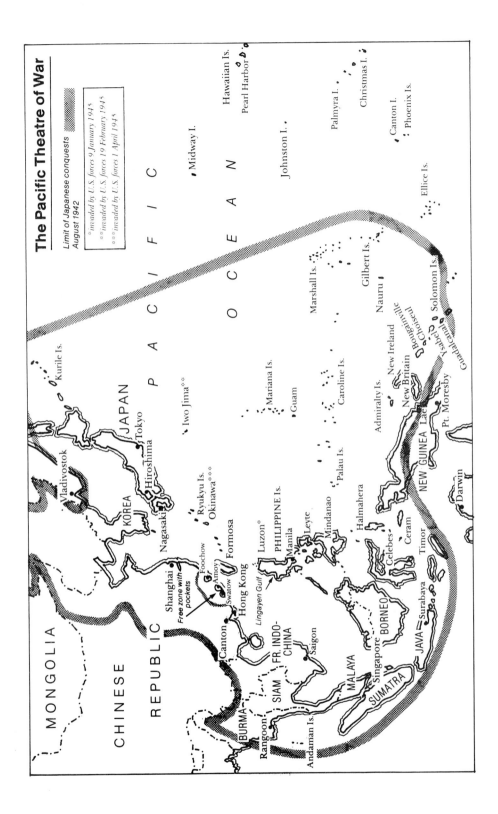

The Pacific Theatre of War

Limit of Japanese conquests
August 1942

° invaded by U.S. forces 9 January 1945
°° invaded by U.S. forces 19 February 1945
°°° invaded by U.S. forces 1 April 1945

MONGOLIA

CHINESE

REPUBLIC

Vladivostok

Kurile Is.

JAPAN

KOREA

Tokyo

Hiroshima

Nagasaki

Iwo Jima°°

P A C I F I C

Midway I.

Hawaiian Is.

Pearl Harbor

Ryukyu Is.

Okinawa°°°

Shanghai

Free zone with
pockets

Foochow

Amoy

Swatow

Formosa

Hong Kong

Canton

Lingayen Gulf

Luzon°

PHILIPPINE Is.

Manila

Leyte

Mindanao

Palau Is.

Caroline Is.

Mariana Is.

Guam

Johnston I.

O C E A N

Marshall Is.

Gilbert Is.

Nauru

Palmyra I.

Christmas I.

Canton I.

Phoenix Is.

Ellice Is.

Halmahera

Ceram

Celebes

BORNEO

Surabaya

JAVA

Timor

Darwin

New Guinea

NEW GUINEA

Lae

Pt. Moresby

Admiralty Is.

New Ireland

New Britain

Bougainville

Choiseul

Ysabel

Guadalcanal

Solomon Is.

FR. INDO-
CHINA

Saigon

SIAM

BURMA

Rangoon

Andaman Is.

MALAYA

Singapore

SUMATRA

made substantial gains there in 1944 and Chiang Kai Shek in his New Year message had admitted that not since 1938 had so much territory been lost or the Chinese people suffered such hardships. He said that they should be prepared for even more violent attacks in the coming year and meanwhile strengthen their forces preparatory to striking back in co-ordination with their allies.

One part of this message which gave encouragement to these allies was that in which he said that as soon as the military situation had stabilised enough for such a counter-offensive to prove possible he would call a People's Congress to enable the Kuomintang to transfer power to the people themselves. The welcome significance of this lay in its implied spirit of reconciliation towards the 80 million Chinese under Communist rule in the north. A considerable part of Chiang Kai Shek's forces had been used to contain the Communists rather than to attack the Japanese. In this respect there was undoubtedly substance in Mao Tse Tung's complaint that Chiang Kai Shek was not as aggressive as he should be against the national enemy. Many observers felt that a full-scale American assault against the Japanese on the Chinese mainland would play an essential part in the eventual defeat of Japan and such developments within China seemed to provide further ground for some optimism in the outlook.

President Roosevelt in his New Year speech to Congress, had sounded a justifiably proud note when he said that in 1944 the United States had conducted the fastest-moving offensive in the history of modern warfare, by driving the Japanese back more than 3,000 miles in the Central Pacific. Admiral Nimitz, the United States' Commander in the Pacific, while also confirming that 1944 had been the most successful year of the war, considered, at a press conference, how 1945 might develop. He sounded a warning note. Previously he had thought that the Japanese might be brought to surrender by the defeat of their armies on the site of their conquests. Now, he said, he had somewhat modified his opinion. He still thought that a landing on the Chinese coast was an objective, but added: 'I think they will fight to the last ditch. . . . The only safe plan is to assume we will eventually have to invade.'

In this assessment of a hard long-term outlook he was supported by a US Army Air Force General, Millard F. Harmon, who had recently written: 'We expect that Japan will be on her feet and fighting in 1946.'

Confidently, Nimitz maintained that the planning for the future in the Pacific was not dependent on a transfer of troops and resources from Europe and would go ahead on its own account. This reassured certain British critics such as *The Economist* which was querying the decision that seemed to have been taken to prosecute both the European and

Japanese wars with equal emphasis. 'This diversion of massive forces to the Far East,' it wrote, 'may well have made the difference this autumn between complete victory and the long-drawn-out fighting which seems to threaten now.'

Summarising the general position against Japan, Nimitz said that at sea the Allies undoubtedly had the upper hand, having destroyed more ships than Japan had the capacity to replace. This was not true of their aircraft production though that had been put under great pressure by the Allied destruction of some 6,000 aircraft in the previous year. They were now only able to use their supply line through the China Sea with considerable danger.

The Japanese mainland itself was soon to come under increasing air attack from carrier-borne aircraft of Nimitz's Fifth Fleet. These were to supplement the raids by B29 Super Fortresses being already carried out from land bases. Indeed the New Year sleep of Japanese on Honshu had been ominously interrupted by intermittent alerts throughout the night, caused by four Super Fortresses dropping incendiaries. Altogether there seemed no reason to think that Nimitz was speaking with unreasonable confidence when he concluded: 'I foresee an unhappy 1945 for the Japanese.'

The *New York Times* military correspondent Hanson Baldwin, looked at what was likely to happen next. He said that everything pointed to an imminent invasion of the main Philippine island of Luzon. It was not going to be easy; the bloody nature of mopping-up operations on Leyte and Mindoro made this clear. The Japanese had scores of airfields on Luzon, and their navy for all its losses was still a force to be reckoned with. An attack on the Mindoro beachhead had been beaten off only a few days before the New Year. The Luzon invasion fleet had to pass through many miles of narrow seas within range of airfields and Japanese carriers as they approached those beaches on the west of the island which were the only ones feasible for major landings. Once ashore, however, American mechanised superiority would make itself felt.

The Japanese General Homma in a radio interview publicly announced that he was expecting a stubborn attempt by the enemy to carry out landing operations on Luzon. He did so in a slightly defensive, if defiant tone. The fact, he said, that the enemy had gained a foothold in the Philippines already did not inevitably 'become a fatal factor in the whole war situation.' He stressed how the raids by Super Fortresses on Japan itself had totally failed to disturb Japanese morale and that the assumption behind these that they could do so was absurd. 'On the contrary,' he said, 'the spirit of resolute fighting will burst into flame.' Tension mounted as on the 1st and 2nd of January the Americans carried out new landings on the island of Mindoro and on the 6th occupied the small island of Marinduque opposite the south coast of Luzon, virtually unopposed. Tokyo Radio broadcast that Macarthur was actually on his way to invade Luzon and that one of three great invasion fleets had reached the Lingayen Gulf, the area in which the Japanese themselves had landed in 1941. Macarthur's own communiqué told only of heavy American air attacks against positions in Luzon. Further Japanese broadcasts said both that 'the Americans may have landed on Luzon,' and that 'Japanese forces in the Philippines were eagerly awaiting the opportunity to annihilate the invader.' Since the Lingayen Gulf was so obviously the best area for an amphibious landing it was certain to be very heavily defended, and indeed the chances of achieving surprise seemed slim. There was no more confirmation from Tokyo of an actual landing but reports continued of American warships shelling the coast of west Luzon 'apparently planning a landing there', and it added that the American naval taskforce which had penetrated the Lingayen Gulf had been continually attacked from the air and by long-range Japanese guns on the Gulf coast, which were giving the incoming convoys 'the hottest reception ever recorded in the annals of war'. 32 warships altogether, including 6 carriers and 18 troop transports were claimed sunk or damaged. The radio added that a solid structure of defence had been built on land and was awaiting the enemy with resolute determination. It was anticipated that a great enemy annihilation battle would be unrolled as soon as he stepped ashore. Reports of the American arrival in the Gulf and attacks on the invasion fleet were splashed right across the front pages of all leading Japanese newspapers on Monday, 8th.

The Japanese General Yamashita said he welcomed the landings. 'If the enemy thinks he may be able to make good his dream of Normandy landings here,' he commented, 'he will in no time learn what is in store – a catastrophic Dunkirk.'

The Japanese were now definitely claiming to have sunk three aircraft carriers, one battleship and either two other battleships or two cruisers. That same night the Tokyo radio broadcast that American troops were 'still unable to secure even a foothold' on Luzon. But again it spoke confusingly both of the Americans 'attempting to land' and also of 'the anticipated landings.' But for Japanese consumption anyway the conclusion seemed fairly optimistic: 'The defenders have already dealt a staggering blow to forces engaged in the attempted landing.' A single column heading on page 3 of the *New York Times* of Tuesday, 9th ran: 'Invasion Pictured Failure On Luzon'. All this time Macarthur remained silent.

Then on Wednesday, 10th January came the official news that at

Luzon, Philippines; the landing at
Lingayen Gulf, January 9th

Philippines; Americans flushing
out Japanese snipers

9.30 a.m. the day before a large American amphibious force had landed on the Lingayen Gulf at four beachheads, and that 24 hours later they had come together to form a 15-mile front. Macarthur himself had waded ashore knee-deep in water with troops from an assault boat. The Commander of the ground troops under him was Lieutenant-General Walter Kruger who had first seen soldiering as a Private in the Philippines in the Spanish-American war.

First losses were described as insignificant. There was almost no ground resistance though they had been under constant air attack for the previous three days and Macarthur's own ship had been narrowly missed by two torpedoes from a midget submarine the night before. The beachhead was already about four miles deep and they were 100 miles from Manila.

The Japanese radio now announced positively that landing operations had begun and that Japanese air and ground forces were engaging the enemy in 'sanguinary fighting'. The battle for the Philippines, it said correctly, had entered its main stage. '300,000 American officers and men,' it added, 'are doomed to die.' But General Honma in an interview with the German News Agency admitted that a serious threat now existed to Japanese positions in East Asia.

Two days later American patrols were already operating some 18 miles in from the beachhead with the main body of troops consolidated to a depth of nine miles. There was some Japanese resistance developing on the left flank to the east but no large concentrations of Japanese troops had yet been encountered though attacks on the ships in the Gulf continued, some even from Japanese swimmers with explosives attached to their bodies.

Macarthur announced that surprise had been achieved and that the Japanese had expected them from the south of the island. They were now, he said, feverishly bringing up troops from prepared positions in the south but it remained something of a puzzle how the Japanese had thus come to be surprised, considering their continuous reporting of the invasion fleet in the Lingayen Gulf. It was difficult not to wonder if they were perhaps not holding back on purpose. Or had they, as Macarthur was suggesting, really been caught so seriously off-balance that they had to reorganise their defence?

Macarthur himself seemed to acknowledge the uncertainty. 'The enemy,' he said in a communiqué, 'is as yet either unable or unwilling seriously to challenge our offensive drive into the central plains', while the Japanese News Agency reported: 'A major grand battle in the northern sector of the central Luzon plain is believed imminent.'

Already the beachhead was 22 miles wide and 12 miles deep, but Joseph Grew, the Acting Secretary of State, warned against false

142

optimism and wishful thinking, saying that the success of the landing would make the Japanese fight even harder than usual. Commentators sounded the same note. It was indeed possible that the Japanese had been surprised despite the appearance in strength in the Lingayen Gulf because an amphibious force of that sort could select a quite different objective in the course of a night's sailing. But a counter-attack had to be expected at any time with even more Japanese fanaticism than usual. Hanson Baldwin warned that the battle for Luzon was only just beginning and 'that chickens must not be counted before the eggs are hatched. . . . What may be a campaign of weeks or months, a campaign involving the largest land battles of the Pacific war, lies ahead.'

It looked as if the most probable Japanese defence line would be on the Agno River ahead of the beachhead which was 26 miles wide by the 13th January. The whole future course of the Pacific war would depend on the result of the battle which seemed about to take place there. It had to be remembered that the conquest of Leyte on which the Americans had landed in October had taken a full two months. That of Luzon, if it were to be successful, would be likely to take longer.

But though Japanese forces were reported to be pouring northwards under American air attack, no major battle developed on the Agno River. By the 17th January American forces were poised south of it, ready for the drive to Manila. It was still only on the left flank that really serious resistance was being met. It seemed that the Japanese, besides expecting a main invasion in the south, had also expected the invasion from the Lingayen Gulf to land on beaches further north, because the river delta on its southern shore was complicated by occasional high surf and also by a maze of fishponds. As the *New York Times* man with Macarthur's troops reported, the road to Manila seemed increasingly open every day.

On the 31st January, with his main force only 25 miles from Manila in places, Macarthur made a new landing on the east coast of the island, virtually unopposed. On the 4th February he announced the first entry of his troops into the Philippine capital. The first cavalry division under cover of darkness had entered to secure the safety of several thousand internees at the Santo Tomas concentration camp. It was exactly 26 days since the landing in the Lingayen Gulf.

No fighting against the Japanese was ever easy or bloodless and they were in fact to fight viciously in Manila often street by street, ruthlessly slaughtering prisoners and Filipino civilians as they went. It was not until the end of the month that Macarthur was in full control of the city. And though mopping-up in the rest of the island was to continue for many weeks and to be as bloody and dangerous as such operations against the Japanese always were, American control of the Philippines themselves was now assured. The most important base for a final assault against Japan, whether it was to be against the Chinese mainland or the home islands of Japan themselves, or both, was now secured. It had been a famous victory, massively expunging the disaster of two years before.

And yet it had to be conceded that victory over Japan itself still seemed to lie in the far distant future. There was, as Joseph Grew, who before the war had once been Ambassador in Tokyo, had said, a long hard road ahead and it was no good the Americans thinking that the Pacific war would not be tough and long. Triumph in the Philippines put the Allies only half-way to Japan.

As a British commentator, Frank Rounds, broadcasting for the BBC said, 'Ten million square miles retaken in the Pacific! Ten million square miles to go! All those miles of evil archipelagos and endless stretches of sea, recaptured from the Japanese by American and British' (and he might have added Australian), 'blood and sweat during the past two years. Ten million square miles of more islands and more land-masses and more ocean areas still to be conquered by the Allies, in the many, many months to come.'

Though the Japanese navy had suffered a catastrophic defeat in the great five-day naval battle of Leyte Gulf in October 1944, yet they still had a great Home Fleet in being. Organising the invasion of Japan was something quite different from organisation of the Normandy landings at D-Day. Planning for D-Day had required consideration of distances measured in scores of miles. In the Pacific they were measured by thousands of miles. It had been a dusk-to-dawn run for invasion craft in the Channel. In the Pacific, bases in the Marianas – Guam and Saipan – were over 1,000 miles from Japan, as were the new bases now acquired on the Philippines. Recent British and Indian successes in Burma included the capture in January of the ports of Akyab, in Arakan, and Moniwa on the River Chindwin. These were to lead to the capture of Mandalay in March and Rangoon itself in May, but did not affect the basic invasion geography. Geography was on the side of Japan.

The next stage was simply to get closer.

Quite apart from which there were the extraordinary qualities of the Japanese soldier to contend with. General Macarthur himself had already summed these up, though with an encouraging qualification:

'The military quality of the rank and file remains of the highest. But their officer corps deteriorates as you go up the scale. It is fundamentally based on the caste and feudal systems and does not represent strict professional merit. In that lies Japan's weakness. Her sons are strong of limb and stout of heart, but weak in leadership.'

Manila; Filipino girl welcomes
American liberators

Mother and child slaughtered by the Japanese before the Americans came

Estimates were that Japan had an army of 4,000,000 men and that her full strength had not yet been mustered. It was true that the Allies had great advantages in air power. The home islands were in range of B29 Super Fortresses operating from China and the Marianas, but attacks so far had been unable to inflict anything comparable to the damage inflicted on German industry by bombing in Europe. Damage would increase as the Allies acquired bases closer to Japan's shores, and these too would facilitate the closer approach of aircraft from carriers of the Fifth Fleet. But in addition to her own home industries Japan now had many which supplied her with strategic necessities from Korea and Manchuria as well. It was calculated that her food production could keep the population going almost indefinitely. Given the religious quality of Japanese patriotism, her morale was likely to be strengthened rather than weakened by the defeat of Germany when it came. Frank Rounds had summed the prospect up well: 'The first 10,000,000 square miles were hard and tough, full of bruises and burns and blood. The final 10,000,000 square miles, I think, will be worse.'

The first thing to do was to try to shorten the distance. Even before the complete fall of Manila, the Americans, after a long series of bombing attacks on the island of Iwo Jima in the Volcano Islands, and an assault by 1,500 aircraft of the US Pacific Fleet against targets in and around Tokyo, landed on the 19th of February on Iwo Jima itself. The Japanese resistance was, as expected, desperately fierce and inflicted heavy casualties on the Americans, of whom some 20,000 were killed before the Stars and Stripes were finally raised triumphantly on March 15th. The distance to the Japanese homeland had been halved. The Allies were now only 750 miles away.

On the 1st April the Americans landed 100,000 men on the west coast of Okinawa, largest of the Ryukyu group of islands only just over 300 miles away from Japan itself. Here, at first, it seemed as if they had secured the same sort of surprise as on Luzon, but within a few days they were again involved in bitter and costly battles against Japanese now fighting directly for the defence of their homeland. (Both Iwo Jima and Okinawa had been, for administrative purposes, part of Japan itself.) The fighting on Okinawa was not to end until June 21st.

The prelude, but only the prelude, to the major battle of the Pacific war was over. There were of course those who said that to think in terms of only one such major battle ahead was quite unrealistic. In view of the tenacious resistance of Japanese pockets long-isolated from all contacts with the homeland to American and Australian mopping-up operations in New Guinea and elsewhere, there was some reason to respect this view. An American commentator, Paul Schubert, broadcasting on the BBC towards the end of February, had said, 'Many observers feel

Liberating the Philippines; a road in Northern Luzon, and (*below*) Manila

that, to deal with the Japanese army, Allied armies will have to land in force on the Asiatic continent and fight a "finish" fight on Chinese soil. That is, that the simple invasion – even conquest – of the Japanese home islands would not be enough.'

For any offensive of that sort clearly there would have to be a wait before the allied resources released by eventual victory in Europe could become available in the Pacific. As another American broadcaster for the BBC put it three weeks later: 'This line of reasoning puts the final operation against Japan rather further into the future than has generally been assumed around here.'

Chapter Fifteen

History is concerned mainly with events of scale rather than incidents, with concepts rather than thoughts, with nations or classes rather than men – or, if with men, then with giants rather than with the usually anonymous individuals from whose lives the events and history itself are formed. But events and their interaction are of course only the product of many millions of personal actions taken by ordinary individuals as well as by the giants who sway them. Although history obscures most of such individuality, in wartime this can surface momentarily in a particular glory, or shame, or in some other singular aspect of its own.

On the 1st January, 1945 Flight-Sergeant Thompson of the RAF was the radio operator placed forward in a Lancaster bomber attacking the Dortmund-Ems canal in daylight. The bombs had just been dropped when flak scored a direct hit in front of the mid-upper gun turret. Fire broke out and the fuselage was filled with smoke until another hit on the nose of the aircraft brought in a rush of air and cleared it. A large hole had appeared in the floor of the aircraft and ammunition was beginning to explode. Thompson, seeing that the gunner in the blazing mid-upper turret was unconscious, went back down into the fuselage to pull him out though he thereby lost all chance of hearing any order from the Captain to abandon aircraft. Edging his way around the hole in the floor he carried the gunner away from the flames, beating out the man's burning clothing with his bare hands. He himself was seriously burned on his face, hands and legs.

Noticing that the rear gun-turret was also on fire, he then went and rescued the rear-gunner, again using his hands to beat off the flames. Clinging to the sides with his burned hands he made his way back across the hole in the floor to tell the Captain what had happened. The air rushing into the aircraft was so cold that frost-bite set in over his burns. The official citation with which he was awarded the Victoria Cross said that his condition on arrival in the cockpit was so pitiful that his Captain failed to recognise him. His only concern was for the two gunners he had left in the rear of the aircraft.

After forty minutes the aircraft crash-landed. Three weeks later Thompson died of his injuries; one of the gunners he had rescued also died, but the other, as the citation put it, 'owes his life to the superb gallantry of Flight-Sergeant Thompson.'

The air war of course furnished many such scenes of horror and heroism, some of which were recorded in citations for gallantry while others will remain always unknown. Of those which did emerge from behind the daily routine communiqués many were bizarre individual experiences or examples of personal courage almost unimaginable to the civilians who read about them at their breakfast-tables.

A United States Seventh Air Force Liberator, bombing harbour installations one night in the Japanese-held Bonin Islands was struck, when flying through heavy Japanese flak, by a bomb from the Liberator flying above it. This crashed through the fuselage and lodged without exploding in the waist of the 'plane two feet from the waist-gunner. He together with the tail-gunner, the bombardier and the navigator, kicked and pushed at it in a desperate effort to get it out of the 'plane before it detonated. Finally the top-gunner, Miles Kennington from Texas, climbed out of his own turret, stripped down the waist-turret guns and using their barrels as crowbars succeeded in sending the bomb toppling down into the sea. The aircraft with a tail section considerably weakened by the impact managed to weave its way back to base 500 miles away.

A less heroic lucky escape was that of Staff-Sergeant Frederick Walsh of Mobile, Alabama, a gunner in a Flying Fortress in collision with another over England. There was an explosion and he lost consciousness for a while; when he came-to he found himself at the bottom of his turret and could see the pilot and co-pilot slumped horribly in their seats. Their bodies were burned almost black. Half of the aircraft seemed to have been blown away by the explosion and as it fell towards the earth he looked round desperately for his parachute. He could not find it. Where the escape door should have been there was open sky. Then he spotted his parachute dangling in space with the harness caught on a jagged edge of metal a few feet away from him. The fear, he said later, of letting it slip from his grasp itself almost prevented him from trying to reach it. But finally he lurched towards it, grabbed the harness and slipping it on, baled out just in time for the 'chute to open a few feet above the bare treetops below.

On earth too, as armies stood poised, or swept forward, or held their ground to alter the shape of history, similar actions of infinitesimal significance to the general course of the war brought individuals to a public attention which would never have been theirs in peacetime.

On the 5th January, 1945 the Victoria Cross was awarded to a bricklayer, Richard Henry Burton, a Private in the Duke of Wellington's regiment, whose father and grandfather had both been bricklayers before him. In Italy in the autumn of 1944, two companies of his regiment were trying to take a German position on a crest 1950 feet high. They were within twenty yards of the top when the leading platoon was mown down by fire from four Spandau machine-guns. The second platoon, of which Private Burton was the runner, was sent in to try the assault again. Running forward firing his tommy-gun he knocked out one Spandau, killing the crew of three, and, coming under fire from two more, rushed towards them firing his tommy-gun until his ammunition ran out. He then picked up a discarded Bren-gun which he fired from the hip, killing or wounding the crews of both. The company was thus able to consolidate its position. The Germans temporarily withdrew. When they almost immediately counter-attacked Private Burton, one of the few members of the company who had been neither killed nor wounded, used his Bren-gun to such effect that the Germans finally retired for good, leaving the crest in British hands. Burton's VC was the 124th of the war.

The 123rd Victoria Cross of the war had been awarded to a Corporal John Harper of Doncaster who in an action in north-west Europe that same autumn had displayed very much the same sort of qualities as Private Burton. Harper was in command of the leading section of the York and Lancaster Regiment ordered to take a strong position which the Germans had established in the building of a local poor-house. This was well-protected, first by a dyke with banks and then by an earthen wall in front of which the defenders had a clear field of fire of some three hundred yards. Against a hail of mortar-bombs and small-arms fire, Corporal Harper had succeeded in leading his section across this open ground to the wall itself where they killed or captured the Germans dug-in there.

The Germans on the other side of the wall started throwing grenades over the top but Corporal Harper, climbing single-handed over it, threw his own grenades back at them and then jumping down and rushing forward against heavy small-arms fire at close range, routed the Germans, shooting a number as they fled. He took four prisoners with him as he rejoined his men on the other side of the wall. Soon afterwards he went back again to see if it was possible to wade the dyke which lay beyond. Finding it too wide and too deep he again returned, only to receive orders to try and establish his section on the far side. He again crossed the wall alone, and making use of the former German weapon pits there gave such good covering fire that the rest of his section were able to cross the wall for the loss of only one man wounded.

Leaving them in position, he then moved alone along the bank of the dyke against heavy machine-gun fire, trying to find a crossing-point. After making contact with a battalion on his right which had found a ford he returned to tell his Company Commander. Taking him back to show him the place, he was hit by a bullet and died beside the dyke.

Such men were of course to be found in the armed forces of all fighting nations. On the day on which Corporal Harper's award was announced, Hitler instituted an even more élite order of bravery than the Victoria Cross: the Golden Oak-Leaves with swords and diamonds to the Knights' Insignia of the Iron Cross. The order was to be confined to a maximum of twelve recipients. The first was Lieutenant-Colonel Hans Rüdel, credited with destroying 463 Russian tanks single-handed.

In order to award a decoration for bravery to a 35-year-old American officer of German origin, from San Francisco, Captain Hermann Bottcher, a special Act of Congress had had to be passed. Bottcher had been a naturalised American citizen but had been deprived of his citizenship for going to Spain in the Spanish Civil War and fighting for the Republicans in the Abraham Lincoln Battalion of the International Brigade. He had, however, managed to join the US army after Pearl Harbor, and won a Distinguished Service Cross fighting in New Guinea when, as a Sergeant, he had taken command of his Company after the officers had been killed, and smashed his way through the Japanese lines to the coast. Congress had then had to pass its special Act restoring his citizenship so that he could receive the medal. On General Macarthur's return to the Philippines, Bottcher had put his jungle experience to new use on Leyte, frequently infiltrating the Japanese lines there with picked men to live off the country and hamper the Japanese retreat by blowing up bridges and sometimes even disman-tling them with his own hands. On the last day of 1944 he had been killed by a burst of mortar fire which had shattered an arm and leg. The General under whom he served praised him in official glowing terms:

'His repeated hazardous reconnaissance missions,' he said, 'deep into enemy territory, played an invaluable part in the 23rd Division's victories in the Leyte campaign.' But one of the men who fought with Bottcher had already paid him a more moving tribute. 'I never feel safer out in the jungle,' he said, 'than when I am with Captain Bottcher.'

19 of the 129 VC's won by the 9th February 1945 had been awarded to the Indian Army. Sepoy Phandari Ram had won his in Burma the previous November when, wounded in the left shoulder and the leg by machine-gun fire he had crawled to within fifteen yards of a Japanese machine-gun post before being hit by grenades in the face and chest. Severely wounded and bespattered with blood, he had then crawled to within five yards of the post and had thrown in a grenade of his own

which killed the Japanese there. Only after his platoon had retaken the position did he allow his wounds to be dressed.

Equally and less dramatic versions of such incidents occur frequently within the stark routine of war. Much bravery goes unnoticed. The Germans and the Japanese referred to in the above events may well have been as brave as the men who killed them. Of the 463 Russian tank crews put out of action by Rüdel, some in their day may have had successes almost as startling as his own. Even heroes have bad luck.

The leading United States Air Force fighter ace in the European theatre, Major George Preddy, a 25-year-old from Greenborough, North Carolina, who the previous summer over Hamburg had shot down six German 'planes in little more than six minutes, was himself shot down and killed in his Mustang on Christmas Day. With ground troops watching below, he ran into a patrol of German fighters. He had shot down two Messerschmitt 109's and was chasing a Focke-Wulf 190 when American gunners below put up a stream of flak to try and get the German fighter for him. They hit Major Preddy's B51 instead. He span into the ground. The Focke-Wulf got away.

The body of the British bomber ace, Wing-Commander Guy Gibson, who had won a Victoria Cross for his part in bombing the Mohne Dam earlier in the war, had just been found as the Allies, having fully recovered all the ground lost in the Ardennes offensive, began to push their way forward towards the German frontier. Gibson had been missing since the previous summer; a retired Wing-Commander wrote to *The Times* to deplore what he regarded as his 'unnecessary' loss, both for the RAF and for his country. He said his courage and initiative had been tried and proved to the hilt and that after his great exploit on the Mohne Dam he should have been restrained from further combat.

'We are spendthrift in our policy to these super-men,' he wrote. 'Surely it was the original intention that these decorations for perhaps the greatest of human virtues should be worn on the breasts of the living.'

A few days later another correspondent wrote to *The Times* to say that the difficulty with such men as Gibson was that they refused to be taken off operational flying. Surely a man of Gibson's attainments and character had earned the right to live or to give up his life as he chose?

'While one realises,' he wrote, 'that the loss of such a man is a terrible thing for his country, relatives and friends, it is up to us who are left behind to see that his spirit and inspiration and that of all those like him lives on as a constructive force: it is only through our forgetfulness of them and all they stood for that their deaths can be a waste and their sacrifice in vain.'

Gibson's photograph and a special obituary appeared in *The Times*, where, as in the American papers, casualty lists recording the deaths of less distinguished airmen and soldiers appeared with routine regularity.

Among the survivors there were some bizarre experiences to be read about, some happy, some horrible. Private Richard B. Goldstein of 1158 East Seventh Street, Brooklyn had in January been billeted in a small town in Alsace when he and eight of his companions were cut off there in the course of a German attack. The house in which they had been living was surrounded and they had just managed to snatch up some basic rations and hide in the attic before the Germans rushed into the building. The Americans had lived up there for three days, scarcely daring to breathe while the local German Commander set up headquarters in the house. Carefully doling out their rations in the cramped conditions under the roof they had listened to the Commander and his staff at work below. None of the Germans bothered to look in the attic until one day a soldier came up in search of an onion. They surrendered at once, banking in any case on American troops soon retaking the town. The Germans moved them downstairs and put a guard over them. A few minutes later an American artillery attack started and a shell hit the roof, completely destroying the attic. The shelling increased and, since it was obviously the prelude to a counter-attack, 'the Krauts' in Private Goldstein's words, 'took off in a big hurry, leaving us behind . . .' He added: 'After that shell landed I sure was glad that that Kraut liked onions.'

Other survivors were less fortunate. When British troops, pushing towards Mandalay in Burma, came into the village of Ondaw north of the Irrawaddy, they found two prisoners of the Japanese, one British soldier and one Burmese, tied up by their feet to the wall of a pagoda with their weight resting on their heads. They had been there for three days, after being bayoneted and shot in the back. They told their rescuers that there was a third prisoner to be found somewhere nearby but he was not discovered for a few days. He had been buried up to his neck and was by then dead. The rescued Burmese eventually died too but the British soldier survived.

The Times correspondent who reported these things proclaimed: 'The Allies can never relent in this war until all these crimes are revenged.'

The first prisoners were being liberated from Japanese camps in the Philippines as the Americans developed their successful drive on Luzon towards Manila. The first such rescue of all took place in a style worthy of Hollywood. Some 400 green clad United States Rangers and Filipino guerillas struck inland to a camp at Cabanatuan in the Luzon hills, 25 miles behind the Japanese lines, where more than five hundred prisoners, mostly American but including twenty-three British, were left with their Japanese guards. The camp had originally held ten thousand prisoners but very many of these had died, and the rest had been moved to Japan.

The Rangers arrived at the camp undetected and entered with guns blazing, killing all the guards after a short fight. When the prisoners had first heard the firing they had assumed that the Japanese had decided to kill them all before withdrawal. They were crouching on the floor, waiting for the end when, according to the *New York Times*, they heard the words: 'Take it easy, fellows, the Yanks are here. We've got this place, folks.'

It took exactly thirty-two minutes to get more than five hundred prisoners, some of whom were too weak to walk, out of the camp and on the road back through the Japanese lines to safety. A guerilla unit had meanwhile been holding off a Japanese attempt at counter-attack. Further counter-attacks took place against the column on the way back and the Rangers reckoned that they killed over 500 Japanese and destroyed twelve tanks before returning to the American lines with the loss of only 27 Rangers and Filipino guerillas killed.

It was from these prisoners that the first stories began to be heard of the sufferings undergone by prisoners building a railway for the Japanese between Thailand and Burma. Thirty thousand prisoners had been engaged on this and half of that number had died. On the way back to safety after the Cabanatuan rescue some prisoners were so weak that they had to be carried on the Rangers' backs while others travelled in carts. Of the raid itself General Macarthur commented, 'No incident of the campaign has given me more personal satisfaction.'

Some five thousand more prisoners and internees were released a few days later when the Americans moved into Manila itself. The civilian camp at Santo Tomas by the University still held 3,700 men, women and children. But a Japanese Lieutenant-Colonel and 63 men had managed to withdraw into the Education Building which was the camp headquarters, taking with them 221 hostages. A bizarre incident then took place: the negotiation of the first truce between Japanese and Americans in the Pacific war. The Japanese Colonel agreed not to harm the hostages if he were allowed to march out with his men and their arms back to the Japanese lines. To this the Americans agreed. The strange scene was then witnessed of a Japanese column marching down the road simultaneously with an American contingent. The Americans were given orders not to fire unless the Japanese did.

'I don't want any of you fellows to be trigger-happy,' their Commander was reported as saying, 'but if they fire – give them Hell!'

At an agreed point the Americans halted. The Japanese passed on, looking about warily. But no incident took place and they disappeared from sight to take part in the last desperate and unsuccessful defence of Manila itself.

For the population of the little town of Binmaley a few miles inland from the first beachhead on Luzon, and the first point at which a Japanese strongpoint could be expected, liberation had been a cause for mixed feelings. The Filipinos who lived there had been warned by leaflet before the landing to get out of the area but, having built themselves dugout shelters, had mostly chosen to remain. As their Bishop, the Most Reverend Mariano A. Madariaga commented: 'It was unfortunate that we did not know more about modern warfare.'

They were subjected to a continuous bombardment for three days, at the end of which the Bishop decided that the Americans would stop if they could only know that there were in fact no Japanese there. So he set out on the ground some pieces of calico and printed on them in charcoal the words:

'WE ARE ALL CIVILIANS AND FRIENDS. NO ENEMIES HERE. HAVE MERCY ON US.'

An American 'plane read the message and dropped a letter reassuring them that they would now be safe. A reporter described those who had survived, starting back to the ruins of their little town – 'pausing for grave melancholy glances at the ruins of their shattered church' parts of which were two hundred years old. The Bishop put a brave face on it. 'We are your friends,' he said. 'There is no hard feeling. There is real joy here that you have come back.'

But the reporter described the Bishop's eyes resting longingly on some pictures he had of his cathedral and of other churches in his diocese, some of which were now either totally or partially destroyed. He recalled that the Japanese behaviour had been vile when they had first come as conquerors and that many had molested the women. But they had settled down and had been quite peaceful since, except towards those families who had sons fighting with the guerillas in the hills. They had not, added the Bishop, interfered with Christianity.

In Manila, in defeat, the Japanese had had little mercy for the Filipinos. The Americans found many bodies of Filipino women bound and shot, lying in the streets and a male carpenter, Isabelo Kabotin, of the Intramuros district survived to tell one story of horror among many which were never heard. He had been rounded-up by the Japanese with some four thousand other men of his district on the 6th February and taken to Fort Santiago where a masked woman escorted by Japanese soldiers had picked out suspected guerillas. These had then been taken to a separate enclosure where in the course of the next eight hours Kabotin saw many shot and bayoneted. He and the remaining others were then put in a garage over which on Friday, 9th February the Japanese poured petrol and set it on fire. He himself had managed to escape by pulling himself up to the ceiling, breaking through the roof and dropping some 20 to 25 feet to the ground and crawling to the Pasing River which he swam to join the guerillas. He had suffered first, second and third degree burns.

But the indiscriminate nature of war ensured that sometimes it was the prisoner's own side which inflicted the horrors. The US War Department revealed on 16th February a report from five Americans from a Japanese prison-ship. This had been sunk by an Allied submarine. Of the 1,800 mainly American prisoners on board they were the only survivors.

There were also those individuals who became singled out from the generality of war not by the unusualness of their experience, or their suffering or their bravery, but by their activity on behalf of the enemy. This was occasioned sometimes by a sort of alternative idealism, sometimes by self-interest, sometimes by personal inadequacy and often by a mixture of all three. One unimpressive such example was Gerald Hewitt, a 44-year-old teacher of English who had lived with his mother in Paris most of the time since 1931, only returning to England to be charged in January 1945 with committing an act likely to assist the enemy, 'namely [that he] supplied literature to one Haferkorn for use by the enemy as propaganda.' Hewitt was the son of a distinguished lawyer who had died in 1928. His was the first case to be brought in the British courts against a British citizen knowingly assisting the enemy for money. He had received a salary of 20,000 French francs a month from the Germans with a rise latterly to 25,000.

After his arrest he had made a long statement expressing his 'deep, sincere and bitter regret and repentance' for his activities, saying, 'My only excuse is the fact that for many years I have been completely out of touch with England and English thought.' He immediately offered to do propaganda work for the Allies against the Germans, but was rejected. It was noted that he had been taking German pay until July, 1944 and had been evacuated from Paris at the time of its liberation with other collaborators to Germany, thereafter moving to Switzerland and finally to Allied-occupied France where his arrest took place. The most telling evidence against him was a letter he had written in 1943 from Berlin where he had gone to make contact with the German Foreign Office and to be introduced to a certain Professor Haferkorn.

'My darling Mummy,' he wrote from the Adlon Hotel back to Paris, 'Well, I arrived this morning after such a tiring journey. They were very nice at the frontier; they have been nice all along . . . I saw enough just to make one appreciate these great people more and more. The

157

splendid camaraderie amongst men, the calm, steady cheerfulness of the civilians – none of the frantic nerviness or stark depression of poor France. They all seem intent on their job and perfectly calm. None of that hysteria which passes as patriotism in England. . . . More than ever I feel the road I have chosen is the right one. When you think what the Germans are doing in . . . "our good cause" and how we all depend on the German soldier to defend us from worse than death it seems that anything we can do is small in exchange, and I, at any rate, will do it readily. I shall do my level best for they are the greatest of all peoples, and the most deserving. To think one is in the capital of the greatest man of all time. It seems incredible. How I would like to see him once, even from afar . . .'

It was said at Hewitt's trial that while in Berlin he had met P. G. Wodehouse and John Amery, son of the British Secretary of State for India. Hewitt had been employed by Professor Haferkorn to write scripts for broadcasting and also to give a few talks himself on the Paris radio, visiting Berlin on a number of occasions for further instructions. Then, in some way he did not clarify, he 'began to become disillusioned about the Nazi régime.' His counsel speaking up for him at Bow Street Magistrates' Court on the 19th February commented: 'It might be that he realised he had backed the wrong horse.' A number of his speeches attacking the Allies and dealing with the deadly nature of Communism were found in the offices of Radio Paris. All, it was said, were calculated to inflame the French nation against the Allies and to cause disaffection. He pleaded Not Guilty but on coming up for trial at the Central Criminal Court on the 5th March changed his plea to Guilty and was sentenced to twelve years' penal servitude.

More distinguished collaborators excited more sophisticated attention elsewhere, particularly in France.

Chapter Sixteen

After the liberation of the greater part of France in the summer of 1944 a purge of collaborators had been carried through, often with summary ruthlessness. No one knew how many unofficial death sentences had been carried out in those early days. By the first week in February 1945 the purge had more or less settled down within the framework of the refurbished Law Courts. There had by then been 3845 official trials and 471 official death sentences. But the functioning of these courts themselves was attracting much controversy.

This arose partly from the ambiguity which had often been at the heart of the collaboration itself. Many of those compromised could plead some justification for their actions by citing the legality of Pétain's Vichy Government. This was in itself a cause of much bitterness and frustration.

That summary justice was still occasionally being applied had been shown by the sentences in January on three FFI officers at Maubeuge for executing reprieved collaborators in 1944 to satisfy a local mob there. Nor had lynch-law ceased altogether by 1945. The former Vichy Mayor of Alès near Nîmes, Farger, sentenced to death for collaboration had been reprieved in January and had had his sentence commuted to twenty years' imprisonment. The local Committee of Liberation, angered by this, ordered the local Sub-Prefect to shoot him at once but found that he had already been sent off by prison van to Montpellier. Their anger now vented itself on others sentenced to death in Alès whom they insisted on having handed over to them and executing in the corridors of the prison. Six of the Liberation Committee then drove after Farger and catching up with the van just as it reached Montpellier, shot him dead. Later in the month at Gap in the French Alps, a girl of 27 accused of denouncing a score of people to the Gestapo was attacked by a crowd as she was being taken from the court, and hanged from a tree outside. The judge had just remanded her for observation of her mental condition.

However, the due processes of law when applied were at least being carried out with proper ritual. On the 9th January a former Naval officer and writer of sea stories who had been President of the Committee for Action against Bolshevism, Paul Chak, was executed in Paris for 'intelligence with the enemy'. Having contritely admitted his errors to the court, he had made a request to command the firing-squad himself but this was refused. On the same day it was announced that the appeal against the death sentence by Henri Béraud, a principal contributor to the anti-British paper *Gringoire* had been rejected. Four days later however this death sentence was commuted to life imprisonment.

Béraud's was one of the court cases which profoundly disturbed that residue of confusion left by the German occupation and still fermenting beneath the surface of French life.

The original sentence of death passed on him had itself been condemned by the distinguished French writer François Mauriac, a man whose own patriotic integrity under the occupation was unquestioned. His criticism therefore of the death sentence on Béraud was all the more disturbing for those who regarded death in such cases as the only fitting revenge for the humiliation and torture they or those close to them had suffered.

Mauriac had himself been complaining that in the past four months the courts seemed to have developed no consistent principle in their judgements: 'All is arbitrary and unpredictable,' he wrote. When, he said, it had been found impossible to keep all those arrested in prison and half of them had been freed, there had been inevitable discontent and resentment that the guilty were evading their just punishment. The Minister of Justice himself had intervened in favour of one collaborator, Gaillard-Bancel, who had denounced patriots and recruited for the Vichy Milice. When he also tried to remove the accused academician Charles Maurras from a court in Lyon to one more to his own liking, this was, according to Mauriac, 'something more than imprudence'. The Court of Appeal in so often reversing the decisions of the lower courts was showing a plain wish 'to thwart the impeccable decisions of patriotic courts of justice'. All this went beyond arbitrariness, it was treason. Such views, which were probably a fair reflection of public opinion, made Mauriac's pronouncement in favour of Béraud, all the more controversial.

The essence of the charge against Béraud had been that by his brilliant expression of anti-British, anti-Communist and anti-Semitic opinions in *Gringoire*, he had helped the Germans recruit Frenchmen for units in the German army, for the Milice, and for actions against French hostages and French Jews. Therefore, it was said, his work consisted of intelligence with the enemy. Béraud, unlike the Naval officer Paul Chak, had defended himself with spirit and subtlety. In the first place it was marginally to his advantage that he could claim to

The price of collaboration; French Miliciens executed in Grenoble. Dutch girls with shaven heads in Zutphen

have expressed the same views before the war as during it. He said he had never been pro-German or a collaborator, though he had always been anti-British. One had, he maintained, a perfect right to be wrong on such matters provided that one was expressing oneself in good faith. Since no one accused Béraud of any other act of collaboration with the Germans than that he wrote articles in the French paper *Gringoire*, there was indeed some difficulty in deciding how to apply the normal concept of treason in time of war to everyday journalism. The court had to admit that Béraud had the right to be anti-British, anti-Communist or anti-Semitic, and that, since France was '*un pays de liberté*', he had the right to express these opinions. But just as individual liberty stopped short at the freedom to steal or commit some other crime, so in time of war intellectual freedom stopped short at the point at which it contravened the general interests of French society.

'You knew,' said one of the judges, 'that your opinions and your hatred played the enemy's propaganda game. . . . You knew that this was so and that you were sowing disunity among Frenchmen, sapping their morale and putting your talents at the service of the Germans . . . you knew all about the shooting of hostages, the fate reserved for millions of our prisoners and for those who had been deported. Sincerity, you say? But sincerity does not authorise treason. You should have kept your feelings and your hatreds to yourself until the day of victory.'

It was a powerful indictment. The assumption that the Resistance and de Gaulle had represented the general interest of French society at a time when a legitimate Government of France at Vichy maintained the opposite was technically open to dispute, but the reminder of what had not been in the interests of so many Frenchmen under that Government was telling. The same newspapers which reported Béraud's trial were still recounting fearful stories of what life had been like for ordinary French citizens under the occupation. In Grenoble, for instance, a few days before its liberation, the Germans had shot a number of hostages openly in the streets in front of passers-by including children and had left the bodies where they were for a time as a grim everyday warning to all.

Telling too was the evidence of Admiral Muselier whom Béraud in *Gringoire* had once ridiculed as a mere washtub Admiral. Muselier testified to the considerable influence which Béraud's pro-German articles had had on career officers of the French Navy. He said that the writings of Béraud and others were passionately discussed among them. Without papers like *Gringoire* and *Je Suis Partout* there would have been no Dakar and no scuttling of the French fleet at Toulon – the whole French navy would have rallied to Free France. Muselier had himself been in charge of the liberation of St Pierre et Miquelon, the French territory off the coast of Canada. After liberation he had held a plebiscite there in which, he said, only fourteen of the inhabitants voted against Free France – all of them subscribers to *Gringoire*. Of the men he had taken with him on that occasion, he said: 'There were 385 of us. Today only 80 are left. A washtub, did you say? Well, admit that we washed the shame of your treason in our blood.'

Mauriac conceded freely that for ten years Béraud had placed his powerful talents at the service of a certain clique – 'and what a clique!' But how did he come to do this? It had not been for money – he was already the best-paid reporter in Paris. No, he was simply possessed of the demonic force of the born polemicist at a time when such men were drawn principally to the Right in politics. At *Gringoire* he was free to indulge himself to the full extent of his redoubtable gifts. That he should be punished and have to pay dearly for taking the wrong course in this way was right, but to execute for treason a French writer who had never committed treason and who, though favourable to the Germans, had never had the slightest contact with them, was an injustice, said Mauriac, which no power in the world was going to stop him from contesting.

Le Monde asked if Mauriac were not being seduced to a certain extent by the fellow feeling of one writer for another. And it countered his point that Béraud had not actually worked for the Nazis, by saying: 'If Béraud could not stop the Nazis from using his articles, he could certainly have stopped giving them such helpful material; he knew perfectly well how effective they were. By continuing to write he inevitably became their accomplice.'

'Béraud,' said *Franc-Tireur*, 'wrote in the same sense as the Gestapo killed. . . . He wrote for the killers, on the side of the killers. And thereby earned a fat living.'

Albert Camus, in *Combat* displayed existentialist acceptance of an unsatisfactory situation. He said that although the Government could not have arrested all the guilty in a matter of a few weeks, it could, in a matter of a few weeks, have laid down suitable legal guidelines which it could have applied for the next six months or a year and thus rid France of a shame which still continued. Now, he said, it was too late. Journalists who did not deserve the death-penalty were being sentenced to death, people who had actually recruited for the Germans were being half set free. 'And sickened by weak justice, the people will continue to intervene from time to time in matters which ought not to be their concern. A certain natural good sense will preserve us from the worst excesses; fatigue and indifference will do the rest. One accustoms oneself to everything, even to shame and stupidity. . . . The face of a nation is reflected in its justice. Ours ought to have something other to show than its present disordered features.'

Perhaps, given the recent past, what was surprising about France, as the Resistance set about transforming itself into a political party within the framework of the new fourth Republic, was not that its features were disordered, but that it could compose its features at all. French logic helped in this. Mauriac accepted that the purge itself was an unfortunate necessity, an unavoidable price to pay for Vichy and the collaboration, but continued: 'We think it is not now too soon to try and find a way out of this unending bloody labyrinth.'

L'Humanité on the other hand, simply applied a crude patriotic counter-logic from the Marseillaise, recommending that blood should flow in the gutters.

Both points of view represented an attempt to escape from the confusion of the immediate past and seek a genuine 'renewal' for France.

Another journalist, Robert Brasillach, the 36-year-old editor of the pro-German and anti-Semitic *Je Suis Partout* was sentenced to death in January. His sentence was not commuted. He was executed on February 6th. 'Long Live France!' he shouted before he fell. Yet another writer, like Béraud an Academician, the Royalist Charles Maurras was sentenced to twenty years' imprisonment for his writings in *Action Française*. His cry from the dock was: 'It is Dreyfus's revenge!' He left the court to cheers of 'Vive Maurras!' Another French writer still, the Resistance Colonel, André Malraux, had entered liberated Strasbourg in January at the head of his men of the Maquis of the Dordogne, the Corrèze and the Lot.

The intellectual debate about the purge was part of a wider need to impose order on a more general social disarray in France. There were many painful anomalies in French life early in 1945. Those who had made vast fortunes during the Occupation, sometimes through the acquisition of Jewish property under Vichy's racial laws, were still forming associations for the preservation of their 'just rights'. (One such person had recently presented a German requisition document to justify his claim.) The racial laws had been annulled after the Liberation but decisions taken under them were still effective as late as February 1945. Many of the top civil servants and members of the officer corps represented a sort of continuity with Vichy, having merely substituted in their offices the portrait of General de Gaulle for that of Marshal Pétain. The only satisfactory resolution of such latent ambiguity seemed to lie in the early trial of Pétain and his one-time Foreign Minister, Laval, both of whom were to be put under arrest but not brought before any court for some months.

At the same time that black market which had been a patriotic requirement under the Occupation, paradoxically providing even collaborators with some semblance of underground activity, was now a virtual economic necessity. 'The black market in France,' declared the BBC reporter Thomas Cadett at the beginning of March 1945, 'is the biggest and best-run racket that Europe has ever seen.' For the ordinary individual Frenchman there was bitter paradox in the fact that at the moment when, after four years of national humiliation, his country was being welcomed back to an honoured position among the United Nations, his own material living conditions should have become more difficult than at any time since the war started.

France had formally become a member of the United Nations on the first day of 1945. The US Secretary of State, Stettinius commented: 'France is herself again.' And President Roosevelt sent a message skilfully calculated to emphasise her individual national pride: 'France was the first ally of our country in our own war of liberation.' In Britain itself *The Times* commented warmly: 'France thus becomes formally what she has long been in fact, and always in spirit, a full member of the Grand Alliance.' But within France itself it was food and fuel shortages which took precedence in the average Frenchman's mind over such lofty recognition of his country's ancient prestige.

General de Gaulle had warned at the New Year that one of France's most difficult years lay ahead and that the winter would be one of the worst. He was right. It was noted that while for the New Year celebrations some of the bars and restaurants seemed to have more heating than for some time and lights burned until dawn in Montmartre and Montparnasse as champagne flowed and the revellers sang the National Anthems of the Allies, in the suburbs people were shivering in their houses and did not even open their doors to greet each other as the chimes of the New Year struck. In such houses every cardboard box and every wooden packing-case had been burned long ago for warmth and people queued in the streets by day for small bundles of kindling wood. On all roads leading from the country into the capital, streams of cyclists could be seen returning from foraging expeditions in the woods. Auction rooms were combed for junk furniture which could be burned. Since few Paris apartments had fireplaces, being reliant upon central heating which seldom materialised, families huddled together in one room trying to warm themselves at a small electric fire or radiator, itself dependent on precarious electricity. Gas for cooking was available for one hour at lunch-time and two hours in the evening. At work only offices occupied by the Allies or by the Government were heated. Employees sat at desks huddled in overcoats.

In the middle of January the fuel shortage imposed a number of severe restrictions in France. All steam trains were to cease to run; there was to be no gas after 8.30 p.m., no electricity between 8.30 a.m. and 5 p.m. with the exception of one hour at lunch-time; all stores were to close at 5 p.m. and there were to be no night clubs. But it was the food shortage and the necessary measures to be taken by individuals to deal with it that were the greatest single source of trouble.

The operation of the black market prevented actual starvation but there were many people in Paris who were consistently under-nourished and the number of babies' deaths there much troubled Allied consciences, particularly in Britain where the weekly illustrated paper *Picture Post* monitored an indignant popular outcry on the subject.

If French families had had to try and survive on the official rations alone, under-nourishment would have been wider still. In Paris there was no butter legally available at all for the first two months of the year and the BBC Paris correspondent Thomas Cadett heard a Frenchman say, 'There's only one way of getting any nourishment out of these confounded butter tickets – it's to eat them.'

At the time butter was even short on the black market itself. Otherwise this had done a fine job; everything else was available though sometimes at a considerable price. There were two sorts of client for which it catered. The first was the ordinary housewife who could not afford to buy on the grand scale but kept her family as well fed as possible. The other clients were the rich, whether feeding at home or in smart restaurants where foie gras, oysters, omelettes, meat, cheese and vegetables in abundance were available, provided you could pay the bill. There was also no shortage of wine, though the nominal ration was a bottle per month per head. The rich could buy what they liked and more than they needed, while those with less money had to get by as best they could. All visitors to France agreed that the standard of food in the private houses of the rich was as high as it had ever been.

Given the essential service provided by the black market – and indeed its respectable ancestry under the German Occupation – it was not surprising that French Government attempts to deal with it were limited. The London *Sunday Times* reported that in Paris, bread, meat and other black market commodities were sold openly under the eyes of the police, who were bribed daily with cigarettes (forty on the day their reporter was present) to look the other way. Shoes could not be bought in France without an official permit but according to Thomas Cadett such permits could themselves be bought at the Prefecture of Police at whatever happened to be the going rate.

Shortage of transport was said to be the principal cause for the absence of an efficient legal market in food. Part of the black market was indeed supplied by individuals plying with suitcases or rucksacks by train or bicycle between the towns and the countryside. But larger operators seemed to have no difficulty in procuring official authorisation of road transport for their own purposes. The real trouble was that the French peasant was reluctant to let more than about thirty per cent of his produce go through the legal channels because he could make so much more money on the black market at a time when he had little faith in an inflating currency.

Nor was it only the French themselves who were involved in black market operations. In the course of January a gigantic conspiracy was uncovered within the American Army in Paris and a number of officers and men were tried and sentenced to long terms of imprisonment, some as long as fifty years, for misusing US army transport and supplies of petrol for the creation of their own fortunes.

How then did the French regard the Allies who had brought them this liberation? Raymond Mortimer, reported tactfully for the *New Statesman* from Paris in January that the Americans 'could not be said to be unusually popular' though he doubted if any foreign army, even when come to expel a detested invader, could hope to go on being liked for long. He said there was something about youthful American exuberance which the French found less attractive than the British did and the French were shocked by the extent to which Americans traded their own army resources on the black market. A small point which rankled was the excessive consideration which, in French eyes, the Americans gave to their German prisoners. Whatever the Geneva Convention might say, they found it difficult to understand how German prisoners could be provided with such luxuries as cocoa while French babies were dying for lack of milk. A lot of the ill-feeling over such matters, wrote Mortimer, could be put right by an increase in the supply of necessities to the French from the Allies.

The French attitude to the British he found 'overwhelmingly friendly,' possibly, he suggested, because now, by contrast with the Americans, they had very few troops in France. The main French fear about British foreign policy was that it might once again encourage the Germans, as it had done in the nineteen-thirties. Then, it had seemed to Frenchmen, Britain had suddenly changed her policy, inducing a weakened France into a war she was unable to fight and finally blaming her for signing an armistice. It had been quite possible for patriotic Frenchman to hate both the invader and their former ally.

As for the Russians, the French Government had just completed a new Franco-Russian treaty. This was welcomed inasmuch as it solemnised the one special link between France and the Soviet Union, lacking in France's links with Britain, namely a common fear and mistrust of Germany. And although in other respects there was a distance between the two countries based partly on ignorance and partly on mistrust of Russian Communism, even sometimes by French Communists themselves, the resulting detachment perhaps suited both parties. The Russians knew that they could depend more solidly on the French to be anti-German than the Americans, while it always suited Frenchmen to think of their country's foreign policy not so much in terms of its relations with other countries but in terms of France's own individual status. Mortimer said that he returned from Paris 'alarmed by the material difficulties of the French, but profoundly impressed by their continued intellectual vigour.' He allowed himself to wonder whether in the long run French sympathy would go chiefly to the Russians or to the British. He thought that both France and Britain had the same wish for radical reforms and the same distaste for revolution and felt that Frenchmen's final choice would depend on whether Britain was to be thought of as the country of banks and trusts or as the country of Beveridge and Keynes.

His comment was interesting in a quite different context from that in which it was made. For it signalled the present inclinations of British intellectuals not primarily politically-minded (Raymond Mortimer was the *New Statesman*'s literary editor) in looking towards the time when the war would be over and their own country would experience its first General Election for ten years.

168

Chapter Seventeen

In none of the countries of western Europe now liberated or partially liberated from German rule had the euphoria of liberation managed to sustain itself for long. Economic hardship, with shortages remedied only by an expensive black market from which the patriotic cachet had been removed, now seemed more frustrating than ever. Political problems had often supervened at once, as in Belgium and Greece. Both economics and politics had to be subordinated to the Allies' over-riding need to win the war.

Italy had lost the war. In February 1945 the coalition democratic government of its 'liberated' area, under Premier Bonomi, received from Mr Harold Macmillan, President of the Allied Commission, freedom for the first time to act without having to refer its laws and decrees to that Commission, and to conduct its own foreign affairs. But economically the country was, in most towns at least, in a near-disastrous condition. The US Congress Representative Clare Boothe Luce who paid a visit to Italy that winter declared that she had found the Italian people 'literally dying of cold and hunger before your eyes by the thousand.' There was some dramatic overstatement in this, but certainly protests and riots over food shortages were common and the distress of many ordinary civilians very great. Posters in the street mocked the name of the Allied Military Governor, Charles Poletti: 'Less Poletti and More Spaghetti!'

The black market played the same economically indispensable rôle as in France. 'Take it away,' an Italian said to the BBC correspondent Godfrey Talbot, 'and we should really starve.' Again, the extent to which one could benefit from it was determined only by money. There was, said Talbot, 'a black market in just about everything, in permits to travel, permits to liquidate money frozen in banks, permits to hold a position to issue permits.' It was a grimmer picture than in France, though Talbot tried to present it as unsensationally as possible. It was, he said, 'a picture, not of starvation but of hunger and poverty; not of anarchy but in places of cynical misbehaviour and dishonesty born of empty bellies, born of the searing tide of war which has passed across the face of the land . . .' He described how in an accident on the road between Rome and Naples his car had skidded and crashed into a tree, finally ending upside-down in a ditch. While he and the driver were still trapped inside, Italian farm workers and children had arrived and, assuming that they were dead or unconscious, started making off with the baggage and engineering tools in the ripped-up boot. On another occasion a well-dressed civilian and his wife, who, he said, 'looked as if they might have a limousine and a palace around the corner,' had asked him if he had a tin of bully beef or a little bread, for which, having no money, the wife said she was willing to barter some of the furnishings in their house.

Armed gangs roamed the countryside, composed of criminals, former anti-German partisans and Allied deserters. The ability of both the Italian Government and the Allied Commission to deal with such conditions was of course limited by the fact that the northern part of Italy which contained the country's industrial wealth was still in the hands of the Germans and Mussolini's Fascist Republic. Not only was this a grave disadvantage in itself but it meant that in southern and central Italy military requirements took economic and every other priority. 'Don't think,' said Talbot of the Allied armies at the front, 'that they are now sitting down and having a picnic in the snow of the Appenine Hills, and the grim, dreary Emilian Plain; know that they are fighting and enduring.'

It was more than the weather that was causing the stalemate which continued to delay the social and economic renewal of Italy. In the middle of February the Germans were proving themselves capable of launching effective counter-attacks at both eastern and western ends of the weather-bound Italian front. An American correspondent, Eric Sevareid of CBS, took a less optimistic view of the campaign than Talbot's. 'Why should we not be frank about Italy,' he asked, 'and admit that Kesselring, on a very small budget, has done a masterful job in making a primary Allied force pay bitterly for every dubious mile of a secondary battlefield?'

Defenders of the Italian campaign would have replied correctly that whatever frustration the Allies were experiencing as a result of skilled and tenacious German defence in mountainous countryside, they were at least thus holding down some twenty-five German divisions desperately needed on the eastern or western fronts. This argument ignored the possibility that the Allied assault might have tipped the scales of the war more effectively in the West where although German resistance was still stubborn and courageous, the terrain would have given the defence less advantage. Italian civilians might have argued that it was the Italian campaign which had loosed upon them a state of affairs often verging on social and economic anarchy, and that for all the moral virtues of liberation from their former allies, it might have been more comfortable for them if this had been delayed until the final defeat of Germany elsewhere.

In Italy as in France, there was the problem of retribution against individuals for their Fascist past, though it was not always so easy to accuse such people of lack of patriotism since the 20-year-old Fascist régime had always claimed patriotism as one of its principal virtues, not least when fighting for three years beside the Germans.

Some of the same overlap at high administrative level as in France between the outgoing and incoming régimes complicated the new Italian justice. When fifteen prominent Fascists (of whom only eight were as yet in custody) were tried in Rome in January they included the Fascist General Mario Roatta who had for a time after the Armistice continued officially to retain the title of Army Chief of Staff given him by Mussolini. The main charge against him, of having committed acts which conspicuously supported the Fascist régime, while plainly true, had a slightly fatuous ring in the circumstances. Fulvio Suvich, who had been Under-Secretary of Foreign Affairs between 1932 and 1936 was also arraigned. Though Roatta disputed the competence of the court to try him and demanded a military tribunal, he was overruled.

Roatta was known to have developed the army's military intelligence under Mussolini into an organisation which specialised in many questionable practices including the murder and kidnapping of political opponents. Suvich was expected to reveal the extent to which Mussolini's Government had been implicated in the murder of King Alexander of Yugoslavia in Marseilles by Croat terrorists in 1934.

To this extent the trial was a disappointment because Suvich insisted he could throw no light on that event. A bespectacled, mild-mannered man of 58 he made what *The Times* called 'a rather lame effort to defend his Fascist past, apparently to show how lukewarm was his faith in the régime.' He made a strong point of the fact that while Ambassador in Washington in 1937 to 1938 he had warned Mussolini of the power of the United States and that she would side with Britain in the event of a conflict.

Some theatrical compensation was made to the public for this poor performance in court when one of the judges was himself charged with 'nodding approvingly' while the Public Prosecutor challenged another of the accused about the preparation by Roatta's men of disease-spreading bacteria to be dropped on the Republican side in the Spanish Civil War. The nods were said to show a 'grave lack of impartiality on the part of a judge.'

But Roatta himself provided the best value. He revealed how until the end of 1936 the activities of his organisation had been directed consistently against Germany and how at the time of the Laval-Mussolini Agreement of January 1935 a pact had been concluded with the French to transport a French army corps across northern Italy to defend Austria, should Germany attack her. This was convenient evidence because one of the accusations against him was of close collaboration with the Germans enabling them to occupy Rome after the Armistice. In the Spanish Civil War he had commanded an Italian division under the pseudonym Mancini. He denied having had anything to do with the murders, which had caused some stir at the time, of the Rosselli brothers, Italian opponents of Mussolini in exile, saying merely that they had presented no real menace. But he hardly absolved himself of the moral substance of the charge when he continued that in his opinion it would have been better to have got rid of men like the Spanish Republican Prime Minister Negrin or the French Socialist Prime Minister Blum. The real sensation of the trial came when on the evening of March 4th, having been admitted temporarily to a military hospital for heart trouble, he slipped through an open door at the end of a corridor on to a first floor balcony and from there dropped down into a yard, from which he gained the deserted embankment skirting the Tiber near the Fiorentini Bridge. He was wearing civilian clothes and made off in a car in which his wife was waiting.

The escape caused widespread indignation. It was asked, with reason, why better arrangements had not been made for his security. The twelve men of the Carabinieri Guard and a hospital attendant who was suspected of having opened the corridor door were placed in detention, accused in an official statement of 'grave slackness'. A week later he was still at large and the Commander of the Allied forces in Rome published a statement making clear that there was an extensive underground active Fascist organisation in the country.

*

One other country in Western Europe was, like Italy, split in two by the war. Northern and western Holland was still occupied by the Germans, while in the south the Allies directed their attention eastwards towards those rivers which presented preliminary obstacles to the major defensive barrier of Germany, the Rhine. Conditions in both parts of Holland were grim, in the occupied north and west a nightmare. Most householders had long ago burned nearly all their furniture as fuel and sat on the floor in their empty houses or lay in bed by day for warmth. The average number of calories per day per person was between six and eight hundred though it was reckoned that two thousand were necessary to maintain health for people in an ordinary sedentary occupation.

In the western part of the occupied territory there was a virtual famine, with people living on one or two slices of bread and a few potatoes a day. It had been a freezing winter and there was no fuel of any sort – no gas or electricity or coal. By February hundreds of thousands of people were leaving the towns and roaming the countryside, desperately searching for fuel and food. One of the Resistance papers, *Het Parool* wrote: 'There is an unending stream of people, old men, women and even children, who for days, sometimes even for weeks, wander around. Many of them have already met death by the roadside as the result of their exhaustion and hunger. Countless numbers do not complete a journey. They turn back half-way, they are ill, with empty hands . . .'

But the Dutch spirit of resistance, both active and passive, remained strong. For five months since the airborne landings at Arnhem in the previous September the entire Dutch railway system had been on strike and some 30,000 railwaymen were living in hiding in the houses of other families than their own. There had been all the normal ruthlessness and bureaucratic human extermination normally practised by the Germans in their occupied territories. Hostages were shot in reprisal for actions of the Dutch Resistance. It was reckoned by the end of February that some 20,000 Dutchmen had died in prison and concentration camps, while 100,000 Dutch Jews had been deported to be gassed somewhere in Poland. Some half a million men and boys had been sent to Germany to work in war factories and, since the railway strike, there had been a particularly merciless intensification of this procedure. The Germans began to deport all men between 17 and 40, organising man-hunts in all the towns. They had arrested 50,000 men in Rotterdam and forced them to march the forty miles to Utrecht without food and without sleep in a little over twenty-four hours. An eye-witness described their arrival: 'They dragged themselves along the streets, deadly pale, completely exhausted. Those who had dropped by the roadside were carried in wheelbarrows, one on top of the other.' On the instructions of the Reichskommissar for Holland, the Austrian Nazi, Seyss-Inquart, a systematic dismantlement of the Dutch economy had begun. The ports of Rotterdam and Amsterdam were largely destroyed; factories were closed and their machinery exported to Germany.

In spite of all this, the Dutch Resistance continued its activity and issued to the world a statement that they were not asking for pity. They knew, they said, what they were fighting for, '. . . A people of ancient culture is threatened with extinction by Hitler's barbarians. . . . We in Occupied Holland stand fast.'

In liberated Holland there was at least freedom from terror and the fear of extinction. Material conditions too were far better, though compared with conditions in Britain they were desperate. A Dutchman who had lived in Britain before the war and returned for the first time early in 1945 was amazed to find living conditions there 'so near to normal'. In his own house in liberated Holland there was gas for only one hour every day, at noon, and electricity was rationed to the use of one 60-watt bulb for about two hours after dark. (The meter was checked officially every day and if the ration had been exceeded the supply was cut off.) However the Dutch food ration was already close to two thousand calories a day; more bread and other rationed food was now actually available, including sugar, of which the Dutch had had none for many months. Their chief anxiety was for their friends and relatives in the occupied territory.

In both parts of Holland therefore, the anticipation with which all Europe inevitably considered the likelihood of the next Allied move in the west had an urgency of its own. It was tempered by a tolerant understanding of the problems still facing British and Americans there, not least of which was that the German fighting spirit remained unbroken.

In two other West European German-occupied countries a similar combination of hope and resignation awaited a new Anglo-American land offensive. Denmark, for reasons of geography, could hardly hope for liberation before Germany's defeat was total; but the resistance movement there remained persistently active as demonstrated by the raid on the V2 component factory at Torotor.

Norway, equally likely to have to wait to the bitter end for liberation of the greater part of her territory, was enjoying a fragment of liberation in the north. Norwegian units co-operating there with the Red Army had begun to push into areas from which the Germans had driven the inhabitants. The Germans had hoped to force them into a mass evacuation but had merely sent them into the forests and surrounding mountain fastnesses.

In occupied Norwegian territory the resistance, as in Denmark and Holland, seemed emboldened by the prospect of a spring and summer in which the war might come to an end. Norway after all had provided the archetypal collaborator, Quisling, the man who had given his name to the political genre. On the 8th February his police chief, head of 'the Norwegian Security Service' was ambushed by the resistance while driving to his office through the streets of Oslo and mown down by machine-gun bullets. Quisling immediately ordered 'all measures needed to maintain public order and security'. What he meant by these was soon made plain. First he summoned a number of prominent Oslo industrialists and told them that they would be held as hostages and executed unless the persistent sabotage were to stop. On the 9th

February, nineteen hostages were shot in reprisal for the assassination. The next day the number was brought up to thirty-four.

Even with the Russians sitting on the Oder some forty miles east of Berlin and the British and Americans again able to look hopefully towards the Rhine, the last year of the Third Reich – if that was what it was to be – still looked like being a painful one for Europe.

Chapter Eighteen

The communiqué issued after the Yalta Conference had spoken of co-ordinated plans for the final assault on Germany from east and west.

In the east, the Russians continued to consolidate the sensational successes of their January offensive. The pace of their advance had been slowed both by the thaw and by the need to deal with strong German 'hedgehog' positions left behind in their path, as at Posen and at Schneidemühl. Progress was made in the north, in Pomerania and in East Prussia, and along the Baltic, while bridgeheads were strengthened on the Oder. But it was still a matter for conjecture whether the Germans might not successfully stabilise a front along that river. The one area in which it seemed the Russians might be able to accelerate again was in Saxony. There, with bridgeheads on either side of Breslau, and the Red Army some eighty miles east of Dresden they appeared to have a chance of turning any such Oder front by a thrust towards Berlin from the south.

Meanwhile, methodically and unspectacularly, the first stages of the British and American and French offensive in the West were developing. In the first week of February, having at last recovered all the ground that had been lost in the Ardennes offensive, American and British armies began steadily pushing their way up to and into the Siegfried Line. Though gains were only often a few hundred yards a day, the names of towns and districts which had last been mentioned prominently in the tentative French Army probes of the autumn and winter of 1939 began to reappear in the communiqués.

Further south towards the Swiss border the still tenacious spirit of the German defence was shown at Neuf Brisach, a moated mediaeval town just west of the Rhine, where American and French troops had to storm the 20-foot walls with rope ladders against Germans fighting to the last to deny them the use of the Rhine bridges. Only on February 8th was the French General de Lattre de Tassigny able to announce the end of what had been at times the worrying battle for Alsace: 'On the twenty-first day of a fierce battle the enemy has been chased from the Alsatian plain and had to recross the Rhine.' It would have been a greater victory, if he had been able to say that they had been destroyed before they could do so.

On the same day Montgomery announced a new British and Canadian offensive south of Nijmegen in Holland after massive artillery preparation. In three days he had advanced some ten miles and British troops after strong opposition had entered their first major German town, Cleves. Only about 50 of the pre-war population of 20,000 remained, sheltering in the cellars. Hundreds of others were said to be dead beneath the ruins of their homes destroyed in a big RAF night attack at the start of the offensive. Other British troops cleared the German forest, the Reichswald, but here too there was strong opposition and the Germans put in a number of counter-attacks between the Maas and the Rhine. The Americans were making a push to capture the reservoirs at the head of the River Roer. None of these moves, it became clear, was the main offensive but only a preparation for it.

The main offensive was being delayed as much by appallingly wet weather as by the German defence. A *Daily Mirror* reporter, George Macarthy, gave a glimpse of why this war in the west so far lacked the dash of the Russian advance. He had just arrived in Kranenburg from Myler, a village on the Dutch-German border 'still smoking with the fires of war'.

'. . . you travel through an avenue of gashed trees along a road that seems to float in mud, a road that is flanked in the north by mile after mile of flooded fields – floods that stretch up to the Rhine itself . . .'

The Company Commander in Kranenburg told him, 'Every man of us arrived here through mud that squelched up to his knees. . . . By the time we got to this town only one of our six tanks was still with us. The rest were ditched somewhere in the mud . . .'

Macarthy said the troops' uniforms were thick and heavy with mud. There was mud on their faces, mud on their hands and mud in their hair. A BBC reporter, Howard Marshall, described how to the mud was added, at night, extreme cold. He found men of British County regiments – the Norfolks and the Warwicks – taking their boots off in their slit trenches along the river Maas and putting their feet into sandbags stuffed with straw, as they sat there whispering and listening to the Germans talking across the water, 150 yards away.

The *Sunday Times* military correspondent, 'Scrutator', summing-up on the 11th February these 'limited operations' said he hoped the main offensive would be postponed until the weather and the nature of the ground had improved. The *Daily Mirror* in a leader sounded a warning note:

'The war is going to end before long, but not so soon as many seem to think. Our duty is not to throw our hats up, but still to take our coats off

177

and keep on with the job. . . . That national pest the crass optimist is about again. Let us be more sensible than this foolish gentleman and view events with common-sense. . . . This war is like no other war. . . . Its end will be like no other end. There may be no formal armistice or peace because there is no one to make it with. Possibly the Allies will have, slowly and completely, to occupy the country. No one can definitely say. We should be well advised therefore to dilute our heady hopes with a dash of sober realism.'

The most powerful blows struck by the Allies in the west were from the air. On February 3rd Berlin suffered one of its heaviest raids of the whole war from 1,000 US Fortresses, escorted by 900 Mustangs and Thunderbolts. Swedish correspondents reported that thousands of refugees from the east then in the city had been killed. The air crews were told that its purpose was to help the Russians now halted before Berlin along the Oder some forty miles away, though the *New York Times* also said that it was 'designed to fan the flames of German discontent.'

Photographs taken after the raid showed about two miles of central Berlin consumed by fire. A week later Swedish reports described the German workmen bricking up the Brandenberger Tor as being 'like undertakers' assistants putting the lid on a coffin'. There was speculation as to where the next capital of Germany would be. Most of Germany's old and great cities had already been razed to the ground as thoroughly as Berlin, though the *New York Times* noted that 'among the cities spared, Dresden is number one'.

On the 6th February, 1300 US Liberators and Fortresses bombed railway and industrial targets at Magdeburg, Leipzig and Chemnitz, in order to disrupt German supply routes to the east. Next day Marshal Koniev was reported to be advancing from the Oder on a front some thirty miles across, sweeping into Saxony to sever vital lateral communications at Dresden, Leipzig and Chemnitz. RAF Mosquitoes over West Germany had been attacking German traffic on roads and railways nearly all of which was moving eastwards. The further east the Mosquitoes went, the heavier this traffic became. And the *New York Times*, while noting that the Russians were checked in the bulge before Berlin, remarked that they were 'hitting out on both flanks. . . . They have smashed through the Oder line in Silesia,' the paper added, 'and are advancing in the direction of Dresden in what may be a vast move to outflank Berlin from the south.'

The next day the *Manchester Guardian* ran a headline: 'More Headway On The Road To Dresden' and that night, the 13th to 14th of February, there took place what *The Times* described as 'Smashing Blows At Dresden'. It described how British and American bombers had struck one of their most powerful blows at 'a vital centre for controlling the

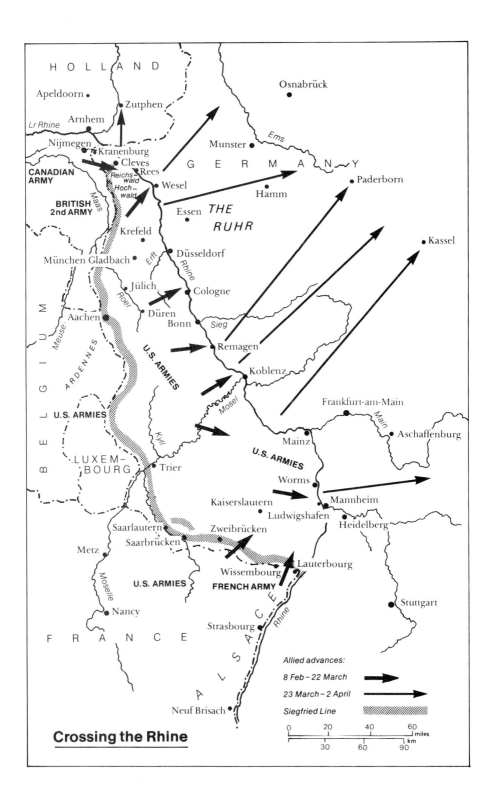

HOLLAND

Apeldoorn •

• Zutphen

Arnhem
Lr Rhine

Nijmegen Kranenburg
           • Cleves
CANADIAN   Reichs- Rees
ARMY   wald
           Hoch-   • Wesel
BRITISH   wald
2nd ARMY

           • Krefeld

München Gladbach •

        • Jülich
              • Cologne
        • Düren
              Bonn
Aachen •   Sieg
                    • Remagen
U.S. ARMIES   Koblenz

ARDENNES

U.S. ARMIES

LUXEM-
BOURG   • Trier

Metz •

        U.S. ARMIES

• Nancy

FRANCE

GERMANY

Osnabrück •

Ems

• Munster

• Paderborn

• Hamm

Essen • THE
         RUHR

Düsseldorf

                    • Kassel

Frankfurt-am-Main •
                        Main
Mainz •   • Aschaffenburg

U.S. ARMIES

Worms •
           • Mannheim
Kaiserslautern •   Ludwigshafen •
    • Zweibrücken   • Heidelberg

Saarlautern •
Saarbrücken •
                    Lauterbourg
    Wissembourg
              FRENCH ARMY

                              • Stuttgart

Strasbourg •
              Rhine

A
L
S
A
C
E

Neuf Brisach •

Crossing the Rhine

Allied advances:

8 Feb – 22 March ➡

23 March – 2 April →

Siegfried Line

0   20   40   60
                   miles
    30   60   90
              km

German defence against Marshal Koniev's army advancing from the east.' In two night attacks 800 aircraft of RAF Bomber Command dropped over half a million incendiaries, a number of 8,000 pound bombs and hundreds of 4,000 pound bombs. The night attack was followed the next day by another from 450 US Fortresses.

At 12.30 p.m. they could see the fires caused by the RAF still burning. The day after that, the city which had put up a relatively small amount of flak was again the principal target for 1,100 Fortresses of the US Fifth Air Force, some of which bombed another railway centre, Cottbus about fifty miles to the west of the Red Army then pushing its way past Görlitz. The *New York Times* headline proclaimed: 'Dresden Hit Twice As Russians Move On It'. It described a two-pronged Russian drive for Berlin and Dresden, towards the last of which it said, 'Koniev lunges on'. A broadcast from Moscow noted how 'Allied air forces are now intervening directly in support of the Red Army'.

The Times said that as the centre of a railway network and a great industrial town Dresden had become of the greatest value for controlling the defence against Marshal Koniev. The telephone services and other means of communication in the city were almost as essential to the German army as the railways which met there. It was a meeting-place of the main lines to eastern and southern Germany, Berlin, Prague and Vienna.

But powerful as this air assault might be, it was the land offensive in the west that people were waiting for. What chance, asked 'Scrutator' of the *Sunday Times*, was there of an Allied move in the west which would close down the Ruhr? He decided that it was still largely dependent on the weather, and hoped that Eisenhower's great offensive would coincide with the dry spell which was often a feature of March. The weather could not be counted on until May but 'no one supposes that this year we can wait till then.'

Aware perhaps of the danger to morale from apathy while the laborious and often hard-fought preliminary stages for the eventual offensive went on, General Montgomery delivered one of his celebrated 'pep' talks in familiar sporting metaphor.

'We stand ready,' he said, 'for the last round. Many of us have fought through previous rounds; we have won every round on points. We now come to the last and final round, and we want, and will go for the knockout blow. The last round may be long and difficult, and the fighting hard but we now fight on German soil. We have got our opponent where we want him and he is going to receive the knockout blow – a somewhat unusual one, delivered from more than one direction. . . . The Germans began this all-out contest and they must

In the aftermath of RAF bombing, British troops move into Bremen

One of Bremen's massive air-raid shelters

Something saved from the ruins

not complain when in the last round they are hit from several directions at the same time.'

However, the Germans were still hitting back. 'Monty's Men Stand Fast' was the *Daily Mirror* headline three days later as the paper described 'non-stop counter blows' being put in by the Germans against pressure on the Siegfried Line.

At 3.30 in the morning of the 23rd February two US armies, the First and the Ninth, under the operational command of Montgomery, launched an offensive in bright moonlight across the River Roer with what the Germans described as 'the greatest assembly of military might since the opening of the Second Front.' They said that 'the hurricane of enemy fire' sweeping the Linnach–Julich–Düren area exceeded that even of the Normandy invasion.

By the next day the Americans had a bridgehead across the Roer two to four miles deep. The town of Julich and half Düren had been taken and the armies stood on the edge of the Cologne plain, in sight of the spires of Cologne Cathedral. Elsewhere General Patton's Third Army was now entirely on German soil – at some points having made its way right through the Siegfried Line.

From Supreme Allied Headquarters General Eisenhower, the Com-mander-in-Chief, made an appropriately solemn pronouncement which, however, also made clear that this major offensive was in itself only a preliminary to that which he hoped would finally knock Ger-many out of the war. He stated explicitly that his present aim was to destroy 'every German west of the Rhine'. Once the Allies had reached the Rhine they would then penetrate into the heart of Germany as fast as weather and terrain permitted. And once the Ruhr as well as Silesia in the east had been lost, he did not believe that Germany could hold out for more than sixty days. But he did not discount the possibility of large-scale guerilla warfare in a southern redoubt. Appropriately in the post-Yalta spirit he drew attention to the fact that the Red Army had 'drawn off considerable German strength from the west' and he hoped to meet the Russians in the centre of Germany after which they would clear up the remnants of German resistance. Liaison with the Russians, he said, had been 'as close and intimate as necessary to meet any situation; they have given us all the information desired willingly and cheerfully.'

The air assault was now in close support of this preliminary western offensive; the day before it started, 6,000 Allied aircraft had met over the Ruhr. The great importance of Allied air superiority at this stage, wrote 'Scrutator', was that it could effectively stop the Germans, who now had much shorter inner communications than the Allies, from switching their forces from east to west and vice versa.

Progress on the ground was at times spectacular, particularly in the Rhineland; German resistance was oddly varied. There were signs in places that it might be breaking down, elsewhere it was actually stiffening. The town of München-Gladbach which still held a population of some 15,000 offered little resistance. But there was very heavy fighting by the German First Parachute army in Hochwald, a pivot of the Siegfried Line's defensive system. Fierce German counter-attacks there actually forced the Canadians back for a time.

This unpredictability of the German response continued to be a feature of the advance. On March 2nd Krefeld was taken, now a mere shell of a town, with only the residential area still keeping its walls around a flattened, burned-out shattered industrial district. Lawrence Fairhall, the *Sunday Times* correspondent found some 120,000 people cowering in deep underground shelters two or three storeys below the earth, where most of them had lived for nearly a year. West of the Rhine opposite Wesel the Germans still fiercely defended a very strong bridgehead some 12½ miles wide and 15 miles deep. Further south their resistance was described as 'hurried and unco-ordinated'.

That there was some method in this lack of co-ordination became clear from a statement issued by Eisenhower's Headquarters. This revealed that although the Siegfried Line had been broken and the Allies had now closed up to the Rhine at a number of points, neither the German First Parachute Army under General Student nor their Fifteenth Army under General Von Rundstedt had been destroyed, in spite of suffering heavy losses. The probability was that most of their heavy equipment had been successfully brought across the Rhine into Germany.

By March 5th the Americans were in a suburb of Cologne, on the west bank of the Rhine, in which they were encountering strong initial resistance. They had strict orders not to fire on the Cathedral. Watching the Allied progress to date 'Scrutator' commented in the *Sunday Times*, 'A process like this, once started, cannot be stopped half-way.' Though Germans might fight to retain a bridgehead or two and possibly contest yard by yard the ruined city of Cologne, the Western Allies were on their way, while in the east the Russians only waited for good weather and supplies.

The Allied air forces continued to help the Russians. On the 26th February Berlin had another very heavy daylight raid: some 1,200 Fortresses and Liberators bombed at noon with 700 Mustangs and Thunderbolts as escorts. Only sixteen bombers and seven fighters were lost.

Cologne, as things turned out, was captured in twenty-four hours, putting up very little resistance at all. Some 150,000 of the normal population of three-quarters of a million still remained in the city, presenting the Allies with the biggest example to date of their new problem: how to deal with Germans. The first orders to the population were necessarily strict. They were told to stay in their homes except for excursions to get food or water. All cameras, radio sets and arms had to be handed in. There was a strict curfew and anyone found in the streets after dark was liable to the death penalty. For the Allied troops themselves strict 'non-fraternisation' with civilians was decreed.

David Walker, a *Daily Mirror* correspondent, who thought it not unreasonable to say that Cologne had been taken by the RAF, wrote: 'It is hard to find words to describe the great mass of destruction that lies in the path of the Allied armies as they move forward into Germany . . . Only when you get into these towns do you see the extent of the devastation.'

In the last raid alone 3,000 tons of bombs had been dropped on the city, some seven times more than had been dropped in the worst of the raids on London; and Cologne had experienced bombing on this scale since May, 1942.

'There are ruins,' wrote Walker, 'where people have lived beneath the ground for two solid years, where shops and stores are beneath street level and where men and women have learned to live like moles.' The desolation, he said, was a triumph for the RAF, a tribute to the very gallant crews who had faced the stiffest flak over these towns. 'It seems to me a good moment as we force our way through these devastated towns, to remember that these places were "Target for To-night" to countless cheerful Air Force crews flying from English fields to this black heart of Germany. It was their courage and their efficiency that helped to make this all possible.'

But people were looking forward rather than back, and, inevitably, with a sort of tired impatience.

'The war against Germany goes on relentlessly,' wrote A. J. Cummings in the *News Chronicle*. 'It also moves fast. Not fast enough, perhaps, for millions of people in this country whose minds not unnaturally are apt to leap far ahead of events. On the Rhine, yes. But why not over the Rhine? How long will it be before the Allied armies are on the other side of the swift flowing river and marching straight into the heart of the Reich?'

Progress to the Rhine was indeed now consolidated all along the west bank except in the Wesel bridgehead where fanatical resistance continued. On the 9th March Bonn was captured. But the day before this, the Allies had had a sensational and unexpected success which, because

184

Liberation; prisoners of war greet American troops advancing into Frankfurt

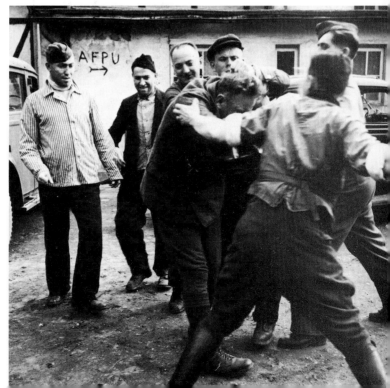

eration; freed Russian slave
abourers have recognized a
i and settle some old scores

it was unexpected, almost seemed to interfere with the methodical procedure of their advance. A bridge over the Rhine at Remagen, south of Bonn, was captured intact.

Within twenty-four hours the bridgehead was five and a half miles wide and three miles deep. A high crest of hills east of the Rhine provided it with a natural defence and with some protection from German artillery which now began to shell the crossing with understandable desperation. Demolition charges had been set on the bridge but owing to what the Germans termed 'accident or chance' had not been effectively detonated before American engineers managed to dismantle them, allowing General Hodges' advance guards to race across. The central span of the bridge was actually to collapse into the water a few days later but by then the Americans were sufficiently established on both sides of the river to be able to repair it in twenty-four hours. A week later the Germans court-martialled and shot three Majors and one senior Lieutenant for cowardice and failure in their duty, a failure which, as *The Times* commented, meant that Allied plans too would now require 'adjustment'. The *New Statesman*'s verse satirist 'Sagittarius' published a poem after Robert Browning, 'Accident In The Allied Camp':

> 'You know Remagen bridge was seized
> A week or two ago –
> The High Command was hardly pleased,
> It almost wrecked the show.
> The bridge they thought as good as blown
> When Ike's assault began;
> Allied Headquarters had their own
> Supreme strategic plan.'

Popular reception of the event was enthusiastic, particularly in America. Alistair Cooke, reporting from there for the BBC said that pictures of the bridge appearing in every US newspaper and magazine had been 'a sign of pride and wonder to Americans, a symbol of the road to victory in Europe.' He said he knew of people who had been rung up or asked by early-morning shoppers if their boy was on the bridge. 'In time,' he wrote, 'I suppose the presence of an ancestor there will become a passport to a hundred per cent Americanism.' In Britain, its capture was hailed as 'a piece of luck, an uncovenanted mercy'. Taking everything into account, it began to look as if organised German military effort could not hold out much longer. Churchill himself on March 15th, possibly under the influence of this piece of good news, talked of the war in Europe ending 'before the summer ends, or even sooner, as it might well do.' Hitherto the Government's date for the end of the German war could only be inferred from the official date for the ending of double summer-time, early in August.

But although the Remagen bridgehead was steadily expanded day by day becoming 25 miles wide by 8 miles deep by the 21st March, this fortune, as 'Sagittarius' had suggested, was to play only a minor rôle in General Eisenhower's final success and was not allowed to disturb his master plan.

His Headquarters had already been able to announce that since the Rhineland battle had started on February 23rd, some 24 German Divisions, including some of the best in the German army had been 'destroyed, battered beyond recognition'. By March 27th all Germany west of the Rhine except for a diminishing triangle with a 30-mile base on the river between Ludwigshafen and Lauterburg was in Allied hands. The quality of German resistance remained varied. In some areas it had completely collapsed; in others it was fanatical. In the triangle German rearguards fought bitterly to cover the main retreat across the Rhine. In Mainz, SS troops had fought a last-ditch battle street by street from strongpoints of rubble.

From dawn to dusk on March 21st the RAF and USAAF carried out some 6,000 heavy bomber and tactical sorties against towns in the lower Rhine defence line, against marshalling yards in the north German plain and against the airfields east of the Ruhr. Then on the night of March 23rd to 24th, under a further shattering aerial and artillery bombardment, Allied troops, by glider, parachute and amphibious boats streamed across the Rhine in bright moonlight to begin the final assault on Germany from the west.

Twenty-four hours later all the bridgeheads had been firmly established and fourteen miles of the east bank between Rees and Wesel were in Allied hands. Except around Rees, where German paratroops fought stubbornly, the expected large-scale resistance had not materialised. Germany's greatest defence barrier had been 'crossed with incredible ease' and the German defences had 'collapsed like a house of cards.' By March 25th the airborne forces had everywhere linked up with the infantry. By March 27th British and American tank spearheads were streaming eastwards, in the style of the Russian offensive, through great gaps which the Germans were unable to plug.

Eisenhower announced from his Headquarters that the Germans were 'a whipped army, incapable of throwing in sufficient strength to stop the Allies anywhere within range of their maintenance sources.' In view of strong sporadic resistance encountered in certain sectors he was careful not to be over-optimistic. It was, he said, the end of one phase and the beginning of another, but it was too early to ring bells. He also released for public consumption an interesting admission about the quality of Allied tanks. 'If the war lasts a few weeks longer,' he said, 'the enemy may be met on the battlefield with something equal to the Tiger and Panther tanks.'

But even the existing American tanks were, as one correspondent in the south put it, 'tearing through the German lines like wolves through a flock of sheep.' The great town of Mannheim had surrendered. On the 1st April Leonard Mosley of the *Sunday Times* wrote: 'All unified and central control of the Wehrmacht has disappeared from the west. The defence against us, where there is any, is completely uncoordinated, sometimes it comes from a surrounded group of para-troopers, and it is bloody if short-lived. Sometimes it comes from a terri-fied Company of Volkssturm, goaded by the local Gestapo, whom they kill or capture, and then surrender themselves as soon as they can.'

'Scrutator' wrote that the Germans had no defensive line left in the west and the paper's military correspondent declared that the situation on the western front could no longer be measured by any military yardstick.

Eisenhower himself issued a message to the German army pointing out that the German Government had ceased to exercise control over wide areas and that the High Command had lost effective control over its units. He gave out his own orders. Those units in contact with the Allies were to cease hostilities and preserve discipline. Those out of contact and scattered were to report to the nearest Allied command, observing the usual signs of surrender.

Officially German morale faced what now looked like an even greater disaster in the west than in the east with the same grim determination. National Socialism, which by definition could not fail Germany, only had to maintain its character to save Germany. Nazi Gauleiters and their subordinate officials were given full powers to muster resistance by the Volkssturm, to organise civilian labour and construct defences, and, wherever defeatism was sensed, to seek it out and destroy it ruthlessly. SS troops whenever present ensured the power with which such tasks could be effected. Announcements that the Mayor of Breslau had been shot in the city's main square by the Volkssturm for wanting to surrender to the Russians, or that high-ranking army officers had been executed for cowardice in East Prussia, were made without any apparent fear that such revelation of weakness in high places might increase misgivings. In this spirit the gravity of the situation could be welcomed as a purifying agent. It ensured that unadulterated National Socialist zeal which made final victory inevitable. To all questions posed by the deteriorating situation ritual responses rather than con-crete answers sufficed. At no stage of the western offensive up to the

PICTURE POST

SALUTE TO DEFEAT

HULTON'S NATIONAL WEEKLY

In this issue:

INTO GERMANY 4^D

MARCH 24, 1945

Vol. 26. No. 12

Rhine and now beyond did the apparent inadequacy of such responses prevent them from being used again.

Doctor Goebbels wrote in *Das Reich*: 'No one can say where and when this war will end. It must however be clear to every German that it must and will only end with our victory. But it is obvious that the question most widely discussed today among our people is whence, in our present precarious war situation, will come new chances to change the fortunes of war.'

The only answer he could provide was one which had to remain equally valid in the weeks ahead: 'Stand firm and do not jump overboard, however high the seas; that would mean certain death.'

A broadcast to the German forces ran: 'Comrades, it seems as if our distress were growing beyond measure. Yet conditions will become still harder and then we shall long for the days and hours which once we thought the limit of what we could bear. You may ask, comrades, where all this is leading, where is the end, and whether there is any sense left in all this. . . . There are no bridges to the lives we have left behind, although most of us yearn to return to the past. This yearning we must bury once and for all.' 'Some,' said another German forces broadcast 'find it difficult to understand when we say that today time is working for us.'

A broadcast to the German people had stated openly: 'At this hour anyone referring to an imminent turn of the tide would find many sceptics.' But the answer to sceptics was always there in National Socialist terms: 'It is only natural that, in view of the situation, wide circles of the people should show a desire to learn how a turn in events can materialise,' ran a broadcast to the German forces. 'But the Führer has stated unequivocally that it will come this year.'

Reciprocally, the German people were told: 'If every German believed as much as we front line soldiers in our Führer, then victory wouldn't be very far distant.'

William Joyce, Lord Haw-Haw, speaking to a British audience, had no such mystical resources at his command and could only speak with a crude bravado wholly ineffectual now compared with some of his earlier attempts to undermine the British people's confidence in their own leadership. 'I am not making a propaganda point,' he had said on March 8th, 'when I say that Churchill was very ill-advised to utter the boast: "We shall soon be across the Rhine." '

A Luftwaffe Major, Immanuel Kant Professor of Philosophy at Königsberg, had been, in his fashion, on safer ground when he broadcast to the German people: 'If there should be only dispersed hosts of Germans left in Europe, the heroic German nation will, in a thousand natural ways, rally them, gather them once more into a nation and lead

Some of the last defenders of the Reich

them upwards. We shall conquer – now or later. We shall be all the more unconquerable, the more the grandiose work of Germany's visible obliteration progresses towards its extreme consequences and the more German self-defence is petrified, as it were, into a weird monument.'

Chapter Nineteen

As it began to look more and more certain that the war in Europe really was at last approaching its end, British domestic political awareness increased.

Churchill had said in Parliament in 1944 that it would be right to hold an election at the end of the German war. It was now known that he would prefer to keep the Coalition in existence until the end of the war against Japan. But the indefinite prospect which this appeared to offer seemed unsatisfactory to Labour leaders; they felt the need to show that they were not afraid of fighting an election. As early as the 6th January, Greenwood, Labour leader in the House of Commons for so long as Attlee remained in the Government, had gone out of his way to refute any idea that Labour were ill-prepared for an election or that, if one were held, they did not really want to win it.

'It has been said . . .' he declared, 'I am out for a sham fight. . . . The idea that we are not going all out to win is absolutely untrue.'

The fact that he felt it necessary to make the statement showed something of the position of electoral inferiority from which Labour had to start. It had suffered overwhelming defeats in the two elections of the nineteen-thirties, and the Conservatives had a majority over it in the present Parliament of more than two to one.

A further wish to display Labour leaders' self-confidence was evidenced by Herbert Morrison who himself accepted the future Labour candidacy of East Lewisham, a seat never before won by Labour and which, at the last General Election, in 1935, had yielded a Conservative majority of over six thousand. In his adoption speech he gave a foretaste of the wide appeal Labour wanted to offer.

'If,' he said, 'Labour is to get an independent and stable majority . . . it must gain the support of large numbers of professional, technical and administrative workers. I am confident that the reasoned appeal of the Labour Party will be accepted by all manual workers and black-coats alike.'

What indications were there of the likely result of such an election, the first in Britain for nearly ten years?

A Gallup poll the previous November had asked the question: 'What form of Government would you like to see lead Britain in the period following the war?'

The replies had been:

> 35% all-party Government
> 26% Labour
> 12% Conservative.

The rest of the total was made up of small percentages for either the Liberals by themselves (4%) or in coalition with Labour (6%) or with the Conservatives (3%). 14% described themselves as uncertain.

When, however, people were asked who they would like to see as Prime Minister after the war, 24% replied Churchill, 21% Eden. Only 7% were for Attlee and 2% for Bevin. As many as 28% of the sample were uncertain. 90% approved of Winston Churchill as the present Prime Minister.

These results were not in general discouraging for Labour. They revealed no monolithic confidence in the Conservative Party as such, though they clearly showed that Churchill's personal appeal as its leader had to be taken into account. But they equally clearly showed a wish for some sort of change from the pre-war political atmosphere. This wish had to some extent already been catered for by all parties including the Conservatives. As early as April 1943 Churchill had announced on behalf of the Coalition a 'Four-Year Plan' to ensure a new social deal from the cradle to the grave, the first aspects of which emerged in 1944 with the Beveridge Report on Social Security, together with a White Paper on the need for full employment and a new Education Act. The strongly emotional sense of the need for change which the war had brought about was well expressed at the beginning of 1945 by the Bishop of Liverpool, Dr Clifford Martin. Devotion to a common cause, he maintained, had broken down barriers of class and social distinction. Many remembered with gladness the comradeship of the shelter on the night of an air raid.

'This,' he wrote, 'is the spirit which has carried us through and brought us near to what we hope may be a victorious conclusion of it all. If and when peace comes it will be disastrous if we just sit back and say the job is done. What chances will be in front of us! The health of the people requiring vast improvement. . . . The rehousing of families with the need of building thousands of houses. . . . The development of culture and the Arts to enable everyone to have a chance of expressing the gifts God has given them. Here is a programme requiring a tremendous sense of devotion.'

The question was: would general feelings of this sort be effective enough to make themselves felt politically?

The first channelling of this sort of emotion into politics had been seen in a small number of by-elections at which Independents or members of the new socialistic Common Wealth party had flouted the electoral truce and either beaten the Coalition candidate or seriously embarrassed the Government by heavily reducing its majority. In February 1944 a Conservative majority in Brighton of 40,000 had been reduced to under 2,000 – though such movement could reasonably be interpreted simply as overall impatience with the electoral truce.

In January 1945 came a pamphlet, 'Why Not Trust The Tories?' from the Labour MP Aneurin Bevan, written under the nominal pseudonym 'Celticus' and published by Victor Gollancz. Bevan's argument was that, given the Tory record of tricking the electorate in the past, its apparent commitment to the social security of the Beveridge Report and the principle of full employment was wholly untrustworthy.

The liberal *Manchester Guardian* described the pamphlet as 'one more ammunition dump at the service of the Left.' But it was critical of Bevan, saying that the alternative to what he hated was hardly visible in his pages. He rightly advised his own side not to be manoeuvred into appearing as the advocates of regimentation against freedom. But that was exactly what would happen unless Labour spent much more time and thought making their own case more attractive than Bevan did in his book. The paper noted that the Tories were still holding their fire. Dr C. E. M. Joad, the BBC Brains Trust philosopher, assessed the mood of the armed forces in a discussion on 'What is the average man fighting for?' in the *Daily Express* in January. He agreed with Bevan that cynical mistrust of the political party which had been in power for eighteen of the twenty-one years before the war was likely to be as potent a political force as any more constructive thinking. There was, said Joad, a distinction growing all the time between what the average man hoped to get out of the war and what he expected to get out of it. '. . . The increasing belief is that he is going to be let down again as he was last time. . . . There is a growth of cynicism and a feeling that the post-war world will not be very much better than 1939.'

There was also, said Joad, general cynicism towards leaders. An army dispatch rider, Albert Foxwell, also taking part in the *Express* discussion, agreed with him.

*

At the end of January Attlee himself made what almost amounted to a public electioneering speech for the Labour party. This was in a way an odd departure for, as Deputy Prime Minister in the Coalition Government, he was responsible for official statements about the mechanism of the election whenever it might be held. He had in fact just announced a scheme enabling the armed forces to vote by post and on the 17th January gave a pledge on behalf of the Government that there would be no snap election. Whenever the election should be decided on, an announcement would be made at least three weeks before the dissolution of Parliament and the normal seventeen days before polling day would then follow.

Now on the 25th January Attlee told a meeting of Labour supporters that the party was 'going into the fight as a party on its own, with its tail well up because we've done our share in winning this war.' He had indications from all over the country that people of all classes were swinging to the Left. A lot of people had come up to him and said: 'I've been a Conservative all my life, but I'm changing now. I've seen the nation come first in war. I want to see it come first in peace.' Not only, said Attlee, were economists but even bankers swinging over to Labour. He warned however against what he called 'stunts and scares'.

A certain amount of such low-key electioneering by Labour leaders while still members of Churchill's Coalition Government continued in February. Ernest Bevin, Churchill's Minister of Labour, made a speech in which he said that the country would need controls after the war. He did not regard controls as a political instrument at all but as a means of getting balanced labour forces and preventing future chaos. 'The old days,' he said, 'of using men and starvation to adjust exchanges and money and currencies have gone and must never come back.' Both Hugh Dalton and Stafford Cripps declared their support for continuing controls after the war, though Lord Beaverbrook's *Daily Express* made clear that the removal of controls would be an essential feature of Conservative policy in peacetime.

Officially the Conservatives still held their fire, presumably because of Churchill's wish to extend the life of the Coalition until after victory had been won against Japan. There was also a tactical reason why a delayed election might have an advantage for the Conservatives. A prominent northern Conservative, Sir Cuthbert Headlam, MP, addressing a meeting of the North Cumberland Conservative Association in January had said that the party was suffering from the fact that when war came it had shut down its party organisation a great deal too vigorously. The Opposition on the other hand had not been so scrupulous, and its propaganda continued incessantly.

It was at the Conservative Party Conference on 15th March that the first serious shot was fired from the Conservative side. Since the Deputy Prime Minister had felt no inhibition about outlining the case for his own side in public, the Prime Minister now also reverted to his rôle of Party Leader.

He first commended Conservatives for devoting their organisation and activities to the national rather than the party cause for so long in spite of 'many provocations from that happily limited class of Left-Wing politicians to whom party strife is as the breath of their nostrils.'

He stressed the freedom for which Britain had been fighting, 'freedom for individuals within the broad and ever-advancing conception of the British Constitution and the British way of life. We have no use here,' he added, 'for totalitarian schemes of government.'

He pointed out that the public declarations of his Labour and Liberal colleagues left no doubt that with the end of the war in Europe they intended to resume liberty of action and bring the Coalition to an end. And after reminding his audience of the enormous tasks which would face the country in peace he went on, 'Our Socialist friends have officially committed themselves, much to the disgust of their leaders, to a programme for the nationalisation of the means of production, distribution and exchange . . . sweeping proposals which imply not only the destruction of the life of our whole existing system of society and life and labour, but the creation and enforcement of another system, or system borrowed from foreign lands and alien minds. . . . It is no easy, cheapjack Utopia that lies before us. This is no time for windy platitudes. . . . No restriction upon well-established British liberties that is not proved indispensable to the prosecution of the war and the transition from war to peace can be tolerated. Control for control's sake is senseless. Controls which are in fact designed to favour the accomplishment of wayside totalitarian systems, however innocently designed . . . are a fraud which should be mercilessly exposed to the British public. At the head of our mainmast we fly the flag of free enterprise . . .'

The *Manchester Guardian* said the speech did him honour because it was so poor, showing that his mind was rightly on the far more important business of winning the war. It was a reversion to 'reach-me-downs from the tub-thumping 'twenties' and his description of the Labour Party's programme 'might have been taken from Conservative Central Office Speakers' Notes for 1926.'

The *New Statesman* answered Churchill indignantly by saying that Labour only wanted to nationalise 'precisely as few of such means as will enable them, when they get into power, to carry out the promises they have made of full employment, living wages, tolerable housing and a reasonable measure of social security.' But at least what had been revealed was an indication of the Conservative line of attack on Labour whenever an election should come.

The first open duel between members of the Coalition, each championing the cause of his own party, took place at the beginning of April. Ernest Bevin, the Minister of Labour, possibly resenting particularly the remark in Churchill's conference speech to the effect that some Labour leaders were not as much in favour of the nationalisation programme as the party itself, deprecated the Prime Minister's 'attempt to resort to personalities . . . when the country is tired and exhausted and nerve-racked and when judgement needs to be nursed but not exploited.' This was not, he said, what one might have expected from politicians who should face all this in responsible mood. He went on to defend Labour's own sense of responsibility shown by declining any more extensions of Parliament's life once the German war was over and its wish to leave the Coalition when that moment came. The Conservative Party, he said, were afraid to face the electors on the record of their own doings that had led Britain into the war. They had completely failed to prepare for defence or adequately warn the country where it was heading. They had run a foreign policy which 'nearly brought us and the whole of civilisation to the dust'. Now they were hoping that the present generation of young electors would know nothing about it and that those who were older would have forgotten it. Big business which had preferred to keep millions of unemployed drawing unemployment pay rather than put them on to useful work had been ready to do a deal with Hitler and his gang. As for Churchill himself, although he had a profound admiration for him, 'it had not been a one-man war or a one-man Government.'

This was an important electioneering point for Labour, historically accused of both inexperience and incompetence in office, and Bevin further stressed it in another speech at Newcastle-on-Tyne the same day when he said the war had completely disproved the assertion that Labour did not have the ability to govern.

The next day Brendan Bracken, Bevin's colleague as Minister of Information in the Coalition Government, replied to what he called 'Bevin's blitz on the Conservative Party'. He said that when he first heard a summary of the speech on the BBC he had thought it must be by Aneurin Bevan. He pointed out that if the Conservatives had failed to prepare for war they had at least been in good company, for Socialists had continually argued against rearmament in the 'thirties and Churchill had been the 'one man' then who had consistently warned against Hitler. As for the country's economic future, 'Britain would never accept the sort of totalitarian State desired by the Socialists. . . . Instead of messing about with nationalisation schemes which must inevitably create confusion, not to say chaos, the whole productive power of the country should be geared up to provide our people with the homes, the

furniture, the clothes and all the other goods they so greatly deserve. . . .
As a nation of enterprisers our future is boundless. As a nation of
form-fillers and restrictionists we have the bleakest of futures.'

Arthur Greenwood, speaking the same night in Southwark said that
the General Election was coming pretty soon now and that Brendan
Bracken, following on Churchill's Tory Conference initiative, had
brought it on even sooner.

Shinwell, in the House of Commons asked if the Minister of Information's salary should not now be borne by the Conservative Party rather
than the Treasury. Churchill replied that Bracken had been speaking
as a member of the Government 'in which,' he added with jocular
reference to Bevin's speech, 'great freedom appears to be allowed.'
Later, in answer to a question he said, '. . . as we are by general consent
moving into dispute between parties it is obvious that divergences of
outward expression will occur.'

The Times summed things up the next day by saying that even the
most vigorous partisans seemed to feel that for the moment honour was
satisfied. 'And so the unreal controversy goes on,' was the *New Statesman*'s comment, awaiting more incisive political debate altogether.

But it began to look as if such generalities might prove to be the real
stuff of the eventual election. On the 21st April the Labour Party
published its declaration of policy for the election, 'Let Us Face The
Future'. The *Daily Mirror* used the occasion to stress that Labour which
had revealed in the Coalition its high sense of national responsibility,
had now 'grown up'. There was no difference, the paper said, between
any of the parties in promising as their aim jobs, homes and food for all.
It was a question of the means by which these aims were to be achieved.
Labour believed that the economic structure must be underpinned by
some State enterprise in the form of nationalisation of coal, iron and
steel, the railways and the Bank of England. For the *Daily Mirror* it was
not so much economic theory itself as an appeal to the record of the past
which was important.

'The Labour Party points to the mass unemployment, mass poverty
and mass misery which was the lot of too many people before the war –
to the prison from which it says free enterprise found no escape. When
Conservative leaders promise jobs for all – Labour men ask: "Why
should we believe you?" '

The *Daily Mirror* pointed out reassuringly that there was no new idea
in 'Let Us Face The Future'. 'No revolutionary proposal tickles the ear
of the blow-everything-up brand of reformer. . . . Labour's declaration
offers a typically British solution for British problems.'

The paper even criticised Labour's declaration of policy for saying
nothing about the future of the Empire 'and the part it alone can play in

sustaining Great Britain as a Great Power in the world of tomorrow.' But its general mood of welcome for what it plainly saw as the real start of Labour's election campaign was summed up by the Zec cartoon of the day. This showed a short-sleeved Attlee and Bevin pulling on a rope round a large top hat marked Privilege while Herbert Morrison pushed from the other side. Emerging from underneath the hat was a lamp marked Labour Party Policy from which a burning flame spelled out the inspiring message: 'The chance for a happy and secure future'. The cartoon was captioned 'Lifting The Blackout.'

It so happened that there had been two by-election results in the previous week. Although the electoral truce was scrupulously upheld by the three main parties of the Coalition, both turned out to be defeats for it. There were however special factors at work and it was not easy to discern any clear auguries for the future.

Both were in Scotland, the first at Motherwell where a Labour Coalition candidate was defeated to let in the first Scottish Nationalist to enter Parliament, a Dr R. MacIntyre. There was a low poll of only 58%, and one of the reasons given for the defeat was that the political bickering between Bevin and Bracken had lessened the sense of responsibility among Unionists and Liberals to support a Labour Coalition man. There had also been a build-up of general Scottish discontent with the way in which the Government had dealt with a number of major Scottish issues.

The second defeat, in the seat for the Scottish Universities, was similarly attributed to Scottish resentment, though here, the size of the victor's majority was spectacular. Sir John Boyd Orr won as an Independent over a Liberal National Coalition candidate by a majority of over 12,000. The only possible pointer to the future in this result was a negative one: the defeated Coalition candidate had been particularly strongly recommended by Winston Churchill. But no such negative interpretation was made by the Under-Secretary of State for Air, Quintin Hogg, who gave it as his opinion that the conduct of international affairs was going to be one of the great issues at the next general election and that it was of paramount importance to have men of the stature and experience of Churchill and Eden to make the frequent contact with other Heads of Government that would be necessary in the future.

The result in a third by-election that April was due a week later, and that certainly could be said to be likely to provide some indication for the future. It was in the constituency of Chelmsford where again the official electoral truce was being observed. But a candidate for the newly-formed Common Wealth Party, a 28-year-old RAF Wing Commander Millington who commanded an operational bomber squadron, challenged the Conservative Coalition candidate on an avowed Socialist programme. The creation of the Common Wealth Party had indeed been largely brought about by a wish on the part of many Labour supporters to be able to express their views while the electoral truce continued. Millington's slogan in his campaign was: 'A vote for Common Wealth is a vote for the people.'

On paper his chances did not look good. The constituency had returned a Conservative majority of 16,624 at the last General Election in 1935. However, many industrial workers had come into the constituency during the war. A further unpredictable factor was that Chelmsford was the first English constituency to poll on the new register and to include proxy votes for Service men and women overseas.

Millington's Conservative opponent was also in the RAF, a Flight-Lieutenant Brian Cook. He had the advantage of receiving a strong letter of support from Churchill, the substance of whose message was what in other circumstances would have been a straight assault on the policy of the Labour Party. Having stressed that victory would not bring automatic solutions to the enormous problems of peace at home and abroad he continued: 'These are no tasks for novices or theorists. They are practical tasks demanding skill, knowledge, patience and a spirit of united endeavour. The choice lies between a firm supporter of the Government that has organised the defeat of Germany and at the same time given the country abundant evidence of preparations for tackling the problems of peace, and a party whose equipment for dealing with those intractable problems is a portfolio of grandiose aspirations and untried theories.' Attlee, as Deputy Prime Minister in the Coalition, found himself in the anomalous position of having to send a letter of support alongside Churchill's to the Conservative candidate.

By polling day in Chelmsford there were many political observers who thought that, for all the vast majority which Millington had to overturn, the result might well be a close-run thing. 'Close Vote Expected Today' was *The Times* headline. The paper judged that if Millington were to defeat the Government it would be a vote for personality rather than policy; it was doubtful, it said, whether many of those who had flocked to his meetings had troubled themselves about the gospel preached there but they had been impressed by the candidate himself.

The poll was high for a by-election in wartime: 69%. But the result was not a close one. Wing-Commander Millington, the Common Wealth candidate, won by a majority of 6,431. The result, said *The Times*, was 'a sign and a portent'. Millington said: 'It shows that the people are tired of the old order and want a new plan. They will have it in Common Wealth.' As far as the forthcoming general election was concerned, the leader of the Common Wealth Party, Sir Richard Acland, was probably more accurately prescient when he said the result showed that 'Socialists had nothing to fear from the myth of the Churchill prestige.'

The Times may well have been right when it said it was foolish to suppose that all Millington's support had come from people in favour of Socialism. But in that case it could be argued that the result was all the more significant for it showed the strength of the general feeling of disaffection with the past at work in the electorate. Millington exaggerated when he said the Conservatives fought the election on Churchill and lost it on Churchill. But at least what the result showed was that it was not possible to win an election on Churchill alone.

Chapter Twenty

It was, all in Britain were agreed, one of the most beautiful springs in living memory.

'Day after day it continues,' wrote L. F. Easterbrook in the *News Chronicle*, 'with the fresh green of the new leaves showing sage-coloured against the pearly sky in the early mornings and then the June warmth under the blue vault of the heavens.' And Robert Lynd in the same paper: 'Never indeed has Nature looked and sounded happier than at this present hour when "what Man has made of Man" gives cause for lamentation beyond anything Wordsworth had in mind. The birds and flowers, knowing nothing of what man has made of man have made of at least one part of the earth the scene of such a jubilee as time can never surpass.'

And all through April the war news was good, unbelievably so if the disappointment with which the year had begun was remembered. Only the exhaustion of five and a half years could sap the enthusiasm with which most days' news was to be greeted.

By the end of the first sixteen days of April the Americans, British and French, driving deep into the heart of Germany east of the Rhine against resistance that was at times hardly even token, at others bitter and fanatical, had taken more than three-quarters of a million prisoners, 144,000 of them on April 16th alone. Nine days later, the Americans who had by then reached the Elbe, were met there by the Russians. Other units of the Red Army were now fighting their way into Berlin itself. Germany was cut in two.

Yet there was still no certainty about how or when the war would end. In the euphoric mood engendered by an advance proceeding often at the rate of many miles a day there had been at one moment the rumour that Churchill might announce V or Victory Day on April 19th, but this was almost immediately discounted. As late as April 22, the experienced American commentator, Drew Middleton, writing from Eisenhower's headquarters in Paris was saying that in view of the formidable German forces still on the North Sea and the Baltic, and the magnitude of the task of reducing the long-predicted southern redoubt

The Advance on Berlin

NORTH SEA

SWEDEN

BALTIC SEA

• Copenhagen

DENMARK

canal

• Flensburg

↑ Kiel
Lübeck •

Königsberg
• Tilsit

Gdynia •
Danzig •

EAST PRUSSIA

Wilhelmshaven

Emden •

• Peenemünde

Stettin

• Schneidemühl

• Torun *Vistula*

Ems

• Hamburg
• Lüneburg

Weser

• Bremen
Verden

Elbe

HOLLAND

Amsterdam
Arnhem •
• Emmerich
Wesel •
Dortmund •

Osnabrück •
Tecklenburg •

GERMANY

Berlin ●

Magdeburg

Frankfurt •

• Posen

Oder

Glogau •

WARSAW

POLAND

• Hildesheim

Munster •
Paderborn

Hartz Mts

Ruhr

• Kassel

Leipzig •

Elbe

• Torgau

Neisse

Oder

• Breslau

• Lodz

Oppeln •

Czestochowa

• Erfurt

Chemnitz •

• Dresden

Gleiwitz •

Vistula

Cologne •

Meuse

Rhine

Frankfurt
-am-Main

Schweinfurt •

• Karlsbad
Pilsen •

● Prague

CZECHOSLOVAKIA

• Cracow

Carpathian Mts

Moselle

Erbach •

Main

Nuremberg •

● Strasbourg

• Stuttgart

Black Forest

Danube

Moldau

• Bratislava

FRANCE

L. Constance

• Munich

• Innsbruck

Linz •

• Salzburg

Vienna

Budapest ●

SWITZERLAND

*Brenner
Pass*

AUSTRIA

HUNGARY

L. Balaton

Danube

• Ljubljana

• Trieste

Belgrade

Po

Venice •

YUGOSLAVIA

• Ravenna

Line of 9 April 1945

ITALY

Riga LATVIA

Vitebsk

THUANIA

Kovno

Vilna

Grodno

Minsk

Niemen

Pinsk

PRIPET

Pripet

Lublin

MARSHES

Kiev

U. S. S. R.

Dnieper

Lemberg (Lvov)

Przemysl

Bug

Dniester

Jassy

Pruth

Odessa

RUMANIA

Transylvanian Alps

BLACK

SEA

Yalta

Ploesti

Bucharest

Danube

BULGARIA

Europe under the
Axis Powers
December 1942

Moscow

Berlin

Stalingrad

Paris

Rome

*Stalingrad approx
270 miles (432km)*

British, American &
French advances

Russian advances

0   100   300
                      miles
    100   km
            400

in south-east Bavaria, the general feeling was that they might be into the summer before organised German resistance ended. This was very much in line with a letter Eisenhower had written to Roosevelt on the 31st March and which had since been published.

'Our experience,' he had told the President, 'is that even when formations as small as a division are disrupted, these fragments continue to fight until surrounded. This attitude if continued will likely mean that V Day will come about only by proclamation on our part rather than by any decisive collapse or surrender of German resistance.'

He foresaw an eventual form of guerilla warfare against isolated groups of paratroops, SS and Panzer units which would require a very large number of troops for its suppression.

The extent of the Allied victory following the Rhine crossing had nevertheless been overwhelming. Its true nature was first indicated by the news on April 1st that two American armies, the First and the Ninth, had linked up round the Ruhr thus cutting off the whole of that great industrial zone from the rest of Germany, which had already lost her other major industrial area in Silesia to the Russians. But the persistence of much National Socialist morale, and the patriotic discipline of many ordinary German soldiers meant that to the end there were to be, as Eisenhower had predicted, pockets of resistance in which the logic of defeat was not accepted. At the point of link-up round the Ruhr itself, at Paderborn, SS units continued bitterly to resist the pressure of American tank spearheads in an attempt to keep an escape gap open for the armies trapped there. There were many individual instances of desperate resistance elsewhere, while at other times Britsh and American armour drove almost unhindered through an undamaged countryside in which white flags fluttered from villages and farmhouses in the spring sunshine.

At Emmerich German paratroops resisted fiercely from houses, cellars and tunnels and had to be burned out with flame-throwers while the town was reduced to rubble.

At Tecklenburg, south west of Osnabruck a battalion of cadets from an NCO training school at Hanover held up British armour and airborne troops for many hours. Osnabruck itself, where Nazi fanatics manned the perimeter of the town, expecting a frontal assault, was surprised by British commandos who penetrated in a lightning coup and took it from within. But the city of Munster, where the German commander rejected an ultimatum to surrender, had to be shelled remorselessly and was captured in ruins.

At Aschaffenburg, the garrison commander had wanted to surrender but had been supplanted by a Major von Lambert who, in accordance with Hitler's orders to deal summarily with all 'defeatists' of whatever rank, had hanged him and carried on a vicious defence for five days. He had conscripted hospital patients, old men and women and children, armed them and told them to fight to the death. The Americans had had to fight from house to house and even room to room, sometimes against fifteen-year-old children hurling hand-grenades. American casualties had been heavy and veterans of the Italian campaign and Normandy said it was the fiercest fighting they had experienced anywhere. A US Sherman tank which the defenders had captured actually fired punitively on a column of German prisoners before escaping from the town, but von Lambert himself eventually came out of the castle under a white flag and surrendered. The Americans found the body of a young German lieutenant hanging on front of a wine shop with a placard on him: 'A coward who betrayed the Fatherland'.

At Königshofen white flags had begun to be put out but SS troops then went round the town destroying the houses that flew them, before the Americans could enter, and bitter house-to-house fighting followed in which many civilian snipers took part.

At Kassel, devastated already from the air, the Americans were attacked at one point by a column of 28 German tanks straight off the assembly line of the factory there, their speedometers registering only the mileage from the factory to the point where they were eventually destroyed.

The ancient late Gothic and Renaissance half-timbered town of Hildesheim had also been devastated from the air, in eighteen minutes of a single raid just over a fortnight before the Americans got there. Its newest building was more than three hundred years old but the town also possessed important railway marshalling yards. One of the Americans who now got there was John McCormac, a *New York Times* reporter who described it as he found it: '. . . the corpse of the once-beautiful mediaeval city . . . a corpse that has not yet returned to dust but still stared sightless at the sky.' Some inhabitants told him how, though the bombing had been a terrible enough experience in itself, the fire which consumed the inner town was worse, roasting alive many who were unable to get out of their cellars in time. But this of course had been a quite common experience for German civilians in the last two years.

On the day on which McCormac reported from Hildesheim, the Russians finally captured the long-surrounded fortress of Königsberg in East Prussia, with 27,000 prisoners. However on the Oder opposite Berlin there was then still no sign of movement. In Austria the Red Army was in the suburbs of Vienna, meeting desperate resistance from

Panzer units, SS and every able-bodied man who could be drafted into the fighting. The contrast indeed between the speed at which the British and Americans were now able to move in the west and the overall tenacity with which the Russians were confronted in the east was a subject for pointed comment by Ilya Ehrenburg in the Red Army paper *Red Star*. He said all that was holding up the British and American advance were the columns of prisoners blocking it, so anxious were the Germans to surrender to them.

A BBC correspondent indeed described them as 'the most polite and the most helpful lot of prisoners I've ever seen.' One stopped him in the road and asked: 'Where is your prison?' Told it was some twenty miles to the rear, he asked again: 'Oh, but please. You have not got one a little nearer?'

In fact what was really remarkable, given the degree to which the Germans had been subjected to propaganda about the savagery of the Bolshevik hordes was that more Germans in the west did not make a more immediate choice of what they saw as the lesser of two evils, and surrender quickly to the British and Americans. Many did, but many did not.

The last chance for the Germans to form anything like an orthodox military defence in the west after the Rhine had lain on the river Weser, and at the beginning of April this had still seemed technically a possibility. Only a week later it was clear that the speed of the Allied advance had forestalled any such development. By the 11th April war correspondents agreed that the whole of the central German front had broken up. Three American armies were virtually racing each other to the Elbe, which one of them – the Ninth – reached at Magdeburg 63 miles from Berlin on April 12th.

Yet at Schweinfurt, already devastated by air raids on its great ball-bearing factory, the garrison of 5,000 refused to surrender even when half of the great pile of stone which was virtually all that was left of it was in American hands. Richard Johnston, a *New York Times* correspondent there with the 42nd US (Rainbow) Infantry Division wrote: 'It is impossible to report house-to-house fighting since there are no houses or buildings recognisable any more.' When the ruins had finally been captured eleven German soldiers were found to have been hanged by the SS and the Bürgermeister, a hardline Nazi who had been taken prisoner, killed himself by jumping from a third floor window of the school-house where he was being held. The SS commander himself, an Oberst Lechner, and the surviving SS withdrew, presumably to fight another desperate battle elsewhere.

In one way such withdrawals seemed at odds with specific orders issued by Himmler, overall chief of the SS that every German town was to be defended to the last man and that death was the penalty for not doing so. The death sentence (*in absentia*) was passed on General Lasch for surrendering Königsberg to the Russians and, since he himself was unavailable, it was announced that 'reprisals' were to be taken against his family. But keeping the spirit of resistance alive could be judged as being even more important than dying immediately. Men like Lechner, the commander at Schweinfurt, could be trusted to do that, and from the Nazi point of view there was need of them.

For Richard Johnston also described how it had been possible to travel hundreds of miles across Germany, avoiding large cities but passing through scores of small towns and villages where all the houses were intact and the fields unrboken, and the only signs of war were the white flags fluttering from some kind of staff from every house in every town and from every cottage. There was even a report of some housewives making sure in true German fashion that they had a clean white flag out every day. The people in such places Johnston found to be on the whole neither arrogant nor humble, friendly nor hostile, but polite. Only where there had been bombing was there hostility. He noticed too that in the rural areas people seemed well-fed and well-clothed – better so, in fact, he thought, than the British.

There was almost no sign of the 'Werwolf' organisation which German propaganda had said would carry out resistance behind the lines. Occasionally an Allied soldier would be attacked in a town in the dark and there was a story of a Canadian asked by a small boy for a bar of chocolate and then being knifed when he reached for it, but these seemed isolated individual instances. The sabotage of a military train near Erbach in the first week of April with a number of American fatal casualties was a rare enough event to make news. The surprise element in the advance was such that even if there had been the civilian will to organise resistance behind the lines systematically there was almost no time in which to do so. Sometimes German military trains were captured steaming through railway stations which they had no reason to know were already in Allied hands. Sometimes villages and small towns were captured ahead by telephone. The Bürgermeister would be rung up and told that the place would be destroyed unless he surrendered, and, provided he himself was not a fanatic and there were none in the vicinity to put pressure on him, the white flags would appear and the Americans drive in.

At this speed it was militarily a bizarre war. Sometimes patterns of war and peace became disconcertingly confused. At Hanover, where the Nazi leader had announced that anyone showing a white flag from his house would be shot, the Americans found the population resentful of their arrival rather than hostile. Even while German and American tanks were exchanging fire, civilians complained to GIs from the doorways in which they sheltered at not being able to get on with their normal lives. 'It sure makes you feel silly,' commented one American officer, First Lieutenant Darrigo of Novotan Heights, Connecticut, 'crouching or dashing around trying to get a shot at a sniper, while a civilian peddles by on his bike and a woman and child just tag along watching.'

Even outside the isolated pockets of resistance it was a strange business. For the supply columns to catch up with the armoured spearheads they drove day and night along the roads into the heart of the Reich with headlights blazing past notices urging 'Hurry up with your supplies'. The corridors of advance were at times little wider than the roads themselves and it was dangerous for war correspondents or others to try to follow too precipitately after the tanks for Germans would appear behind these to try and seal the spearhead off. Frank Gillard of the BBC reported that men and vehicles were lost in ambushes of this kind every day, but that the price was well worth it. The supply columns themselves went up in escorted convoys as at sea, with screens of armoured cars and light tanks instead of frigates and destroyers, while fighter bombers circled overhead.

At the same time massive air assaults by thousands of American and British bombers continued day and night against the Germans' own military transport, their airfields and, in support of the Russians, Berlin itself. Though the Luftwaffe was being smashed by attacks on airfields where its aircraft were increasingly grounded through lack of fuel, its fighting qualities were by no means extinct. On April 7th it had managed to send up 300 fighters, perhaps a third of them the jet-propelled Messerschmitt 262's, which were more advanced than any the Allies had yet been able to put into the air in such quantities. In the next four days the Allies estimated that, including attacks on 61 airfields, they had destroyed 765 aircraft, and that number had risen to over a thousand two days later, with 112 destroyed on the ground on 12th April alone. By the 14th the total was 1,392, and on the 17th alone 905 more were reported destroyed (again mainly on the ground). And yet some Luftwaffe pilots may still have believed that there was truth in the leaflets they had been dropping over Rhineland cities to the effect that the German army would be back there by May 1st. As late as April 30th, the day before Hitler himself died in Berlin and the British, Americans and Russians had joined up along a large section of the Elbe the Luftwaffe still had the spirit to attack all day the Allied bridges across the river and lost 42 of their aircraft shot down. Undaunted, they were back again next day in what must have been some of the very few Focke Wulf 190's and Me 109's left, attacking the same targets. Their determination was equalled by a German below them, a swimmer captured while trying to fix a mine on one of the bridges.

What did such men conceive themselves still to be fighting for?

At the beginning of April German broadcasts to both troops and people had managed to harmonise ritual exhortations to faith in National Socialism with a certain rational approach.

'Germans ask themselves anxiously,' ran one broadcast to the armed forces, 'How can we still win this war?'

The posing of such an open question transmitted National Socialist realism as well as mystical strength. The inadequacy of the reply offered was of secondary consideration.

'Germany's chance to withstand and beat back this onslaught remains,' went on the broadcast lamely.

Or as Goebbels himself put it: 'Before we reach the lowest limit of material resistance we can reach a point when our empty canisters have again been filled and our empty pockets stuffed full.' He complained that while Germans had their hands full with 'criminals' in the east, the British were 'stabbing them in the back in vile treachery.'

Since this implied that the British should have been on the German side, there seemed some further implication that it might one day turn out to be the case. But painful realism was also increasingly blended in broadcasts with stern rigour: 'Our sufferings seem sometimes unendurable. It can be easily understood that weaklings feel they can no longer stand it, and yearn for an end to their ordeal whatever the cost. . . . For those who try to shirk the struggle, the bullet, which has hit so many fighters for freedom in this war, is too good. They will die the death of ignominy.'

And while there was a bleak readiness to acknowledge what Goebbels called 'a kind of lethargy among the lax and weak . . . weakness and apathy among those most afflicted by the war,' inspiration for triumph over such weakness and every adversity was found from the one unassailable, because by now remote mystical source, the Führer.

'Where,' asked a broadcast on April 5th, 'where in these bitter days, does the homeland's almost god-like strength come from? From the Führer. Many live only for their faith in the Führer. We shall never succumb, we can never be altogether broken, because the Führer dwells within us.'

The reality of life among the Nazi hierarchy was indeed now shrouded in obscurity. Even Hitler's whereabouts were uncertain. Some thought him to be in the southern redoubt possibly at his mountain fortress of Berchtesgaden. But there was also speculation that he might be in Berlin and on April 20th, Hitler's birthday, Hans Fritzsche announced on the radio that he was indeed leading the capital's defence. Opinion in the West was uncertain about the truth of this.

Speculation continued too among the Allies about his psychological condition. There was a report from two high-ranking Wehrmacht officers taken prisoner in March who had received decorations from him the previous November. They described him as neurotic and paranoiac but still holding the political system together. He looked broken, they said and sat through most of the interview talking of the anguish he was suffering, but seemed mentally alert. Goering, they said, was then already in disgrace because of the failure of the Luftwaffe to cope with the Allied air offensive. Goebbels was described as 'an intellectual without character.'

From the hordes of prisoners and the many refugees now streaming into British and American occupied territory the impression gained was that though they themselves conceded that Germany had lost the war, it would be kept going for weeks by the political leaders and that the German people would go on working and fighting for as long as they had to.

Perhaps a British reporter, Richard Dimbleby, had seen as far as it was possible to see, into the opaque attitude to defeat of many Germans when, in early April he had sat in the kitchen of a country hotel near the Weser, the river on which the Germans had failed to build an effective defence line and which the British 11th Armoured Division were even then crossing. Listening on the radio together with the family which owned the hotel to news of the British at Hanover and the Americans at Wurzburg, he had watched the family fetch a map of central and southern Germany and pore over it, marking the places as mentioned. He saw on their faces '. . . not one sound or sign of regret . . . no shock, no despair, no alarm. They just picked up what was said, checked it on the map and noted it just as if they were a bunch of neutrals . . . neutrals in their own country. They seem to have lost the power of passion or sorrow. They show no sympathy for their army, for their government or for their country. To them the war is something too huge and too catastrophic to understand.'

Such too, possibly, were the feelings, together with thankfulness for survival, of the tens of thousands of Wehrmacht prisoners trudging west down the roads daily to the prison cages. On the other hand the Wehrmacht also continued in certain instances to perform in accordance with the highest principles of German military tradition. In northern Holland, the greater part of which was still under German occupation, the Canadians were meeting bitter resistance at Gröningen and in their drive to Apeldoorn. (The news coincided with a bleak announcement from the Dutch Government in London that, as part of the effort at liberation, an RAF raid on V2 sites round the Hague in March had rendered 25,000 people homeless and killed and injured an unknown number of others.)

At Magdeburg on the Elbe which the Americans had reached by April 11th there was bitter resistance in the town itself by a garrison of three thousand and on April 15th one of two bridgeheads which the Americans had established on the east bank of the river had to be abandoned before a strong German counter-attack. American casualties were considerable and the *New York Times* described the withdrawal back across the river as 'a miniature Dunkirk'.

One of the many incidental oddities of this last stage of the war in Europe was that Dunkirk itself, the scene of such a critical moment in its early days, was still in German hands with the civilian population largely removed under a truce, and the garrison there relatively inactive but still refusing to surrender to the mainly Czech units of the British army which contained them.

On the Atlantic coast a stronger German pocket held out until mid-April on both sides of the mouth of the river Gironde preventing access to the port of Bordeaux. Then a drive was launched by French troops to dislodge them. It was only successful after 1,300 Flying Fortresses had first bombed the pocket round Royan – 35 miles long by 12 miles deep – drenching it in half a million gallons of liquid fire. French warships in their first big action since 1940 carried out a heavy bombardment from the Atlantic. Even so there was fierce fighting in the town of Royan itself before the Germans finally surrendered.

In Germany itself fanatical resistance continued at a number of points. At Nuremberg, scene of the great Nazi rallies of the past, it was only to be expected and duly experienced. The city was taken by the Americans on Hitler's birthday after five days in which elements of many German army units, Volkssturm and civilians had been rallied by part of the 17th SS Infantry division and had fought 'like madmen' against overwhelming odds. There was not a building in the centre of the city which by the end had not been destroyed or damaged either by bombs or gunfire. Any apparently intact building found as the Americans advanced towards the centre had to be blasted to get at snipers who held out until they were killed. Some were beaten to death by liberated Russian prisoners with clubs. There was so much rubble in the streets that the very direction of these was difficult to find. Civilians sometimes armed only with pick-axe handles, axes and shovels had to be shot down in close hand-to-hand fighting in the ruins.

On the eve of this, his 56th birthday, Hitler himself had responded to good wishes from the Nuremberg Gauleiter, Karl Holz. 'We are now,' he replied, 'starting a battle as fanatical as that we had to fight for our ascent to power years ago.' And so it was at Nuremberg, only this time it was the end. Before his birthday was over the Stars and Stripes flew above the Adolf Hitler Platz, and GIs were photographing the rostrum from which he had so often proclaimed his harsh creed to the ranks of bannered National Socialists below and millions of Germans beyond. (While firing was still going on in Nuremberg, the American reporter Ed Murrow had been asked by an American Corporal, 'Hey, Mack, do you know anywhere round here where I can get some films developed?')

A similar last stand had been made in Leipzig, captured the day before. The Americans had had to fight all the way from the outskirts to the great granite fortress built as a monument to the defeat of Napoleon there in 1813. In this fortress, decorated on the outside with huge Germanic figures thirty foot high, some 150 Germans had fought on behind six foot thick walls. These had withstood the bursts of more than seventy eight-inch howitzer shells knocking chunks off the masonry before the garrison finally surrendered. Surprisingly large quantities of food and ammunition were found inside.

For the Leipzig Bürgermeister and other officials in the town hall it had been easier. He and his wife and daughter, as also the City Treasurer, his wife and daughter and four Volkssturm men had committed suicide in various offices. The Volkssturm men had shot themselves; the Treasurer and the Bürgermeister with their families had taken poison, the officials sitting at their desks, and wives and daughters in armchairs and on a sofa opposite. It was said by the caretaker that the Bürgermeister had wanted to declare Leipzig an open city but had been overruled. He was found slumped slightly backwards at his desk so that in death he appeared to be staring up at the picture of the Führer that hung on the wall.

On the approach to Bremen where the British Guards Armoured Division was meeting increasingly strong opposition and into which the German 15th Panzer Division withdrew to defy all calls to surrender, the District Commissioner of Verden committed suicide in similar fashion after the town had been taken.

To encourage his men in this uncertain but at times exhilarating form of warfare as they pushed towards Bremen and the other major north German port of Hamburg, beyond which were waiting uncommitted German armies in Schleswig Holstein and Denmark, Field-Marshal Montgomery delivered himself of one of his periodic addresses.

'It has been a long journey,' he began, 'but the end is in sight,' adding in a curiously inappropriate phrase, 'The Germans have no possible hope of doing any more good in this war.' Of the German army itself, he said, '. . . chunks of it will be chopped off until the whole thing

Field Marshal Montgomery on the outskirts of Bremen; '. . . the end is in sight'.
Germans look on as the Allies occupy their town (*below*)

disappears. It will gradually decrease in size and lose cohesion, like an iceberg which melts and falls into the sea . . . Because of that you cannot really say when the war will be finished.'

Not all the chunks were melting so easily, as the Americans had yet again experienced on 19th April when Germans trapped in a pocket in the Harz mountains carried out a surprise offensive with 10,000 infantry and some 20 to 30 tanks to try and break through behind the American lines to the Elbe. One column advanced fifteen miles before it was stopped, and took a number of American prisoners.

But by that time the blow required finally to seal the fate of the Third Reich for ever had been struck. The first news of it had come in an Order of the Day issued by Hitler himself to all German armed forces, though the finality of the event was given a different interpretation:

'For the last time,' said Hitler, 'the Jewish-Bolshevist arch-enemy has hurled his masses into the attack. . . . This time Bolshevism will suffer the fate which has always befallen Asia. It must and will bleed to death in front of the capital of the German Reich . . .'

As so often before there was a delay before the Russians themselves made any reference to their new offensive. Then on April 19th they announced that the Oder-Neisse line had been crossed and that the Red Army had made deep penetrations into the German armies beyond. They now closed in on Berlin. The next day Marshal Zhukov's men were in the green belt area of the city, in the Hangelsberg Forest eight miles from the centre, while Marshal Koniev, further south, thrust simultaneously towards Dresden, towards the Americans on the Elbe and up through Juterbog and Lückenwalde to Berlin too. Berlin radio admitted that there had been a grave deterioration in the situation but said that, though very serious, it was not hopeless.

Such hope, apart from faith, as the German people could now, with any vestige of reason, muster for their cause lay in the possibility of some split in the alliance between the western democracies and Russia. For one wild moment a piece of news which on April 12th had shattered the world with its suddenness seemed to lend some plausibility to this hope.

*

Before he had set out for Yalta, some questions had arisen about the state of President Roosevelt's health. Vice-Admiral Ross T. McIntyre, Surgeon-General of the US Navy, had already made a statement on the subject. Roosevelt's health, he said, compared favourably with that of most men of sixty-three. 'Everything's fine,' he said. 'He went through the campaign in fine shape. . . . He's had no colds this winter.' He said Roosevelt was five to ten pounds lighter than the 185 pounds he had been, and that he needed a short rest after lunch. Some reporters had found his hearing not so good and Admiral McIntyre admitted that his left ear had always been 'a little down'.

At about 1 p.m. local time on April 12th Mrs Elizabeth Schoumakoff, a smartly-groomed American woman in her late forties who had been staying in a cottage beside President Roosevelt's retreat in Warm Springs, Georgia, entered the room where he was working with his aides, to make sketches of him for a portrait. She had already completed one portrait of him which hung in the White House.

Roosevelt had started the morning in excellent spirits and when Mrs Schoumakoff came in was surrounded by documents he had signed lying out on furniture around the room because the President's signature had to dry without being blotted. One of his officials referred to these as his 'laundry', a joke which made him laugh. Mrs Schoumakoff described him as looking younger than the day before, 'strangely well' was how she put it. He was sitting in his chair being sketched when he suddenly complained of a very severe headache at the back of his head and soon afterwards lost consciousness. He never recovered it and died at 3.35 local time of a cerebral haemorrhage.

Though the news was a shock to the world, those who had been close to Roosevelt had noticed recently a marked change in his appearance and manner, and the photographs published of him with Churchill and Stalin at Yalta had shown something of this. In Washington there had, over the past months, been some speculation as to what the effect of his death might be on the national and the international scene. For the world he had personally symbolised America and its commitment to total war against Germany and Japan to be followed by a just peace. Without him there was suddenly the possibility of a question mark over future American international identity.

This was what, for instance, Georges Bidault, the French resistance hero who had become de Gaulle's first Foreign Minister in his Provisional Government, meant by saying that the news was not only sad but 'a great disaster'. One of the three greatest personalities who had made the Grand Alliance of America, Britain and Russia work had disappeared.

It was on this aspect of the news of Roosevelt's death that the German National Socialist propaganda machine seized, revealing to a public which had after all long learned to follow it, a ray, however faint, of far-fetched hope. The German Press described it as a miracle of the sort which had saved the Führer on the 20th July, an act of divine justice. Goebbels drew an analogy with the moment in the eighteenth century when Frederick the Great of Prussia seemingly at the mercy of the Grand Alliance ranged against him, had been saved by the sudden

217

death of Catherine the Great of Russia. Now more than ever, wrote Dr Robert Ley's paper *Der Angriff*, it was worthwhile to resist the enemy at any price.

All over the allied and neutral world tributes were paid to Roosevelt. In Britain the House of Commons adjourned for the day out of respect, after Churchill had spoken of 'the loss of the famous President of the United States whose friendship for the cause of freedom and for the cause of the weak have won him immortal fame.' In Moscow black-bordered flags flew from Stalin's residence in the Kremlin and from all Government buildings.

At a meeting of the Supreme Soviet the Chairman exhorted, 'Let us insure that in future the friendship between our peoples will stand as a memorial,' and Stalin and all present stood for a minute in silence with bowed heads.

The solemnity of the moment epitomised the uncertainty over the immediate future. Roosevelt had had the natural affinity with Europe of the American leisured classes. Harry S. Truman, who had replaced Henry Wallace as Vice President in January, was a relatively unknown quantity. A senator for Jackson County for the past nine years, he had been a former employee in the mailing-room of the *Kansas City Star*, a time-keeper for a railroad contractor, and had worked in two banks as well as helping his father on the family farm. On his induction as Vice President, one of the telegrams of congratulation he had received ran, 'Dear Harry, when you came home from World War One to the home farm you sold your mules and saddle-horse. We all knew you were going somewhere. Congrats.'

Truman took the oath as President the evening Roosevelt died, and four days later addressed Congress in a speech eagerly awaited all over the world. The manner of his beginning revealed something of the very different personality now to represent the awesome power of the United States. The small figure entered the chamber just after 1 p.m., dressed in a dark suit with a black tie and a white handkerchief in his breast pocket, and went straight to the rostrum to applause which he cut short with a smile and nod, before starting to speak. 'Mr Speaker –' he began as if still just an ordinary Senator. Speaker Rayburn interrupted him:

'Just a moment, let me present you, will you, Harry?'

Truman stopped and Rayburn announced:

'The President of the United States.'

The speech itself quickly sought to dispel the tentative anxieties which Roosevelt's death had aroused. It made nonsense of any German hopes of a *volte face* within the Alliance, though its terms at least did not disregard their existence.

'So that there can be no possible misunderstanding,' said Truman, 'both Germany and Japan can be certain beyond any shadow of doubt, that America will continue to fight for freedom until no vestige of resistance remains. We are deeply conscious of the fact that much hard fighting lies ahead of us. . . . America will never become a party to any plan for partial victory. To settle for merely another temporary respite would surely jeopardise the future security of all the world. Our demand has been, and it remains – unconditional surrender. We will not traffic with breakers of peace on the terms of peace. . . . Nothing shall shake our determination to punish the war criminals, even though we must pursue them to the ends of the earth. Lasting peace can never be secured if we permit our dangerous opponents to plot future wars with impunity at any mountain retreat . . .'

He concluded by emphasising the world's need for a peace that would endure, saying that it must be a peace built on law and justice.

In the universal praise with which the speech was received for its combination of strength and personal humility, these last words drew special acclaim from such traditional Republican opponents as Senator Taft of Ohio and Ferguson of Michigan. The former scented 'material changes' for the better – meaning more regard for the rights of less powerful nations – to be made in the Dumbarton Oaks proposals for the post-war peace-keeping organisation. Such thoughts sharpened anticipation of the conference of the United Nations due in only nine days' time (April 25th) at San Francisco, which was to try and turn those proposals into something concrete. Meanwhile, as Truman had said, there was hard fighting ahead, not only in the Pacific where the main assault on Japan was still a matter for fearful contemplation, but in Europe.

The successful German counter-attack against one of the Magdeburg bridgeheads took place on the day Truman spoke. And as the *New York Times* said, this put paid to any extravagant hopes that at that stage the Americans might be able to race into Berlin itself. 'The Germans,' the paper wrote, 'have abruptly resolved any rising doubt that they meant to defend Berlin against the swift American advance. They mean to defend it with all the strength they have left.'

And yet the end could only be a matter of time, as the start of the last great Russian offensive, which also took place on the day of Truman's speech, made clear. By the 26th April the vast Ruhr pocket had already surrendered, yielding over three hundred thousand prisoners, Berlin was encircled, the British were finally taking Bremen and massing for an assault on Hamburg while the Americans and the Russians had linked up on the Elbe. On that day Representative Buell Snyder of Pennsylvania who had just come out from a meeting with Truman was reported as forecasting that official German resistance would probably not end before June 1st, while individual pockets would continue to fight until the beginning of July. The Pacific War, he said, would probably last from nine months to a year longer 'but we should prepare for two or possibly three years of Pacific fighting.'

The street fighting in Bremen had been particularly fierce, with the British encountering a number of women snipers. The German commandant General Becker was supported in his last stand in a massive air raid shelter in the north east district of the city by Bremen's no less diehard Nazi evangelical Bishop Weidemann.

The meeting with the Russians had taken place on the afternoon of Wednesday, April 25th. There was some competition for the honour of being the first American unit to make contact. The radio talk of Russian tank crews across the Elbe had been heard for some days beforehand and liberated Russian prisoners of war had been enlisted by the Americans to try and get in touch with the Red Army on the other side of the river. But there had been no response and on at least one occasion this had simply resulted in such prisoners of war raising hopes prematurely by getting in touch with each other.

The final honour may have belonged to a column of six jeeps with twenty men under a Lieutenant Albert Kotzebue from Houston, Texas, which met the Russians in the outskirts of Riesa, twenty miles southeast of Torgau and thirty-eight miles east of Leipzig at three o'clock that afternoon. An hour and forty minutes later Lieutenant William Robertson and three GIs met a Russian private on the sloping girders of the partly-destroyed railway bridge at Torgau itself. By the next day the respective Generals of the American 69th Armoured Division under Hodges and the Russian 58th Guards Division under Koniev were together exchanging congenial toasts to victory, their leaders and each other. A *New York Times* correspondent wrote of 'almost a continuous party', adding: 'Our soldiers and the Russians have got along beautifully so far.'

An Order of the Day from Stalin in Moscow decreed a salute of 24 salvoes from 324 guns for 'the valiant troops of the 1st Ukrainian Command and our allied British and American troops' and in a special message he greeted 'the valiant troops of our Allies now standing shoulder to shoulder with Soviet troops on German territory.' Alexander Werth, the *Sunday Times* correspondent in Moscow watched children in the street there playing a game of the Torgau meeting, and crowds gathered in many Russian cities to celebrate the event. President Truman, speaking of the link-up drew a moral for the future.

'Nations,' he said, 'which can plan and fight together shoulder to shoulder in the face of such obstacles and of distance and of language

'Our soldiers and the Russians have got along beautifully so far'

and of communications as we have overcome, can live together and work together in the coming labour of the organisation of the world for peace.'

On another front altogether – the most disappointing for the Allies of the whole war – there now came at last news of a break-through. On April 16th in Italy, Field-Marshal Alexander had announced that an allied offensive against the Germans on their line across the Appennines was in full swing, that they were 'very groggy' and only needed 'one mighty punch to knock them out for good.' He warned that it would not be a walk-over, adding that 'a mortally-wounded beast can still be very dangerous.'

But this time expectations were not to be disappointed. The line was broken and although the Germans fought a number of fierce rearguard actions to try to cover their retreat across the river Po, the Allies were across it themselves south of Mantua by the afternoon of April 23rd and driving into the Lombardy plain. At the same time a major Italian Partisan revolt broke out in Milan, Turin and Genoa and quickly spread throughout the whole of Northern Italy. In the course of this the Italian dictator, Benito Mussolini, who after the Italian armistice of 1943 had been rescued from his mountain hotel-prison by German paratroops, and ever since had run a vicious Fascist Republic with German help from the town of Salo, came himself at last terribly to grief. Perhaps no other single event hitherto so clearly demonstrated that not just the war but a whole era was at last coming to an end and a new phase in the history of Europe was about to begin.

Of the European dictators Mussolini had always been the most theatrical. His end had the quality of Grand Guignol.

On the evening of the 28th April a furniture van drove into the Piazza Loretto in the centre of Milan, the city where Fascism was born, now in the hands of Partisans. The Piazza had recently been re-named the Piazza dei Quindici Martyri, in honour of fifteen Partisans shot there not long before by Mussolini's Fascists. Now Mussolini himself came onto the scene, his body dumped there from the back of the van together with that of his 25-year-old mistress Clara Petacci and twelve prominent Fascists who had all been caught by Partisans and shot after a short trial the day before. Mussolini had been taken from a column of thirty cars moving up the western shore of Lake Como in the direction of the Swiss frontier. He had been wearing a black coat over his uniform but had been recognised by one of the Partisans who had stopped the column. He was reported to have died badly, yelling 'No! No!' to the firing squad commanded by a 40-year-old Republican veteran of the Spanish Civil War.

Now his body, with two bullet-holes in the head lay all night in a heap

A British contribution to the Russian war-effort

with the others in the Piazza until the next morning when word got round the city of what had happened. Milton Brackler of the *New York Times* came on the scene about 9.30 and found Mussolini's body lying on the rim of the heap across Clara Petacci's. A large mob was being kept back by Partisans who were occasionally firing shots into the air. Brackler saw two young men break through and aim kicks at Mussolini's skull. One kick simply glanced off but the other landed full on the jaw with a hideous crunch disfiguring the once proud face. His small eyes were open. Brackler found it the final irony that this man who had so often thrust his chin out for so many official photographs should now have to have his yellowing face propped up with a rifle butt to turn it towards the light for an Allied cameraman. Later in the day Mussolini's body was hung upside-down in the square alongside Petacci's and cursed and spat upon by the Italian crowd.*

The German radio had again officially announced that Hitler was in Berlin conducting the defence of the capital. Taking no chances, 350 RAF Lancasters on the 25th attacked his famous Berghof at Berchtesgaden which Chamberlain had visited before the Munich Agreement of 1938. Together with the conventional 4,000-pound and 1,000-pound bombs they dropped a number of 12,000-pounders for deep penetration and photographs showed that the central building had been severely damaged.

In Berlin itself a savage street-by-street and house-to-house battle was in progress with casualties very high on both sides as they had been on the whole advance from the Oder, before the city was encircled. Much of the battle was being fought beneath the city in the underground railway and the sewers. A Soviet war correspondent, Nicolai Asanoff described the scene. Berlin, he said, was a place of sudden spurts of flame, deafening explosions and avalanches of brick and stone thudding into the street. The water system had ceased to function because reservoirs and canals were filled with corpses, sewage and general wreckage. Motorised Russian water tanks came rumbling from unit to unit rationing out supplies. Soldiers with blackened faces would come up from the sewers to gulp a few ladles and then drop back down again after the Germans still fighting there. The Germans mined pedestrian subways and tunnels and occasional great underground explosions split the pavements while spurts of flame spouted up through the cracking streets.

*The blow, and perhaps others, to Mussolini's skull deprived Professor Mario Cattabani of Milan of all but the upper third of the brain for the autopsy he carried out. From this however he was able to conclude confidently that Mussolini had not been suffering from syphilis as had been supposed, that he manifested no clinical signs of abnormality, and might well have lived to be a hundred.

In the streets and houses themselves, Wehrmacht and SS backed by Volkssturm and civilian snipers often fought desperately using the anti-tank weapons and grenades in which they had been trained. Every house was teeming with snipers, many of them civilians. Inexorably, though, the Russians were compressing a ring round the centre of the city within which presumably Hitler was trapped.

The first sign of anything like an official acknowledgement by the Germans that all was lost transpired in a Reuter report from Stockholm on the 28th April to the effect that Himmler, who had been having secret meetings in Berlin with Count Bernadotte, nephew of the King of Sweden, had offered unconditional surrender to the British and Americans though not to the Russians. This seems to have been the source of the rumour which swept New York that evening that Germany had at last unconditionally surrendered. A crowd of about 10,000 people assembled in Times Square to celebrate, but just after half-past nine Truman announced that there was no truth in the news. The Himmler offer had, however, been made. It was communicated at once to the Russians to forestall the embarrassment it had been intended to create, and was rejected with unequivocal re-statement of the position that unconditional surrender could only be made to America, Britain and Russia together.

Another remarkable indication of collapse in the internal system of the Third Reich came from no less a National Socialist shrine than Munich. The Americans had advanced so rapidly into Bavaria that, taken in conjunction with the Allied break-through in Italy, any chance of building the once much-vaunted 'southern redoubt' had disappeared. At half past seven on the morning of the 28th April a programme on Munich radio was interrupted for about five minutes 'for technical reasons'. When it came back on the air a proclamation was read out calling on foreign workers to rise in revolt and the German army to lay down its arms to save unnecessary bloodshed. 'Bavarians!' it declared, 'The hour of Freedom has struck! The clique of ruling Nazis has been arrested . . .' This was followed by light music which was interrupted at ten to eight by a broadcast purporting to come from General Ritter von Epp, the Governor of Bavaria, proclaiming that 'the yoke of Nazism' was being thrown off in the name of humanity as well as common sense and ending: 'Long Live Liberty!'

There followed more light music when suddenly there was the brutal scratch of a needle and a new voice interrupted to say that the previous broadcasts had been made by traitors trying to exploit National Socialist names, that National Socialism was again in charge and that the fight went on. In fact this proved no more than that Munich radio station was once again in orthodox hands. It seemed that the incident

225

masked a struggle between the Party and certain army units over whether or not to surrender the city without a fight to the death. On the 29th April the Americans entered Munich without much difficulty and learned that an attempt had indeed been made by a Wehrmacht Major to clear the road for them into the city. He had had the tacit support of some 200 Wehrmacht officers in the vicinity who, however, had been reluctant to move before he had eliminated the Nazi Bürgermeister. His attempt to do this in fact failed after a bloody shoot-out with the SS in the cellar which was the Bürgermeister's headquarters, but the subsequent resistance to the Americans had been undermined and the Major survived to tell them the tale.

On the 29th too a large-scale surrender of intact German fighting units – even greater than that of the Army Group in the Ruhr – took place. After tentative negotiations which had in fact been going on with an SS General for some weeks, all German and Italian Fascist forces in Northern Italy and Western Austria surrendered unconditionally.

Fighting in Berlin was now getting closer and closer to the central Government quarter. Around this, remnants of the Wehrmacht and fanatical SS kept up a desperate resistance. They knew themselves to be totally surrounded. They knew too that their Führer was in their midst. Then at 9.30 in the evening of May 1st, Hamburg radio, one of the few German radio stations still able to function, interrupted its programme to tell listeners to stand by for an important announcement. The music of Wagner was played. An hour later came the announcement itself:

'Our Führer, Adolf Hitler, has fallen this afternoon at his command post in the Reich Chancellery, fighting to the last breath against Bolshevism and for Germany. On April 30th the Führer appointed Grand-Admiral Dönitz as his successor. Our new Führer will now speak to the German people.'

Dönitz came to the microphone.

'. . . The German people,' he said, 'bow in deepest mourning and veneration. . . . His battle against the Bolshevist flood benefited not only Europe but the whole world.' Dönitz proclaimed his own first task as being to save the German people from Bolshevism. That was the only reason the fight continued. As long as the British and Americans hampered that fight it would continue against them too. He asked for trust and appealed for order and discipline.

In an Order of the Day to the Wehrmacht Dönitz said that Hitler had 'died the death of a hero . . . With his passing, one of the greatest heroes of German history has passed away.' He added that the oath of allegiance sworn to the Führer now applied to himself.

But the mystical spell had been broken, though there were even now desperate attempts to preserve its power. General Blaskowitz, the German commander in Holland, who still held the main western part of that country, including Rotterdam, Amsterdam and the Hague addressed his troops on Hitler's 'hero's death' with the words. '. . . It is now your task to keep up his faith in Germany. He was and he remains our Führer . . .'

Frank, the Minister of State for Bohemia and Moravia went further still. 'For us, the Führer is not dead,' he said. His only qualification was: 'The oath of allegiance we swore to him is from now on valid for every German to Admiral Dönitz.'

General Eisenhower at once attempted to spike any legend about Hitler's death by revealing the information given by Himmler when negotiating with Bernadotte on April 24th that Hitler had had a brain haemorrhage and then only had a few days to live. This information was inaccurate, as a Wehrmacht doctor who had seen Hitler regularly up to the 15th February disclosed when taken prisoner a few days later. He described Hitler as having been in 'above average' health for a man of 56, with heart, lungs and blood pressure all in good shape; it was impossible that he could have suffered a cerebral haemorrhage so soon. But only one physical detail was now relevant; he was dead. It was the living myth that had helped hold Germany together. To preserve that myth in death within the total disintegration of the Germany he had built was not possible.*

A Soviet war correspondent described the state of even the most hardline Germans as they now began to surrender in Berlin: 'Shaggy headed, bearded and grimy, they emerged wearing white armlets, from bunkers, drain-pipes, tube stations and piles of ruins. Some threw their weapons away with sullen faces; others were ingratiating and stacked

---

*Only in the British publication *Who's Who* did Hitler achieve a certain temporary immortality. His entry there, between Henry Luxmoore Hitchins, CBE, a retired naval Captain whose club was the Golfers, and Ernest Walter Hives, CH MBE, the Managing Director of Rolls Royce remained, inevitably, as it had been throughout the war, unaltered until the end of the year. He was described as born 20 April 1889 'of an old Upper Austrian peasant family . . . religion Catholic'. His address was given as Wilhelmstrasse 77, Berlin and telephone number 11 6191, and Obersalzberg, Berchtesgaden, Bavaria. He was survived into the next year in reality and *Who's Who* by both Goering and Ribbentrop, Goering's address still being given in 1946 as Leipziger Strasse 3, Berlin W8 while among other landmarks in Ribbentrop's career it was mentioned that he had been made SS Gruppenführer in 1936. His recreations were given as 'sport and music'. All three re-appeared in *Who Was Who 1941–1950*, the deaths of Goering and Ribbentrop being left discreetly inexplicit on the 15th and 16th October 1946. As for Hitler's religion, an alternative view was expressed by A. J. P. Taylor in a review of a book about him in the *Manchester Guardian* of May 14th. Hitler he said, was 'in the true sense Anti-Christ, the negation to which men turn when they have lost faith in all else.'

their rifles where they were told; many laughed hysterically and could not stop laughing as they trailed through the shattered city.'

As a bewildered SS man who had fought to the last in Nuremberg had said to his captors, everything they had ever learned had to be unlearned; they had to start in life all over again.

On May 3rd all fighting in Berlin came to an end.

By that day the whole German defence system in North West Europe had collapsed. The western Allies were experiencing the bizarre military phenomenon of a rout moving towards them rather than away from them. Panic-stricken units of the Wehrmacht crowded down roads already seething with liberated foreign workers and prisoners of war in an effort to avoid being taken prisoner by the Russians. At the same time the roads running northwards out of Schleswig Holstein were crammed with German transport escaping into Denmark. That Dönitz might still try to make a temporary stand there and in Norway, to give himself some bargaining power, was not quite beyond the bounds of possibility. Hundreds of small ships were trying to escape from the North German coast and being attacked by Meteors, Typhoons, Tempests and Spitfires in great strength. People continued to die as if the war were not coming to an end at all. But it was, and for the living it was only the end that seemed important.

Over the past few weeks there had in Britain been some irritation with newspaper correspondents for having, at the time of the Rhine crossing, given the impression that all was over, when plainly, as day followed day, it still was not. For five years, until September 1944, the war had seemed virtually unending. Then, with the thrust at Arnhem a sudden end had come into sight, only to recede with that defeat and remain tantalisingly distant throughout the winter and early Spring. The fear of further disappointment had aggravated inevitable impatience since the victory on the Rhine. Weeks seem exasperating stretches of time at the end of a long war. On the 3rd May a letter appeared in *The Times* from Alan Moorehead protesting that war correspondents like himself simply relayed the progress of the war as they learned of it and could not be held responsible for over-optimism in Britain. Nor could they control the general irritation of soldiers on hearing broadcasts or reading newspapers which apparently concluded that the war was over when they were actually engaged in fighting of a particularly dangerous kind.

But the end was at last being signalled even to the Germans themselves by their government – that remnant structure of the Third Reich which still sought to assert some National Socialist control over events from Dönitz's headquarters in Flensburg.

On the evening of May 2nd, 24 hours after Dönitz's assumption of

Shoulder to shoulder on the Elbe

An American war correspondent talks to Russian officers and women after the link-up at Torgau

the rôle of Führer, his Foreign Minister, Count Schwerin von Krosigk, who had replaced Ribbentrop, broadcast to the German people and beyond them to the world.

'The world,' he began, 'is still echoing to the din of weapons. German men are still fighting in their last fight to defend their Fatherland. In the streets of still unoccupied Germany a great stream of desperate and famished people is rolling westwards, pursued by fighter bombers, in flight from indescribable terror. In the East, the iron curtain, behind which, unseen by the eye of the world, the work of destruction goes on, is moving steadily forward. In San Francisco they are deliberating on the organisation of a new world order which is to give mankind security against a new war. The world knows very well that a Third World War will not bring about the fall of a nation but of humanity. The terrible weapons which there has been no time to apply in this war would take full effect in a third war, and would sow death and destruction around humanity.

'We Germans have felt more than any other people in the world the fullest force of what war and its destruction means. If therefore from the very hearts of tortured women and mothers a fervent prayer rises to heaven that the world may be spared the horrors of a new war, it comes most strongly from the heart of the German people . . .'

There was a familiar political note to his conclusion: '. . . A Bolshevised Europe will be the first step on the road to world revolution which the Soviets have been following for twenty-five years. The achievement of their goal or a Third World War are the inescapable alternatives.'

The next day Albert Speer, the man who more than anyone had effectively mobilised the German people for war, now exhorted them to face the consequences with equal resolve, admitting that 'the direction of our lives is no longer in our hands. The bearing of the German nation in this war,' he said, 'has been such that in times to come, future generations will look upon it with admiration. Let us not stop to cry our eyes out about the past. To work!' He called upon them to repair railways and factories, to get food supplies moving and basic public services working again.

The Wehrmacht was signing off. At half past six on the evening of May 4 after discussions with Field-Marshal Montgomery in a caravan captured from the Italian General Bergonzoli in the victorious Libyan campaign of 1941, five German plenipotentiaries including Admiral von Friedeburg, who had succeeded Dönitz as head of the German navy, signed, in a tent on Luneburg Heath the unconditional surrender of a million men in North West Germany, Holland and Denmark. (It was understood that the surrender of Germans in Norway would follow as a matter of course.)

The End of the Road; Russians in Berlin, May, 1945

The surrender had been to all three major Allies though the German radio now operating from Flensburg sounded an ambiguous note by saying that 'resistance against the Soviets is continuing to save as many Germans as possible from the Soviet terror.' The next day it broadcast instructions to the population not to carry out Werwolf activity 'in enemy occupied western territories.'

The German armies fighting the Russians north of Berlin and falling back, had also offered to surrender but to the British alone. Montgomery refused this although he did accept the personal surrender of their commanders, Generals Manteuffel and Tippelskirch and a number of other senior officers. 'And so tonight,' reported the BBC correspondent Chester Wilmot, 'In the woods and villages between the Baltic and the Elbe there are tens of thousands of Germans from Army Group Vistula vainly trying to find someone who will accept them as prisoners . . . only those in direct contact with the Russians continue fighting – fighting rather than yield to the Red Army. The fact is that at all costs the Germans want to avoid surrendering to the Soviet troops. They know how great are Germany's crimes against Russia and they know that the Russians won't forget.'

The armed forces and the Third Reich itself were disintegrating simultaneously. Wynford Vaughan Thomas of the BBC described the wreckage of the Wehrmacht rumbling bumper to bumper in defeat through the white-flagged ruins of Hamburg, directed by their own traffic police under British orders while the population looked on dumbfounded. By next day even the population had been cleared from the streets by a forty-eight hour curfew. Thomas surveyed the aftermath of victory.

'We thought Bremen was bad,' he said, 'but Hamburg is devastated. Whole quarters have disintegrated under air attacks and there are miles upon miles of blackened walls and utterly burnt-out streets, and in the ruins there are still nearly a million people and fifty thousand foreign workers living in the cellars and air raid shelters.'

It was a microcosm of the plight of the whole German people – their only comfort to be found in Albert Speer's exhortation: 'To work!'

At 2.41 a.m. on May 7th, at General Eisenhower's headquarters at Rheims, in the presence of American, Russian and French Generals, General Jodl representing the German High Command and what was left of the German state, signed the unconditional surrender simultaneously to the Allied Expeditionary Force and the Soviet High Command of all German land, sea and air forces in Europe.

When the signing was over Jodl stood up and speaking in German said to Bedell Smith, Eisenhower's Chief of Staff, 'General, with this signature the German people are, for better or for worse, delivered into the victor's hands. In this war which has lasted for more than five years, both have achieved and suffered more than perhaps any other people in the world. In this hour I can only express the hope that the victor will treat them with generosity.' Bedell Smith barely nodded and the German delegation left the room.

Jodl's signature was confirmed by Field-Marshal Keitel in the additional ceremony in Berlin the next day, May 8th.*

German-occupied territory by now consisted of Norway, parts of Czechoslovakia and Austria, small pockets in Latvia and on the Atlantic and Channel coasts (St Nazaire, Lorient, La Rochelle, and Dunkirk), some of the Greek and Dodecanese islands, part of Crete, and the Channel Islands. Nearly everywhere the transition to allied rule occurred smoothly. In Norway the Resistance movement took over, as the Danes had done in Denmark (there was some shooting in Copenhagen which principally involved collaborators but cost the lives of over 50 people). Only in Prague where a rising against the Germans had started on May 5th did SS units refuse to accept the Rheims surrender and try to act as if they were still the masters they had been there for the past six years. As late as May 8th the resistance radio in Prague put out a desperate call for help to the Americans only 45 miles away in Pilsen but it was the Red Army who arrived as liberators after receiving indirect help from the Russian traitor General Vlassov, whose troops in German uniform fought to keep SS reinforcements out of the city. Some 5,000 civilians, it was reckoned, had been killed in the course of the rising.

All German broadcasts of the last days stressed the German right to feel proud in defeat. There was no suggestion anywhere that the cause had not been a good and great one, only that, as Schwerin von Krosigk put it on the day of the surrender at Rheims 'after almost six years of incomparable hardships, Germany has succumbed to the overwhelming power of the Allies.' Flensburg radio had just proclaimed: 'Germany's contribution towards the civilisation of mankind rests on timeless achievements.' And the same station continued fulsome tributes to the dead Führer.

'In choosing a soldier's death,' it said on the 5th May, 'he set an example of inexorable will-power and singleness of purpose. Will not even in the hostile world every personality of character be moved by the purity and greatness of this man?'

The last German High Command communiqué of all which went out on May 9th spoke of 'a heroic struggle' and the honour of the Wehrmacht which had succumbed to enormous material superiority. It went

*See pages 1–2.

233

on, 'The unique performance of front and homeland will find a final appreciation in a later, just verdict of history. Even the enemy will not withhold his respect for the performance and sacrifices of German soldiers on land, on sea and in the air. . . . Every soldier therefore may lay aside his arms, proud and erect and set to work for the undying life of our people . . .'

It was presumably stirred by such feelings of self-justifiable pride that a young German naval officer, Kapitän-Leutnant Arnim Zimmerman set out in a battered mine-sweeper to rendezvous on the afternoon of May 8th four miles off Guernsey with two British destroyers, the *Bulldog* and the *Beagle*, to help conduct the surrender of the Channel Islands.

When the minesweeper had anchored in the vicinity of the two British ships Zimmerman set off from it in a rubber dinghy with his brief-case and three German sailors. Swamped by the waves on his short journey, he arrived at the *Bulldog* soaked to the skin but coming up on deck gave a smart Nazi salute, which he repeated several times in a rather exaggerated fashion when entering the wardroom for formal discussion of the hand-over of the Channel Islands. There he revealed that he had no credentials to negotiate a surrender, only an armistice. Since the Rheims surrender, though signed on the 7th, did not come into force until the second minute of May 9th, he was technically within his rights. He was promptly told that there was no question of negotiating an armistice but that he must return on the next day empowered to surrender. He replied with spirit that in the meantime the *Bulldog* and *Beagle* should withdraw from offshore waters or the German commander would consider their presence provocative. He then himself withdrew, saluting pointedly in the Nazi fashion and returned to his mine-sweeper.

Just after midnight Zimmermann returned in an armed trawler to a new rendezvous outside the harbour limits, together with a white-haired Major-General Heine in full uniform to represent the Admiral in command of the Channel Islands. They were rowed across to the *Bulldog* under the powerful beam of one of her searchlights in a white eight-oared cutter. The General was piped abord but did not salute. Down in the wardroom, where he had a little difficulty in standing to attention because of the rolling of the ship he replied, 'Ja' to his instructions including one to haul down all German flags, and just after seven o'clock signed, in drizzling rain, on an upturned rum barrel on the quarter-deck, the unconditional surrender of the only part of British soil ever to have come under Hitler's New Order.

The ceremony was really unnecessary because since one minute after midnight any German who had resisted would have put himself beyond the rules of war under the general surrender agreement. But such formalities are designed to reassure both sides that there is something neat, even civilised after all, about the chaotic horrors from which they have just emerged and to acknowledge not just the victor's triumph but the honour and dignity of the vanquished in defeat. This time they failed to cheer in the last respect. A guard of honour with fixed bayonets was drawn up as Major-General Heine left the ship and the pipes again shrilled but as he walked slowly past he again did not salute and once back in the cutter, went over to the far side and gazed silent and alone, out to sea.

By contrast, in another corner of the crumbling Reich, Goering, its one-time joint architect, had surrendered with a show of ebullience that was to cause some embarrassment to his captors. He shook hands ostentatiously with the American Brigadier-General Stack of the 7th Army to whom he had sent an envoy and, after a bath in the castle near Kitzbühel where he was staying with friends, changed into his favourite uniform with medals for photographers whom he told to hurry up because he was hungry. Holding a sort of press conference he was happy to stress what a difficult time he had been having in recent months with Hitler. He was moved to a suburban house near Augsburg but continued to lord it there for a while, being interviewed over a lunch of chicken, potatoes and peas (which he was reported as tackling with gusto) by the American Major-General Dahlquist. Accounts of such goings-on caused indignation both east and west in view of the fact that his name was, with some plausibility, being placed on the list of war criminals. The London *News Chronicle* wrote plainly that he was 'an evil murderer to whom justice must be done.'

Other individual captures made momentary news. Von Papen, the diplomat of the First World War who had helped Hitler to power, and was said to have been ready to present himself as some sort of respectable political alternative now that Hitler had fallen, was arrested in the Ruhr pocket wearing Tyrolean outfit. He said he himself had known the war was lost after D-Day but the majority of the German people had realised this only after the crossing of the Rhine. This did nothing to improve his standing with the Russians. The Communist Youth version of *Pravda* indignantly demanded that he should be hanged, saying that the time had come to get busy with those criminals who had started the war in Europe.

A more impressive First World War survivor, Field-Marshal von Mackensen, now 95, had been found on his farm near Hanover in the middle of April. A journalist from the *News Chronicle* who interviewed him found nothing of the dotard about him at all. There was, in fact, he wrote, 'a frightening vitality in this incarnation of the old Germany that had ravaged Europe a generation ago.' Mackensen had seen no point in continuing the war by then. It was lost and that was that. There had been too much political interference with the Generals. Too many of the Generals had been ill-educated. His voice was strong, often violent as he slapped the table or pounded the floor with a heavy black stick. As to the future, all he would say was, 'The first thing, the only thing is the Fatherland!'

The French had found the eldest son of the Kaiser, 'Little Willie' at a hunting lodge in Mittelburg. He said he had always said the war was madness and had known it was lost after Stalingrad. Of Hitler he said he had had immense powers over the German people but surrounded himself with second-raters as a pretty woman surrounds herself with ugly ones. He, 'Little Willie' had always thought the persecution of Jews and Catholics a mistake.

Figures of the more immediate German past were not so easy to find. Goebbels was reported to have died with Hitler. But the whereabouts of Himmler, Ribbentrop, Ley, Kaltenbrunner, Bormann and other members of the once-arrogant Nazi hierarchy were unknown and, as the cease-fire sounded, methodical intelligence teams went into action to track them down as wanted criminals. A minor success that stirred an early memory of the war for the British was the capture near Luneburg by two British officers looking for firewood for a 'brew-up' of William Joyce, who, nicknamed Lord Haw-Haw, had broadcast so raspingly from Hamburg in tones which sometimes suggested fuller possession of the truth than was wholly comfortable to those who laughed him off. He had been well-dressed and had a German passport in his pocket in the name of Hamsen but when in English he had told the officers that he too often went there looking for firewood, his voice had been recognised. Challenged, he had put his hand into his pocket and one of the officers, thinking that he was reaching for a gun had shot first, wounding him in the thigh, though not seriously. He was in fact not armed. As he lay in the back of an army vehicle which was taking him to hospital, soldiers had crowded round to stare at their notorious prisoner. He told them he had always thought civilised people treated a wounded man with some respect.

There were many suicides.

Sometimes the shame of surrender was too much not just for party men but for officers too. When the general in command of the city of Augsburg was persuaded to surrender he agreed to give orders down the telephone to his garrison to lay down their arms. A Lieutenant-Colonel on his staff asked permission to leave the room. Soon afterwards a shot was heard and he was found dead with his revolver beside him. An allied correspondent reported how elsewhere two junior

236

German officers shot each other dead simultaneously by agreement after surrender formalities had been completed.

As the canvas of the war itself had been composed of millions and millions of small personal experiences so the cataclysm of the war's end was on one level a vast accumulation of individual adjustments to tragedy, triumph and plain relief. Deaths in action at the very end of a war particularly emphasise its tragedy and raise disturbing thoughts about the value of individual sacrifice. Particularly tragic and futile seemed the deaths of Dutch civilians who were celebrating their liberation in Amsterdam with British troops actually in the streets. Some German Marines who were, under Blaskovitz's surrender of the 4th technically prisoners of war, fired on the crowds either in panic or in a spirit of revenge or both, killing and wounding many. British troops were unable to fire back effectively from fear of increasing the slaughter.

But even at the end of a war, a man's preparedness to risk his life in the belief that it is right to do so is an inspiring thing. One of the last deaths in action of the war was that of a German Major named Braun. He was the commanding officer of some 40 Wehrmacht soldiers guarding Schloss Itter, a castle in South Tyrol in the Inn valley between Innsbruck and Salzburg, at which a number of prominent prisoners including French politicians and Generals had been held. They included Paul Reynaud, Edouard Daladier and Generals Gamelin and Weygand. On the 6th of May the garrison surrendered to eight Americans who appeared before the castle with a tank. It was found that the prisoners had been well-treated and well-fed.

They were welcoming their liberators when shells began to fall about the castle, one of them hitting its tower. These came from a party of some 300 SS who were in a position in the nearby woods and who, hearing of the castle's surrender, were determined to recapture it and continue the fight against the Americans. Immediately Major Braun and his men joined forces with the eight Americans to fight back. Meanwhile one of the former prisoners, Jean Borotra, an international tennis player who had been Vichy Minister of Sport, managed to slip out from the castle and through the woods to contact the United States 142nd Regiment at Wörgl. From there he led a column of infantry and some tanks of the 32nd US Armoured Division back to relieve the castle. They were only just in time. The mixed garrison of Americans and Germans had been hard-pressed. The German Major Braun was killed in the course of the fighting.

The next day, for everyone, the war in Europe was over. Only in Prague did Death work the streets and doorways a few hours longer. To those who cared to notice such things, there was a bitter irony in the fact

237

that the first western democratic capital to fall a victim to German conquest, in March 1939, should be the last to be delivered from its terrible grip.

Chapter Twenty-One

North of Prague a discovery was now made which, had not world opinion in recent months become numbed by new evidence of what Man could do to Man, would have seemed impossible to accept. A town surrounding the ancient castle of Tierzin, some 40 miles from the capital of Czechoslovakia, had been turned into a concentration camp for the extermination of Jews; it was labelled Theresienstadt. In it, Jewish children under 15 and Jewish adults over 40 had been gassed 'like bugs', as one survivor put it, while the rest were worked until they collapsed from sickness or exhaustion when they were gassed too. Over 50,000 Jews had died here altogether. But by May 9 this was just one more shocking enormity to add to an already ghastly German record.

But for the revelations of the German concentration camps in the early months of 1945 the legend of honourable German defeat which the Dönitz Government sought to foster for posterity might reasonably have carried some conviction. But what was seen to have happened in these concentration camps was also seen to have been carried out by the same leadership as had commanded the Wehrmacht's loyalty and devotion in the field. Distinctions, which Germans sought to point out between the activities of the SS and the Wehrmacht, or between the Waffen-SS (an indisputable part of the Wehrmacht) and the political SS, became meaningless beside the unpleasant truth that the same German patriotism had been responsible for both. All German honour in this war, even the most chivalrous and brave, was stained by the scale of what was now revealed.

That scarcely credible brutalities were practised in German concentration camps particularly against Jews, had been known from first-hand accounts of experience even before the war. British newspapers had published such accounts and the British Government in October 1939 had issued a White Paper detailing many of these from reports of its Consular agents in Germany. But some reluctance to believe the worst of Nazi Germany on the part of those who had hoped to avoid a Second World War, and a general suspicion of atrocities as a result of Allied propaganda in the First World War, made it difficult for many to

239

appreciate the reality of these accounts. Later, when reports of far more horrific brutality on a literally unbelievable scale began to arrive from the East, distance and the more immediate considerations of war made them still seem strangely remote.

From time to time summary information which reached western governments, particularly from the Polish Government in London of German actions perpetrated in their own country, had been communicated to the House of Commons. In February 1945 Churchill had reported the slaughter of three and a half million Polish Jews, describing it as '. . . probably the most horrifying act of cruelty which has ever darkened the passage of man on this earth.' But even then such figures tended to remain statistics.

Eye-witness reports of discoveries in the course of the Russian advances in the east began to be published, among them that of Iris Morley the British journalist whose account of what happened at the 'Folkestone Girls' School' in Estonia had been broadcast on the BBC. There were some short factual reports of Red Army discoveries of concentration camps at Maidanek and elsewhere. One of the most terrible concerned a camp at Oswieczim in Poland, though few factual details other than that it had contained chambers in which the prisoners were gassed were available in the newspapers. The impact of such things within the general turmoil of the war's quickening events was slow to make itself felt.

Incontrovertible evidence that the Germans were gassing some of their prisoners had in fact already become available at first-hand in the west. The very first day of 1945 saw a report in the *New York Times* of a camp that had recently been overrun by the Allies in the Saint Die valley of Alsace. The camp had once contained between 50,000 and 60,000 men and women of whom at least 15,000 had been killed in one way or another. Witnesses told how two German specialists had come one day to test the use of new gases and some 80 women including 16-year-old girls had been sent to the 'fumigation unit', their screams terrifying all within hearing. Their bodies were examined afterwards to chart the effects of the gas.

The *New York Times* reporter who saw the gas-producing mechanism in the camp, as well as a torture chamber with hooks at a height at which a man hung by his wrists would barely touch the floor, a dissecting table for human experiments and the crematorium and urn room, said something which was to be repeated in one form or another over and over again by journalists and others who came to see such things for themselves. In spite of the evidence of his own eyes he wrote, 'It remains hard to accept such stories'. They were 'outrages too great to be believed even in the face of the physical evidence.'

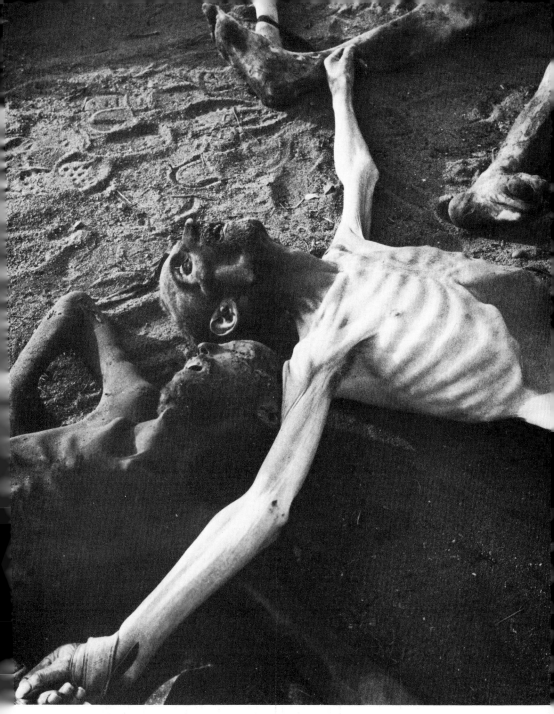

The New Order; Belsen

Still in the first week of January the British 21st Army Group published a 79-page report on a concentration camp they had found at Breendonck, near Malines, Brussels. The killing there had been by shooting, hanging or excessive torture only. Tortures included routine beatings with truncheons and cat-o'-nine-tails, the thrashing of victims in mid-air after hoisting them up to the ceiling on a pulley and then releasing them to fall on sharp pointed wooden blocks, crushing fingers in a mediaeval style screw-press and burning with a four-pointed electrical needle.

The gap by which the ordinary public in the western democracies were still distant from such realities was well illustrated by Patrick Kirwan in the London *Evening Standard*, when he wrote: 'The idea of torture is so abhorrent that it is not easy to believe that practices associated with the Spanish Inquisition could be carried out by twentieth century Europeans.'

A French Colonel Poujade, who had been commander of the French Normandie Air Squadron fighting in Russia had entered Lithuania with the Red Army. In the ghetto at Kaunas which had at one time contained 40,000 Jews of whom some 30,000 were reckoned to have died since 1941, he saw the bodies of the remaining 10,000 or so who had been machine-gunned or burned to death in the Germans' last night there. The corpses of men, women and children lay in great heaps in the streets and in ruined cellars. Alive, they had been massed together in one square kilometre of the ghetto. The houses had then been set ablaze. Machine-guns had been turned on all those trying to escape from the smoke and flames. Poujade said he had been inclined to be sceptical about some of the atrocity reports which had been published in Russia, until he had seen the results of this Kaunas crime with his own eyes.

Another Frenchman, a Master-Sergeant who had been taken prisoner in 1940 and was liberated in early May by the US Ninth Army described many hitherto unbelievable things which he had seen in the course of his stay in the Third Reich. At Rawa-Russka in Polish Galicia he had seen the bodies of some hundred Jewish men, women and children who had been jammed into a railway cattle-truck after being stripped of all their possessions and then machine-gunned. Later in Rawa-Russka itself all Jews had one day been ordered indoors. The doors of their houses had been locked. The houses were then set on fire. All those trying to escape were shot. He had been on a working party with Jewish women and children engaged principally in breaking large stones into little ones. The Jews had been worked until there was no more work to be got out of them, then they were shot. Anyone straggling on the way to work was also shot. He had seen a woman with a

242

'. . . the whole world and all mankind is involved . . .'; Nordhausen

SS men are forced to bury the dead at Belsen

two-year-old child shot in this way. By far the worst things he had seen had been at Lwow in Poland where too the ghetto had been set on fire and had burned for eight days. Tens of thousands of Jews, he thought, must have died there.

But now, moving into Germany, British and Americans began to see these things for themselves. They saw them with a cold horror; it was like looking at Hell after the fires had gone out. In the German camp above the town of Trier, Gene Currivan of the *New York Times* learned of the experiences of some of the thousands of former slave workers of many nationalities who had been kept there like animals. He talked to a former Captain in the Italian army taken by the Germans from Trieste in September 1943 after the Armistice, first to Hanover and then to Tarnopol in Poland. On the journey between Hanover and Tarnopol he had been one of 70 packed into a cattle-truck without food or water or sanitation for seven days. On arrival he had been made to work twelve hours a day, seven days a week in a tank factory, and later, had been brought back across Europe to Germany to dig trenches in the front line.

Currivan also talked to Serb army officers who had been digging trenches before Trier under US artillery fire. They had been working with 400 or so others for a fortnight, in the course of which 18 of them were killed. When, pleading that this was wholly contrary to the Geneva Convention on the treatment of prisoners of war, they had rebelled, one in five of them had been taken out and shot. There were many stories in the camp of the killing of Jews in Poland in lethal gas chambers.

'The veracity of these accounts,' wrote Currivan, 'can no longer be doubted. They come in various forms, but follow the same general pattern from Belgians, Bulgarians, French, Dutch, Greeks, Poles, Russians, Yugoslavs, Czechs and Italians, and all other tortured souls who pass through here.'

On the 4th April, the Americans came upon a camp at Ohrdruf, nine miles south of Gotha where slave-workers had been starved and worked until they were able to work no longer and were then clubbed to death or shot. Some 4,000 had been killed in this way in the last eight months, some 70 of them on the day the US army arrived.

The Americans made local German civilians visit the camp to see what had been done in their name. After such a trip the local Bürger-meister and his wife committed suicide by slashing their wrists.

One of the inmates liberated there had been a former President of the dissolved Hungarian Democratic Party, Dr Bela Fabian. He had written books published in the United States and had even once lunched with President Roosevelt. He had, he reported, been in a camp at Auschwitz (the German name for Oswieczim which the Russians had liberated in January). There, he said, the Germans had killed five million Jews. All Jews over the age of 50 were automatically gassed; the rest were worked to death or to the point of death when they were also sent to the gas chambers. Fabian imitated the wave of the hand with which the German officer in charge would single out members of a Jewish transport on arrival to send them on their way to the gas chambers. His story of what happened at Auschwitz was corroborated by others at Ohrdruf and indeed 35 French women liberated from Auschwitz in January had just reached Marseilles from Odessa with the same stories.

But there seemed to be some conflict over the exact figures involved there so that the horror, only beginning to be known about from those who had experienced it, still retained some statistical remoteness compared with what British and Americans were beginning to see with their own eyes. (The Polish Ministry of the Interior had said the year before that half a million Jews had been gassed and cremated at Auschwitz, while later the International Churches Ecumenical Movement had spoken of one and three-quarter million. The American Jewish Committee Library in New York spoke of four to five million.)

Colin Wills, a writer for the London *News Chronicle*, visited the town of Celle, near Hanover in the second week of April. He wrote, 'This is a charming town, except when the wind blows the wrong way. . . . In the gardens of the prosperous houses about the green parks rise the towering candelabra of the magnolia trees and the breeze wafts a sweet scent from the blossom – except when it blows the wrong way. That is when it blows from the concentration camp. It is only a small concentration camp; perhaps that makes it easier for the citizens of Celle to ignore it as they stroll in the sunlit streets, well-dressed and well-fed. When we got there, there were 197 prisoners alive – if you can say that men live who cannot walk but shuffle inch by inch across the ground, heads hanging on their chests, arms dangling at their sides, their leg-bones bent at the knee – you cannot say legs; only the bones are left. Their faces were ashy-black . . . starvation does that to the complexion. . . . I did not count the dead.'

Many such camps both large and small were discovered by the Allies in these days. At Nordhausen 3,000 living skeletons were found and 2,700 dead ones unburied. There tortured foreign workers had been hanged from time to time on a wall by iron hooks through their mouths. Local Germans were now made to bury the dead, though they objected strongly. Some became violently sick and one man died from a heart-attack. At another camp at Gardelegen where the SS had burned over 1,000 prisoners to death before evacuating the camp, local Germans were again made to bury the dead, first digging individual graves for them six foot by six foot by three.

At a foreign workers' camp at Langenstein in Saxony the US Eighth Armoured Division of the Ninth Army found over 1,000 Poles, Russians, French, Belgians, Dutch and Czechs. John McCormac of the *New York Times* wrote that in their clay-like pallor and the flat contours of their bloodless bodies they were almost assimilated to that dust which had claimed already so many of the original inhabitants. These were mainly professors, lawyers, doctors, civil servants and officers who had been employed in an underground factory making aircraft parts. The working day started at 4 a.m. with coffee but no food and an hour-long parade. It ended at 6.30 p.m. Camp records showed that 450 workers had died in the previous year, 450 in January 1945, 550 in February, 570 in March and 191 up to the camp's liberation on April 12th. McCormac was shown a gallows on which six prisoners could be hanged at a time, specially constructed so that their toes just touched the ground to make the torture of their deaths longer. Prisoners had been forced to watch such deaths with SS guards also looking on, laughing and smoking.

At Mieste near Gardelegen the Ninth Army found a smouldering human bonfire of 700 Polish, Russian and Hungarian slave-workers who had been put into a barn with petrol-soaked straw and burned to death by young SS guards. Ten men had somehow survived to tell the tale. The 700 had been part of a transport of 2,000 slave-workers brought from an aircraft factory in Eastern Germany. 600 had died in cattle-trucks on the way and when the train stopped at Mieste for the camp at Gardelegen those reckoned to be too weak to work had been taken and burned. Those refusing to go into the barn had been shot.

An American sergeant from Long Island who had helped liberate the camp said, 'I never was so sure before of exactly what I was fighting for. Before this you could have said those stories were propaganda, but now you know they weren't.'

Frederick Graham of the *New York Times* visited the small town of Thekla on the 20th April. He described it as 'a quiet, dull-looking place' with old, well-kept stone houses and neat intensively-cultivated kitchen gardens bordered with flowers and evergreens. Fair-skinned, blue-eyed, flaxen-haired happy children were to be seen playing in the streets. On the western edge of the town there was a factory which until the day before had been turning out aircraft wings for the Luftwaffe. And until the day before there had been a camp there of about 5,000 prisoners, 1,600 of them political prisoners and the rest Polish, Russian, Czech, Belgian and French slave-workers. The camp was surrounded by an electrified fence. It was entered through a first courtyard in which were neatly-kept flowerbeds with pansies and tulips. In the inner courtyard Graham found a mass of waxen-looking once-human figures, now hairless and grotesque, burned and full of bullet-holes. In the very centre was a solid mass of melted human flesh, the product of another burning of prisoners by the SS before they left. A Frenchman, named Pierre Gentil, who had witnessed their slaughter was described by Graham as 'himself a mere ghost'. He said the dreadful pyre had burned for five hours. 'Now we want a great peace.'

It became clear from captured orders that there was a cruel and macabre system in all this. Those workers who were too weak to be used any more were to be destroyed like rubbish; the others were to be evacuated for further use. Sometimes the useless were found undestroyed.

At Flossenberg about nine miles north-east of Weiden, 1,600 prisoners were found left from a complement of 15,000 the week before. Half of those remaining had typhus. Methodical entries in the German camp record office revealed that since 1938 when the camp had started, 12,500 prisoners had been killed by hanging, shooting or injection. As late as April 1st, 13 US Paratroopers had been hanged there. One of the prisoners who worked in the record office, a Frenchman, Pierre Bertrand, said he thought the Austrian Chancellor Schuschnigg had been hanged shortly before the withdrawal, but this turned out to be incorrect, for Schuschnigg was later found safe, elsewhere.

By now the general public in the western democracies was personally aware of the full nature of those horrors which had for so long been an inseparable part of the character of the Third Reich. In recognition of a certain tardiness in acquiring this sensitivity the *New York Times* in an editorial reminded its readers that 'the revealed conditions that are now shocking so many are only a continuation of a record which the Nazis have been writing in blood since they came to power in 1933.' But what had most vividly shocked both the British and American publics that month had been the recent discovery of two major German concentration camps, at Buchenwald and Belsen.

On the 10th April the 38th Division of the Third US Army successfully negotiated, without having to fight for it, the surrender of the German town of Weimar, celebrated for its association with Goethe. In a wood some four miles to the north of it they found one of Germany's oldest concentration camps and, so said some of the inmates who had seen others, the best of them. Records showed that 32,705 prisoners had died there since the camp was established in July 1937, on the gallows, in its torture-rooms, in dissection rooms and laboratories for human experiments, of starvation, brutality and neglect. Table-lamps with shades made from the parchment of human skin were on view there. Some 20,000 human beings were still alive in the camp when the Americans arrived, though the *New York Times* reporter Gene Currivan described them as 'human skeletons that had lost all likeness to anything human. Most of them,' he added, 'had become idiots but they still had the power of locomotion. Those in the sick-bay were beyond all help – packed into three-tier bunks which ran to the roof of the barn-like barracks'.

One of the first reporters into the camp was the American broadcaster Ed Murrow. He commented first on the Germans he saw in the countryside round about, 'well-clothed . . . well-fed and healthy, in better condition than any other people I have seen in Europe.' He began his report with an example of that compelling modesty which had made him a great journalist, 'Let me tell this in the first person for I was the least important person there, as you shall hear. There surged around me an evil-smelling horde . . . men and boys reached out to touch me. They were in rags and the remnants of uniforms. Death had already marked many of them, but they were smiling with their eyes. I looked over that mass of men to the green fields beyond where well-fed Germans were ploughing . . .' He went into a building which he had been told had once stabled 80 horses, in which 1,200 men now lay, five to a bunk. 'The stink was beyond all description.' A man came up to him. 'You remember me. I am Peter Zenkl, one-time Mayor of Prague.' Murrow remembered him but couldn't recognise him.

As in all German concentration camps proper records had been kept: 242 men out of 1,200 had died in those barracks in one month.

'As I walked down to the end of the barrack, there was applause from the men too weak to get out of bed. It sounded like the hand-clapping of babies.' He passed through into the courtyard; a man fell dead and he saw two elderly figures crawling towards a latrine. He was taken to a small courtyard with a wall about eight feet high. It adjoined what had been a stable or a garage which he entered.

'There were two rows of bodies stacked up like cord-wood. They were thin and very white. Some of the bodies were terribly bruised, though there seemed to be little flesh to bruise. Some had been shot through the head, but they bled but little. All except two were naked.' He counted them as best he could: 'All that was mortal of more than 500 men and boys lay there in two neat piles.' Even an experienced and acclaimed journalist like Murrow seemed almost distraught at the thought that what he was describing was too terrible to be believed. 'I pray you to believe what I have said about Buchenwald,' he said. 'I have reported what I saw and heard, but only part of it. For most of it I have no words.'

248

Many more words of course were to be used to try to convey the unconveyable about Buchenwald. Harold Denny of the *New York Times* visited it a few days after Murrow. He went into one of the barracks and an inmate opened a cupboard door for him. Twenty or so half-naked corpses lay piled on top of each other inside. 'Last night's crop,' said the inmate in an unconcerned sort of way.

Denny walked down the corridor between the rows of bunks.

'On either side were men, or what had been men, only a little less dead than those in the closet. Most of them lay comatose on their filthy shelves. Some stared with piercing eyes in shrunken faces and with mouths idiotically gaping . . . there was hardly a man of those hundreds in the barrack who could be restored to humanity now.'

In a last spiteful gesture SS had wrecked the water system of the camp before leaving. Although US Army trucks were bringing up water, there was not nearly enough nor were the Americans able to supply enough food. Bread and hot watery soup was still the ration, though the ex-prisoners described it as good. There was some milk for the sick. Some International Red Cross ambulances were at work but there was little they could do for many of those shrunken faces with their idiotically gaping mouths on the shelves.

For all the strong picture which he gave of the scene, Denny too seemed worred by the fact that he could not convey it in its full horror. 'Even a hint of the present hygienic conditions would be unprintable,' he wrote. 'An indescribable stench of filth and death hangs over the camp.' And he added, 'I had not intended to write about Buchenwald. By nature I am cautious about atrocity stories, and I merely wanted first-hand knowledge so that if anyone ever asked me about German concentration camps I could tell them the unexaggerated truth. What I saw was so horrible that I would not have believed it if I had not seen it myself. . . . The world must not forget such things.'

Some of the German population of Weimar were brought up to see what had been done in their name, so close to the town of which they were so proud and in which they were resentful of some damage done to Goethe's house by Allied bombing. They were sceptical at first about such an exhibition arranged for their benefit by the Americans. But there were too many of their own countrymen among the prisoners to tell them of what had been there. Men went white and women turned away from many of the scenes.

'Never has a nation claiming to be civilised,' wrote the London *News Chronicle*, 'treated men and women so brutally. . . . No German in prosperous circumstances can disclaim responsibility for Hitler. At best he will have been a passive accessory to the degradation of all man's decent instincts.'

To some Germans the truth of this was already beginning to strike home. When Nuremberg was taken on April 20th the *New York Times* reporter Richard Johnston penetrated after the battle into one of the evil-smelling shelters in which the population had been taking refuge. In the dim light he saw a number of dirty, frightened people who had not yet found the courage to go up into the streets to investigate the silence. Among them was a man in German officer's uniform with a Red Cross brassard on his left arm. This man had been out during the battle to bring both American and German wounded into the shelter. He spoke excellent English, having been a ship's doctor on the North German Lloyd line.

'We took too many orders,' he said, 'obeyed too many commands, listened to too many words, believed lies. We are a beaten people. We are a shamed people. We are reaping the whirlwind. I am a doctor. I am a German. I am proud of being a doctor.'

General-Leutnant Heinrich Kircheim had won the highest German award in the First World War, Pour Le Mérite and the Knights Cross of the Iron Cross in the second. He renounced the latter when he heard of the concentration camps and, having been taken prisoner, agreed to make a personal broadcast over the Allied radio to Field-Marshal Keitel. 'In the present situation,' he said, 'no officer can consider himself bound by his oath. As soldiers they are duty bound to end this hopeless battle at once. . . . Whoever still wavers should be convinced by the ghastly murders in Nordhausen, Buchenwald and Gardelegen.'

Those who had been through the experience of such places personally were as aware of those who came upon them from the outside of the virtually unbridgeable gap between what had happened there and communication of what had happened. A British Captain Burney who had spent a long time in Buchenwald told a BBC interviewer:

'The means of execution in the camp were varied, and applied with great frequency. Sometimes there had been no offence at all, sometimes offences which they considered were offences but which no civilised person would consider as offences. Anybody who escaped was automatically – if he stayed out for three days – accused of pillage and was brought back and hanged. There were other means of execution. They shot, they had patent traps where you stood on a trap-door which let off a bullet into your neck, they electrocuted, they injected with phenol, they injected with air, they injected with milk. . . . I feel as though I have been absolutely out of the world. It's been shocking, but on the other hand it is so stunning, it's almost unreal, and I think probably when one has been back amongst people for a while one just forgets it. Everything which happened here was without relation to anything which had ever happened before . . .'

On the same day as the BBC recorded that interview, 19th April, another of their reporters, Richard Dimbleby, went into the barracks of another concentration camp which the British 11th Armoured Division had just overrun near Hanover. Its name was Belsen. Dimbleby reported: 'I picked my way over corpse after corpse in the gloom, until I heard one voice raised above the gentle undulating moaning. I found a girl. She was a living skeleton; it was impossible to gauge her age for she had practically no hair left, and her face was only a yellow parchment sheet with two holes in it for eyes. . . . She was trying to cry but she hadn't enough strength.'

Outside, in the shade of some trees, he walked among a great pile of bodies 'all so thin that their yellow skin glistened like stretched rubber on their bones. Some of the poor starved creatures . . . looked so utterly unreal and inhuman that I could have imagined that they had never lived at all.' It was perhaps such individual glimpses that most successfully conveyed the enormity of what had happened. It was the scale of the horrors – which in any case was only just beginning to be revealed – which both made them unique in human history but also difficult to apprehend.

When six Norwegian police who had been in Stutthof concentration camp near Danzig reported that a transport of 18,000 Jews marked for death had arrived there early in the year and had been shot because the Germans had had no time to gas them systematically before the Russians overran the camp, this too was little more than a statistic. The closer such things could be brought to personal perception the easier they were to try and take in. Even the fact that the SS guards at Belsen had shot, it was said, perhaps as many as 2,000 prisoners on the day before the British reached the camp was less easy to take in, than the fact that they had, in some cases, actually continued shooting them after the British had arrived, on the grounds that it was necessary to keep order. Small details continued to insist on the human suffering contained in the appalling scale of the statistics. A *News Chronicle* reporter described one man in Belsen as looking 'like a yellow stick wrapped in a grey rag'. Another, had an ivory skull on which the moustache and spectacles which he had somehow managed to retain seemed enormous as they stuck out above a hanging rag of striped cloth. 'It was as if the head were being paraded on a pole.'

R. W. Thompson of the London *Sunday Times* experienced the common journalistic sense of desperation that what he had to write about might not be believed. 'It is my duty,' he wrote, 'to describe something beyond the imagination of mankind. . . . You must read and you must believe. We few who have had the opportunity to view this atrocity against mankind have the right to demand your attention. . . .

Our words, our honour must suffice that this terrible deed against the human spirit may be known to all the world.'

In trying to communicate what he saw he neatly identified the source of the difficulty which obsessed him and so many other good journalists. 'When,' he wrote, 'for hours you gaze on the human body distorted beyond recognition, and come to the point where there is literally no difference between the living and the dead, you are beyond shocking because you are beyond normal standards. . . . The living and the dead lie often side by side and the only difference is the purely physical one of the still-beating hearts. Clothing is without meaning for these bodies are no longer people. In a sense they are less offensive naked than in the grey striped filthy rags that hang on them, serving only to accentuate the awful shame.'

Here a British prisoner told the reporter how each day the dying had been taken out of the barracks with the dead and laid with them in a latrine trench before being taken to the morgue. Anyone trying to rescue those still alive was punished but he himself had one day gone to the morgue to which a still-living French army Colonel who was a friend of his had been taken. He had heard his voice calling out from among the corpses: 'For God's sake, save me. Don't leave me here.' He had somehow brought him back to the barracks but what the French-man needed was food and there was none to give him. Next day he was again taken alive out to the latrine trench and then to the morgue where this time he duly succumbed.

This British prisoner in Belsen had worked for a time taking bodies to the burial ground. In doing so he had noticed curious wounds on many of them about the thigh. On drawing the attention of one of his workmates to this, he had received the reply, 'Don't you know what that is? People eat the flesh.' Even he, at the very centre of these horrors, had the problem of belief. 'I did not believe it,' he said, 'until the next day when I saw a man doing it.'

Testimony to cannibalism was found at all levels. Prince Frederick Leopold of Prussia, who was in Dachau concentration camp at the end of the war described how towards the end of March 1945 a transport of prisoners arrived at the camp. 'Many were dead on arrival,' he said, 'the living were terribly starved. As the carriage doors were opened, the dead fell out. Some of the prisoners in this new arrival had existed by eating human flesh.'

Dachau itself, with some 32,000 prisoners still alive, was liberated by the 42nd and 45th Divisions of the US 7th Army on the 29th April, soon after lunch. In a railway siding nearby were 39 cattle-trucks crammed with the corpses of Poles who had been brought there and been left without food or water for several days. One man was dragged out, still alive. Within the camp the by now familiar horrors were discovered including gas chambers camouflaged as showers.

Here the problem for the human mind of dealing from the outside with what could not be dealt with, was partially solved, in a manner only available to those who saw these things at first hand, immediately and on the spot. An Associated Press reporter with the American troops described what happened. 'Dozens of German guards fell under withering blasts of rifle and carbine fire as the soldiers, catching glimpses of the horrors within the camp, raged through the barracks for a quick clean-up.' They were joined by French and Russian prisoners who grabbed the weapons of those who fell. The Americans stormed through the camp 'with tornadic fury'. Food was still cooking in the guards' kitchen. An officer with a bullet through his head sat slumped over a plate of beans. Outside, in the railway siding, '. . . in the wake of the storming Americans the bodies of the trimly-clad German guards lay scattered like ten-pins bowled over as they sought to flee.'

The camp was surrounded by a ten-foot high electrified wire fence and a fifteen-foot wide moat. Some of the prisoners in their elation tried to climb over the fence and were electrocuted. Some of the guards still in their watch-towers made the mistake of revealing themselves by firing down on the prisoners. They themselves were immediately riddled with bullets by the Americans. The AP reporter saw their bodies fall into the moat and heard from the prisoners 'a roar unlike anything ever heard from human throats.'

There, and in some other camps where prisoners took revenge on their guards, for a time at any rate, the problem had been dealt with. Elsewhere, and for the rest of time, it was not to be so easy. In both Britain and the United States assimilation of what had been revealed was something with which people wrestled. It had, wrote A. J. Cummings of the *News Chronicle*, 'stirred the people of Britain to the very depths.' Many, in both countries, took refuge in a response similar to that of the American GI's in Dachau, softened only by the differences of time and place. Those responsible for such things, they insisted, must be hunted down and swiftly and rigorously punished. Many culprits – large and small – Commandants and ordinary SS guards, were indeed found and punished though, in the west, often not all that swiftly or rigorously. Many disappeared for ever into respectable anonymity. A list of major war criminals was being prepared. A War Crimes Commission was established but it had no power to investigate or indeed to act at all unless approached by national Governments.

For intellectuals the dimensions of the problem were infinite. C. E. M. Joad, the BBC resident philosopher, writing in the *New Statesman* described how the accounts of the camps had evoked in him 'a bewildering mixture of thought and feeling.' But even he, 'trying to sort out the threads in the tangle,' could not at first get beyond emotional horror. These things, he said, were as horrible as any things that human beings had ever done to one another – more horrible in that they had been done on a larger scale. But there was the problem that they were 'atrocities', and 'atrocities' had been devalued by their use for propaganda purposes in war, particularly the First World War. And yet this time the horrors did indeed seem to be every bit as bad as they were made out to be. He heard of some people who '*even now* refuse to believe and say that this is merely a newspaper stunt or is Government propaganda.' He described that refusal as partly a natural defensive mechanism of the mind against the admission of the intolerable; there were certain things, one was tempted to think, whose perpetration was easier to human beings than the admission that they were perpetrated.

That what had happened might have had more to do with the nature of Man than with the nature of German National Socialist Man, was something which the journalist Alan Moorehead, writing in *Horizon*, edited by Cyril Connolly, tried to face, after his visit to Belsen.

'It was all like a journey down to some Dantesque pit, unreal, leprous and frightening. And now that one emerged into the light again, one's first coherent reactions were not of disgust or anger or even, I think, of pity. Something else filled the mind, a frantic desire to ask: "Why? Why? Why? Why had it happened?" With all one's soul one felt "This is not war. Nor has it anything to do with here and now, with this one place at this one moment. This is timeless and the whole world and all mankind is involved in it. This touches me and I am responsible. Why has it happened. How did we let it happen?"' And he concluded, '. . . The physical evidence of all those horrible places will soon have been wiped out. Only the mental danger remains. The danger of indifference.'

On a simpler level public reaction continued to be a combination of horror, indignation and bewilderment. Films of at least the gruesome aftermath of what the Germans had been doing were shown both in Britain and the United States, newsreels of starkly realistic scenes appearing among the glossy productions of Hollywood. In Britain audiences sometimes took refuge in affront and walked out. In the United States it was made marginally easier to take in the nature of what had been happening because of an increasing number of reports of the brutal treatment of American prisoners of war by the Germans in recent weeks.

Atrocities against prisoners of war had hitherto been limited to untypical individual instances, as in the shooting of over a hundred American prisoners during the German offensive in the Ardennes at

Malmedy in Belgium. On the whole the British and American prisoners of war liberated in the last days of the European fighting had testified to correct treatment for themselves from the German armed forces, though they had witnessed barbarity practised on others, particularly Russians. Their chief complaint had been that in the last few months the supply of Red Cross parcels which had kept them alive over the years, had stopped owing to the disruption of German communications. But more and more instances began to appear in the last weeks of the war of callous and inhuman treatment meted out to American prisoners on the long marches into which they had often been forced from prison camps in the east under pressure of the Russian advance. They had covered up to twenty miles a day for several weeks on very little food, spending the nights in the open without covering, and they were often beaten and shot when they collapsed. There had been many deaths. A picture of emaciated American prisoners at Marktreidweitz which appeared in the *New York Times* on the 27th April showed them looking very like the worst of the concentration camp victims. The experience of all in such places was brought directly home.

Just how barbarically the Germans could behave on forced marches was revealed in many accounts of the attempts to move prisoners from the concentration camps ahead of the Americans' own advance. Several thousand had left in columns from Buchenwald at the beginning of the month, among them a 34-year-old Frenchman, Marcel Cadet, whose wife lived at 34 Riverside Drive, New York. He described how they had been driven out of the camp with clubs, rifles and rubber truncheons. He had seen some fifty men beaten to the ground and pounded until dead, then, on the way to a train at Weimar for the first part of their journey, some hundred others had been shot before the column reached the station. Later on the road to Flossenberg concentration camp: 'They shot when a man stopped to tie his shoe-laces or when he tried to pick up a blade of grass to eat. I saw comrades piled ten foot high.'

When the column was intercepted by the 90th US Infantry near Posing, the route it had taken was marked by a litter of shrunken corpses, broken bodies and common graves. Such burials as were carried out had been the work of special parties of Poles and Jews who were themselves then shot in turn. The last deaths had been the result of a further attempt to evacuate the prisoners from Flossenberg itself on the appearance of advanced US troops. Five minutes outside the camp, Cadet said, shooting started again, and men dropped every ten yards or so. US Piper Cub aircraft had appeared above the column and then tanks and vehicles marked with Allied white stars could be seen coming towards it. The SS machine-gunned 200 prisoners at the end of the

255

column in order to form a human roadblock against the Americans.

Broadcasting from Chicago in the week after VE Day, Clifton Utley said he thought that the continuing revelation of German atrocities in newspapers and in cinemas otherwise concerned with Bing Crosby and Betty Grable, had played a rôle in eliminating what might otherwise have been a difference of American and European opinion about the severity with which Germany was to be treated. A party of senior American editors including Joseph Pulitzer of the *St Louis Post-Dispatch* who had been to Europe to verify the sort of stories that had been appearing in the press, reported on the day after VE Day. 'We found,' said Pullitzer himself, 'that they were not exaggerated. As a matter of fact they were under-stated.'

Gideon Seymour, the executive editor of the *Minneapolis Star Journal* said: 'We've got to police Germany for the next twenty years if the American people will stand for it.' They described the gas-chambers which they had seen disguised as showers, rooms of about 30 feet by 20 feet with perforated pipes overhead dispensing not hot water but gas, and glass peepholes in the walls for the SS to look through. 'We found no feelings of remorse among the Germans,' said Stanley High, associate editor of *Readers' Digest*; 'If you talk to a German now you wouldn't think there were any Nazis left – or at least, only one, and that would be Hitler or the fellow next door.'

Representative Claire Boothe Luce was also just back from Europe. She gave an account of the Nordhausen concentration camp from which many thousands of prisoners had been sent each day to work in an abandoned salt-mine in the nearby mountain, like Nibelungen, in a vast underground network of tunnels making parts for V1 and V2 rockets. Prisoners from that camp, she said, which had held some 50,000, were still dying at the rate of many hundred a day as indeed they were in other camps where, even after VE Day, the Allies could still often do little to help victims over whom the Third Reich had won its only lasting triumph.

Of course the worst was not yet in any full sense known. It was only in the slowly emerging account of prisoners now rescued from Buchenwald, Belsen, Flossenberg, Dachau, Nordhausen and many other such abominable places, that the full story was to be learned of what had been happening for so many years behind what the German High Command, in its last communiqué issued from Flensburg, on May 9th, described as the German Wehrmacht's 'heroic' and 'honourable' struggle. On the 23rd of April the *News Chronicle* had had a story which it was still able to present as something new. 'There is a concentration camp,' it wrote, 'worse than Buchenwald. It is Auschwitz. . . . Prisoners in Buchenwald revealed that when the world is told about

Auschwitz, it will hear the most ghastly story of all to come out of Nazi Germany.' The problem of taking such things in would remain the same.

In a letter quoted in the London *Times* of the 28th May, 1945, a Rabbi expressed in language all the more poignant for its similarity to that of an English nursery song, the impossibility of ever really coming to terms with what had happened: 'If all the heavens were paper and all the water in the world were ink and all the trees were turned into pens, you could not even then record the sufferings and horrors.'

That letter was quoted in protest against a small incident which had occurred in a neutral country at the end of the war, namely a visit to the German Embassy in Dublin by the Prime Minister of Eire to convey his condolences to the German Minister there on the death of Adolf Hitler. Seen from the twilight world of the concentration camps, or even from a world beginning to have the reality of those camps brought home to it, this was indeed, as the letter-writer put it, a most strange tribute. But nothing epitomised more neatly the distinction men had to maintain between that twilight world and the world of political pragmatism in which they are ordinarily engaged. De Valera was not concerned with respect or otherwise for Adolf Hitler. His visit was simply one more carefully calculated move in his long campaign to establish the unassailable political reality of separatist Irish nationalism. It was the final point of punctuation in that campaign which itself had been successfully concluded by the maintenance of official Irish neutrality throughout the war.

It was to such a world of everyday practical political considerations, their compromises, their deviousnesses, and their routine shrinking of ideals, that the international community as a whole was now to return.

Chapter Twenty-Two

The end of the war in Europe meant that the period of shadow electioneering in Britain was now also over and that the real thing would soon have to begin.

The Labour Party had first thought, like Churchill, that once the Germans had been beaten the Coalition Government should come to an end. But it was at the same time anxious that there should be no rushed election. The new voting register had been compiled in a hurry and was known to be imperfect. Arrangements for the Services to cast their votes either by post or through proxies had not always been satisfactorily completed; it was reckoned that some 10% of servicemen and women would be disfranchised. Time also was needed for returning Service candidates to make themselves known to their constituents and for those constituents to think over the issues involved. Labour therefore let Churchill know that, while they would withdraw from the Coalition as soon as notice of the dissolution of Parliament should be given, they would prefer that not to take place until the autumn.

Churchill, in a letter to Attlee dated 18th May, said that if there were to be a delay, it would be better for the Coalition to continue until decisive victory had been won over Japan.

Attlee replied from the Labour Party Conference then taking place in Blackpool where the matter had been discussed. He turned down the suggestion and repeated the case for an autumn election. The date of the defeat of Japan was uncertain. If it were to take long, the sort of pre-electioneering which had already been disturbing to the sense of government unity would inevitably become even more embarrassing. He ended his letter with the warning that if Churchill decided on an election in July, the nearest alternative date, '. . . the responsibility must and will, of course, be yours.'

Churchill decided on an election in July. He went to Buckingham Palace to see the King at noon on May 23rd and resigned as Prime Minister after more than five years in office, returning at 4 o'clock that afternoon to receive an invitation, which he accepted, to form a new

From *Punch*: 'Since there's no help, come let us kiss and part.'
The end of the Coalition Government

Government. In accordance with the arrangement for a special three-week delay, the dissolution of Parliament was announced for June 15th with polling in the General Election to take place on Thursday, 5th July.

Labour and those organs of the press supporting it, notably the *Daily Mirror*, the *Daily Herald* and the *New Statesman*, immediately complained that the election was being rushed by the Conservatives. But Churchill had made a fair point in his last letter to Attlee when he said that it was specifically in order to avoid a sense of rush that, at the request of the Labour leaders themselves the three-week delay had been introduced. Attlee himself as Deputy Prime Minister had announced it. A 'snap' election, however was how the *Daily Mirror* and the *New Statesmen* now referred to it and there was a strong implication that Labour was not being given a fair chance. The *Daily Mirror* reckoned that the margin of error in the new register was more than enough to sway the election one way or the other and when it discovered that hundreds of thousands of voters were going to be away on holiday on July 5th it said that the election was 'in danger of becoming a farce'.

The principal advocate for the tactic of this 'snap' election was assumed to be Lord Beaverbrook who was thought to have overcome Churchill's own scruples. The purpose behind the tactic was, said Sir Stafford Cripps at a Labour meeting in Lancashire, '. . . to cash in on the victory atmosphere and the Prime Minister's leadership as quickly as possible, since apparently they believe that his reputation and power will so quickly decline as to make an autumn election less favourable for them.'

This was not a reasonable charge. Churchill had offered a postponement until after the defeat of Japan, a date generally assumed to be later than the autumn, without apparently fearing a waning of his appeal. Nevertheless, heavy emphasis on Churchillian national leadership was, as Quintin Hogg had indicated, to be the Conservatives' single strongest card, and was the first item in a twelve-point statement of policy now put out by Conservative Central Office.

The Chelmsford by-election result had cast some doubt on the value of this particular election appeal. But the very strong and widespread sense of gratitude to Churchill for his national leadership, undertaken at a time when another Conservative Prime Minister (Chamberlain) had brought the country to the brink of defeat, meant that in a national General Election many undecided voters would find it difficult to reject him.

There was also still a war to be fought, if to many of the people of Britain a rather remote one. Many Americans indeed looked to Churchill's victory as a guarantee that Britain would go through to the bitter end against Japan. But as the *Chicago Daily News*, which was critical of Britain for having an election at all while the Pacific War still lasted, correctly assessed, the Pacific War did not in Britain give the same sense of urgency to national leadership as the European War had done. Electors felt released to think of other things. A letter which appeared in the *Daily Mirror* on June 5th was probably of wide application. 'I am a married woman with a family of three,' wrote Mrs Jean Hanson of Coventry. 'I shall vote Labour because I believe it will be best for my family. We shall never cease to thank and praise Mr Churchill for seeing us through the dark years of the war, but neither we nor our children can exist on gratitude.'

Other items on the Conservative twelve-point policy included 'the fullest opportunity for individual initiative, and the removal of wartime controls as the necessity for them disappears . . . a determined policy for full employment and a rising standard of living . . . a prosperous and healthy agriculture . . . an all-out drive for more and better houses . . . the removal of need from the home, by carrying out complete schemes of national insurance and family allowances, and improved health and hospital services; and an educational system giving equal opportunities for all . . .'

The *Daily Mirror* on the day on which it published these proposals also published a cartoon by Zec showing a pot-bellied, top-hatted gentleman orating in a working-class street while clutching a list of promises – 'Better homes,' 'Full employment,' and so on. A working-class mother in a doorway pointed him out to her young son with the words taken from the title of the popular Tommy Handley radio show: 'Alfie,' she said, 'It's That Man Again!' The street in which she was living was marked 'Slum Street' and in brackets underneath those words was written 'Thanks to years of broken Tory pledges.'

While the Coalition had still been in existence and the eventual election only theoretically envisaged, the Labour Party had made a point of asserting that its own return to party strife would be gentlemanly. The National Executive had expressed the hope that, when what had been 'a great partnership' came to an end, the dissolution should be accompanied with good feeling and that it would be 'an unworthy thing for so great an adventure to end in squalid bickerings'. Something of this spirit did manage for a while to survive the early election campaign, but as the distance to polling day shortened so inevitably did rivals' tempers. Before the end of the month Michael Foot in the *Daily Herald* was to be describing it as 'the dirtiest of all elections.' The tension built up slowly at first.

On the 31st May Churchill, who had just formed his new all-Conservative 'Caretaker' Government, had toured with his wife in a small open car his newly-redistributed constituency at Woodford for six hours. He made a point of avoiding election issues beyond denying that it was a rushed election. Indeed, he used the fact that they were having forty days instead of the usual seventeen before an election as his excuse for not making any campaign speeches that day. 'We must not,' he said, 'use all our powder and shot in the early days of the battle.'

He expressed 'grief' that his Labour and Trades Union friends and the Liberals should have felt it their duty to their parties to leave the National administration but proudly accepted the title of caretaker for the new Government, which he continued to call 'National'. It meant, he said, that they would 'take very good care of everything that affects the welfare of Britain and of all classes in Britain.' Finally he congratulated the party faithful around him on looking so well, in spite of the recent cut in rations announced soon after VE Day by the Minister of Food. (Cooking fats were to be reduced from 2 ounces to 1 ounce a week, bacon from 4 ounces to 3 ounces a week, and there was to be no Christmas bonus of extra sugar this year.)

He had already started to face his old colleagues as opponents in the House of Commons. It was the first time in five years. The experience seemed to amuse him. Asked by Herbert Morrison if he could give a rough estimate as to how long it would take 'to despatch Goering to his proper destination?' Churchill replied, 'I know no more than I did the day before yesterday when I shared this want of knowledge with the Right Honourable Member.'

The campaign proper began with a broadcast by Churchill on the evening of 4th June. He in turn began with a rejection in typical style of the charge that he was pushing the country into a rushed election. 'It was impossible,' he said, 'to go on in a state of "electionitis" all through the summer and autumn. This election will last quite long enough for all who are concerned in it, and I expect many of the general public will be sick and tired of it before we get to polling day . . .'

He devoted the greater part of his broadcast to a full-scale attack on 'this continental conception of human society called Socialism, or in its more violent form Communism.' It was, he said, '. . . abhorrent to the British ideas of freedom and struck not only at property in all its forms, but at liberty in all its forms . . . inseparably interwoven with Totalitarianism and the abject worship of the State . . .

'How is an ordinary citizen or subject of the King to stand up against this formidable machine, which, once it is in power, will prescribe for every one of them where they are to work; what they are to work at; where they may go and what they may say; what views they are to hold and within what limits they may express them; where their wives are to go to queue up for the state ration; and what education their children

Electioneering; Lord Buckhurst at Bethnal Green, and (*below*) Ernest Bevin canvassing for Wandsworth Central

are to receive to mould their views of human liberty and conduct in the future. . . . But I will go further. I declare to you from the bottom of my heart that no Socialist system can be established without a political police. . . . They would have to fall back on some form of Gestapo, no doubt very humanely directed in the first instance. This would nip opinion in the bud; it would stop criticism as it reared its head, and it would gather all the power to the supreme party and the party leaders . . .'

He confronted the argument, perhaps awkward in this election for Conservatives, that Socialism in some form had been necessary for the conduct of the war. This, he indicated, was just one of the horrors and dangers of war through which they had now so successfully passed:

'We cast off the shackles and burdens which we imposed on ourselves in times of dire mortal peril, and quit the gloomy caverns of war and march out into the breezy fields, where the sun is shining and where all may walk joyfully in its warm and golden rays.'

With one last swipe at a Socialist government, which once it started 'monkeying with the credit of Great Britain would see that there is no man or woman in this country who has, by their thrift or toil, accumulated a nest-egg, however small, who will not run the risk of seeing it shrivel before their eyes,' he reminded his listeners of the tremendous task still ahead in fighting the Japanese and concluded, 'On with the forward march! Leave the Socialist dreamers to their Utopias or their nightmares. Let us be content to do the heavy job that is right on top of us. And let us make sure that the cottage home to which the warrior will return is blessed with modest but solid prosperity, well-fenced and guarded against misfortune and that Britons remain free to plan their lives for themselves and for those they love.'

On the next evening Clement Attlee replied to Churchill in a broadcast on behalf of the Labour Party.

He began drily 'I am also addressing you tonight on the wireless for the first time for five years as a party leader . . .' but he paid a warm tribute to his colleagues of all parties in the wartime Coalition and particularly Churchill. 'No political differences,' he said, 'can efface the memory of our comradeship in this tremendous adventure . . .'

He spent some time justifying Labour in calling the election now against the Prime Minister's wishes and emphasised that the fact that it had been called in no way altered the Labour Party's firm resolve to do its utmost to win the war against Japan. He was nearly half-way through his broadcast before he arrived at the main theme of Churchill's attack. He confronted it with academic dismissal, reminding listeners that Socialist theory had been developed by Robert Owen in Britain long before Karl Marx, and that the only time Britain had known a political police had been under the Tory Prime Minister, Lord Liverpool, in the years of repression after the British people had beaten Napoleon. Churchill's own mentor, he said, in his present political theory appeared to be an Austrian professor of the name of Friedrich August von Hayek. 'Any system,' said Attlee, 'can be reduced to absurdity by this kind of theoretical reasoning, just as German professors showed theoretically that British democracy must be beaten by German dictatorship. It was not.'

Attlee's own main attack was on the Conservative belief that if every individual sought his own interest, somehow or other the interest of all would be served. 'A pathetic faith resting on no foundation of experience,' he called it. Labour, he said, believed in mobilising resources for peace in the same way as the last Government had so successfully mobilised them for war. As for individual freedom, 'I entirely agree that people should have the greatest freedom compatible with the freedom of others. But there was a time when employers were free to work little children sixteen hours a day . . . there was a time when people were free to neglect sanitation so that thousands died of preventable disease. For years every attempt to remedy these crying evils was blocked by the same plea of freedom for the individual. It was in fact freedom for the rich and slavery for the poor.'

He pointed out that the Labour Party was no longer the class party that it had been forty years before, and that its candidates were people from all walks of life, including 120 from the fighting services, so that youth was well represented. '. . . The Conservative Party remains, as always, a class party . . . it represents today, as in the past, the forces of property and privilege.'

Attlee's broadcast provided such a complete contrast in style with Churchill's that it was difficult to compare the two talks at all for their likely effects upon the electorate. It could be seen that Churchill's would delight many by its robust assault on the dreaded fantasies of Socialism, would cause misgivings among some Conservatives or floating voters for having gone too far, and that it would be laughed to scorn by those who were going to vote Labour anyway.* It could be seen that Attlee's talk would strike robust Conservative voters as excessively dim, that it might cause misgivings among Labour of floating voters who wished he could have shown himself a more obvious match for Churchill, and that it would satisfy by his articulate reasonableness those who had already decided to support him. But to weigh

---

*The *Manchester Guardian* political correspondent found some Tory MP's 'who say he overdid it.' D. N. Pritt, the left-wing Labour MP said it was worth 50 votes to Labour.

one up against the other was a feat which seemed to defy the normally straightforward mechanism of electoral analysis.

At least, though, the main battle-lines of the election were now drawn. From these positions, with occasional diversions on the flanks, the electoral issue was to be decided. The unprecedented length of time since the last general election, the fact that no one under the age of thirty-one had ever voted before, the vagaries of the new register, the unknown factor of the services' proxy or postal votes, and above all the unpredictable personal factor of Churchill's national appeal across party lines, all made the outcome almost impossible to forecast, though the Conservatives as the traditional party of government could be said to have a natural psychological advantage and Labour with its electoral record of failure a corresponding disadvantage.

There was also an unpredictable factor in the intervention between Labour and Conservatives of the once-great Liberal Party, which, under Sir Archibald Sinclair, the Coalition's Secretary of State for Air, was fielding candidates in the majority of constituencies. Finally the fact that when polling closed on July 5th there would be a three-week delay before the results were known, in the course of which service votes would be collected and counted, somehow made the result seem an even more indiscernible and remote prospect.

The British press divided predictably enough, though *The Times* seemed to stand more on the sidelines than had been usual for this traditionally Conservative organ in previous elections. Often stressing how much the parties had in common, it appeared to regret the Coalition's breakup. *The Daily Telegraph* and the *Daily Express* provided the big Conservative guns. The latter, reflecting Lord Beaverbrook's extensive influence on Conservative policy, worked up the more extravagant pitches of election feeling. The *Manchester Guardian* and the *News Chronicle*, while anti-Conservative, and therefore in a way helpful to Labour, were specifically loyal to the Liberals. The *Daily Herald* and above all the *Daily Mirror*, with a daily correspondence column open to Labour and Liberal supporters for an expression of their anti-Conservative feelings, were the mainstay of the Labour Party's attack.

The *Mirror* equalled in emotional intensity the analogous appeal of the opposing *Daily Express*. In reply to Churchill's charge that Labour would introduce a Gestapo it hurled back at him one of his own famous wartime questions, 'What sort of people does he think we are?'

Nobody said very much about Mr Attlee's broadcast. Much of the pugnacity in the Labour campaign in these early days came from Ernest Bevin who, replying to a charge of Oliver Lyttelton's to the effect that the Labour Party wanted to make queues permanent, replied, 'For twenty years there were permanent queues outside the Labour Ex-

266

'. . . We have played our part in shaping recent great events.' Ernest Bevin puts the case for Labour

changes of people drawing a miserable dole and facing the Means Test, while Mr Lyttelton, friend of the Bank of England, was fixing-up tin pools and companies. I hurl it back at him that for twenty years he and his City friends . . . have been responsible for more permanent queues than anybody else in the country, the queues of starving men.'

A certain amount of early bickering over whether the electoral truce needed to have been broken, and who broke it, over who forced the election and whether or not it was a rushed election, persisted for a time. But the *Mirror* was probably in tune with public opinion in general when on the 14th June it said its only comment on all this was: 'Who cares?' And *The Times* too deplored what it called the continued bickering over the 'Who killed Cock Robin?' issue. 'The electorate is concerned for the future, not the past,' it added, as did almost identically the *Mirror*. 'The future is the thing that matters,' it maintained, insisting that the most important single issue for the electorate was housing, and that Ernest Bevin was the only man who could get the houses built. Its correspondence columns continued to repeat familiar but strong generalities. 'The Conservatives are going to fight controls,' wrote one reader. 'Well, if controls helped to win the war, they can do so for the peace.' Another pointed out, 'Churchill was persistently cold-shouldered by the very Conservatives who now exploit him as a hero. When the country was drifting to destruction they kept him out of office . . .'

For those who preferred steadier intellectual fare there were regular nightly broadcasts by luminaries of each party. Those who found the brashness of the *Express* or the *Daily Mirror* unsavoury could hear Sir John Anderson proclaim, 'It would be a betrayal of the interests of the nation to secure the worst of every possible world by encouraging a wholly delusive belief in the speedy extension of national control and thereby in obscuring the absolute necessity of giving to private enterprise the conditions necessary to its success.'

Mr Tom Johnston, for Labour, countered with a complaint about an arcane financial moment in March, 1926 when a finance house lent money to the Skoda works in Czechoslovakia at an interest rate more than double that at which British thrift and savings were being rewarded.

Sir Archibald Sinclair played on listeners' literary susceptibilities. 'You have been listening,' he began, 'to a series of political broadcasts from representatives of the three main parties; first the Conservatives, after them the Socialists and then the Liberals: Goneril, Regan and then Cordelia. Remember what happened to poor King Lear when he thrust out his third daughter . . . I ask you to give your Cordelia – the Liberal Party – its chance.'

The National leader;
Churchill arrives at
Walham Green on his tour
of London

The Challenger; Clement Attlee at the Labour Party Conference

A correspondent, signing himself 'Disgusted Elector' wrote to *The Times* of 'inexpressibly tedious nightly sparrings on the wireless – a really menacing development.'

It remained difficult to assess what all this was doing to the opinions of the electorate. Kingsley Martin, the editor of the *New Statesman* said that he hadn't met a single person who had liked Churchill's broadcast. But such criticism, if it came his way, did not deter Churchill from returning to his theme when he made another broadcast on the night of June 13th. He said of the Socialist leaders, 'If and when the plans to which they are publicly and irrevocably committed come into force in their entirety, and we had a complete Socialist system, all effective and healthy opposition and the natural change of parties in office from time to time would necessarily come to an end, and a political police would be required to enforce an absolute and permanent system upon the nation.'

He went on to emphasise the dedication of the Conservative party itself to social welfare. 'We are determined,' he said, speaking of his new National Government's commitment to the free school milk, school meals and other benefits introduced by the Coalition, 'We are determined to secure the nation's future by seeing that from birth and even before birth, every British infant is well-nourished and given the chance to grow up sturdy and strong. . . . Equal opportunity for all under free institutions and equal laws: there is the banner for which we will do battle against all rubber stamp bureaucracies or dictatorships.'

The *Manchester Guardian* found this second election broadcast of Churchill's 'certainly an improvement on his first.' But the paper found it 'hard, with the best will in the world, to accept his picture of a Conservative party all fired with enthusiasm for social reform . . . he speaks as one handicapped by his friends.'

James Griffiths who broadcast for Labour five days later was wholly unimpressed. 'I would like to tell Mr Churchill,' he said, 'that we are not frightened by his phantom Gestapo. What we are afraid of are the real terrors we cannot forget – unemployment; the dole; the Means Test.'

The *New Statesman* had already warned that the Conservatives might try some election stunt or scare such as the Zinovieff Letter, a scare about Russian Communist influence on Labour which was reputed to have won them the election of 1924. In the middle of June such a scare materialised. Mr Harold Laski, a Professor of Political Theory at London University and Chairman of the Labour Party National Executive for the year, helped provide it.

Laski's very name – not far removed in simple public imagination from some dangerous or Bolshevik-associated caricature – lent verisimilitude to the scare. The *Daily Express* was at one point to print it, intentionally, as Laskee, and the *Manchester Guardian*, accidentally, as Laskie. The Conservative supporter Lord Croft went out of his way to refer to him with sarcasm as 'that fine old English Labour man.' Laski, in any case, it could be said, went out of his way to ask for trouble.

On the 14th June, the day before Parliament was dissolved, Churchill announced to the House of Commons that a meeting between himself, President Truman and Marshal Stalin was about to take place. He could not yet say where or when exactly but it would be before the results of the election had been announced (on July 26th). He was inviting Mr Attlee to come too lest anyone were to say: 'Why are you committing yourself to something when in the ballot box there may be something which strips you of your authority?' He said he and Attlee thought alike on the foreign situation and agreed together, and there would be an opportunity to show that 'though Governments may change and parties may quarrel yet on some of the main essentials of foreign affairs we stand together.'

All parties in the House received this information with approval. There was no Labour back-bench criticism, even from Aneurin Bevan who had tried to trip Churchill up with a point of procedure over making the statement at all. But the same evening Harold Laski in his capacity as Chairman of the Labour's National Executive drew public attention to the fact that the Big Three Conference would be discussing matters which had not been debated by the Labour Party Executive. Thus, he said, the Labour Party itself could not be committed to decisions arrived at by the Conference. He said that Labour's foreign policy differed from and was 'sounder' than that of a coalition dominated by Tories and that therefore neither the Labour Party nor Mr Attlee could accept responsibility for any agreements concluded by Churchill at the Conference. 'It is,' said Laski, 'essential that if Mr Attlee attends this gathering he shall do so in the rôle of observer only.'

The next day Churchill formally issued his invitation to Attlee by letter but in it drew attention to Laski's remarks and said that while the Government of course would bear responsibility for all decisions, his idea had been that Attlee 'should come as a friend and counsellor and help us on all the subjects on which we have been so long agreed.' He said that if Attlee were to come as a 'mute observer' this would be derogatory to his position as leader of his party. In other words what Churchill was suggesting was that even though they were in the middle of an election and indulging in sharp domestic exchanges, the spirit of the Coalition would continue as far as foreign policy was concerned.

Attlee replied that after consulting with his principal colleagues in the House of Commons he had pleasure in accepting the invitation. He commented tersely, 'There was never any suggestion that I should come as a mere observer.' That this was a rebuke for Laski rather than Churchill was made clear by subsequent sentences of Attlee's letter in which he went out of his way to stress the 'great public advantage in preserving and presenting the unity on foreign policy which has been maintained for the past five years.' His letter incidentally disclosed for the first time that the forthcoming conference was to be held in Berlin.

In the face of this, Laski momentarily appeared to climb down. 'Everything,' he said, 'has been satisfactorily cleared up,' and he told the *Manchester Guardian* that it was precisely to obtain such clarification that he had made his intervention. But all in fact that had been cleared up, at least temporarily, was that Attlee was ignoring what Laski had said. Laski had no need to worry. What he had said would not go away until the election was over.

Hore-Belisha, the former Transport and War Minister at Coventry the very next day put the charge which Churchill himself was to take up as a major election issue and to which the *Daily Express* and other Conservative papers were continually to return. 'If Mr Attlee returned as head of the Government, that Government would have to take its orders from the executive of the Labour Party. What a hamstrung leader Mr Attlee would be as Prime Minister of Great Britain. He would be talking to Marshal Stalin and President Truman on a footing of complete inequality. If he strayed outside his detailed mandate he would be liable to censure and repudiation. . . . This is not the kind of Government we can afford to have in Britain at this time.'

Laski was no pragmatic politician but a left-wing party intellectual who had in the past expressed, as one might expect such a man to do, some qualified admiration for Lenin. In the 'thirties he had been in favour of admitting Communists to the Labour Party. The *Daily Express* was quick to pick up what he had written in a Socialist League publication about the monarchy, namely that it was 'not in the long run compatible' with social democracy. He was not a man to keep his convictions about a correct political analysis to himself, election or no election. Ignoring the sharp rebuke to him in Attlee's letter to Churchill he warmed to his theme the following day, speaking at Scunthorpe. 'I repudiate,' he said, 'altogether the notion that the doctrine of continuity of foreign policy is a doctrine that the Socialist Party ought to accept, and that it is our business to keep foreign policy above party . . . when Mr Attlee goes to Berlin it is vital that there should be no implication on our part.'

As the *Manchester Guardian* put it: if Laski was taking Attlee's rebuke lying down, he was only half lying down. Attlee, speaking the same evening, ignored any embarrassment Laski might be causing him, only making one oblique but very characteristic reference to the subject. He said he did not suppose anyone would be taken in by the Government's 'stunt'. It was 'an attempt to apply a kind of continental logic to the British people, but the British people are not that kind of people.' But Laski ploughed remorselessly on. At Croydon on the 18th June he repeated the importance of a clear understanding that 'we Socialists are only committed to decisions which result in coherence with Socialists. I have no apologies for holding that view.'

The Daily Telegraph, which from Attlee's very first intervention had talked of a 'socialist split' now proclaimed 'Major Crisis in Socialist Party'. 'Who Rules?' asked its leading article, a question echoed by the *Daily Express* with 'Who is the real boss of the party?' and extended by Mr Harold Macmillan, the Under-Secretary of State for Air, with the words 'Who is this Gauleiter Laski to tell British statesmen what they are to do?' The *Manchester Guardian* had advised Laski that he 'should trust the good sense of his countrymen and not try to force the pace.' But the pace was now forced by someone else.

On the morning of the day in which Laski spoke at Croydon there appeared in the correspondence columns of a respected provincial paper, the *Nottingham Guardian*, a letter from a Conservative Councillor, H. C. C. Carlton of East Leake who said he had heard Laski say, at a meeting in Newark that if socialist reforms could not be had by fair means 'we shall use violence to obtain them', and that when a Member of the audience had protested at this invitation to revolution Laski had repeated, 'If we cannot get reforms we desire we shall not hesitate to use violence.' 'Violence' was immediately picked up by both *Express* and *Telegraph* to fan the flames of the Laski affair.

In fact Carlton's was a slightly blurred account of what had happened at the Newark meeting. The sequence of events was that after Laski had finished his address a former *Daily Express* journalist, J. Wentworth Day, who listed among his recreations in *Who's Who* 'taking the Left-Wing intelligentsia at its own valuation,' had asked Laski why he had openly advocated revolution in two speeches in 1941. (What Laski had said then was that there was a choice between revolution by consent then or revolution after the war.) Wentworth Day said that in reply to his question at Newark, Laski had cited the French Revolution and said, 'We shall have to use violence even if it means revolution.'

THIS MAN LASKI, announced the *Express*, printing the *Nottingham Guardian* letter, together with Wentworth Day's account of the event, 'He is the Power Behind the Party.' Laski served writs for libel on both the *Nottingham Guardian* and the *Express*, effectively stopping any further specific discussion of the violence question, but in no way removing himself as a personal issue from the Election.

273

In fact on the very day on which the *Express* published the news of the writ, its OPINION leader column, while technically refraining from any further comment on the matter of violence sailed reasonably close to the *sub judice* wind with the words, 'The Socialist Party is a many-headed monster. . . . But there is one notion in every head. And that is: socialist revolution even if it means the wholesale slaughter of the ancient rights and liberties of the people . . .'

To judge the effect of all this on voters' minds was no easier than it was to determine the trend in general of the election. The *Express* was after all the largest circulation paper in the country, and indeed the world, being able to announce for the month a record sale of 3,300,000 copies. The *Wall Street Journal* was of the opinion that 'Professor Laski's exhibition of the Führer complex' had given Labour a bad start; it was the disunity displayed in the party that made the worst impression. *The Times* reported that it had caused much embarrassment to Labour. It was to be several days before Attlee himself again alluded to the matter in public.

'Red Herring' was the *Daily Herald*'s summing-up of the affair. In fact it had not been above trying to distract attention with an anti-Tory foreign affairs scare of its own. 'This is the Election Cry the Tories Fear,' it had run its headline two days after Laski's first intervention, 'A Vote For Churchill Is A Vote For Franco.' And since it was to the conduct of foreign policy that the Laski issue immediately applied there was some general attempt on Labour's part to discredit Conservative foreign policy in the past. The arrest which had just taken place in Germany of the fugitive Ribbentrop inspired Tom O'Brien to ask at his adoption meeting for Nottingham West on the 18th June, 'Who fêted Ribbentrop? Not the Workers. The very people who are now claiming to be "National" fawned and flattered him. They vied with each other for his favours and smiles. Ribbentrop was never seen in the houses and haunts of the people, but in the salons and clubs of the Tory privileged classes.'

Aneurin Bevan who on the 17th June had already revealed that 'the Labour Party can speak a language the Soviet people understand' told 7,000 Metro-Vickers workers from the top of an air-raid shelter outside their factory in Manchester on the 20th that after the last war, Britain had helped wreck any international system of peace and that after this one 'unless Russian suspicion of British and American capitalism were removed there is no chance of preventing a third war.' Sir Stafford Cripps, in a broadcast on the 21st, said it did not bode well for the country that so many of Mr Chamberlain's collaborators (sic) were back again in the revived Tory Government.

But, in any case, the importance or otherwise of foreign affairs was an

274

uncertain element in the election. The *Daily Mirror* banked on other priorities and dealt with the whole Laski issue as a subject for contemptuous dismissal under a leader headline, 'EYES ON THE TARGET'.

'There are a lot of electioneering games going on,' it wrote. 'In particular there is "Bogey Man", a game specially designed to scare those who possess a childish mentality . . .' And it listed the four vital issues of the election in order as Housing, Full Employment, Social Security and International Co-operation. It conceded that all parties believed in these things and had put them in their programmes but said that the record of the past was the only way to decide which of them really believed in such things.

'Examine the records of the parties,' the *Mirror* said. 'If you do you will find that the men who failed to keep their pledges in the past are the same men who are now diverting attention from their record by trying to frighten the electors with stunts about revolutionary violence and totalitarian rule.'

When Attlee did finally speak out on Laski it was in such a way as to gain in effect from his delay, for he treated the subject as one which need never have excited any fuss in the first place and thus enabled his earlier rebuke to the Party Chairman to be forgotten. Asked by a questioner at Mile End on the evening of 25th June if it might not be a question of 'mein Führer Laski' he said it was curious that the Conservatives had not realised the nature of his relationship with the executive of the Labour Party during all these years. (A telling point, since it had been exactly the same throughout the five years he had been Deputy Prime Minister and no one had ever brought it up before.) 'Everyone knows,' he went on, 'that our policy is settled by the rank and file. The carrying out of that policy is for the Parliamentary Labour Party when it is meeting. . . . Mr Laski is Chairman of the Labour Executive for one year. That's all there is in this. It's an absolute ramp put up by people who pretend not to understand.'

*

Difficulty in assessing the way the election was going was made greater by the fact that though most candidates and observers, particularly on the Left, said that there was noticeable interest (in London the shortage of available halls for meetings as a result of bomb damage or official occupation was a problem), there had not yet, except in the newspapers, seemed to be a great deal of excitement. The *Manchester Guardian* in an article headed 'How Is The Electoral Fight Going?' said 'they would give their heads off at party headquarters to get even an approximately trustworthy answer to the question. There never was such an electoral "leap in the dark." ' So many voters had never taken part in elections before or even attended political meetings. There was not the same contact as in previous elections between the party organisations and the electorate. The considered utterances of the leaders were now confined through the microphone to 'the void' and no one knew what the millions were making of them in the privacy of their homes. The suspicion was growing that 'Disgusted Elector' of *The Times* might not be alone in becoming bored with them.

The overseas service vote was particularly inscrutable. The *Manchester Guardian* reported bewilderment about the election among the British Forces in Germany saying that the transformation of Churchill from national leader into the man who made the 'Gestapo' speech had puzzled men everywhere and that the continued 'mud-slinging' in the election had 'added to a general feeling of dazed incomprehension.' The *Mirror* was publishing pro-Labour servicemen's letters such as one from 'a whole roomful of hard-hitting commandos' which urged 'all servicemen to stand up for their rights and give Labour a fair chance.'

A few opinion-sounding indices were available though there was no great confidence in their reliability. The *News Chronicle* had published the result of a Gallup poll on the 28th May, before the campaign started. This, in answer to the question, 'If there were a General Election tomorrow, how would you vote?' gave 40% Labour, 24% Conservative, 12% Liberal and the rest Others or not voting. Little attention seemed to be paid to it. The *News Chronicle* itself correctly pointed out that since in the last election twice as many Labour votes were needed to win a seat as Conservative, it was not a very accurate guide as to who would actually win the Election. Moreover service voters had not been included. More than a fortnight later, on the 15th June (before the Laski 'scare'), the *Daily Express* published the result of a straw poll which it said had been conducted in 500 constituencies. The result gave the Conservatives a majority of 58 over all other parties: 49 Socialist gains were projected and 21 Conservative losses.

Three days later a Centre of Public Opinion poll published answers to the question: 'Whom Would You Like To See As Prime Minister After The General Election?' The results were:

Churchill	48%
Eden	18%
Attlee	13%
Bevin	5%
Cripps	4%
Morrison	4%
Sinclair	1%
Greenwood	1%

Except for the improvement in Attlee's own rating this seemed to indicate little basic change from the similar poll the previous autumn. The overwhelming majority for Churchill may have had something to do with an idea which Sir William Beveridge as a Liberal was putting forward, namely that it was somehow possible to throw out the Tories and yet retain Churchill as a national leader. (Churchill went out of his way to repudiate this, taking the opportunity to add that he hoped many Liberals would indeed support the 'National Government' and put country before party.)

Working thus in the dark were the political commentators who at least had to appear to have something to work on. Those on the Left tended to say the Left was doing well, those on the Right, the Right. The *Manchester Guardian* political correspondent went no further than to say that he thought the chances of Labour's securing a majority of between 30 and 40 seats were difficult to assess. But he did discern 'a general opinion that there had been a big swing of feeling to the left.'

Reporting from Birmingham where there were 10 Conservative seats in 12 constituencies, a Special Correspondent of the *Manchester Guardian* found the Tory party on the defensive. Many Labour Party workers there believed that there was a chance of capturing as many as six of these seats, though the Conservatives, putting their faith in the great political machine which Joseph Chamberlain had bequeathed the City, derided the idea as ridiculous. As the Special Correspondent pointed out, an upset of this nature for the Tories had occurred in 1929. '. . . But can it be said that the wind blows as propitiously for Labour as in 1929? . . . All the careful observers of sign and portents are prepared to say at the moment is that the breezes are variable and the Tory barometer shows a tendency to fall.'

The barometer of the London Stock Exchange told a different story. The market which had fallen quite sharply with the uncertainty introduced by the announcement of the election, had steadied and begun to develop an increasingly strong undertone by the third week in June. The *Daily Telegraph*'s City column commented, 'There seems little doubt that while the more cautious are still content to keep to the sidelines, the bolder type of investor has begun to take a sufficiently optimistic view of the Conservative prospects of victory to justify buying on a moderate scale.'

A great fillip was then given to Conservative confidence by the one stirring public event of the election, something in the nature of a triumphal tour which Churchill made of the Midlands, the North of England and part of Scotland in the last week of June.

Travelling by car during the day and joining each night a special train which he used as a mobile office for his work as Prime Minister

277

and Minister of Defence, as well as somewhere in which to sleep, he was, as he moved up through Britain, greeted everywhere with a rapturous enthusiasm which newspapers of every political persuasion faithfully reported, though those which did not share his politics remained unclear how far the affection expressed for him was for him as Party Leader and how far for him as a national hero. Known to the British people throughout the war from photographs, newsreels and his rallying eloquence in the intimacy of radio, Churchill had in fact been seen in person only by Londoners and then not frequently. Now he was touring Britain for the first time since 1940.

The tour was in a way a belated climax to the celebrations of VE Day. Churchill himself, continually maintaining that he was standing in the interests of a National Government may have found it easy to blur his rôle. One of his most heartfelt pleas in the course of the tour was to electors 'not to throw away their votes and leave me with a weak and feeble Government incapable of carrying out the people's party's programme.' The *Manchester Guardian* reported that the crowd which greeted him in that city was probably the largest ever assembled there. *The Times* wrote that the scene was 'astonishing for the vastness of the assembly and the cordiality of their welcome. Scores of thousands were surging and eddying round his car.' 'It was,' wrote the *Guardian*, 'the magnificent reception that everyone expected and it is his due. It is his victory tour and the people are right in paying him tribute as a national hero. Whether that means that a cheer for the victor preludes a blank cheque for the Party Leader is more disputable.'

It was noticeable that in Lancashire he was astute enough to remind audiences of his first loyalties in politics which had been to the Liberals. At Oldham he said; 'I am as much a Liberal as I am a Tory. I don't understand why the Liberals are pretending to differ from us.' The next day he took care to quote from the former Liberal Leader, Asquith. It was arguable however that people had come to see him rather than listen to him. *The Times* seemed to confirm this when it reported how in Manchester, perhaps because the loudspeakers were not working properly, he was quite inaudible less than 20 yards away throughout his 15-minute address. 'But nothing could have exceeded the manifest pleasure, good humour and affection with which people watched him talking into the microphone, making occasional gestures and ending by taking off his hat and waving it vigorously.' On the way to Oldham the streets were filled with many thousands of workpeople, men in dungarees and girls in bright overalls who had left their factories to greet him.

For the *Daily Express* the triumphal tour was simply further confirmation of a foregone conclusion. 'Churchill's joyous reception,' it commented, 'over hundreds of miles of fair England which might have felt the German jackboot shows that the people have not forgotten his contribution to their steadiness and calm in the evil days. Yesterday's scenes represent an immense encouragement to Mr Churchill that he is also the man the people expect to beat Japan and bring the armies in the east home again quickly.'

In Glasgow he received probably the most tumultuous welcome anywhere in his whole journey. A great line of Tory cars had wound their way through Lanarkshire, Stirlingshire and Linlithgowshire, counties dotted here and there with coalmines, shipyards and iron works. When it arrived at Ibrox and Shettleston in Glasgow there was, reported the *Express*, 'a tempest of cheering and shouting and flag-waving, compared with which even some of the exciting scenes which the Prime Minister had seen this week were a mild vapour. Down through the Paisley Road, past rows and rows of typical Glasgow tenements, there were masses of girls standing on lorries, families were leaning out of the tenement windows, men from the Clydeside in their boiler suits were waving their arms and cheering.'

In Sauchiehall Street ticker-tape snowed from the windows and everywhere on the pavements was a solid block of people, with office girls perched on window-frames sometimes fifty to sixty feet up. In Edinburgh he addressed a crowd of 50,000 cheering Scotsmen and women in Princes Street Gardens, speaking with relish of 'a certain Mr Laski.' And here again he said he wanted a large majority and added, 'It is no use people saying you can vote for the Liberals and Labour and "the old man" will be in it anyhow.'

The next day Churchill returned to London, having travelled more than a thousand miles in four days and made about forty speeches. Obviously deeply satisfied by the warmth of his reception, he appeared somewhat tired but in good health and high spirits. The next night he gave his fourth and last election broadcast. Having expressed with some moving sincerity his gratitude for the reception on his tour he put forward in equally simple terms what was plainly the strongest single case for a vote for his party in the election. 'It may be,' he said, 'the last time I shall so address you through this medium as Prime Minister. That rests with you. I am convinced that I can help you through the dangers and difficulties of the next few years with more advantage than would fall to others, and I am ready to do my best. I await your answer. It must be Aye or No.'

He then reverted to what had clearly been decided was the most effective tactical point scored by his party in the course of the election, what he called 'the Laski episode'. He drew attention to the fact that Laski had in no way withdrawn his instructions to the Labour Party.

'On the contrary, he has shown himself the master of forces too strong for Mr Attlee to challenge by any effective counter-action.' 27 members of Labour's National Executive, few of whom were Privy Counsellors, would have to discuss the most difficult and secret aspects of foreign policy including military matters and they would be primarily responsible to the Crown or to Parliament. He concluded by stating his belief in 'the instinctive wisdom of our well-tried democracy. I am sure,' he said, 'they will speak now in ringing tones and that their decision will vindicate the hopes of our friends in every land and will enable us to march in the vanguard of the United Nations in majestic enjoyment of our fame and power.'

After a day's rest on Sunday, July 1st he was out on the road again on Monday evening, touring the west, south-west and north of London, looking, as *The Times* said, fit and fresh, smoking a long cigar and wearing a dark overcoat and the type of hat which he had made famous. There were cheers everywhere he went, with some occasional booing from hecklers, but only at Paddington where he tried to speak for Brendan Bracken was he unable to make himself heard. At Camden Town and again at Holloway there was a somewhat mixed reception but, according to *The Times*, 'it was undoubtedly a friendly people who listened to him. There was some booing, but above all the cries of "Good old Winnie" resounded.'

The following day, Tuesday, 3rd July, Churchill addressed at Walthamstow Stadium in London his biggest meeting of the whole campaign and, as it turned out, one of the stormiest of his long career. He spoke from a platform draped in red, white and blue, supported by 28 Conservative candidates from various London constituencies. Charles Curran, the candidate for Walthamstow West opened the proceedings and it became clear at once that hecklers were not overawed by the national colours or by the presence of Churchill behind them. 'Every time he mentioned Churchill's name,' wrote *The Times* the next day, 'there was a strong barrage of boos mingled with cheers.'

When Churchill himself rose to speak, shielding his eyes from the evening sun with a black felt hat he had borrowed, the boos and catcalls started at once, although the cheers were louder still. 'This is a peculiar meeting,' he began unperturbed, 'in which both sides are taking part.' He made a great play of testing the microphone. 'Are we downhearted?' he asked, and secured the required thundering response: 'No!'

He then went on to make a distinction between, on the one hand, the right to cheer and boo politicians as much as one liked, which was one of the freedoms for which the war had been fought ('The winners cheer,' he added, 'and the beaten boo!') and, on the other, interruptions intended to stop free speech. That was the sort of thing that Hitler and

Mussolini had stood for. 'Anyone,' he said, getting into his stride, 'who interrupts in an organised manner a great public gathering is guilty of those very crimes which our soldiers have swept away across Europe with fire and sword.'

He said he had come to this, the first great meeting he had addressed in London to say first of all something that was not at all controversial: to congratulate London on her wonderful record in the war. 'Would you like to boo that?' he added. There was silence, but interruptions soon started again. 'There has been a gentleman on my left,' said Churchill at one point, 'who keeps hollering about policies. I will answer his enquiry. Our policy is in the first place to beat Japan.'

There were loud cheers at this. But loud interruptions started again when he brought up the need for homes and houses after the bombing and the loss of six years' building work. A statement that 350,000 houses had been built in one year before the war caused the most trouble. 'Look out,' said Churchill. 'Hold on to your chairs. This one you will not like – two-thirds of those houses were built by private enterprise. Have a good boo about that; have a good boo – private enterprise!'

Six years of building at that rate had been lost in addition to all the houses the bombing had destroyed. When he himself posed the question: 'Why have we not repaired and rebuilt those houses?' there were interruptions from all over the stadium and this increased to what *The Times* described as 'pandemonium' when Churchill skilfully closed the trap into which he had enticed his hecklers.

'Well,' he said, 'you can ask Mr Attlee and Mr Bevin, and that great London hero Mr Herbert Morrison –' he had to wait a while before he could finish his sentence, '– because if we are to blame, they are to blame too. But some of the Socialists and Labour's friends will be relieved to hear that I do not think they were to blame, nor are we. The reason why –' here Churchill had to stop for the booing, to which characteristically he allowed full rein: 'Another two minutes will be allowed for booing if you like.' And when the audience took advantage of this, he added: 'Get it off your chest all right.'

When he started again, he said the reason why we did not build – here an organised chant of 'We want Labour!' started up and he interpolated: 'That is exactly the cause – we want the labour.' The builders were at the war, we could have had houses but the war would have been dragging on from summer into the winter. 'That is the excuse I offer on behalf of Mr Attlee, Mr Bevin, and Mr Morrison – and of myself.'

The rest of his speech continued in much the same manner. In addition to the determination to build more houses he drew attention to what he called the 'Four years plan' to implement Beveridge's 'great insurance scheme which covers everybody from the cradle to the grave' and a planned development of the health services and implementation of the Education Bill. To renewed and repeated cries of 'We want Labour!' he said that the enormous tasks ahead could be achieved 'provided we are not thrown into foolish faction fights about idiotic ideologies and philosophical dreams of absurd Utopias – a world which will only be seen by great improvement of the human heart and the human head –'

To the booing which broke out at this Churchill said; 'I am sorry that one hurts – but I repeat – improvement of human hearts and human heads before we can achieve the glorious Utopia that the Socialist wool-gatherers place before us. Now, where is the boo party? I shall call them hence forward in my speech the booing party – everyone have a good boo – where I think the booing party are making such a mistake is dragging all this stuff across the practical tasks we have to fulfil. They are spoiling the tasks that have to be done in order to carry out their nightmares. They have no chance of carrying them out. They are going to be defeated at this election in a most decisive manner . . .'

When one of the Conservative candidates proposed a vote of thanks to Churchill he said, accurately enough that the majority of the audience had been with him, and this was in itself greeted with rounds of applause. Nevertheless the extent of the booing had been a surprise to many, for all Churchill's skills in dealing with it. In expressing his thanks for the vote of thanks he added, 'I give my entire forgiveness to the booers. They have this to take away with them – I am sure they are going to get a thrashing such as their party has never received since it was born.' He then embarked on a drive through some of the north and north-east London constituencies, making a number of impromptu speeches, in the course of which he continued to receive a mixed if, as *The Times* put it, 'preponderatingly loyal' reception.

That the Labour leader, Attlee, had his own sharp skill was demonstrated the same evening when he replied immediately to a letter he received from Churchill at 11.30 p.m. This was the final stage of the 'Laski episode'. Churchill drew attention to the phraseology in the Labour party's constitution to the effect that 'The work of the party shall be under the direction and control of the party conference . . .' and that the executive committee of the Labour party 'shall, subject to the control and directions of the party conference, be the administrative authority of the party'.

Attlee's reply was characteristically terse: 'I am surprised that you, who are apparently becoming acquainted with the constitution of the Labour Party for the first time, should . . . seek to attach to its provisions meanings other than those accepted by myself and others who have spent years in the service of the Labour Party. Much of your trouble is due to your not understanding the distinction between the Labour Party and the Parliamentary Labour Party. This leads you to confuse the organisational work of the party with the actions of the Parliamentary Labour Party. . . .'

However, that the charge was worrying Labour was perhaps shown by the vigour with which it was seen necessary to reject it. Herbert Morrison, speaking at East Lewisham that same night said that it was an example of the Prime Minister 'racking round the Tory garbage-bin with a view to distracting the public by bogies, inventions, scares and irrelevant matters.' He said that the public just didn't believe the fable that Labour Ministers ran their departments under the orders of the Labour Party Executive. He said he had been a member of two Cabinets and had never had the experience 'of being sat upon the ventriloquist's knee . . . and I need hardly say that I would not tolerate any such situation.'

Harold Laski himself, speaking in Essex that night said that at every election since 1918 the Conservatives had needed a scapegoat and that he had been selected for that rôle on this occasion, 'as scapegoat number one.' He said that at about 10 o'clock on July 5th (the evening before polling day) he would be returning to the obscurity from which he had emerged. The real truth was that the Tory Party had gone in for this stunt because they did not know what to say about their own policies. 'It is shameful to think that a man who up to VE Day had so eminent a reputation, should have staked that reputation by descending to matters of this kind.'

Ernest Bevin that same evening, at Streatham, sought to dispose of another scare of which the Conservatives had made consistent play, namely that only two men in the country, Churchill himself and Eden, were capable of handling Britain's foreign affairs. 'I cannot accept that view. Let me assure you that although the Labour Ministers have not taken the curtain every time, we have played our part in shaping recent great events.'

The ability thus to point to Labour's experience in government through the Coalition did indeed effectively seem to deal with what might otherwise have been a telling charge against the party, namely that in their only two periods of office, in 1924 and from 1929 to 1931 they had proved incapable of managing the nation's affairs.

There were now only some thirty hours before the greater part of the country went to the polls. The Services – who were able to vote either by proxy or by post – had already started voting by post overseas. The ballot boxes, the use of which had been scrupulously invigilated by

NCO's and Officers, were in some cases already on their way to Britain by air. In 23 constituencies specially affected by local holidays and one – East Hull – in which a candidate had died after nomination, polling was to take place a week or a fortnight later, but the national campaign came to an end with the last speeches of the evening of July 5th. Votes were to be counted on July 26th.

Churchill, touring South London on this last night, was said to be in 'supremely confident' mood, telling his audiences that he was going to let them into a government secret and, in the hush that followed, revealing: 'It is that we are going to win!' In Ernest Bevin's constituency of Wandsworth, he asked for a strong, definite result. 'How else are we going to get the houses built, the peace made, and the Japanese war finished?' To which a heckler replied, 'By voting Labour!'

But Churchill then warned that if there were a landslide to the left, it would be a signal for many countries in Europe to slide not into Socialism but Communism. 'If we go down,' he said, 'all the mountains of Europe will fall.' He left that meeting to the strains of 'Land of Hope and Glory'.

Throughout this last London tour Churchill's reception continued to be mixed, in the manner of the Walthamstow meeting of the night before. At Tooting Bec he had one of his nastiest experiences in the campaign when a youth threw a firework at him, which narrowly missed his face as it exploded. At Camberwell Green so many thousands of hostile Labour supporters massed in the roadway yelling and jeering that his car could not get through. Police had to clear a way for him. An attempt to speak outside the Southwark Conservative Offices in the Walworth Road had to be abandoned in boos and catcalls. Mounted police had to clear a path for his car. Thereafter, however, there were cheers and cries of 'Good old Winnie!' most of the way back to Downing Street.

The extent to which Churchill's dominating political personality and universally acknowledged position as the nation's successful leader in wartime would determine the result for the Conservatives was still difficult to gauge. The fact that the Conservatives throughout the campaign had no inhibition about exploiting his prestige to the full could itself be turned to Conservative disadvantage. Churchill himself could be accused of subscribing to this. Hugh Dalton, a former Coalition colleague, speaking as Labour candidate in his constituency at Bishop Auckland was able to say sadly, 'He has surrendered to the worst of his advisers and has allowed himself to be degraded into a petty Party boss.'

All this helped Labour to strengthen its strongest emotional appeal throughout the campaign, namely a protest against the sort of Britain which Tories had stood for in the 'twenties and 'thirties, a Britain of unemployment, class rule, working-class poverty and – though Churchill himself could be exonerated from this – sympathetic appeasement of that very Nazi Germany and Fascist Italy which the country had just spent six painful and exhausting years destroying. 'Mr Churchill's prestige is no more than an umbrella,' said Harold Laski, speaking on the last night of the campaign in Kensington.

On the other hand the Conservative candidate in Wembley South was proclaiming simply and point-blank, 'Are you going to sack Winston Churchill? That is the issue.' And very many people felt the force of what Mrs Churchill herself was able to say unashamedly at an eve-of-the-poll meeting in the Prime Minister's own Woodford constituency, 'I would like my husband to have a very great majority,' she said, 'and a great demonstration of your confidence in him. I would like very much for him to know that when you vote for him you do it because you feel he has done a good job of work, and that he will serve the nation well in the future.'

The reason why any meetings at all were held in the Woodford constituency even though the Labour and Liberal parties, out of respect for Churchill as war leader, had agreed not to oppose him, was that most unexpectedly there had appeared an Independent candidate in opposition to him. This was a Mr Alexander Hancock whose motives seemed somewhat obscure. He said that he had no ambition to enter Parliament himself, nor was he trying to keep Mr Churchill out. He simply wanted to focus attention on his 'philosophic plan'. The gist of this was that the necessities of life should result from a compulsory basic production by all able-bodied citizens who, he reckoned, would thus have to work no more than one hour a day. The rest of their time could be spent producing non-essential commodities. Asked if he thought he had a chance of defeating Churchill, Mr Hancock shrugged his shoulders and replied: 'Could anyone?' Certainly no one expected serious opposition to the Prime Minister from that quarter.*

On polling day *The Times* summed-up the campaign. It deplored the acrimony with which the election had been fought and particularly the fact that the constructive cases which the successors to the Coalition had been able to present had faded from view and been allowed to be dominated by the Laski affair. Whatever else was to be said of Professor Laski's indiscretions, they did not, according to the *Times*, furnish the grounds on which the nation should choose a Parliament which was

---

*Before Mr Hancock, William Douglas-Home, brother of Lord Dunglass, had announced his intention of opposing the Prime Minister at Woodford but had withdrawn early.

going to face responsibilities 'at least as heavy and even more intricate and exacting in their way than those which rested upon its predecessors in the darkest days of 1940.'

The Times found it difficult to forecast the probable result of the election. While paying full tribute to Churchill's qualities as a national leader, it suggested that he fell short of that rôle when applying his fighting spirit to his party's cause. The Gestapo jibe in his first election broadcast had shocked public opinion. This *Times* leader, which concluded simply with a clear injunction to all to cast their vote, could not be interpreted as recommending a vote for any one party, although inasmuch as it contained more strictures for Mr Churchill than for Mr Attlee it could have been seen as recommending much closer scrutiny of the Conservative Party tactics than the paper's readers had been accustomed to find in its leading articles on such occasions in the past.

The *Daily Mirror* was in no way so equivocal. While not specifically recommending its readers to vote Labour, as the *Daily Herald* did, the *Mirror* told them to vote for the men who would not be there, the men who had fought and died, and had brought victory. 'You failed to do so in 1918,' it declared. 'The result is known to all. The land "fit for heroes" did not come into existence. The dole did. Short-lived prosperity gave way to long, tragic years of unemployment. Make sure that history does not repeat itself.'

The Conservative press was assured and confident as polling day arrived. 'We trust,' the *Sunday Times* had written the weekend before, 'that the election will give the Government a majority so large that its National character will again be demonstrated to the world.'

The *Daily Express* had already decided not only that Labour had lost the election but that Labour had so decided too. 'Socialists Decide They Have Lost' was one of its last headlines. The ensuing story disclosed that orders had gone out to Labour Party election workers 'to work even harder for a big vote on Thursday, not any longer in the hope that they will lead to the election of a socialist government but to impress the Government with the fact that there is a strong opposition.'

Daily Telegraph readers of its City Column could note that the main stimulus to markets just before polling day came from 'forecasts of a large Conservative election victory.'

The *Manchester Guardian* was happy to see polling day arrive, but for a different reason. 'Today,' it wrote, 'the most hateful election in recent memory comes to a close. . . . A bad dream, a disfiguring page after a chapter of unexampled glory.' It had found the whole campaign 'hateful' because it had dismantled the splendid figure of Churchill, who had dominated the imagination of the world, and

286

turned him into a mere Tory. 'Nothing,' it summarised, 'could be worse than another House of Commons in which the Tory party was all-powerful.'

Americans had followed the whole campaign with interest but a certain tactful respect for the privacy of a British occasion. News of it occupied little space in newspapers in the United States which were more concerned with the extremely bloody fighting still continuing against Japanese trapped on Okinawa and the sombre prospect this presented for the eventual bloody assault on the Japanese home islands themselves. In such American comment on the British election as did appear there was little doubt that Churchill would be returned. 'If he and his party don't win this election,' wrote the *Daily News*, 'there is no gratitude in England.'

The *New York Times*, impressed by Churchill's last broadcast, wrote, 'What ever victory the Conservatives may achieve, they can attribute it in large measure to him.' The paper's correspondent in London, Herbert Matthews, reported that both Churchill and his party leaders seemed confident that they would get a majority of around a hundred. Other observers, he said, were more cautious. The latest Gallup poll, which had only been conducted in 195 of the 640 constituencies gave Labour a six and a half point lead. Reuter's, reporting at the end of polling day that there had been a heavy poll, said that this was in itself something favourable to Labour and that some people were predicting a close race between the Tories and Labour when the votes were counted in three weeks' time.

The fact that there was now to be this three weeks' delay both accentuated such uncertainty as might be in the air and at the same time created a sense of anti-climax as the uncertainty itself went into cold storage. 'Tonight,' wrote Herbert Matthews of the *New York Times*, 'there is a sensation like the deflation of a balloon.' He did not take the pessimistic view of the campaign which had been expressed by the *Guardian*, or agree with Michael Foot's judgment in the *Herald* that it had developed into an extremely bitter one. In comparison with an election in Italy or France, he wrote, it had been 'mild and good-humoured.'

Certainly polling day itself had passed without incident. People had voted traditionally, as one observer put it, 'quietly and without fuss'. There had, however, been a different atmosphere from that of earlier elections, wrote the *Manchester Guardian*. The speeches on the wireless had changed things. These wireless speeches were repeatedly churned out by loudspeaker vans. Concentrated election rallies of the old style with political speakers appearing like gladiators had largely disappeared. The electorate too had changed. A large part of it seemed to be at a distance from all parties and to be making their own way towards independent judgment. This detachment baffled the party managers.

It had, however, been possible to discern at Tory headquarters a certain unease about the fate of three Ministers, Ernest Brown, Harold Macmillan, and Sir James Grigg. Friends of Sir Donald Somervell, the Home Secretary, were also said to be nervous for him in his constituency at Crewe. As for Labour, Ernest Bevin was thought to be possibly in some danger at Wandsworth, though it was thought that Herbert Morrison would get home at Lewisham.

As the day of counting of votes (July 25th) approached, a certain amount of interest was focussed on the question of how the result might affect participation in the all-important conference with the Russians which had already started at Potsdam on July 17th. 'If,' wrote the *Manchester Guardian*, 'Mr Churchill finds on Thursday evening that he is in possession of a working majority, or one still bigger, he can go back to Potsdam at once. Anything else, however, must mean an interrupted conference. Were Labour returned with a working majority, Mr Attlee would have to form his Government before he could go back to Potsdam, and first he would have to find a Foreign Secretary to replace Mr Eden. He would want a week for this task.' Of course it was true that the Tory central office would say, 'Don't bother your head about these sombre contingencies. We are in with a big majority.' 'Well,' wrote the *Guardian* political correspondent, 'they may be but they do not know, and if it is a very big majority then Labour has done worse than its least optimistic managers believe.'

Talking to former MP's, one or two of them Ministers, on the eve of the Declaration, the same correspondent found that hardly one of them was prepared to risk a prediction. One unnamed Government supporter of long experience who had had a hard fight in a northern industrial constituency thought that Churchill had 'done it', but also that there would have been a marked swing to the left in industrial England and Scotland and that the Tory majority would be modest. There was pretty general agreement that the women's vote had on the whole gone to Churchill, though younger women, like those working in the munitions factories, were thought to have moved leftwards. Many seemed to agree that Labour had done better than expected in some of the counties. As for the Service vote, it seemed to have fallen far short numerically of what had been expected, but most people who had a chance of testing Service opinion thought that it too had gone to the left. One safe conclusion seemed to be, 'At the very best it's going to be no runaway victory for Churchill.'

But there were even some Labour men who would have it that there was not going to be a Conservative victory at all. One of the most sober-minded and influential of Labour leaders known to the *Manchester Guardian*'s political correspondent said that he thought it was going to be 1929 all over again.

In 1929 Labour had won 288 seats to the Tories' 260.

Chapter Twenty-Three

The British people, waiting for their election result, experienced a hiatus for the second time in two months; the end of the war in Europe had itself provided the first.

'Well,' J. B. Priestley had said in a broadcast just after VE Day, 'we are here. One long stage of the journey has been passed.' He likened the sensation to that of people who have been travelling all night in a railway carriage, and, seeing the thin grey daylight behind the blinds and feeling the slackening of the speed of the train, take down their battered suitcases and feel rather dirty, hungry, a bit empty both in mind and body – but still vaguely triumphant. 'We've arrived – yes – and it's beginning to be daylight; but the scene is grim and ruinous; and the journey must continue. There is still another war to finish. Europe . . . must be put together again. The world, which is now one indivisible whole of suffering and despair or hope and human triumph, must be nursed into something of security and growing sanity, a new sanity and not the old mere appearance of it with delusions and nightmares lying in wait.' Or, as the *News Chronicle* put it; 'We still have to settle accounts with Japan and try to make the world a place in which our youngsters can be reasonably happy. Meanwhile we took a couple of days off.'

Now with the issue of the Election in abeyance, attention could be focussed on the meeting of the Big Three due in Berlin at Potsdam on the 15th of July. The all important question was whether those three Powers would be able to keep their alliance together for peace.

In the United States there seemed less time to catch breath. There on VE Day the need to win the war against Japan had dominated public attention to a far greater extent than in Britain. In Richmond, Virginia, awareness of the fact that the war was only half won had, according to the *New York Times*, 'put a damper on any inclinations to blow the lid off.' A few wisps of ticker-tape floated conventionally out of Richmond office buildings but in general people simply stood about on street corners reading the newspapers and commenting calmly that now everything could be thrown against Japan. Almost as important it seemed was the news that Mrs Pauline C. Conlon, a dancing teacher, had just asked a Richmond Court for a divorce from her fifteenth husband, alleging that he hit her on the head with his artificial leg.

Right across the nation, with the obvious exception of New York, reports about the way in which the end of the war in Europe was received were similar. In Boston the contrast between the almost religious sense of restraint this time and the exuberance of Armistice Day, 1918 was noted. In Chatanooga the streets seemed even quieter than on a typical Monday. In New Orleans the street-sweepers said they had an easier time than after a normal New Year's Day celebrations. In Omaha there was, so the *New York Times* said, 'no more than the feeblest flicker of public emotionalism and that soon snuffed-out for want of participation.' All along the West Coast, awareness of the need to intensify the drive against Japan had been the chief reaction.

Moreover there were immediate practical considerations to dampen the general mood. Both rationing and military conscription were to continue and some two million Americans now in Europe were to be transferred to the Pacific, many of them without home leave. The more sombre mood in the United States was thus perhaps better adjusted to those difficulties with the Russians which presented the most important single aspect of the post-war world.

Since Yalta there had been disturbing fluctuations in the quality of the relationship between the Big Three. The end of the war against Germany, by removing the need to keep the Alliance together at all costs, had accentuated its fragility.

Russia had after all been in a state of co-operative neutrality towards Germany for the first twenty-one months of the war. After Germany had attacked her, her interests and those of Britain and America had coincided. But this obvious coincidence of interests was now over. There was now presumably a community of interest in a wish to preserve peace. But that was a goal hedged round with greater complications and obscurities than the pursuit of a clear-cut military objective.

There had indeed been times after Yalta and even before final victory over Germany, when relations seemed to be deteriorating sharply.

British journalists at the San Francisco Conference to establish the new organisation for world peace, in session since April 25th, had been struck by the lack of inhibition on the part of the American public about the real purpose behind the meeting. Not only were people asking, 'Would it stop wars in future?', but more specifically, 'Would it prevent a war with Russia?' Kingsley Martin, editor of the *New Statesman and Nation*, who was there at the start had found fear of Russia common and expressed everywhere. Francis Williams, editor of the *Daily Herald*, who attended the closing stages, reported a conversation in which an American friend had said to him, 'Wherever you go in America you will find the people already talking about the next war. Some of them want it soon, while we are still in trim. Some of them hate the idea of it. But a great number think it's coming. As for San Francisco, that simply convinced them that talk of co-operation in matters that really count is just silly at this stage.' Even though the Conference was to conclude with a technical success, such talk had increased considerably in the course of it and was to be found all over the United States. It summarised a sense of realism with which the Americans had emerged from the European war.

The Conference had often been held to be a sort of peace conference, though its specific purpose was only to agree the machinery of the new organisation and define its Charter. But it had been constantly attended by dark overtones from elsewhere. Even before the start a most disturbing occurrence had activated suspicion of Russia on the most sensitive of all issues between her and the West: Poland.

The Yalta agreement had prescribed a new broad-based Provisional Government of Poland to consist both of members of the Russian-recognised Provisional Government (the former Lublin Committee) and members of democratic parties other than Communist in and outside Poland. On the 10th March the London Government received a written invitation from Colonel Pimienov of the NKVD (the Soviet Secret Police) proposing that representatives of that Government in Poland should meet General Ivanov of the First White Russian Front to discuss a matter of exceptional importance. They were offered a safe-conduct and Colonel Pimienov gave his word as an officer of the Red Army that this would be honoured. The offer was accepted and conversations took place in a friendly atmosphere, the purpose of which, it was revealed, was to discuss the coming into the open of those Polish political parties which had not so far revealed themselves to the Soviets, 'in order to include them into the general current of democratic powers in an independent Poland'.

The Polish delegates asked permission to go to London to consult both the Government there and also Mr Mikolajczyk and other leaders of the opposition outside Poland. On March 20th Pimienov agreed that twelve delegates could go to London to confer and said he would make arrangements for their visit and return. On March 27th the Polish Deputy Prime Minister of the London Government, the Chairman of the Council of National Unity, together with the last Commander of the Polish Home Army, General Okulicki, presented themselves to General Ivanov in accordance with the invitation. The Polish Ministry of Information in London reported, 'They have so far not returned from

From *Punch*: 'Trouble with some of the Pieces'

this visit and have given no sign of life either to their families or to anyone else.' ·

On the 28th March three Cabinet Ministers of the London Government, together with eight members of political parties and an interpreter – twelve in all – presented themselves to the Soviet authorities for the visit to London. The Polish Ministry of Information in London reported, 'They have also not returned from this visit. There has been no further news about their fate and the whereabouts of any of those fifteen persons who had been invited by General Ivanov.' This news naturally aroused some anxiety in London and Washington but there were rumours to the effect that the fifteen missing men were in fact in Moscow discussing the constitution of a new Polish Provisional Government. By the middle of April nothing official had been heard of them.

Yalta had set up a special Commission consisting of the British and American Ambassadors, Archibald Clark Kerr and Averell Harriman to work with the Russian Foreign Minister, Molotov to implement the Polish clauses of the Yalta agreement. But the Commission seemed to know nothing of what had been taking place and the British Ambassador pressed personally for information, without result.

One new development did little to make minds easier. Vincenty Witos, leader of the Polish Peasant party for thirty years, who had been exiled by the Colonels' régime of the pre-war years and later spent some time in a German concentration camp, had also vanished, making a total of sixteen disappearances in all. There was no word from any Russian source about what was happening. 'Such reserve,' wrote the *Manchester Guardian*, 'only aggravates suspicion . . . disquiet prevails.'

In the middle of April there were further rumours that a new Polish Provisional Government had been formed in Moscow, to include Witos. But there was no official news, and even if this rumour were true, unilateral action by the Russians was a curious deviation from the Yalta agreement. In London, Mikolajczyk, hoping for the best, declared once again his acceptance and loyalty towards the decisions of Yalta. 'I consider,' he said, 'close and lasting friendship with Russia the keystone of future Polish policy . . .'

American unease was partially deflected by news on a quite different subject altogether, even closer to American hearts than Poland. On April 5th Russia exercised her right to renounce the Russian-Japanese Neutrality Pact one year before its expiry date in 1946.

The news was of the greatest significance for the future of the war in the Pacific where the Americans were only just beginning to contemplate the enormous scale and cost of the operation which they would soon have to launch against Japan. Though in theory renunciation of the Pact meant that it would end only in 1946, the terms in which Molotov had delivered the statement, accusing Japan of helping Germany in her war against the Soviet Union and saying that this deprived the Pact of any meaning, suggested clearly that Russia felt justified in skipping the technical notice period and declaring war at any time. This was at least one consequence of Yalta, kept secret at the time, which did something to compensate for Russia's unsatisfactory attitude to the clauses in the agreement concerning Poland.

One of her first demands at San Francisco had been that, in total disregard of the terms of Yalta, the Lublin Provisional Government should be present at San Francisco as the legitimate Government of Poland. On the face of it this was such an absurd demand that many commentators supposed it had been put forward only to be retracted as a concession for subtler points in Russia's favour. Outright rejection of the demand by Britain and the United States led to a denunciation from Moscow radio of 'this unfair and absolutely unjustified insult to the Polish people.' Further it was announced that the Russian Foreign Minister, Molotov, would not be attending the San Francisco Conference, and that Russia would be represented only by her Ambassador to the United States, Gromyko.

A preliminary technical dispute there had concerned an American demand for an additional two seats to equalise with the additional two seats granted at Yalta to Russia for the Ukraine and White Russia. Eventual withdrawal of the demand, followed, after the personal intervention of Truman, by a change of heart on the part of Stalin who decided to send Molotov after all, led to an opening of the Conference in a more optimistic – though still guarded – atmosphere than had at one time seemed likely. The effect of Molotov's last-minute attendance was indeed rather to make him something of a star, or at least a respected centre of curiosity, in the opening stages. His speeches were heard with particular attention.

Such prestige was to stand him in good stead when on the 4th May he suddenly announced the solution to the mystery of the missing Poles. They had all been arrested by the Russians.

The shock to Stettinius, the US Secretary of State, and Eden, the British Foreign Minister, was understandably great, particularly as only the day before Molotov had been disclaiming any knowledge of what had happened to the Poles. Now, according to a Tass Agency statement, they were accused of preparing diversionary acts in the rear of the Red Army, as a result of which more than a hundred officers and men of the Red Army had lost their lives. They were also accused of installing and maintaining illegal radio transmitters in the rear of the Red Army. Molotov added that they had not simply been engaged in diversionary activities but also in sabotage and wrecking. The London *Times* commented that three of the arrested Poles had actually been proposed by the British Government as suitable for inclusion in the future Provisional Polish Government. Another six were on the list of Mikolajczyk, the Peasant Party leader who had actually resigned as Prime Minister of the London Government because of the other members' intransigent attitude towards the Soviet Union. Indignantly the US and British Foreign Ministers suspended all further discussion of the Polish issue in protest.

The London *Times* had commented that for the Conference to have no representative from Poland, the country which had been the first to take up arms in self-defence against Hitler, would be 'a singularly inept and unhappy augury'. The Conference not only so began but continued to be without any representative of Poland throughout its deliberations. There were expressions of the deepest concern in Britain and the United States over what seemed a flagrant violation of the Yalta agreement. Mikolajczyk issued a statement making clear that all the arrested Poles were in favour of co-operation with the Soviet Union. He repeated that they had specifically made a request to London that they should come out into the open in response to the Soviet invitation. He added two factual pieces of news. Witos, taken away on the 31st March, had returned home after five days. But there had been further arrests in addition to the original fifteen. 'Most of these men,' said Eden at a press conference on the 10th May, 'were just the type who should, in our view, have been consulted about the new National Government in Poland.'

Thus in the very first days of peace, while in San Francisco the Big Three and lesser powers laboriously but conscientiously defined the mechanism of the new United Nations Organisation to maintain that peace, the Big Three were themselves so disastrously split on an issue of fundamental importance that only by ignoring it and removing it temporarily from all further discussion were they able to proceed with their relationship at all. It was, as *The Times* had predicted, an unhappy augury.

The need to proceed as if the issue did not exist was seen at a small ceremony which took place in Moscow on the day after Eden's press conference. Mrs Winston Churchill was visiting Russia as President of the International Red Cross, which had been of help to the Russian people in their years of suffering, and was acknowledged to have been so by Stalin himself. At this ceremony it was actually Mrs Molotov who conveyed the Soviet people's thanks. She presented Mrs Churchill with a diamond ring. 'I hope,' she said, 'this ring will continue to gleam in years ahead as a bright symbol of Anglo-Soviet friendship.' The gulf which now separated the two countries over Poland might not have existed.

A week later Stalin openly addressed the British people on the question of Poland, replying in public to a letter in which *The Times* correspondent in Moscow had asked him for clarification. Stalin began with a human enough apology for the fact that the reply was some eight days late. 'But this,' he wrote, 'is understandable if one bears in mind how busy I am.' The rest of the letter was unconcerned with niceties. The arrest of the Poles, said Stalin, was in no way connected with the question of the reconstruction of the Polish Provisional Government. They had been arrested by virtue of the law dealing with the safeguarding of the rear of the Red Army, 'analogous to the British law of the Defence of the Realm.' It was not true that they had been invited for any negotiations. The Soviet Union did not negotiate with law-breakers. The concluding sentence of the letter had a surrealist flavour: 'As regards the question of the reconstruction of the Polish Provisional Government,' said Stalin, 'this can only be settled on the basis of the Crimean resolution.'

The London *Times* produced a leading article once more reminiscent in softness of tone of its appeasement leaders in the late 1930's. The question of the guilt of those arrested must, it said, be left to be determined in the forthcoming judicial proceedings. It pointed out that Stalin's denial that the Poles had been invited did not in itself represent any conflict with the statement that some of the names had been put forward by the British and American Governments as possible candidates for the new Provisional Polish Government. It found the Russians' lack of candour regrettable, together with the fact that unwarrantable statements about the Poles' 'mission' to Moscow had been allowed to circulate. But no such reservations prevented the paper from accepting Stalin's statement about Yalta as 'ground for encouragement'. In any case the main story in the news concerned the growing feeling that a meeting between Churchill, Truman and Stalin offered the best hope of straightening out difficulties between the three. The next day it was announced that the President's advisor Harry Hopkins was going to Moscow while Joe Davies of the State Department was travelling to London. The White House press secretary said that a meeting of the Big Three was in the offing, though he did not say where or when it was likely to take place.

Certainly something of this sort seemed needed. At San Francisco, there had been an increasing polarisation of Eastern and Western attitudes in disputes over details of the new United Nations Organisation mechanism. The London *Sunday Times* correspondent in the States, Kenneth Crawford, reported that the Anglo-American relationship was now more cordial than at any time at the height of the war. Conversely, difficulties between the American and the Russian delegations – often aggravated by the need for the Russians to delay the issue of points in dispute by referring them to Moscow for decision – had dramatised a growing gulf in American-Russian understanding. Anti-Russian views on foreign affairs were now a majority view at San Francisco though two prominent American commentators, Drew Pearson and Walter Lippmann, stressed the need not to let Russia get the feeling that her former allies were ganging-up on her. 'If German aggression is to be ended for ever,' wrote Lippmann, 'the United Nations must renounce any notion that they are setting up an organisation here to police the Soviet Union. . . . At the bottom of all Soviet policy, of all Soviet suspicion, there is the determination to counteract the powerful interests in the western world which, though they do not avow it, openly have this purpose in mind.'

A bizarre situation which had aroused Soviet suspicions, at least for effective propaganda purposes, was that which the Western Allies had allowed to continue after the German surrender at Flensburg. Here the vestiges of the Third Reich's Government, under Hitler's successor as Führer, Dönitz, had been allowed to continue in being with former German Ministers such as Speer and the new Foreign Minister Schwerin von Krogisk holding office together with General Jodl, Hitler's Chief of Staff and Admiral Friedeburg, Commander-in-Chief of the German Navy. Here they had had their headquarters in a naval barracks, while one of their Generals, General Lindemann, guarded by steel-helmetted Germans carrying rifles and wearing Nazi emblems, maintained an independent presence in Denmark. It was all indistinguishable, though now only in miniature, from the governmental apparatus which had held down Europe for the past five years. Behind this grotesque phenomenon there was a certain temporary logic. Many hundreds of thousands of German troops had to be controlled, kept under discipline and fed. The simplest administrative way of doing this was to allow their Commanders to continue to take responsibility for them. At times such a principle was to achieve obscene effects as when the German Commander in Holland, General Blaskowitz, who had summoned his troops to continue to fight for the Führer in memory even after his death, borrowed, after the surrender, ten rifles and 100 rounds of ammunition from the Canadians so that his disarmed troops could shoot for desertion five of his men who had attempted to make off home. The narrow military logic of this short-term procedure brought with it dangerous political pitfalls.

Dönitz and his entourage at Flensburg, granted pragmatic status by the Western Allies, continued to act as if they had acquired it by right.

For the first week after the surrender, Flensburg radio, while passing on Allied orders, had continued to broadcast for its own purposes, referring to itself as the 'Reichsrundfunk' and conveying the last greetings from commanders of the garrisons at Dunkirk and in the Channel Islands. Its news commentaries made a point of stressing the divergencies of opinion between the Western Allies and the Soviet Union.

Field-Marshal Busch broadcast as 'Commander of all military and civil authorities in Schleswig-Holstein and the areas of the troops occupied by Field-Marshal Montgomery' as if somehow those military and civil authorities enjoyed an identity distinct from Montgomery's occupation. Dönitz even suggested that his present authority might be of indefinite duration. He said in a broadcast that it would rest with the occupying powers 'whether or not I and the Reich Government appointed by me will be able to function'. Schwerin von Krogisk proposed to the Allies the appointment of a certain Wilhelm Stuckhardt as Minister of the Interior and Culture. The man had been Himmler's deputy and an SS General.

The Yalta Agreement had specifically decreed the break-up of the German General Staff, yet here at Flensburg was a nucleus which could ensure its perpetuation. After the somewhat fulsome acceptance of Goering's surrender this maintenance of a skeleton form of the Third Reich at Flensburg aroused indignant protest both in the Soviet Union and the liberal press of the West.

Sensitive to this, Eisenhower's headquarters put out a statement on May 11 to the effect that the Germans at Flensburg were prisoners of war, yet this did not alter the fact that the 'Ministers' continued in being with their secretaries and offices and their own steel-helmeted guards in the naval barracks at Flensburg. The London *News Chronicle* conceded that temporary maintenance of the German High Command had been useful in disarming the enormous number of troops in Schleswig-Holstein but, it added, 'Only extreme political blindness can excuse this parody of government. The harm done to our relations with Russia can easily be seen by anyone who takes the trouble to study the Soviet press in the past week. It is difficult to imagine anything more likely to arouse Soviet suspicion (never a very difficult matter) than the whole of the Flensburg episode.' By the time the decision was taken, on the 23rd May, to place the 5,000 Germans in the Flensburg 'Government' including 300 high-ranking officers, under close arrest, the damage had been done.

'The hard, harsh fact which must be faced,' wrote the liberal British commentator Vernon Bartlett of the two halves of the Alliance, 'is that there is now more distrust between these nations than at any other time since Hitler and the Japanese brought them together.' The *Manchester*

Guardian wrote on the 19th May that it would be foolish not to recognise that there had been recently a growth of cynicism about the state of international relations which had some most alarming signs, and confirmed that there was increasing talk in the United States of a third World War; '. . . a sign of how far we have drifted from those high principles to which the three major Allies have pledged themselves and how remote has become the picture of close working co-operation in the treatment of the defeated enemy and the rehabilitation of the liberated peoples which, after Teheran and Yalta, we had all set before us. The moral deflation of the Allies has been as spectacular in its way as the military collapse of the Germans.'

To remedy this situation a new initiative had plainly been required. As at the time of Yalta, only a Big Three Conference could be expected to supply resolution of outstanding problems, or if such were not available, the crafted appearance of such a thing. Hence the relief with which the White House press secretary's announcement of the forthcoming meeting was received on both sides of the Atlantic. Furthermore, the omens for it were given a newly-favourable look by an unexpected development in the Polish situation. While there was as yet no further news of the arrested Poles it was announced from Moscow on the 12th June that the three-man commission established at Yalta to deal with Poland (the two Western Ambassadors there and Molotov) was inviting democratic leaders from Poland and outside to meet in the Russian capital with members of the present acting Polish Provisional Government to discuss a new Polish Provisional Government of National Unity. There were to be four members of the present Acting Provisional Government: Bierut, Osubka-Morawski, Kowalski, and Gomulka. The three democratic leaders from abroad (*i.e.* London) were to be Mikolajczyk, Stanczyk and Zakowski. There were to be five 'democratic leaders' from Poland itself but the only one of these widely-known was the former leader of the Peasant Party and pre-war Prime Minister, Vincenty Witos. At least two of the others were understood to be supporters of the former Lublin Committee and one of them, a non-party economist and historian named Kutrzeba, had been given the post of Rector of Cracow University by that Committee.

Though *The Times* admitted that there was some disappointment in Polish circles that the choice of 'democratic leaders' from Poland had not been more widely made, it hurried to express a profound sense of relief: 'Satisfaction,' it stated in a leader, 'will be general that at long last effect is being given to the Crimean compromise, and strong hopes are now held that a solution of a difficulty which has poisoned relations among the three major Powers . . . has been found.'

News that the third member of the London trio, Julian Zakowski, declined to go to Moscow did not dampen *The Times*' enthusiasm. It warmed to its theme the next day, repeating that profound satisfaction had been felt everywhere and that a new approach to unity among the Big Three promised well for their forthcoming meeting. It felt confident enough to revile the Polish London Government, still the only official Polish Government recognised by Britain and the United States: 'The presence in London of the reactionary and intransigent Polish Government whose anti-Russian proclivities have been no secret has not been the least of the many obstacles in the way of a settlement.' Success of the negotiations now, it continued, would lead automatically to the joint recognition by the three Powers of a Provisional Government and this step would by itself go a long way towards removing 'the wholly unnecessary friction which the Polish imbroglio has generated.'

News that Witos, the best-known of all the non-Communist political figures, was after all too unwell to make the journey to Moscow – still affected, it was said, by the stroke he had suffered in a German concentration camp – and that the replacement for Zakowski in the London trio was to be Anton Kolodzief, a former Secretary of the Polish Seamen's Union in London – the first external body to come out in favour of the Lublin Committee – did nothing to undermine the general feeling of relief to which *The Times* gave expression.

Talks between the groups of Poles began on June 17th. It was thought a hopeful sign that Mikolajczyk had brought a good deal of luggage with him, not presumably expecting to return to London in a hurry. The Soviet press published two further items of news on the same day. The first was that a village in Poland had been attacked on the 6th June by persons dressed in Polish uniform, describing themselves as members of the National Armed Forces; 194 civilians had been killed. The second was that the trial was opening that day of those other Poles who had hoped to be able to take part in such a meeting but who had been arrested instead. The Soviet press confirmed that there were now, as Mikolajczyk had revealed earlier, eighteen of these.

The Poles continued to meet for four days under the auspices of the Three-Power Commission, though without its participation, and on the 22nd June it was announced that full agreement had been achieved and that a new Polish Provisional Government was to be constituted. The two democratic leaders from Poland who were to become part of it were Kiernik, who had replaced Witos, and Wyceka, while Mikolajczyk, Stanczyk and a new addition, Thugutt, were to join from London. These five were to be in a minority of more than three to one.

The names, apart from Mikolajczyk, meant little to most people in the west. The fact that agreement along the lines of Yalta could now be said to have been reached meant everything. Walter Lippmann wrote that never before had there been a more representative Polish conference and that there was little doubt that genuine agreement had at last been reached on what the Yalta formula meant. 'We must not assume,' he said, 'as many of us do, that being a neighbour to the Soviet Union, Poland's independence must be a sham.'

All that remained to be done now before the United States and Britain recognised the new Government was for a pledge on free, secret and unfettered elections on the basis of universal suffrage to be given, to complete the provisions agreed at Yalta. It could be assumed that the necessary steps for this would be taken in the course of the forthcoming Three-Power meeting.

In the mild sense of euphoria which now prevailed, few remembered what the British Foreign Secretary, Eden had said immediately after Yalta: 'We would not recognise a Government which we did not think representative. The addition of one or two Ministers would not meet our views. It must be, or so far as it can be made, representative of the Polish political parties as they are known and include representatives of national political figures. This is what we mean.' It could be said of course, with truth, that five additional Ministers were a great deal better than one or two.

Alexander Werth reporting for the *Sunday Times* from Moscow the 'warm and cordial' atmosphere in which the agreement had been achieved and the consequent feeling in Moscow that the only serious obstacle to Anglo-US-Russian relations had been removed, felt it necessary to add, 'It should be emphasised that this was not in any sense a Munich.'

The need to feel that things were coming right again within the Big Three Alliance, or at least that they were not going disastrously wrong, was compulsive. Wrangles at San Francisco and the earlier gloom over the Polish situation, had produced much unease. 'Europe's situation a month after victory,' the London *Sunday Times* had written on the 10th June, 'remains difficult and dangerous and for many more months it is likely to continue so. . . . Let us make no mistake about it. The urgent problem is not this or that San Francisco amendment . . . it is the reaction of the Big Three to one another. . . . Nothing less than a negotiation at the highest level at a conference of Churchill, Truman and Stalin – holds promise of removing these disagreements.'

Peripheral problems added to the general anxiety. In Vienna the Russians had unilaterally set up an Austrian Government in which the only strong active personalities, including the Minister of the Interior, were Communists. There had been tension in Trieste between Allied troops and Tito's Partisans. The Russians complained with some justification that the Western Allies were slow in dealing with war criminals. Most prominent Nazis had been captured in the western-occupied territories but not one of them had yet been tried. A delay in repatriating Soviet citizens taken prisoner in German uniforms of one sort or another had led to sharp complaints from the Russian General Golikov, in charge of such matters. The clear Russian intention of regarding those territories occupied by the Red Army as their own spheres of influence and their refusal to allow access there to western journalists added to the general sense of mutual mistrust. The west was open to Soviet journalists; every place the Russians occupied was shut off from the world and nothing known about it but what they themselves chose to reveal. At San Francisco at the beginning of June when so much detail for the new organisation seemed at last to have been successfully agreed, all was for a moment in jeopardy as the Russians insisted that not only Security Council action but discussion as well should be subject to the veto. Only personal intervention by President Truman with Stalin himself resolved the crisis with a Russian withdrawal.

The strong wish for a good relationship between the United States and Russia was expressed in an article by Henry Wallace, Roosevelt's one-time Vice-President, in the *New Republic*. Western Europe, he said, was no longer the centre of world power. This now lay between America and Russia, who had something important in common inasmuch as neither of them believed in colonies. Both however believed in peace and claimed to respect the rights of small nations though they had 'occasionally stepped over the line' where national defence was concerned. But he stressed the potential bond, quoting an article from *Pravda* which revealed how at Teheran in 1943 the British had blocked discussion of a plan put forward by the Russians and supported by the United States for 'an early liberation of the entire colonial world.'

There was indeed some discomfort in Washington that the State Department was sometimes seen merely as the tail of the British kite, and a recent diversion from the main stream of international events, in the Middle East, had illustrated such potential embarrassment in curious fashion. In Syria, de Gaulle's Provisional French Government, picking up the tangled vestiges of the old French League of Nations Mandate, had moved against nationalist elements there, and had gone so far as to bomb Damascus. The British had intervened to put a stop to the fighting. This could hardly be seen as anything but an impeccably anti-colonial intervention, though there were those in Washington who accused the British pot of calling the French kettle black. Some also suspected that the British might use the resulting sympathy they acquired with the Arabs as an aid to restriction of Jewish immigration into Palestine, and of course the opening of the concentration camps had made this a newly urgent issue. But the State Department supported the British action, and there could be no grounds for criticism of it on the part of the Soviet Union. Nevertheless there was some feeling in Washington that for the United States to be an independent mediator, whatever the problem, was more in accord with the new realities of the post-war world. The lesson for British statesmanship, wrote the London *Sunday Times*, seemed to be that political co-operation with the United States which was so necessary for the welfare of both countries, should be earnestly pursued but little talked about and never gloried in.

While Winston Churchill was Prime Minister of Britain, even though engaged in an electoral campaign to preserve his national authority with another sound majority in the House of Commons, it was not easy to recognise that Britain's position in the world was likely to be a lesser one than before the war. His presence at the forthcoming Big Three meeting with the Russians (the first occasion on which President Truman had encountered Stalin), seemed central to the optimism with which it could be anticipated.

As a good preliminary omen on the 26th June the United Nations Charter was signed in San Francisco after eight long weeks of compromises. 'It may well rank,' observed the *Sunday Times*, 'with Magna Carta and the American Constitution as documents of the ages.'

On the 5th July, in a move which further improved the auspices for the Three Power meeting, the British and United States Governments officially recognised the new Polish Provisional Government, merely 'recalling' that Yalta had provided that such a government should be pledged to the holding of free and unfettered elections by secret ballot on the basis of universal suffrage. This was also the day which was Polling Day in just such an election for the British people, and Winston Churchill took himself off for a well-earned holiday at Hendaye in the south-west of France. Ten days later in the early evening of 15th July he landed at Gatow airport in Berlin in the thirteenth 'plane of a flotilla of transport aircraft which had been landing there all afternoon with Western statesmen and their diplomatic and military staffs and advisers. Clement Attlee, the British Opposition Leader was there too. Churchill looked rested after his holiday, Eden drawn and rather pale after the illness which had kept him in the background of the election campaign. The Conference site was to be at Potsdam.

President Truman, who had arrived in Europe on the USS *Augusta*, the ship on which Churchill and Roosevelt had promulgated the Atlantic Charter in 1941, had first driven from Antwerp to Brussels, whence he flew on to Berlin to be greeted by Marshal Zhukov's delegate, General Vassily Sokolovsky.

Moscow predicted success for the conference. *Pravda* wrote that a certain amount of controversy which had sprung up the previous week in Berlin between the Allies had been merely 'an excuse for subversive intrigues by the enemies of the peace'. It said that there was a clear connection between the plans of Nazis and the German General Staff and the attempt now made by reactionaries in Europe and America to undermine Anglo-Soviet-American unity. Stressing the immense value of personal contacts between the Big Three, it maintained that this unity would be further consolidated at Potsdam, thus frustrating German imperialists. Friendship and co-operation between the Big Powers had won victories in war, was surmounting difficulties today and would continue to surmount them in the future.

The *New York Times* struck a more restrained, though basically no less hopeful note. Potsdam, it said, was the nearest thing there would ever be to a Peace Conference. 'Never,' it said, 'have three mortal men borne so heavy a responsibility for the welfare of their peoples and mankind.' It was their task to establish an enduring world peace. The paper pointed out with satisfaction that unlike President Wilson at Versailles after the First World War twenty-seven years earlier, President Truman had behind him in the States a virtually united public opinion which was at last convinced that the road to peace lay through international co-operation. The Senate Foreign Affairs Committee had just approved the United Nations Charter all but unanimously, thus assuring its final ratification.

On the other hand, Anne O'Hare MacCormick in the *New York Times*, comparing Truman's task with that of Roosevelt in previous Big Three conferences, pointed out that Truman's was much the more difficult. Questions which could be laid on the shelf while the prime concern was to keep the Alliance together for victory over a common enemy, now had to be fully examined, and decisions which involved the future pattern of Europe could no longer be postponed.

The London *Times* was basically optimistic, saying that hitherto the decisions of the three Powers had in themselves been for the most part 'wise and far-seeing', and had encouraged the world to believe that effective unity of purpose among the principal Powers which was the only pledge of lasting peace.

The opening of the conference was delayed a day. There was still no official news of the arrival of Stalin. Truman and Churchill spent the day independently touring the ruins of Berlin. Outside the wreckage of the Reichs Chancellery Truman, wearing a grey hat and a 'natty' blue suit, was heard by a *New York Times* reporter to observe:

'The destruction is a terrible thing, but they brought it on them-

305

selves. It just demonstrates what Man can do when he overreaches himself.'

Churchill and Eden arrived at the same site ten minutes later. Eden pointed out a bomb-shattered room where he said he had had dinner with Hitler in 1936. Churchill commented, 'You certainly paid for that dinner, Anthony.'

A vast array of the world's press had assembled with due accreditation at Potsdam to report the conference. They were kept at a long arm's-length from it throughout. The conference area itself was sealed-off from the rest of Berlin by thousands of Allied troops and a curfew was imposed on the inhabitants. Journalists at Zehlendorf had to do as best they could, by speculation and occasional unofficial contacts with members of the delegations, to supplement the official handouts which were concerned almost entirely with trivia of the conference's life-style, and details of the delegates' menus. Anne O'Hare MacCormick strongly criticised the prevailing secrecy for two unfortunate effects: one, that Potsdam thus appeared a fat oasis amid the ruins of Europe in which nothing but a round of lavish lunches and dinners was taking place, the other being that since it was the Russians who had set the tone the impression was given that in order to co-operate with them it was necessary to turn a blind eye to unenlightenment. 'Insofar as it suggests that compromise,' she wrote, 'the news blackout at Potsdam is an extremely serious matter.' The British press was equally critical, exposing the contradiction between Churchill's and Truman's acquiescence in the secrecy and their complaint against exactly the same secrecy imposed by the Russians in their own areas of liberated Europe. 'Never,' wrote the US Army paper *Stars and Stripes*, 'has so little news been available about so much.'

Beyond a statement issued five days after the opening of the conference disclosing that it was 'going ahead and much serious business was being done', no official news emerged at all until its conclusion on August 2nd. Nevertheless certain indications of what was going on became available, based on such information as the journalists could extract from private contacts and embellish with intelligent guesswork. It was a foregone conclusion that the future administration of Germany was under discussion and the US delegation let it be known on the 21st July that Stalin, Churchill and Truman had made considerable progress towards agreement on that matter. The knowledge that both Truman and Churchill had in their delegations a number of top experts on Japan made it certain too that the Pacific war was on the agenda.

On the 25th July it was announced in London that Admiral Lord Louis Mountbatten had just returned from consultations at Potsdam and this clearly confirmed that the war against Japan was under

Potsdam; Churchill, Truman and Stalin

discussion. There was even one quite sensational rumour that Russian entry into that war might soon be expected. A few days later Truman and his new Secretary of State James Byrnes were reported by 'sources close to the US delegation' to have established a most cordial relationship with Stalin and 'to have reached a stage of understanding considered impossible before the meeting had opened.' Once again there was talk of an 'accord' with Russia over Japan.

On the day Mountbatten returned to London a most important proclamation was issued from Potsdam, not specifically about the conference, though the fact that it was issued from there still further confirmed that Japan figured in the conference deliberations. The Soviet Union was not mentioned in the proclamation which was addressed by Churchill and Truman to the Japanese people and offered them an opportunity to end the war in stern language:

'The prodigious land, sea, and air forces of the United States, the British Empire, and of China,' it ran, 'many times reinforced by their armies and air fleets from the West, are poised to strike the final blows upon Japan. . . . The results of the futile and senseless German resistance to the might of the aroused free peoples of the world stands forth in awful clarity as an example to the people of Japan. The might that now converges on Japan is immeasurably greater than that which, when applied to the resisting Nazis, necessarily laid waste the land, industry and methods of life of the whole German people. The full application of our military power, backed by our resolve, will mean the inevitable and complete destruction of the Japanese armed forces, and, just as inevitably, the utter devastation of the Japanese homeland.'

It demanded the unconditional surrender of all Japanese armed forces, said that 'there must be eliminated for all time' the authority and influence of those who had deceived and misled the Japanese people into embarking on world conquest, that Japanese sovereignty would in future be limited to the home islands and that until Japan's war-making power was destroyed these would be occupied by the Allies. The proclamation added that the Japanese would not be enslaved as a race or destroyed as a nation but stern justice would be meted out to all war criminals including those who had visited cruelties upon prisoners. Of these terms it said, 'We will not deviate from them. There are no alternatives. We shall brook no delay.'

The day on which the proclamation to the Japanese people was issued from Potsdam was also the day on which the results of the British General Election were declared. (Five days earlier, in Berlin there had been a review of British troops in the Tiergarten. As Churchill, followed in another vehicle by Attlee, drove up to the reviewing stand there was a loud cheer from British soldiers on the other side of the street. Churchill, assuming that these cheers were for him, raised his hand in the traditional V-sign. But then the troops began to chant: 'Attlee! Attlee! Attlee!' Churchill dropped his hand, realising that the cheers were for the man who was his colleague at the conference but his rival at home.) By 7 o'clock that evening Churchill was at Buckingham Palace handing in his resignation as Prime Minister to the King. Half an hour later Attlee was received there and agreed to form a Government. The Labour Party had won a sensational landslide victory. It was the first time it had ever won an overall majority. It was of a size which almost no one had thought possible. Out of 640 Commons seats altogether Labour's majority over the Conservatives was to be 202; its majority over all other parties combined: 158. In Birmingham where the most optimistic forecast had given Labour six gains it had ten. Churchill personally had won handsomely at Woodford, but his eccentric Independent opponent with his 'philosophic plan' for the revitalisation of human society by one hour's work a day had won over 10,000 votes against him. The largest majority in the country was that of Emanuel Shinwell at Seaham – over 32,000 – and 26 other Labour Members had majorities of 20,000 or more.

Attlee issued a statement in which he said a new era had begun for the British people. Two days later, on July 28th, he returned without Churchill to Potsdam as Britain's Prime Minister, accompanied by the new British Foreign Secretary, Ernest Bevin.

After another four days of talks the Potsdam Conference came to an end with messages of gratitude to Churchill and Eden for their work for peace signed by Truman, Attlee and Stalin. The last sentence of the message to Churchill ran, 'The whole world knows the greatness of his work, and it will never be forgotten.'

On the same day the first and only full communiqué of the conference was issued, claiming that the ties between the three Governments had been strengthened and the scope of their collaboration and understanding extended, with renewed confidence that their Governments and peoples, together with the other United Nations, would ensure the creation of a just and enduring peace. A Council composed of the Big Three's Foreign Ministers plus those of France and China was set up to continue in this spirit and to make the necessary preparations for the eventual peace settlements. The Council was normally to meet in London where the first session was to be held not later than September, 1945.

The greater part of the long communiqué concerned itself with the future of Germany, which was to be completely disarmed and demilitarised, with all arms and aircraft industries eliminated. There was to be uniformity of treatment of the German population in all occupied zones. While for the time being there was to be no central German Government, local self-government was to be restored on democratic principles and an eventual reconstruction of German political life to be prepared for on a democratic basis so that Germany could eventually co-operate peacefully in the international community. War criminals were to be brought to judgement and all members of the Nazi Party who had been anything more than nominal participants in its activities were to be removed from any position of public responsibility. A proportion of the industrial equipment of the western zones was to be removed in addition to the dismantling of industrial equipment in the eastern zone to compensate for the particularly heavy damage which the Russian people had suffered at the hands of the Germans. The only specific territorial change agreed immediately was the transfer of Königsberg to Russia and the provisional acceptance of a Polish western frontier on the Oder-Neisse Line. The agreement reached by representative Poles for a new Polish Provisional Government of National Unity was noted with pleasure, as were the facts that the British and US Governments had withdrawn their recognition from the former Polish Government in London which, in the words of the communiqué, no longer existed. It was recognised that there would have to be a transfer of German populations from parts of Poland, Czechoslovakia and Hungary and it was stipulated that these should be effected in 'an orderly and humane manner.' In a rider, General Franco was punished for his sympathy with the Axis powers by the exclusion of Spain from the United Nations on account of the undemocratic nature of its régime.

World opinion in general was that the conference had been a success. The London *Sunday Times* had no doubt of it: the conference had taken a number of definite decisions over a wide range of problems and on Germany nearly all the urgent questions had been answered; although the final communiqué was not a fully worked-out document like the Treaty of Versailles, it would not be very difficult to translate it into one; the new Council of Foreign Ministers might prove to be one of Potsdam's most useful achievements. In the United States too, reaction was generally favourable on the assumption that performance would equal promises. The fullest satisfaction was expressed in Moscow. *Izvestia* wrote that Potsdam showed that collaboration between the three Great Powers rested 'on the firm basis of vital common interests which at the same time meet the interests of all peace-loving people.'

On the matter of Poland, there was now officially no more anxiety on the part of the western Allies. They had recognised the new Polish Provisional Government and the new member of that Government whom they regarded most highly, Mikolajczyk, was himself now saying that Poland was 'on the right road'. Little concern was expressed for

A new era? Attlee hears the news
of his Election victory

Changing the guard at Potsdam

those Poles who had hoped to join that Government but instead had been arrested by the Russians and put on trial.

This trial took place and was concluded during the early days of the Potsdam Conference. All except one of the accused were found to admit the charges against them, wholly or in part. All except one were found guilty of action hostile to the Soviet Union. The sentences were considered relatively light. The longest was given to General Okulicki, the Commander of the Polish Home Army, who had been parachuted into Poland from Italy in May, 1944. He pleaded guilty to retaining arms, ammunition and radio equipment and ordering that they should not be given up, to retaining illegal staffs, forming an illegal organisation and maintaining contact with London (i.e. the Government officially recognised at the time by Britain and the United States). He pleaded guilty also to hostile propaganda against the Red Army and the Soviet Union. But he insisted that he was not guilty of any acts of terror against the Red Army. 'My great mistake,' he added, 'was lack of confidence in the Soviet Union.'

For that he was sentenced to ten years' imprisonment.

There was no mention of Japan in the communiqué, though the final sentence under the heading 'Military Talks' might be read as an oblique reference to it. This ran, 'During the conference there were meetings between the Chiefs of Staffs of the three Governments on military matters of common interest.'

Post-war Germany; scavenging to survive

Chapter Twenty-Four

General Marshall, addressing a US House of Representatives Sub-Committee about Japan towards the end of May, had said, 'The war will be longer and tougher than is generally expected, and there can be no big reduction in expenditure during 1946.'

Of the 3,000,000 square miles which the Japanese had occupied since Pearl Harbor only seven per cent so far had been liberated. The nearest Allied base to the Japanese home islands was 325 miles away on Okinawa, the island in the Ryukyu group on which some of the fiercest fighting of the whole war had taken place and where organised Japanese resistance was still not at an end. Possession of the greater part of this base, however, made bombing of the Japanese home islands much easier than before and Tokyo in particular was now being subjected to intense air raids comparable in effect to those suffered by German cities. On the early morning of the 26th May special fire-raising tactics in such raids had achieved more damage than ever before. A 70-mile-an-hour gale fanned the flames and the business centre which had been untouched in former raids was laid waste. The Japanese paper *Nippon Times* reported that the destruction was greater than that caused by the 1923 earthquake when two-thirds of the city had been destroyed and 60,000 people killed.

But though such raids could be expected to continue and would undoubtedly damage a war-potential badly needed to replace Japan's losses at sea and in the air, it was on land that the real battle would have to be fought and a vast Japanese army of between 70 and 100 divisions stood ready at home to fight it against the 60 or so divisions which Americans, British and Australians mustered in the Pacific at the end of the European war. The transfer of many divisions from the European theatre together with the newly-available aerial and naval resources was an essential prelude to the eventual assault. Writing at the beginning of June, 'Scrutator' in the London *Sunday Times* reminded his readers that the summer monsoon period which lasted until October was a strong discouragement to any major military operation. Nothing much except aerial warfare could be expected for the next four months,

314

the sort of period which would be required in any case to effect the redeployment from Europe.

From the point of view of strategic back-up for the assault whenever and wherever it might start (and there were still many people who thought that the first attack would be against the mainland of China), the Allies were favourably placed. The persistently successful campaigns of the last two years in the Pacific had secured them the major staging-posts of the Philippines, while the British 14th Army had recently taken the all-important Burmese port of Rangoon. But the superb qualities of the Japanese soldier revealed in the course of those campaigns made clear what a formidable enterprise lay ahead when the home islands themselves were eventually attacked.

On Okinawa, where at first there had seemed virtually no resistance, the Americans had had to fight for 82 days, killing some 90,000 of the 100,000 garrison. And though their own casualties were proportionately far lower they had included more than 10,000 killed. Earlier, on the tiny volcanic island of Iwo Jima, only some five miles long, containing a Japanese garrison of between 10,000 and 15,000, they had had to fight just as desperately. Although in the first week over 10,000 tons of shells and rockets had been directed at the Japanese by US naval guns in support of the marines' land offensive, it was not until over a fortnight later that the Stars and Stripes were formally raised on the island and even then there were isolated pockets of resistance at the northern end of the island where hundreds of Japanese had to be 'cleaned-up' in caves with flame-throwers and high-explosives. As for the Philippines it was not until the 5th July that General Macarthur was able to declare that campaign officially over. Even then minor isolated guerilla actions were still being fought in remote mountain country. Total American casualties in the Philippines campaign were 54,891 of whom 11,921 were killed. No one had any illusions about how bloody an invasion of Japan itself, or even a landing on the Chinese mainland as a preliminary to the final assault, was likely to be.

On the 10th July the Allies initiated what Admiral Nimitz called the 'pre-invasion stage': a massive naval and aerial bombardment of the Japanese home islands concentrating on industrial targets. It was 'like the fourth of July in Hell' wrote one correspondent. Richard O'Malley for the *New York Times* described how US 'planes covered the skies, while 800 shells were fired from the battleship *Iowa* alone, directed at the Nippon Steel Works and Wanishi Iron Mills at Mouroran. 'It was terrifying enough,' he wrote, 'even aboard the battleship. The guns seemed to shake the sea and sky.'

Such bombardments now continued day after day with the British Pacific Fleet task force joining in, in great strength, to form 'the most

315

powerful striking force yet assembled.' The *Iowa* and the British battleship *King George V* steamed boldly and contemptuously up and down the Japanese coastline, bombarding the Hitachi area north-west of Tokyo.

What came as a complete surprise was the almost total absence of any resistance by the Japanese either at sea or in the air. This failure to rise in defence of the home islands was one of the most puzzling events of the war to date. That Japan's navy and air force had suffered crippling losses and were husbanding their strength for the final invasion battle could be presumed. 'Too much significance should not be read into Japan's feeble defence against our ranging fleet,' wrote the *New York Times*. 'She is clearly conserving her dwindling air power and the remnants of her sea power to hurl it all against the American invasion she is convinced is coming.'

The American Vice-Admiral Barbey in a radio interview for NBC said he thought that the Allies might well not wait for the end of the monsoon and typhoon season before invading China or Japan. 'It will take more than a big wind to stop us,' he said. 'The invasion force could be ready in 30 to 90 days.' Barbey was untypical in thinking that the landings might be able to be achieved without very heavy casualties. He pointed out that the US forces, with their ability to range up and down the Japanese coast, and their overwhelming control of the air, could pick their own invasion sites at will.

Meanwhile Washington published a list detailing the percentage of Japanese cities with war industries which had been destroyed by the USAF's fire bombs. Top of the list were Takamatsu at 78% Tokushima at 74%, and Himaji at 72%. 51% of Tokyo was reckoned to be obliterated.

Undoubtedly the hope persisted that the Japanese surrender could somehow be achieved without the bloody invasion which so many were dreading. Only in Britain itself was apprehension to some extent dulled by the remoteness of the Pacific war, for all the involvement of the British Fleet and the 14th Army in Burma now being reinforced by a new Army, the 12th. The sense of relief at the end of the European war and the recent domestic excitements of the General Election sometimes made it seem further away than ever before. 'Scrutator' felt reason to upbraid his readers early in July, 'The country would do well to bestow more thought than it has yet upon our remaining great war, the war with Japan.'

The naval correspondent of the *Sunday Times* again sounded the alert which the British seemed reluctant to heed. He said that the bitter and costly fighting on Okinawa with its substantial losses for the Americans were a warning that the battle of the Japanese homeland 'if and when it

Americans meet continued Japanese resistance as they press on for victory

comes, may be a very tough and expensive affair.' But for all such attempts by responsible British journalists to direct attention to the war against Japan their assessment that the invasion would probably have to wait until the end of September when the rains were over gave the public an excuse for putting it temporarily to one side. Before then the Japanese might well give in.

As, day after day, the massive aerial and naval bombardment continued, rumours persisted in the United States that peace proposals of one sort or another had been directly or indirectly received from the Japanese Government. On the very day on which the bombardment had started, July 10th, Joseph Grew, the US Under-Secretary of State had categorically denied that any such proposals had been received. A week later the State Department said that this was still the case, yet the stories continued. Senator Homer Capehart of Indiana said that he had reason to believe that 'peace feelers of a very definite nature have been made.' But the *New York Times* said that this talk was merely a triumph for enemy propaganda, arousing false hopes and spreading doubt or confusion in the Allied ranks. It reminded its readers that for all the victories in the Pacific war against Japan to date, the war was no further advanced than had been the war against Germany in the autumn of 1942. 'Only an all-out effort,' it wrote, 'by the combined might of all the Allies can shorten the agony.'

The only definite voices to be heard from Japan were those of the radio and newspapers, and these breathed in the main bold defiance. *Asahi* said that the fighting spirit of a hundred million Japanese had now to be boosted by total effort for the Japanese war objective which was to 'win security for the existence of the race.' Only the opposition paper *Yoniuri Hochi* struck a different note, strongly urging the country's leaders to take a realistic view of the world situation and not to succumb to 'political superstition that dissensions among the Allies will pave the way for Japanese victory.' It said that it had been a tragic lesson of the German war that the Germans had made the 'fatal blunder' of thinking that the United States and Great Britain would eventually quarrel with Russia. 'This tragic lack of understanding of international relations,' wrote the paper, 'finally cost the Third Reich its very national existence.'

What no one inside or outside Japan doubted was that should the Japanese Government decide on a fight to the last, it would be exactly that: almost every Japanese soldier would fight, as he had done on Iwo Jima and Okinawa, until killed. The continued failure or refusal of the Japanese air force and navy to respond to the continuing daily attacks by the Allied fleets and air forces conveyed menace rather than reassurance.

318

On the 21st July, preceding the Potsdam ultimatum, the United States had broadcast a call to Japan to surrender, threatening that a refusal would result in the virtual destruction of the country and a dictated peace. Surrender must be unconditional but it would be on the basis of the Atlantic Charter with its commitment on the part of the Allies to no territorial aggrandisement for themselves. 'Your opportunity is rapidly passing,' went the message. 'As soon as our redeployment is completed it will be lost for ever.' Another United States broadcast said that the first US divisions to be redeployed from Europe via the United States would arrive in the Pacific about December 1st.

A British naval commentator, Captain Russell Grenfell, RN in an assessment of the Japanese defensive system headed 'Preparing the Way for Invasion', reminded the public that there were no short-cuts in war. The Germans, who had taken the lead in looking for new weapons to do just this and who had undoubtedly led the way in their progress with jet aircraft, the flying bomb, rockets, acoustic mines and many other clever devices, could be said to have lost the war by such diversion of effort. 'Through all history,' wrote Grenfell, 'wars without exception have been decided by armed conflict, by the victory of one side's fighting forces over those of the other. But mankind, being eternally hopeful, has constantly tried to find an easier way to success which would avoid the hard test of the armed struggle. Yet no such attempt . . . which did not have armed supremacy behind it has ever succeeded.' Nevertheless as the *Sunday Times* correspondent in Washington wrote, 'The public vainly attempts to suppress an almost guilty hopefulness that the story may end sooner than it has any right to expect.'

The spate of rumours about Japanese proposals for surrender had had one embarrassing effect. There had been a sharp break on the New York stock market as a result of these rumours. 'It is always unedifying,' wrote Frank MacDermott, the *Sunday Times* correspondent, 'when moneyed interests are revealed as benefitting or believing themselves to benefit more from war than from peace.'

There was, however, still no peace around Japan. The official Japanese reply to the Potsdam ultimatum of July 26th came on July 27th. It was curt and unbending. It said that, unlike Germany, Japan was not on her knees and pointed out that not a single enemy soldier stood on the Japanese mainland. 'Japan,' it said, 'is determined to battle tooth and nail for every inch of her sacred soil.' The naval and aerial bombardment designed to make this battle unnecessary continued relentlessly.

On the same day as the Japanese reply, American Super-Fortresses dropped leaflets over eleven Japanese towns, warning the populations that they would be targets for heavy air attack and urging them to leave immediately. From US Headquarters on Guam the American General Lemay said, 'We are able to attack any targets we choose, and their defences can do nothing about it. . . . The Japanese have nothing to look forward to except the total destruction of their country.' Six of the named towns were heavily bombed the next day, while British and American 'planes from carriers made a prolonged raid on what was left of the Japanese fleet in the Inland Sea, sinking two battleships and putting three cruisers out of action. Some heavy opposition was met in the air but this was now a rare occurrence, and losses from the force of a thousand and more British and American aircraft attacking Japan almost every day were slight. Allied battleships too were able to approach within a few miles of the shore and bombard ports and industrial centres with impunity. On the 31st July the inhabitants of twelve more Japanese cities were warned by leaflets to save themselves and leave immediately. Nagasaki, which was not one of those warned, was attacked by a large force of fighter-bombers, flying from Okinawa. The next day four of the warned cities in the last batch were attacked by 882 Super-Fortresses which dropped a greater load of bombs than in any of the raids on Germany. It was described by the US Headquarters in Guam as 'the biggest aerial strike in world history'. Nagasaki, though still not one of those cities warned by leaflets, was bombed again on the 2nd August. On the 5th August, US Headquarters in Guam announced that 31 Japanese towns had now been warned of devastation by air attack, 10 of which had already been devastated. General Macarthur had issued a statement in which he said he was taking command of all forces in the Ryukyu Archipelago from the southern tip of Japan to Formosa. 'With the Philippines these islands form a great semi-circular base from which a mighty invasion force is being forged for the final conquest of Japan.'

On the 6th August 1945, President Truman had a statement to make. It was the most momentous ever made by a United States President, or indeed any other statesman in the history of mankind. He had travelled from Potsdam to Britain, where, after meeting King George VI, he had sailed from Plymouth for the United States on the cruiser *Augusta*. He broadcast his statement in mid-Atlantic. He said that the day before the United States air force had for the first time used a bomb against Japan which was more than 2,000 times more powerful than the largest bomb ever dropped.

'It is an atomic bomb,' said Truman. 'It is the harmonising of the basic power of the universe . . .'

It was, he said, to spare the Japanese people from utter destruction that the ultimatum of July 26th had been issued from Potsdam. Their leaders promptly rejected that. If they did not now accept the Allied terms they might expect 'a rain of ruin from the air the like of which has never been seen on this earth.'

Hanson Baldwin, the *New York Times* military correspondent wrote, 'Yesterday we clinched victory in the Pacific, but we sowed the whirlwind.'

The target had been a city called Hiroshima, on the southern tip of the main island of Honshu. It was described as 'an important army centre', with a population of about 350,000. It had not been on the list of cities whose inhabitants were urged to evacuate them. So tremendous was the force of the explosion that it was 48 hours before any aerial reconnaissance could assess the damage. The Japanese too announced that the devastation was so great that it was impossible at first to ascertain its full extent. They were not even at all clear how it had happened. They were under the impression that a small number of aircraft had dropped a few bombs which descended by parachute and exploded before they hit the ground. The last detail was correct, but there had been only one aircraft and only one bomb.

Two days later both sides were in a better position to judge the effects. The report issued by United States Headquarters on Guam, where unofficial estimates reckoned that perhaps as many as 100,000 people had been killed, contained an almost lyrical note, 'What had been a city going about its business at a quarter past nine on a sunny morning went up in a mountain of dust-filled smoke, black at the base and towering into a plume of white at 40,000 feet.' More than half the city's total area of seven square miles had been obliterated.

The Japanese broadcast a report in their foreign services:

'Most of Hiroshima no longer exists. Blasted corpses too numerous to count litter the ruined city. The impact of the bomb was so terrific that practically all living things, human and animal were literally seared to death by the tremendous heat and pressure engendered by the blast. Buildings were crushed or wiped-out. Those outdoors were burned to death and those indoors killed by the indescribable pressure and heat. . . . The dead were burned beyond recognition.'

By comparison, four of the towns which had been on the warning list and had been devastated by high-explosives and incendiaries from 580 Super-Fortresses the same morning – Saga, Imabari, Maebashi and Nishinomiya-Mikage – attracted small attention.

Next day the three principal members of the crew of the Super-Fortress which had dropped the bomb on Hiroshima held a Press Conference. The 'plane had been named *Enola Gay* after the mother of the pilot, Colonel Paul Tibbets. The bomb-aimer was Major Thomas Ferebee and also at the Press Conference was Captain William Parsons of the US Navy, who had been in charge of the bomb itself.

321

Tibbets described how the trip from the Marianas had been without incident: the weather clear, a bright sun shining. Their target, which, he disclosed, had only been given them when they made their landfall over Japan, lay clear below them. There were no Japanese fighters in the sky and there was no anti-aircraft fire. After dropping the bomb he had banked steeply in a 270-degree turn, putting on throttle to get away from the blast effect which in fact had been relatively slight.

'It was hard to believe what we saw. Below us, rising rapidly was a tremendous black cloud. Nothing was visible where, only minutes before, the outline of the city, its streets, buildings and waterfront piers were clearly apparent. It happened so fast, we couldn't see anything and could only feel the heat from the flash and the concussion from the blast. . . . What had been Hiroshima was going up in a mountain of smoke. First I could see a mushroom of boiling dust – apparently with some shelves up to 20,000 feet. The boiling continued for three or four minutes as I watched. Then a white cloud plumed up from the centre to 40,000 feet and an angry dust-cloud spread all round the city. There were fires on the fringes, apparently burning as buildings crumbled and the gas-mains broke.'

Parsons, asked if he had had any reaction as the man responsible for the bomb about the unleashing of destruction and terror below, had replied that he had had none except one of relief when the great flash signalled that the bomb had, in fact, exploded.

Although an obvious immediate question was what impact this new bomb was likely to have on the outcome of the war with Japan, there was at the same time an awareness at once of a frightening new dimension into which mankind had penetrated, which for a moment almost overshadowed the tactical considerations. 'Its implications for good or evil,' wrote the *New York Times*, 'are so tremendous in so many directions that it will take months before our minds can really begin to envisage them.' 'We have turned one of history's corners,' wrote the *Manchester Guardian*. 'There is a power abroad in the world that could destroy, if not all life, at least all civilian life.'

Churchill said: 'The revelation of the secrets of Nature, long mercifully withheld from Man, should arouse the most solemn reflection in the mind and conscience of every human being capable of comprehension. We must indeed pray that these awful agencies will be made to conduce to peace among the nations.'

Leader-writers on both sides of the Atlantic echoed him. '. . . In the face of the unlocking of the inconceivable energy of the atom,' wrote the *New York Herald Tribune*, 'the victory or defeat of armies, the fate of nations, and the rise and fall of empires are all alike in any long perspective: they are only the ripples on the surface of history. We must

322

hope that mankind, which has shown curiosity and cleverness in making this advance into the mysteries of Nature, will also show the wisdom to employ the powers grasped for some other end than self-extinction.' Over the next few days while the most dramatic possibilities in the outcome of the war began to unfold, the newspapers and their readers who wrote to them returned often to the wider theme.

'In the bewilderment that such a stupendous event must bring,' wrote the *New York Times*, 'one consequence stands clear: civilisation and humanity can now survive only if there is a revolution in mankind's political thinking.' 'Beyond all doubt,' wrote the London *Times*, 'unless atomic power is turned to serve the aims of peace, it can speedily make an end of civilised life on earth . . . in a terrible and most literal sense it is a choice of life or death. Humanity must bear the burden of its own power.'

President Truman, in his announcement to the world, had sketched the history of the bomb's progress. Even before American entry into the war, in October 1941, a joint American-British team had been set up at Roosevelt's suggestion to operate in the United States. By the summer of 1942 expanded research had confirmed the earlier forecasts of scientists and the decision had been taken to invest the vast amount of productive capacity necessary in development of the bomb. It had, said Truman, been one of the boldest gambles in history, but it had paid off. The whole burden of execution, including the setting-up of the plant and many technical processes connected therewith in the tactical sphere, constituted, he said, 'one of the greatest triumphs of American – or indeed human – genius of which there is record. . . . By God's mercy Britain and American science outpaced all German efforts.' The bomb had been tested for the first time at 5.30 a.m. on the 16th July on Alamogordo air base, 120 miles from Albuquerque, New Mexico.

Though public questioning of the morality of use of this bomb was immediate, it was not clear to what extent morality had been one of the considerations affecting its use. The *Baltimore Sun* had a report that until early June, 1945 the President and military leaders had been in agreement that the bomb should not in fact be used, but that the High Command had reversed its policy in the last month or two. There was also no indication why Hiroshima had not been on the list of over 30 Japanese cities whose inhabitants had been warned to leave them.

The moral outcry from Japan was of course immediate and strident. The Domei News Agency said, 'It brands the enemy for ages to come as a destroyer of justice and mankind, as the public enemy number 1 of social justice.' Tokyo radio said that by employing new weapons designed to massacre innocent civilians the Americans unveiled to the eyes of the world their sadistic nature. 'Such bestial tactics reveal how thin is the veneer of civilisation the enemy has boasted of.'

There were not lacking voices in the west to point out that charges of inhumanity came with little force from a nation which had itself waged the war with such conspicuous inhumanity. But other voices, recording moral horror at what had been done, continued. A correspondent wrote to the *New York Times*, 'horrified at the inhuman and indiscriminate and un-Christian bombing,' and reminding Americans of how aghast they had been at the bombing of Coventry. Similar letters appeared in the British newspapers. It was noticeable that this new type of bomb occasioned a moral indignation which had been relatively silent when civilian populations had been subjected to 'conventional' Allied bombing. The British liberal newspaper the *Manchester Guardian*, while accepting that man was 'at last on the way to mastery of the means of destroying himself utterly' found it possible to legitimise the use of the atom bomb on this score. It said it was illogical to judge the morality of bombing by the size of the bomb used. The Allies had in fact dropped the equivalent of one and a half times the Hiroshima bomb on Cologne. 'We have done enough to create a precedent for its use.' Its use would shorten the war against Japan and therefore was 'entirely legitimate'. More than one reader wrote to that paper complaining of this use of the word 'legitimate', among them the publisher Victor Gollancz, who said that the Allies had committed a 'further debasement of the human currency' and described their use of the atom bomb as a 'blasphemous presumption'. Another reader asked: 'Of what value will it be to mankind if we end the Japanese war now, six months earlier, but in so doing accept and use methods that will . . . help to destroy some of the faith in mankind that is absolutely essential to world peace?'

The *Manchester Guardian* summed-up what was probably general public response to such sentiments in a leader in which it said that though there was 'no doubt some moral discomfort at the way the atom bomb has blasted us into final victory . . . many lives have been saved and the nation's gratitude should be freely and joyfully expressed.'

This was certainly the point of view of Lord Louis Mountbatten. 'If the bomb kills Japanese', he said, 'and saves casualties on our side I am naturally not going to favour the killing of our people unnecessarily. . . . I am responsible for trying to kill as many Japanese as I can with the minimum of loss on our side. War is crazy. It is a crazy thing that we are fighting at all. But it would be even more crazy if we were to have more casualties on our side to save the Japanese.'

Moral disapprobation came from sources at the Vatican, though it was not clear how official these were. The Swedish liberal paper

Aftonbladet categorically described the bombing of Hiroshima as a war crime. But scruples of the Allied leadership were confined, along the lines Lord Louis Mountbatten had indicated, to bringing the war against Japan to an end as quickly as possible. On the 9th August the dropping of a second atom bomb, said to be more sophisticated than the first, on the already-bombed city of Nagasaki, was treated more laconically. The US Air Force General Spaatz reported from Headquarters at Guam simply that the results were 'good', though so much of the area had been obscured by smoke that it was not easy to assess damage. At the same time 3,000,000 leaflets were dropped over Japan proclaiming: 'We are in possession of the most destructive weapon ever designed by man. . . . Before using this bomb again and again to destroy every resource which your military leaders have to prolong this useless war, we ask that you now petition your Emperor to end the war. Take steps now, or we shall resolutely employ this bomb promptly and forcefully.'

The Nagasaki bomb made clear that such words were no bluff, though the next day only conventional bombs were used, some 1,200 'planes attacking targets in the northern part of Honshu. But a conventional blow of much greater magnitude, in its effect as potent as the atom bomb, had struck Japan on the same day as the bombing of Nagasaki. Russia had implemented an agreement secretly made at Potsdam and had entered the war on the side of the Allies. Twenty-four hours later part of her Far Eastern armies were 100 miles into the heart of Japanese Manchuria.

Joseph Harsch, broadcasting a few days before the dropping of the atomic bombs and Russia's declaration of war, saw the probability of very strong and very stubborn resistance to the coming Allied invasion, even though Japan was no longer a naval power and even if the remains of her air force, which she was obviously keeping in reserve, were eventually destroyed. He likened Japan's position to that of Germany as the Allied armies in Europe came up on opposite sides to the Rhine and the Oder. However, he thought it might take longer than it did in Europe before the Allies were ready for their final attack and that the fighting afterwards might last much longer. If Russia were not to come in, then the Japanese armies on the mainland might hold out for a very long time.

Now Russia had come in and the atom bombs had been dropped. Instead of waiting to see what the Allies would do next, the world watched Japan for her reaction. The Japanese press evinced an inscrutable mixture of sombre realism and defiance: '. . . No matter what the hour may bring we must be above despair. Never before have the Japanese people needed a clearer outlook, a stronger determination for

325

a new racial life. If we keep our traditional culture we can live on as Japanese. . . . This is the worst moment in our racial existence. We must stand by our comrades in our combined efforts to perpetuate our existence. . . .'

Of the atomic bomb itself the Japanese radio in Singapore broadcast: 'This outrage against humanity calls for the intervention of the civilised world. This is not war, not even murder, it is pure nihilism. But it will not in any way alter the Japanese war aims or upset her morale, but merely strengthen her will to fight to the last.' Of Russia's entry into the war, *Tokyo Shimbun* wrote: 'The only thing left to be done is to think how to cope with this stark reality. There is no escape from reality. What is most urgently needed is great courage, not blind courage.'

The world did not have long to wait. In contradiction to the spirit expressed in the Singapore broadcast the Japanese Government sent a message to the Allies via Switzerland and Sweden on the 10th August to the effect that they were prepared to accept the terms of the Potsdam Declaration with one proviso: namely, 'that the said Declaration does not comprise any demand which prejudices the prerogatives of His Majesty as sovereign ruler.'

There was a delay until the afternoon of August 11th while the Allied Governments consulted about this. Then a reply from the American, British, Russian and Chinese Governments was sent back via the Swiss Legation in Washington, defining their attitude to 'the prerogatives of His Majesty as sovereign ruler' as follows: 'From the moment of surrender the authority of the Emperor and the Japanese Government to rule the State shall be subject to the Supreme Commander of the Allied Powers, who will take such steps as he deems proper to effectuate the surrender terms.'

It was a neat formula by which Japanese face could be saved by maintenance of the authority of the Emperor, while that authority could be simultaneously used by the Allies and their Supreme Commander, General Douglas Macarthur to enforce their will. It had the added advantage that their will could probably only be effectively enforced without disorder and bloodshed, through that authority. Deep anxiety for those still surviving Allied prisoners of war who had already suffered extreme deprivation, cruelty and hardship under the Emperor's authority was a concern only secondary to the need to get the Japanese armies all over the Pacific to stop fighting. The reply to Japan contained the clause: 'Immediately upon the surrender the Japanese Government shall transport prisoners-of-war and civilian internees to places of safety, as directed, where they can quickly be placed aboard Allied transport.'

326

The disadvantage of the formula was that it did indeed accord honour to the man in whose name and for whose glory the Japanese war of conquest, with all its attendant cruelties, had been conducted. 'Damn the Emperor!' said the Democratic Senator Capehart. 'He is a war criminal and I'd like to see him hung up by his toes.' Dr Evatt, the Australian Minister for External Affairs agreed with him in more diplomatic terms. He found the retention of the Emperor's prerogative 'entirely unacceptable' and added that no one in Japan of whatever rank should be given immunity from proved responsibility for policies of aggression or for atrocities.

There was considerable public discussion both in Britain and the United States about whether, after what had happened, it was tolerable to accord Hirohito his required dignity, however nominal. Some thought that the Allies should have insisted that the unconditional surrender of the Potsdam Declaration meant exactly what it said. Others, like a man interviewed by a *New York Times* reporter on Pennsylvania Station, New York, thought, 'Let them keep their precious Emperor. Anything to get this war over.' And this seemed, on balance, the general view.

For the next two and a half days, however, it was by no means certain that the Allied formula would be accepted by the Japanese. From Japan there came only official silence while the Cabinet there met and was in contact with the Emperor. No time-limit had been attached to the Allies' last communication, but a certain restlessness began to be felt in both London and Washington by the evening of the 12th, and it was thought in Washington that if no reply were to be received by the following day there was every prospect of a pent-up Allied fury being unleashed against Japan, including the use of further atom bombs. President Truman after all had already made quite clear that he was not squeamish about them. He had said on the evening of August 9th, the day of the Nagasaki bomb, 'We shall continue to use it until we completely destroy Japan's power to make war. Only a Japanese surrender will stop us.'

Conventional war was in any case proceeding in the meantime. Throughout the two days of waiting, three Russian armies continued to penetrate further into Manchuria, while British and American ships and aircraft attacked the Japanese home islands. On August 12th, 500 Super-Fortresses carried out one of the largest conventional raids of the whole Pacific war against Kumanoto, a military supply centre on Kyushu island. 'A major US warship' was reported to have been torpedoed off Okinawa on the same day.

The tension of waiting for the Japanese reply was heightened in the United States, as had been that preceding the German surrender, by a false news flash, prematurely reporting that the surrender had taken place. This time it was the United Press which was at fault.

The flash, which appeared on the evening of the 13th August was denied within two minutes, but in New York where it was estimated that 100,000 people were waiting in Times Square, and elsewhere in the States, it triggered wild celebrations. A cacophony of car horns blended with the steamship whistles and hooters from New York harbour and waterfront for fifteen minutes. There were fireworks and mass outbreaks of impromptu dancing in Greenwich Village. A similar false start to the celebrations was reported from Washington, Rochester, Miami, Boston, Chicago, and Battle Creek, Michigan. In Canada, where bells started pealing all over the country, the State itself became involved in the erroneous jubilation in an embarrassing manner. A special recording which the Prime Minister, William Mackenzie King had made four hours earlier in anticipation of official receipt of news of the Japanese acceptance of the Allied note, was broadcast as if this had been in fact officially received. A hasty correction had to be broadcast immediately afterwards.

The false news flash did not affect Britain since it was not received in London and news of it and its denial two minutes later was only to be heard of in the middle of the night. In Britain the *Manchester Guardian* leader-writer considered, under the head-line 'Son of Heaven' the paradox in which the Pacific war might well be likely to end. On the one side were the Allies with their immense fleets, armies and air forces to which was now added the terrible menace of the atomic bomb. On the side of Japan there was little except 'an obscure and feeble simpleton who embodies the primitive religion of a Polynesian myth.' Yet the Emperor was proving more effective than the bomb. For the Allies, however they might phrase it, were being forced to accept something less than the unconditional surrender for which they had asked at Potsdam. 'Yet,' concluded the paper, 'most people will agree that if it makes the difference between full peace now and full peace in six months' time, between the end of slaughter and its continuance, then it is justified.'

The Allied formula was more effective than the *Manchester Guardian*'s leader-writer allowed. It was the unconditional surrender of the unbeaten Japanese armies some millions strong which the Allies wanted, and on the evening of the 14th August they got it, handed by that Emperor's authority which was now theirs, through the Swiss Foreign Office in Bern. As Attlee put it in his characteristic manner in a short broadcast at midnight on August 14th: 'Japan has today surrendered. The last of our enemies is laid low. . . . Here at home you have a short rest from the unceasing exertions which you have all borne without

328

flinching or complaint for so many dark years. . . . Peace has once again come to the world. Let us thank God for this great deliverance and His mercies. Long live the King!'

August 15th was proclaimed a holiday in Britain as VJ Day and the British, in a renewal of that gratitude and relief they had expressed three months before, could now join in those final celebrations on which Americans had prematurely embarked.

The holiday started slowly, partly because many people were not aware of it until after they had set off for work only to find that there was no work to go to. In places a reverse rush-hour at the wrong end of the day developed, together with some annoyance that many shops and places of refreshment were closed. Relief that the years of war were really over at last eventually got the better of mixed feelings. In London massive good-natured family crowds were soon perambulating the central streets as they had done on VE Day. By a fortunate though also slightly bizarre coincidence the day was also that for the State Opening of the new Labour-dominated Parliament and the King and Queen drove down to Westminster in an open carriage in the morning rain. Crowds larger than those which would normally have watched held newspapers over their heads against the rain. Once at Westminster, sitting in pomp and full ceremony on his gilded throne, the King solemnly announced the nationalisation of the mines and of the Bank of England.

The only piece of Parliamentary business done that day, out of deference to the victory celebrations, was the voting of an address of thanks to the King on the conclusion of the Japanese war. Back at the Palace, similar scenes to those of VE Day were repeated with continual cries of 'We want the King!' and many appearances of the Royal Family on the balcony. Crowds were paddling in the waters of the Victoria fountain in front of the Palace and climbing all over its allegorical figures. One reporter noted that the only cross word he heard all day was addressed by a policeman to a small boy on one of the heavy stone angels,

'You come down. You'll break off that wing, and then where will you be?'

In the evening there were traditional crowds in Piccadilly Circus and round about. In the countryside and in many towns of Britain there was dancing and the pealing of bells and the building of bonfires. In Newcastle-on-Tyne and Brighton fire brigades were called out to deal with bonfires that had got out of hand. Near Swindon in Wiltshire a South African air ace, Lieut.-Col. Pierce Joubert, DSO, who had fought in the skies over Normandy and Arnhem and had led one of the first squadrons to take Paratroops over the Rhine that March, was killed by a home-made firework which he had constructed from a Verey light and an iron tube.

The Second World War was over.

Something about the different emphasis which British and Americans had all along attached to the Pacific war was exemplified in this celebration of VJ Day. Some Americans had always thought that some British were a little too ready to turn their backs on that war too easily. In the United States it was officially announced that VJ Day would have to wait until the elaborate mechanism for the formal Japanese surrender had been arranged, and this was likely to mean a delay of many days yet. President Truman, having announced this together with details of the Japanese note of acceptance at a press conference, appeared afterwards in front of the White House and addressed the crowds. 'This is a great day,' he said, 'the day when Fascism finally dies, as we always knew it would. This is a day for Democracy – but,' he added, 'our real task lies ahead.'

Just for a while, though, it could not help being a time for looking back. Of the three great architects of Allied victory, Churchill, Roosevelt and Stalin, the first was out of office, the second dead, and only the third still a figure on the world stage. Yet Stalin had been in benevolent association with Hitler himself when the war started and although both in Britain and America there were strong and even emotional feelings of friendly gratitude to the Red Army without which the war in Europe could not have been won, it was to the memory of Roosevelt and above all to the surviving presence of Churchill, for all his political dismissal, that sentiment was drawn in looking back over the long years of anxiety, terror, boredom, hardship, frustration, sorrow and exhaustion which the Allied peoples had come through. On the day after VJ Day, in the House of Commons, after the Address in reply to the King's Speech from the Throne had been moved by Major John Freeman and seconded by Mr Fred Willey, Churchill rose to congratulate the Government on 'the very great improvement in our prospects at home which comes from complete victory gained over Japan and especially on peace throughout the world.'

He told how only a month before at Potsdam he and President Truman had approved the plan submitted to them by the Combined Chiefs of Staff for a series of great battles and landings in Malaya, the Netherlands East Indies and in the homeland of Japan. He said those operations had involved an effort unsurpassed in the war and that no one could measure the cost in British and American life which they would require, still less how long it would take to stamp out Japanese resistance in the many territories she had conquered, and especially in her own homeland. He said it was while they had been at Potsdam that news of the successful trial of the atom bomb in New Mexico had arrived ('success beyond all dreams crowned this sombre, magnificent venture of our American allies') and that he and Truman had there and then taken the decision to use it, informing Marshal Stalin of the fact. The Potsdam Declaration of July 26th calling on Japan for unconditional surrender, had been thought a necessary preliminary before its use. ('This we owed to our conscience before using this awful weapon.') In addition attempts had been made to secure evacuation of the inhabitants from the threatened cities.

Churchill did not seem to be aware that neither Hiroshima nor Nagasaki had been on the lists of such cities warned by the pamphlets dropped from aircraft. But his ultimate defence of the use of the bomb was effective. 'I am surprised,' he said, 'that very worthy people, but people who in most cases had no intention of proceeding to the Japanese front themselves, should adopt the position that rather than throw this bomb we should have sacrificed one million Americans and 250,000 British lives in the desperate battles of an invasion of Japan. Future generations will judge this dire decision, and I believe if they find themselves dwelling in a happier world from which war has been banished and where freedom reigns they will not condemn those who struggled for their benefit amid the horrors and miseries of this grim and ferocious epoch.'

There was of course an alternative point of view and it continued to receive expression on both sides of the Atlantic. The Dean of St Albans refused to hold a service of thanksgiving in his cathedral because the war had been brought to an end by the bomb. A correspondent wrote to the *New York Times* of the bomb as 'a stain upon our national life. When the exhilaration of this wonderful discovery has passed, we will think with shame of the first use to which it was put.' The BBC's staid weekly publication in London, *The Listener*, printed a letter which ran: 'It may be a subject for relief that our side discovered the atomic bomb, but we can never escape the condemnation which must fall on those who first used it for war. We can no longer pretend that our morality is higher than that of the Nazis or the Japanese . . .' And the London *Catholic Herald* said that use of the bomb was 'not only utterly and absolutely indefensible in itself but the reaching of this appalling goal lights up for us all the immorality along the path we have been treading.'

Perhaps it is only possible to say that all war is immoral, but that within the paradox of the nature of Man, whose morality can drive him to war, some immoral actions are more excusable than others. The quality of intention can be held to play a part in determining which these are.

The world war had been fought for nearly six years. If any one man, among the millions on the victorious side who had fought it, deserved some personal acclamation for his part, the tribute which Clement Attlee, the man who had ousted Churchill for Britain's peacetime leadership, paid him in the House of Commons in the first Debate of the new Parliament seemed fitting:

'In the darkest and most dangerous hours of our history this nation found in Mr Churchill the man who expressed supremely the courage and determination never to yield which animated all the men and women of this country. In undying phrases he crystallised the unspoken feeling of all. "Words only", it might be said, but words of great moment in history are deeds. We had more than words from Mr Churchill. He radiated a stream of energy throughout the machinery of government, indeed throughout the life of the nation. Many others shared in the work of organising and inspiring the nation in its great effort, but he set the pace. . . . I had the honour to serve with Mr Churchill in the War Cabinet throughout the whole of the Coalition Government from the days of Dunkirk to the surrender of Germany. There are many things on which we disagree, but I think it right to take this early occasion, before we turn to controversy, to express the gratitude and admiration for his leadership in war which we feel. His place in history is secure . . .'

And Attlee added, 'History will link with the name of Winston Churchill that of another great leader of democracy, the late President Roosevelt. One is present with us here today; the other did not live to see victory, but his service to the cause of freedom history can never forget.'

So much for history.

Britain, the United States and the Soviet Union now had to look to the future of the world they had fought for.

Epilogue: The Confusions of Peace

In war, objectives can seem relatively clear and simple: the war has to be won. Other considerations become secondary. The war against Germany and Japan had been won. The framework it had imposed on people's everyday lives, on relations between the Great Powers, and on many complex local situations subordinate hitherto to the greater concern, was now removed. Together with relief and thanksgiving at the lifting of the horrors of war came the need to adjust to the confusions of peace.

Even the technical business of starting the peace with Japan was full of difficulties. She had surrendered but the greater part of her army was unbeaten, much of it even untried and intact, with perhaps as many as two million men under arms on the home islands. If the dismantling of the proud Japanese war machine and the consequent occupation of Japan itself by her enemies was to proceed smoothly, some formality was required which would be both delicate and firm enough to skirt the hazards. The manner in which Japan had surrendered unconditionally contained an element of face-saving which, it soon became clear, the Allies were prepared to acknowledge.

The Emperor Hirohito's broadcast to his peoples on August 15th, in which he told them his decision, showed no penitence for the fact that Japan had declared war and some hypocrisy about her motives in doing so. 'Indeed,' he said, 'we declared war on America and Britain out of a sincere desire to enable Japan's self-preservation and the stabilisation of East Asia, it being far from our thought either to infringe upon the sovereignty of other nations or to embark upon territorial aggrandisement.'

However, the war situation had developed 'not necessarily to Japan's advantage' and the nations of the world had all 'turned against her interests', in addition to which the enemy had begun to employ 'a new and most cruel bomb'. He therefore had to accept the Potsdam Declaration. But he exhorted his people to further nobility of spirit and work with resolution so that they might enhance 'the innate glory of the Imperial State'.

333

The Japanese radio announced, 'We have to remedy our shortcomings. We have lost, but this is temporary. . . . Japan's mistake was a lack of material strength and the necessary scientific knowledge and equipment. This mistake we must amend. . . . We did not lose the war spiritually. We are still fighting for the independence of East Asia. Our ideals are not wrong about that.'

The Emperor had told General Macarthur that he was issuing an Imperial rescript on the 16th August to all armed forces to cease hostilities immediately. Delays in implementing the surrender, often unnecessary since broadcast communications could be virtually instantaneous, had to be tolerated. The consequences were often painful to those still suffering in Japanese prison or internment camps, and aroused indignation among all who thought of the savagery and lack of respect for the dignity of their enemies with which the Japanese had fought. The clause in the Allied note about immediate transport of prisoners-of-war and civilian internees to places of safety where they could quickly be placed aboard Allied transport, seemed a dead letter. As late as the 22nd of August the Japanese in Indo-China were refusing to allow Allied representatives to make contact with the prisoners there. Indeed, the Japanese-controlled Saigon radio announced: 'We might be forced to fight in self-defence, in accordance with orders of Imperial Headquarters, in the event of any of your forces coming too close to areas where our forces are stationed.'

A similar defiance came from Malaya where two Japanese Field-Marshals, Sugiyama, and Shunroku Hata, in charge of undefeated Japanese armies conceded only that negotiations for surrender were under way 'in spite of the fact that the unchallenged dignity of the Imperial Japanese army remains supreme, and what is more, is fully prepared to crush the foreigner if ever he should come.' They added the warning that to disarm or disband such units while alien armies occupied Japan might be too much for some of the officers to bear.

It was not until the 23rd August that the Japanese Commander in Burma confirmed the cease-fire. No Japanese units there had surrendered in the interval since 'VJ Day'. Not even over Japan itself was the new peace total. Several days after the official surrender two Liberators on a photographic mission over Tokyo were attacked by Japanese fighters and an American crew member in one of them killed.

However, in piecemeal and dilatory but generally co-operative fashion, local Japanese surrenders took place all over the Pacific in the ensuing weeks. One of the most moving of all was in Nanking on September 9th when a million Japanese troops in China formally acknowledged 'complete military defeat' at the hands of the Chinese after eight years of a war in which it was reckoned by Britain's 'Aid to China' Society some fifty million Chinese had been driven from their homes and two million children orphaned. But for China the end of one agony was only the beginning of another. Tension between the Communist provinces in the North under Mao-Tse-Tung and Chiang-Kai-Shek's Kuomintang, long barely suppressed by the need to show some unity against the Japanese, was soon to lead to civil war.

When also on September 9th all Japanese forces in the Netherlands East Indies surrendered – though still with the exception of those in Borneo – the Australian Commander-in-Chief, General Blamey, addressed the Japanese delegates in terms which other Allied representatives had avoided in their respect for the face-saving niceties. 'In receiving your surrender,' he said, 'I do not recognise you as honourable and gallant men, but you will be treated with due but severe courtesy. I recall your treacherous attack on China in 1937 and on the British Empire and on the United States in December 1941. I recall the atrocities and maltreatment of our nationals as prisoners-of-war and internees. In the light of these evils I shall enforce most rigorously all orders issued to you.'

The official surrender of the Japanese in South-East Asia took place on September 12th, in Burma on September 13th.

These multiple surrenders were supplementary to the major official ceremony, which had already taken place on board the US battleship *Missouri* in Tokyo Bay on September 2nd. The occupation of Japan by the first of some 400,000 American troops followed from a great ring of battleships and under a vast umbrella of aircraft. The dilatory protocol could be justified by the success of the American occupation. For it proceeded from the first day virtually without a hitch, and through the authority of the Emperor the imperialist glories of a militarist Japan were fully and peacefully dismantled.

Meanwhile a Japanese technician at the Japanese Air Defence General Headquarters had been surveying the ruins of Hiroshima and Nagasaki. He found that 60,000 people had been killed outright at Hiroshima and 10,000 at Nagasaki, but added, 'Many who were burned cannot hope to survive because of the uncanny effect the atom bomb has on the human body. Those who received only minor burns looked quite healthy at first, but for some unknown reason, weakened after a few days and many have died.'

After the Japanese delegates had withdrawn from the *Missouri* General Macarthur had expressed the sense of ideological triumph with which men can congratulate themselves at the end of wars, 'A great tragedy has ended, a great victory has been won. The skies no longer rain death, the seas bear only commerce. Men everywhere walk

335

upright in the sunlight. The entire world lives quietly at peace. The holy mission has been completed . . .'

President Truman, proclaiming 'VJ Day' for the United States immediately after the *Missouri* ceremony, gave his own version of that sense of achievement. 'This is a victory of more than arms alone,' he said. 'This is a victory of liberty over tyranny. . . . We know now that that spirit of liberty, freedom of the individual, and the personal dignity of man are the strongest, toughest, and most enduring forces in the world. So on 'VJ Day' we take renewed faith and pride in our own way of life. We know that under it we can meet the hard problem of peace which have come upon us.'

There were hard problems of peace all over the world. The rest of the year was to be spent meeting them.

*

The most delicate problem of all was the underlying one of relations between those three Great Powers who hoped to make the peace endure. This was first faced again at the meeting of the Council of Foreign Ministers prescribed by the Potsdam Agreement.

It took place in London on the 11th September. It was a disaster. Its purpose had been to draft formal peace treaties for Italy, Finland, Rumania, Hungary and Bulgaria. It broke up on the 2nd October, with the three Powers unable even to agree on the terms of a communiqué to express their failure. It was indeed argued by some that this total breakdown was preferable to an attempt to cover failure with insincere formulae. Russian mistrust of the United States' unwillingness to share with the United Nations the secrets of the atomic bomb seemed a deep underlying cause, though it was disagreement about the political evolution of the states of Eastern Europe that provided the explicit material for the breakdown.

Both Britain and the United States had, even before the conference, made clear that, in the words of Ernest Bevin, the Governments in Hungary, Rumania and Bulgaria 'do not in our view represent the majority of the people and . . . do not impress us as being sufficiently representative to meet the requirements of diplomatic relations'. Russia on the other hand maintained that all three countries now had satisfactorily democratic régimes and that the elections due to be held in them would leave nothing to be desired. Subsequent developments after the breakdown of the conference, in which there were many other matters of procedural dispute, did something to justify both attitudes.

In Hungary, municipal elections in Budapest in October gave a majority to the Smallholders Party over a combination of Socialists and Communists, whereupon an attempt was made by the Russian Com-

336

mander-in-Chief, Marshal Voroshilov, to procure only a single list of candidates for the general election due in November. The Smallholders, however, felt strong enough – and presumably confident enough of genuinely democratic conditions – to resist this request, and, while giving a pledge to maintain a Coalition Government after the election, in fact fought it independently and won a considerable majority over all other parties including Socialists and Communists. The result itself was some indication that the elections had been technically as free as could be reasonably expected; Britain recognised the new Government.

In Bulgaria the elections had originally been scheduled for August. But they had been postponed after strong representations from both United States and British Governments that neither the Coalition Government, formed with Red Army help from a Communist-dominated Coalition, nor the electoral arrangements seemed likely to lead to free elections. When, regardless of the London Conference's collapse, these elections took place in November, they did so in circumstances which gave few opportunities to any genuine opposition and were predictably rejected by both Britain and the United States as insufficiently democratic.

In Rumania, where no election was immediately due, the King, Michael, maintaining by his presence some show of national independence, survived for the time being in uneasy relationship with the Communist Prime Minister of his Government, Dr Groza. This Government was not recognised by Britain or the United States.

In one Balkan country however, which might well have been expected to add difficulties to the increasingly strained relationship between the Big Three, Yugoslavia, the situation turned out to be one which all the important parties were able to accept as reasonably satisfactory. Indeed, Marshal Tito, in an interview with *The Times* in November, while admitting that in one way the circumstances of war made the maintenance of good relations between allies easier, said that on the whole relations between Yugoslavia and Britain were now even better. This was a result of what could only be seen as a triumph for the process, to be applied in time to Hungary, Rumania and Bulgaria, of making things look correct when to accept that they were so was the only choice.

A dispute with Britain in May over Yugoslav occupation of much of Venezia Giulia, including Trieste, and parts of Austria in the area of Klagenfurt and Villach to which Yugoslavia laid claims, had ended with a reluctant Yugoslav withdrawal on the understanding that such claims were to be entertained at the eventual Peace Conference. A matter of equal concern was the evolution of Yugoslav democratic society, for which Britain had taken some responsibility.

337

Under British pressure King Peter of Yugoslavia had given his approval to the agreement between his Prime Minister Subasitch and Tito by which the country was pledged to a democratic future based on free elections and freedom of speech, while Tito's National Liberation Front was to continue administration the country in co-operation with King Peter's Regents.* Reports from inside Yugoslavia suggested that the sort of society emerging was different from the liberal democratic order so hopefully ordained.

'A British Soldier Lately in Yugoslavia,' writing in *The Times* in May, had said it was a society of secret political police, judicial murders of political opponents, and the arrest and disappearance of civilians for no other reason than that they spoke English or had exchanged civilities with British troops. He suggested that now the war was over it was time to stop attributing heroic virtues to anyone who had shared our quarrel and to stop suppressing all notice of their crimes. A similar account came from a *New York Times* correspondent writing towards the end of July. He reported a clear conflict between the expressed high democratic ideals and the oppressive strong-arm methods with which the Government was ruling. 'It is a tyranny,' he said, 'exercised in the name of the people by a minority too well organised and too heavily armed to be disputed.' All opposition to Tito was labelled 'Fascist' and to wear a royalist button, even though the State was still technically a monarchy, was to ensure arrest by the powerful secret police, the OSNA. Most Yugoslavs thought that war between Britain and America and Russia was imminent.

It was Tito himself who took the initiative in bringing the nominal situation into line with reality. On the 7th August he announced to the Yugoslav National Congress that the monarchy was obviously completely incompatible with the new form of government being developed in Yugoslavia. King Peter replied to this statement, not without reason, that it amounted to the final repudiation of the Tito-Subasitch agreement, 'a process which began almost immediately after it was signed.' He condemned the Tito régime as a full-scale dictatorship in which freedom of opinion, the press, public meeting and the right to form political parties were a dead letter. The situation was soon seen to be rather subtler than this but the King's statement was not an undignified one and he ended it by removing his personal sanction for the present state of affairs, which he said was 'abhorrent' to him, and by withdrawing authority from the Regents.

The Times commented on this development with more of the masterly shiftiness with which, in other times, it had combined democratic

*See earlier, pages 70–73.

rectitude with appeasement of authoritarian régimes. 'It cannot be expected,' it wrote, 'that a parliamentary system of western freedom and flexibility should spring fully formed from this foundation, that in these turbulent conditions of national rebirth such a system would be workable. . . . It can however be expected that every effort be made to honour the engagements which have been made to establish more liberal systems, stage by stage. . . . Immediate vituperation of the kind contained in King Peter's statement cannot conceivably do anything but harm.' There had been no such words in the Tito-Subasitch agreement as 'stage by stage'. The leader ended with an exhortation to remember that politics was the art of the possible and to 'avoid the perfectionist snare which entraps the best intentions.'

On the 11th October, in case anyone should be wondering what had happened to Subasitch himself, nominally Yugoslavia's Foreign Minister, it was reported that he was resigning, as was Sutej, another of the three royalist Ministers who had joined Tito as part of the agreement. There was some talk of Subasitch in any case being in poor health. Two days later the Press Attaché of the Yugoslav Embassy in London simplified matters by announcing that all three members of the London Government who had signed the Tito-Subasitch agreement had 'left the Government'. Tito himself expressed 'astonishment' at Subasitch's resignation in view of earlier statements on his part that the agreement was being carried out. He said his resignation was part of a calculated campaign on the part of reactionaries at home and enemies abroad on the eve of the forthcoming elections, to prevent those elections from being held.

Tito, as a result of his wartime campaign against the Germans and the accompanying political organisation of the country by local committees enjoyed genuinely wide popular support in Yugoslavia. He was in the odd position for a dictator of being able to afford elections almost as free as the most enlightened western liberal might require and certainly free enough to give the convincing impression that they were in fact just that. Members of other political parties than the Communist were already included in the National Liberation Front's list of candidates. But Tito could afford something better than this traditional Communist façade of democracy. Paradoxically, his apparent willingness to allow a genuine Opposition ran up against that Opposition's decision to boycott the election. It was, its leaders maintained, subject to intimidation and other unacceptable pressures and it therefore refused to put up candidates.

One such Opposition leader was Dr Milan Grol, the third Minister from London to sign the Tito-Subasitch agreement on behalf of the King. He was now editing the opposition paper *Demokratiya* and conducting in it an uninhibited campaign of criticism against Tito's régime. Doing something to substantiate the Opposition charges, Tito banned Grol's paper in the week before the elections. But the Opposition's boycott campaign was in turn thwarted by Tito's own decision to insist on the presence of special ballot boxes for an Opposition vote in every polling station.

The method of voting was by taking a rubber ball and placing the hand which held it into the National Liberation Front box and an Opposition box in turn. (There were two of the former to one of the latter in the voting for the Assembly.) The final results when published on the 23rd November revealed, as no one had doubted they would, a triumph for Tito's National Liberation Front. 88% of the electorate had voted and 90% of them for the National Liberation Front. The percentage of Opposition votes was marginally higher in the towns, amounting to some 15% of those cast in Belgrade. A British Parliamentary Mission which had been in Yugoslavia to observe the elections was reasonably satisfied with what had passed. They reported that they had heard much talk from the Opposition of terror and intimidation but 'all we could be sure of was that there was a certain uneasiness, and that even where guarantees for freedom of speech and liberty of the person exist on paper, Yugoslav opinion today has other standards of fair play and tolerance than those sustaining in this country.'

They added that there was no practical alternative to the present régime and that therefore it should be accepted and encouraged. A British Government statement was issued shortly afterwards, saying that while some aspects of the elections had not been satisfactory the British Government regarded them in the main as reflecting the popular will and recognised the Constituent Assembly of Yugoslavia as an elected body with sovereign rights.

*

It was of course the 'free and unfettered elections by secret ballot' in Poland that were the most acute concern of the British and American Governments. Ernest Bevin, Britain's new Foreign Secretary, had told the House of Commons in August that at Potsdam he and Attlee had met the Polish representatives there three times and had been assured that the elections would be free, secret and held as early as possible and in no case later than early 1946. The right of the world's press to cover the elections uncensored was equally accepted and it was stressed that the Provisional Government expected all the main Polish democratic parties to take part in them with full liberty to make their own programmes and maintain freedom of expression. Bevin said he had enquired of Stalin if the Russian troops were going to be withdrawn and was assured by him that they would be with the exception of the small number required to maintain communications with the Red Army in Germany. On another matter Bevin sounded less comfortable. He said that there was also the question of the prisons and the security police in Poland, and that that still needed to be 'cleared-up'.

Anthony Eden, the former Foreign Secretary, said that when he had seen the Poles on the night before leaving the Potsdam Conference, to which he did not return, he had not been happy about the position of the post-war parties in Poland and he hoped that the Government would do everything it could to ensure that they had a fair and free chance in the elections.

But the end of the year came and there were no elections in Poland.* Hector MacNeill, Labour's Under-Secretary of State for Foreign Affairs, told the House of Commons in December that Molotov had said that all Russian troops had now been withdrawn except those needed to maintain the lines of communication with Germany. But, MacNeill said, the Government had no wish unduly to hasten the elections as there were still many Poles abroad. He added, as if somehow this were a detached problem, that there were concentration camps in Poland and that the prisoners in them were mainly there for political reasons.

*

In Greece, for which since the bloodshed at the beginning of the year, it had been Britain's particular concern and responsibility to try and foster some satisfactory political evolution, there was little sign of one. The Varkiza Agreement of January between the Government and the ELAS (mainly Communist) forces still held but was already looking strained. Tensions within the Government itself had led to a succession of Prime Ministers with, in October, the Regent himself, Archbishop Damaskinos finding it necessary to take on the Premier's rôle. Both the promised plebiscite on the monarchy and the due elections had to be postponed. Damaskinos' attempt to form a suitable caretaker Government while the stated aim of 'a representative Government on the broadest national basis' was further pursued, itself collapsed. He resigned, even as Regent, in the middle of November, though he was soon afterwards persuaded to resume the last rôle. A disconerting shape to the future was outlined by a statement from the left-wing opposition coalition EAM (the political parent of ELAS) which called on its supporters 'to continue the struggle for recognition of the resistance

*The Polish elections were held in January, 1947.

341

movement and for a general amnesty for the resistance fighters, and for the formation of a truly representative Government.'

There were no elections in Greece by the end of the year either.

*

Within the general framework of concern for relations between the three great Powers, other countries were becoming more and more absorbed by the national problems with which the war had left them. Britain, after the General Election in July, had already embarked on a new political course, but the economic effects of the war struck her nine days after VJ Day.

On the 24th August President Truman announced abruptly the ending of Lend-Lease – the arrangement by which Britain had received material aid from the States which she did not have to pay for at once or could return later. This had enabled her to adapt her industry to the war effort instead of having to earn cash by an export trade. Reconversion of industry, dependent in any case on demobilisation of manpower, could not be immediate. The only alternative to extreme austerity, harsher than anything yet experienced in wartime, seemed to be the negotiation of some new dollar-credit arrangement for the purposes of which the Labour Government at once sent Maynard Keynes to Washington.

After twelve weeks an agreement was reached by which Britain could draw for the next six years on a loan of 3,750 million dollars with interest at 2%, the capital being repaid in 50 annual instalments beginning on the 31st November, 1951. (It could be repaid earlier if Britain could manage this.) Other terms were that Britain should accept the Bretton Woods plan for an International Monetary Fund and restore sterling convertibility in the sterling area within twelve months.

These conditions were thought harsh in Britain and though Churchill (he had called Lend-Lease 'the most unsordid act in history') agreed that there was no alternative but to accept them, he thought the Government should have got better terms and he led the Conservative Opposition to abstain on the vote in the House of Commons. But 71 Conservatives voted against the loan and 23 Labour Members opposed their own Government. The Conservative Robert Boothby described it as 'an economic Munich', while *The Times* called it 'an economic Dunkirk'.

The loan agreement was seen by the Left in Britain, in the words of the *New Statesman*, as a 'devastating appeasement of American capitalism'. In the States it was seen as a progressive move, opening up trade and supplying a mechanism for repayment of Britain's Lend-Lease obligations so that relations between the two countries would not be bedevilled by war debts as after 1918. The average Briton was left with the feeling that he could now have a reasonably happy Christmas.

In the States, by American standards, Christmas was to be a restricted affair. It was epitomised by a cartoon which Clifton Utley described on the BBC: a crowd of women round a department-store counter towards which yet another woman was advancing, purse in hand, calling out: 'What are they selling, how much does it cost, and how many to a customer?'

Neither nylons, radios nor vacuum cleaners were readily available; men's and children's clothing was 'scarce', and there were only 50,000 new cars for the whole nation. But compared with Britain, where clothing was still severely rationed, the American scene was, as Utley said, one of 'sheer abundance'. King George VI did not need to tell his people on Christmas Day that: 'We all have to make a little go a long way.' But he did well to remind them that they, in their turn, were lucky. 'In the liberated countries,' he said, 'millions will spend this Christmas under terribly hard conditions, with only the bare necessities of life.'

*

In France peace had still brought little economic relief and there were few material comforts without resort to the black market. Political evolution however had not been so painful. An overwhelmingly positive vote, on a referendum had, with General de Gaulle's approval, ushered in a new Republican Constitution. The resulting Constituent Assembly had unanimously elected de Gaulle as Head of the Provisional Government.

A national trauma less easily dissolved than the Third Republic had also, after a fashion, been dealt with. Pétain himself had at last gone on trial in July, in proceedings which had not always been as dignified as the occasion seemed to demand. The jury was composed half of former Resistance members and half of former politicians of the Third Republic. The five men in scarlet robes who sat in judgement on Pétain had all in their time sworn loyalty to him as Head of the State. The Prosecutor himself admitted that he too would have done so had he not been made exempt by his retirement in 1939. He blandly explained that he would have done this because it was not, in the summer of 1940, clear that Pétain would betray the nation's trust as, he alleged, he was later to do. The trial made clear how confused even the most patriotic Frenchman had sometimes been at that time, and it was thus not easy wholly to remove from the Marshal the attribute of patriotism, as many would have liked to be able to do.

343

Evidence from a former Prefect named Donati probably illustrated Pétain's dilemma accurately. He said Pétain had once told him that in childhood he had been taught the maxim: 'When two paths, each seeming to present the path of duty, present themselves, always choose the harder.' When, however, this witness went on to call Pétain's trial a political error of the first magnitude there were howls of anger from the jury. The Vichy Ambassador to the Germans, de Brinon, put what was substantially the same point more acceptably when he said that de Gaulle had ensured France's interests in the event of a British victory, Pétain in the event of a German one. Evidence from Admiral Leahy, the American Ambassador to Vichy in 1941 and the early part of 1942 made much the same point. Leahy said he could not believe that Pétain had had any other motive than concern for the welfare and protection of the helpless people of France in the circumstances of defeat. And what seemed to emerge from the trial was that Pétain had thought that, by openly collaborating with the Germans, he could best serve the eventual interests of France and protect the French people who were in his care.

There was some evidence that particularly in the earlier years he had occasionally been able to use his good standing with the Germans to save lives and protect individuals. But what also emerged, not only from the trial but from the historical facts of the Occupation, was that he had become so overwhelmed by the situation in which he found himself that he had increasingly had to concur with what was happening.

A distinction was made between Pétain's attitude and that of his Foreign Minister Laval, whom in the early days of the Unoccupied Zone, he had for a time arrested. But the thinness to which that distinction eventually dwindled was revealed by evidence about a broadcast which Laval had made in 1943. It was a strongly pro-German broadcast and actually contained the statement that he hoped for a German victory. Pétain, who had been shown the script beforehand, had said that he thought that particular sentence ought to be removed. Laval had broadcast it without alteration and Pétain had afterwards been heard to observe that he 'thought that had been taken out.'

The trial, in the stifling heat of the courtroom that Parisian summer, had considerable historical interest. Politicians of the Third Republic, including three Prime Ministers, gave their accounts of the historic days of 1940: Paul Reynaud, self-possessed and voluble; Daladier, tired, aged and awkward, describing himself as 'a University lecturer'; Léon Blum, the Socialist, who had shared German captivity with them, describing Pétain as 'the man with the greatest prestige in France

344

[who] had been prepared to tell the people that dishonourable conduct was honourable.'

It had also had grotesque aspects, sometimes comic, sometimes moving. Pétain himself, aged 89, refused to speak except through his Defence Counsel and sat in the dock with a secretive, hard and contemptuous expression, clasping and unclasping his freckled hands in nervous impatience, sometimes appearing not to hear at all what was being said, at other times listening closely. After General Weygand had given evidence Pétain got up suddenly, to the evident dismay of his Counsel, and paid tribute to Weygand, regretting that he had been unable to follow all he had said, owing to deafness. *The Times* reported that a hush of astonishment fell on the court as if the dead had spoken.

When the blind old General de Lanuren gave evidence and closed with an appeal to the jury to beware lest in condemning Pétain they increased dissension and bloodshed in France, almost the entire court except for the judge and the jury burst into applause. Pétain again rose, to thank de Lanuren and to say that he had had no idea that he had been coming to give evidence. As he spoke he moved forward and clasped the blind man's arm. Each was then led separately away.

There could be little doubt what the verdict and sentence would be. The Prosecutor had asked for the death sentence, and death for a man who had presided over the destinies of France while its traditional enemy had shot in cold blood 150,000 Frenchmen, deported 110,000 to Germany and removed 120,000 French Jews of whom only 1,500 had returned, seemed the only appropriate sentence in the circumstances.

Both jury and judges had received many threatening letters from Pétain's supporters. One such ran: 'Beware! I am sitting not far from you in court.' The jury was out for six hours but just before 4 o'clock on the morning of the 14th August, the day on which the Second World War came to an end, they found Pétain guilty of treason, adding a recommendation to mercy on account of his age. He was duly sentenced to death and soon afterwards, as everyone had expected, had his sentence commuted by General de Gaulle to life imprisonment.

For Laval himself there could be no mercy. After almost succeeding in escaping the ignominy of execution by taking poison on the day allotted, he was rushed to hospital and sufficiently restored to be shot at the stake as a traitor. Also executed by firing squad the same week was Joseph Darnand, who had been in charge of the Vichy Milice and State Secretary for Security in the last year of Pétain's rule. The disturbingly complex nature of the experience which France had been through in the past four years rose again to the surface as he cried, when the order to fire was given: 'Vive la France!'

*

345

Similar trials were taking place all over Europe, part ceremonies of justice, part formal acts of revenge, but all an attempt somehow to come to terms with the enormities of the immediate past which in fact could never be exorcised, and with injustices for which no justice could ever be adequate. In the Balkans the scale of retribution was in conformity with tradition. In Bulgaria for example, earlier in the year it was estimated that as many as 2,000 prominent supporters of King Boris had been executed together with the three Regents and a far larger number of humbler functionaries of the old régime in the countryside.

In Yugoslavia too it was quite impossible to assess the extent of the revenge taken against those Serb Chetniks who in their anti-communism had sometimes negotiated truces with occupying forces in order to fight Tito's partisans.

Western European countries dealt with their own versions of the trauma of occupation in similar manner to France. Many of those accused and at first imprisoned for collaboration were eventually released. But here too, for the worst offenders, and there had been terrible offences in all occupied countries, death seemed the only appropriate measure. Obliteration of the past was what was needed; and since that was impossible obliteration of some of those who had shaped it was the next best thing.

In Denmark, where the death penalty had long ago been abolished, it had to be re-introduced, though of the three death sentences passed only one was carried out by the end of the year. In Norway the archetypal collaborator, Quisling, was given a meticulous trial, in the course of which, taken at one point to the scene of executions carried out under his own régime, he had expected to be shot there and then. The correct process was nevertheless completed and after his appeal against the death sentence had been turned down, he was executed on October 24th.

In Holland, where at one time over 90,000 people had been imprisoned for collaboration, the Dutch Nazi Anton Mussert was condemned to death on December 12th, to be executed in the New Year.

In Belgium, where there was sufficient debate over King Leopold's contacts with the Germans to prevent his return to the country but insufficient to make him abdicate, some 2,000 death sentences were passed.

In Czechoslovakia the German Mayor of Prague was hanged in public in September.

Even in Britain, which except for the Channel Islands, had never been exposed to the dangers of collaboration, there were two traitors to be hanged. Their executions were more a sort of tribute to their own flawed personalities than testimony to any danger they had constituted to the State. William Joyce, 'Lord Haw-Haw', now recovered from the bullet-wound in his thigh, was held to owe allegiance to the King by reason of his British passport, though in the course of the war he had become a naturalised German, being awarded the Kriegsverdien-stkreuz by Hitler. His needling broadcasts from Germany were dignified with the name of High Treason and he was appropriately condemned in December. John Amery, son of Leo Amery who had been Secretary of State for India in Churchill's Government, was revealed as a rather feckless personality crossed with a certain warped idealism. In the name of British patriotism he had tried to raise a force among British prisoners-of-war to fight on the Eastern Front. He gave what seemed a meticulous and sincere account of his wartime movements and motives in the preliminary judicial hearing, after pleading 'Not Guilty'. But he changed his plea to 'Guilty' at his trial, recognising presumably that in the climate of the time and after such a war there was only one penalty for having got things so wrong.

On the other side of the world Britain was involved, in India, in a trial of 300 traitors around whom was to centre much of the Indian nationalist emotion now itself liberated from the conflicting loyalties of wartime. These were members of the Indian National Army organised by the Nationalist Subhas Chandra Bose, from among Indian prisoners-of-war of the Japanese, to fight in turn on the Japanese side for Indian independence.* Some 20,000 Indian soldiers had joined altogether, though the great majority of the Indian Army prisoners had remained true to the Raj in spite of cruel pressure put on them by the Japanese. The 300 on trial were those alleged to have collaborated most willingly, often to the extent of maltreating their former comrades.

What made the trial more significant than a mere strict issue of military discipline was the prevailing nationalistic mood in which India, though anti-Japanese, had emerged from the war. Her politicians were impatient to move fast towards that self-government to which the British had long been saying they were prepared to lead her, and to turn that self-government into outright independence disregarding British reluctance to proceed without first resolving Hindu and Muslim differences. Chief Counsel for the Defence of the 300 INA soldiers on trial was a man who had not practised law for some thirty years but was a leading figure of the All-India Congress Party, Pandit Jawaharl Nehru.

*

*Bose himself died in an air crash before the Japanese surrender.

Another trial, harrowing and meticulously laborious, was being conducted in Germany under British auspices: that of the Commandant of Belsen concentration camp, Kramer, and 44 of the SS guards there. Most of the accused, including Kramer himself, had been active in Auschwitz before the Russian advance in January. It was at this Belsen trial that the first fully-authenticated details of what had happened in Auschwitz became painfully available to the general public. Kramer himself and ten of the guards, including a notoriously sadistic woman guard Irma Grese, were hanged after a trial lasting many weeks and nineteen guards were sentenced to terms of imprisonment, varying from one year to life.

On the 20th November, twenty-four of the leading political, military, naval and diplomatic leaders of the Third Reich, including Goering, Hess, Generals Jodl and Keitel and Admiral Dönitz were put on trial at Nuremberg. The tribunal consisted of British, French, Russian and American judges. It provided at least some reassurance that the three major Powers could co-operate successfully in a Germany which was otherwise becoming split into an Eastern (Russian Zone) Germany and a Western (British, American and French Zone) Germany.

In this new Germany, while the Allies both collectively and individually sought to punish those responsible for the horrors of the recent past where they could find them (and many like Himmler escaped through suicide or, with successfully-concealed identities, down escape routes to South America), new horrors of a man-made sort, overshadowed only by the details of German cruelty revealed at the various trials, were being inflicted on the Germans themselves. Those who suffered were mainly women and children expelled, often at a moment's notice and in circumstances of considerable harshness from the Sudeten areas of Czechoslovakia and that former part of Germany east of the Oder-Neisse Line into which the Poles were moving in compensation for their own territories lost to Russia in the east.

The Potsdam Agreement had stipulated that such expulsions should be carried out 'humanely'. But already so many had taken place in conditions to which that term could hardly be applied that the sort of control once envisaged remained theoretical. In the Sudeten territories from which all expulsions had not yet taken place, the Czechs had deprived Germans of most of the normal rights of citizens, placed them on lower rations and compelled them to wear yellow armbands to signify their race, rather as the Germans had once made Jews wear the Star of David.

No one knew how many people were on the move in Europe; their numbers were far too great to be assessed accurately. Those expelled from Czechoslovakia and Poland were perhaps as many as seven million. In addition, millions of slave workers and prisoners of war were making their way home. Germans were moving voluntarily from the Russian zone to the West. The total was thought to be somewhere between twelve and fourteen million – one of the greatest mass population movements in history.

Among those not moving, but wanting to do so, were those former wearers of the Star of David who had managed to survive the extermination camps. Many still lived on the sites of such camps and among the people whose doctrine had thought it reasonable to exterminate them.

A British Government had once proposed Palestine as a 'national home' for Jews. This now seemed the desirable alternative to their predicament since no country, including the United States, was prepared to ease its immigration restrictions to admit them in any numbers. But Britain, operating a Palestine Mandate conferred on it by the old League of Nations, felt compelled to enforce restrictions on Jewish immigration there to fulfil the Mandate's obligation to the Arab population. The immigration quota was still 15,000 a year as it had been since the Palestine White Paper of 1939. But since 1939 the greatest racial tragedy in history had overwhelmed the Jewish people. In August President Truman wrote to Attlee asking him to admit 100,000 Jewish immigrants to Palestine immediately. Attlee was unable to comply.

There had been no change of attitude to Jewish immigration on the part of the Arab population of Palestine who, with some logic, asked why their social, cultural and economic heritage should be imperilled to pay for Europe's crimes. Responsibility for resolving this seemingly unresolvable crisis rested with the British Government. In the circumstances, it could find little to do but enforce what it saw as the provisions of the Mandate. These became increasingly unenforceable as Zionist activists devoted their energies to the transport of illegal immigrants into Palestine. Terrorist extremists, disowned by moderates who shared the same Zionist cause, carried out their own actions with increasing effect. Violence in Tel Aviv and Jerusalem towards the end of the year, as Britain continued to refuse President Truman's request presaged a darkening future. In Palestine as in India, Britain, encumbered with redundant obligations from another era was embarked on a painful process of re-adjustment which would eventually leave her no alternative but to abandon such obligations altogether.

In other parts of the world which were no direct concern of hers but in which she was circumstantially involved while the superannuating forces of history were at work, she became entangled in other painful anomalies. To maintain order against nationalist elements in parts of

349

Indo-China, pending the return of French administration, Japanese troops had occasionally to be used; in the former Dutch East Indies, again with a responsibility to maintain order, Britain found herself in bloody engagements with Indonesian nationalists fighting with weapons they had obtained from the Japanese.

*

It was a restless peace. Over all the many widespread individual problems with which the world was confronted, the uneasy question mark about the future relations of the three Big Powers who had won it continued to be raised.

'Russia – is it hopeless?' was a phrase which Alexander Werth, who had been reporting the war from Moscow, heard uttered often in London in the autumn of 1945. He said that in the five months since VE Day people seemed to have forgotten everything Russia did during the war, and were almost accepting that she was the inevitable aggressor of the near future. The breakdown of the London Conference, in which the Russians had certainly been unpredictably and enigmatically difficult, was mainly responsible for this feeling. But Werth put the Russian attitude there largely down to the psychological blow which they had been dealt by the Americans' possession and deployment of the atomic bomb while showing small willingness to share its secrets. At the same time, on the question of whether the Russians wanted war, Werth stated categorically that what she both needed and hoped for was fifty years of peace.

At the end of October President Truman, whose immediate importance on the Three Power scene was that he was not President Roosevelt but a man from the Middle-West with no particular Liberal sympathy for what might seem best in Russian ideology, made what was officially described as his most important speech on United States' international policy since taking office. In it he gave his own answer to the question which Werth had heard so often in London and which was being asked just as cogently in the United States about what one British correspondent there called 'the steady and ominous downward spiral in Big Three relations since the Potsdam Conference.'

'Differences of the kind existing today,' said Truman, 'among nations that fought together for so long and so valiantly for victory are not hopeless or irreconcilable.' At the same time he stated firmly, 'We shall approve no territorial changes in any friendly part of the world unless they accord with the freely-expressed wishes of the people concerned.' He said there was an urgency now about the situation which no one would have dreamed of six months before: 'The atomic bomb does not alter the basic foreign policy of the United States. It means that we

350

A
lasting
peace?

must be prepared to approach international problems with greater speed, with greater determination, and with greater ingenuity, in order to meet a situation for which there is no precedent . . .'

A free exchange of scientific information would take place with Great Britain, Canada and 'later with other nations' but, Truman emphasised, such discussions would not concern the processes of manufacturing the bomb. 'The possession in our hands of this new power of destruction,' he said, 'we regard as a sacred trust. Because of our love of peace the thoughtful people of the world know that that trust will not be violated, but it will be faithfully executed. Indeed, the highest hope of the American peoples is that world co-operation for peace will soon reach such a state of perfection that atomic methods of destruction can be definitely and effectively outlawed for ever.'

Such expressions of the highest aspiration, as in Roosevelt's time before the atomic bomb had added its particular note of urgency, had somehow always to be brought into line with awkward realities without losing the substance of the vision. The first Assembly of the United Nations Organisation was due to meet in London in January 1946 and it was essential that once again appearances should be made to conform as far as possible with the highest hopes. The Council of Foreign Ministers was re-convened.

It met in Moscow on December 15th. Its deliberations were anticipated with some trepidation. If what the London *Sunday Times* called the serious cleavage between Russia and the other Allied Powers in the past two and a half months was not somehow mended, the whole United Nations Organisation might well be threatened with collapse. 'To avert such an immense calamity,' it wrote, 'something had to be done.' It was an appropriate time of year for such a meeting. At Christmas itself, Bevin, Byrnes and Molotov were able to report that goodwill had prevailed.

Once again it was agreed that draft treaties for Italy, Rumania, Bulgaria, Hungary and Finland should be prepared. Agreement was reached on a resolution to establish a Commission on Atomic Energy, to be put to the General Assembly of the United Nations.

An additional grievance was met by the American concession to allow in Japan, hitherto administered by the United States single-handed, some system of joint Allied control similar to that which existed in Germany.

But what of the matter which had caused the final breakdown at the London Conference: the régimes in Rumania and Bulgaria which the United States and Britain found too undemocratic to recognise?

This awkward problem was solved by the appointment of two extra Ministers in both Rumania and Bulgaria who were to join the existing unrepresentative Governments to make them representative. They were to be nominated and pledged to 'work loyally with the Government.' It was impossible, in the circumstances of Russian occupation of the two countries, not to see this as a mere token gesture. However, the fear of another London-type breakdown was paramount. Without waiting to see whether the assurances of the new 'more representative' Governments about the holding of free elections and the maintenance of the freedoms of democracy were met, both Britain and America gave their recognition to them. The worst had been averted.

James Byrnes, the US Secretary of State said it was 'a constructive Conference. Relations were established which should make decisions easier on other matters in the future.' Ernest Bevin's tone was more cautious. 'I do not believe,' he said, 'in creating in the public mind the impression that one Conference has solved all problems. . . . It achieved what was humanly possible under present circumstances, and its actual significance depends on implementation of the agreements reached.'

It was difficult not to remember Yalta and Potsdam and to understand the need for his caution. But at least it could not be denied that, in harmony with the spirit of the season, sounds of goodwill were in the air. The diplomatic correspondent of the London *Sunday Times* was able to write, 'The Old Year ends on a note of optimism.'

It was difficult to remember the gloom with which the year had started. The Allies had still been suffering from the shock of the German Ardennes offensive. There had been peevish bickering between Britain and the United States. There was dulled realisation that the German war was far from won, and that victory over Japan was still more remote. At least now in Western Europe and in the United States people could turn to their predictions for the coming year in a happier frame of mind than twelve months before.

The British journalist Hannen Swaffer, writing in the *Daily Herald* twelve months before had commented on forecasts that were being made for 1945. Clever Bernard Shaw had said: 'Even I do not know what is going to happen in 1945.' But Swaffer then recounted something he had heard from a five year old boy over the New Year. 'A big bomb will bring down all the earth,' the child had said. 'It will bring down God!'

Now, towards the end of that year, it had been possible to read in the newspapers the following account from an American member of the air crew which had dropped a bomb on Nagasaki:

'Awestruck, we watched the pillar of fire shoot upward like a meteor coming from the earth instead of from outer space, and becoming ever more alive as it climbed skyward through the white clouds. It was no longer smoke or dust or even a cloud of fire, it was a living thing, a new species of being, born right before our incredulous eyes. At one stage of its evolution, covering millions of years in terms of seconds, the entity assumed the form of a giant square totem-pole, which at its base was about three miles long, tapering off to a mile at the top. Its bottom was brown, its center was ember, its top white, but it was a living totem-pole, carved with many grotesque masks grimacing at the earth. Then just when it appeared as though the whole thing had settled down into a state of permanence, there came shooting out of the top a giant mushroom that increased the height of the pillar to a total of 45,000 feet. The mushroom top was even more alive than the pillar, seething and boiling in a white fury of creamy foam, sizzling upwards and then descending earthward. . . . It kept struggling in an elemental fury like a creature in the act of breaking the bonds that held it down. In a few seconds it had freed itself from its gigantic stem and floated upwards with tremendous speed, its momentum carrying it into the stratosphere to a height of about 60,000 feet. But no sooner did this happen than another mushroom, smaller in size than the first one, began emerging out of the pillar. It was as though a decapitated monster was growing a new head.'

*

In his 1945 Christmas Day broadcast King George VI addressed himself particularly to the young, and spoke of the fine spirit of service they had devoted to destruction of the country's enemies. He went on: 'You have known the world only as a world of strife and fear. Bring now all that fine spirit to make it one of joyous adventure, a home where men and women can live in mutual trust and walk together as friends. Do not judge life by what you have seen of it in the grimness and waste of war, nor yet by the confusion of the first years of peace. Have faith in life at its best and bring it your courage, your hopes and your sense of humour. . . . Let us face the future with hope . . .'

British dead were officially: 296,521 soldiers, seamen and airmen, and 60,585 civilians killed in air raids; total British Empire dead: 466,035. American dead were 396,637. Of their allies, some 20,000,000 Russians had been killed; among others, 1,685,000 Yugoslavs. For the enemy the estimates of dead were 3,000,000 German soldiers, seamen and airmen, and 350,000 civilians killed in air raids; 1,219,000 Japanese.

Four months after the end of such a war the hope was above all for peace. Forty years later in a reality in which the vision of the airman above Nagasaki and that of the monarch in his study had still to be reconciled, the hope was still for peace.

Illustrations

Acknowledgement is made to the following:

The trustees of the Imperial War Museum, London
(p. 3, p. 7 (*top*), p. 45, p. 51, p. 65, p. 119, p. 181, p. 185 (*bottom*), p. 191, p. 215 (*top*), p. 241, p. 243 (*bottom*), p. 307, p. 311 (*bottom*))

BBC Hulton Picture Library
(*frontispiece*, p. 7 (*bottom*), p. 9, p. 11, p. 15, p. 35 (*top*), p. 41, p. 263, p. 267, p. 269, p. 313)

Topham Picture Library
(p. 141, p. 145, p. 147, p. 215 (*bottom*), p. 309 (*top*), p. 317)

Novosti Press Agency
(p. 5, p. 221, p. 223, p. 229, p. 231)

Punch
(p. 17, p. 53, p. 87, p. 259, p. 293)

Photo Source
(p. 35 *(bottom)*, p. 93, p. 185 (*top*), p. 189)

Associated Press
(p. 161)

Camera Press
(p. 351)

Barratts
(p. 243 (*top*))

While every effort has been made, it has not been possible to locate the copyright-holder for the illustration on p. 13.

Index

Evening Standard, 242

Fabian, Dr. Bela, 243–4
Fairhall, Lawrence, 183
Falaise gap, battle of (1944), 52
Ferebee, Major Thomas, and dropping
   of atom bomb, 321
Ferguson, Senator, 219
Finland, 78, 94, 352
Fish, Representative Hamilton, 57, 106
Flensburg, continuation of Dönitz's
   Government at, 298–9
Flying Fortresses and Super-Fortresses,
   150, 178, 180, 183, 213, 319–21, 327
Foot, Michael, 261, 287; on Poland, 115
Foreign Ministers, Council of: set up at
   Potsdam, 309; failure of London
   meeting, 350–3; reconvened in
   Moscow, 352
Forster, Gauleiter of Danzig, 96
Foxwell, Albert, 195
France, 122, 125, 167, 309, 343–4, 345;
   the Resistance, 16, 21, 162, 164,
   343; and the United Nations, 125,
   165; purge of collaborators,
   159–60, 162–4; lynch law, 159;
   official trials, 159, 160; black
   market, 165–7, 343; shortages,
   165–7; attitudes to the Allies, 167–8;
   Franco–Russian treaty, 167;
   Communists, 168; plebiscite, 343;
   Constituent Assembly, 343; trial of
   Pétain, 343–4, 345
   See also French Army
Franco, General Francisco, 82, 310
Franc-Tireur, 163
Frank, Hans, 227
Frederick Leopold of Prussia, Prince, in
   Dachau, 252
Freeman, Major John, 330
French Army: battle for Alsace, 176;
   drive into Germany, 203; fighting on
   Atlantic Coast, 213
Friedeburg, Admiral, 230, 298
Fritzsche, Hans, 82, 211
Funk, Walther, 92

Gaillard-Bancel, collaborator, 160
Gallacher, Willie, 64
Gamelin, General Maurice, 237
Gardelegen concentration camp, 244,
   246, 250

Gasperi, Alcide de, 23
Gavin, Representative, 27
General Election: prospect of, 193–4;
   fixed for July 5, 258, 260;
   beginning of campaign, 262;
   standpoints of the Press, 266, 268;
   nightly political broadcasts, 268,
   276; the Laski controversy, 270–5;
   progress of the campaign, 275–7;
   overseas service votes, 276, 288;
   opinion polls, 276, 287; polling,
   287–9; labour victory, 309
Geneva Convention on prisoners of war,
   244
George VI, King, 320; and victory in
   Europe, 2, 12; VE Day, 4, 6, 8; VJ
   Day, 329; Christmas Day
   broadcast, 343, 353
German Army: First Parachute Army,
   183; Fifteenth Army, 183; 15th
   Panzer Division, 214; 17th SS
   Infantry Division, 213; battle of
   the Ardennes, 18, 27, 28, 30, 33,
   40, 44, 46, 48–50, 85–6, 88, 96,
   134, 153, 254; and the Russian
   advance, 81–3, 85, 95, 96; resistance
   and counter-attacks in Italy,
   170–1; defence on eastern front,
   176; fighting near Swiss border,
   176; battle for Alsace, 176; on
   Dutch-German border, 177;
   counter-attacks in Rhineland,
   183; and the Rhine crossing, 186–8;
   High Command loses effective
   control, 188; pockets of resistance,
   206–10, 213–14, 216, 219; anxiety to
   surrender to British and
   Americans, 208; central front breaks
   up, 208; resistance on Atlantic
   Coast, 213; surrender to
   Montgomery at Luneburg Heath,
   230; surrender to Eisenhower at
   Rheims, 232–3
Germany: 'New Order', 16, 80; and
   unconditional surrender policy,
   43, 94–5, 98; resilience of war
   production, 48; atrocities in
   Poland and Estonia, 80–1; morale,
   85–6, 88–90, 92, 94, 96–100;
   Hitler's speeches in January,
   88–92, 97–9; evocation of
   fanaticism, 96, 99–100; and Yalta,

Germany – *cont.*
    123, 126; ruthlessness in Holland, 172
  attempts to sustain morale, 188–90,
    192, 206, 211; and Roosevelt's
    death, 217–18; total collapse of
    defence system, 228; refugees from
    the Russians, 228, 230–2; transfer
    of remaining occupied territory,
    233–5; capture of prominent
    individuals, 236–7; concentration
    camps, 233–5; treatment of
    prisoners of war, 243–4, 246–7; and
    Potsdam Conference, 306, 309–10;
    casualty figures, 16, 18, 354
GI brides, 37
Gibson, Wing-Commander Guy, 153
Gillard, Frank, 210
Goebbels, Josef, 82, 86, 92, 96, 97, 99,
    100, 190, 211; broadcast to German
    people (Jan 5), 86; and Roosevelt's
    death, 217–18; death, 236
Goering, Hermann, 227n., 262;
    surrenders, 235, 299; tried at
    Nuremberg, 348
Goldstein, Private Richard B., escape
    of, 154
Golikov, General, 303
Gollancz, Victor, 324
Gomulka, Wladyslaw, 111, 300
Good Housekeeping, 37
Graham, Captain Alan, in Yalta
    debate, 129
Graham, Frederick, 246, 247
Great Britain: and liberated countries,
    20, 22–6; reactions to US
    criticism, 29–30; rationing and
    shortages, 33–4, 38; incidence of
    crime, 39
  and Poland, 78, 115–16; misgivings
    about Soviet policy, 107;
    reactions to Yalta decisions, 121–2;
    Foreign Office and London Poles,
    124; Commons debate on Yalta,
    125–31; and Roosevelt's death,
    218; and the German surrender,
    1–2; victory in Europe, 2, 4, 6, 12;
    recognises new Polish
    Government, 304, 310; VJ Day,
    329–30; and ending of Lend-Lease,
    342; economic agreement with
    USA, 342; casualty figures, 16, 354
Greece, 57, 58, 61–4, 66–9, 88, 122, 130,

169, 341–2; struggle for control in
    Athens, 24–6, 43–4; EAM and
    ELAS, 24–6, 43, 44, 61–4, 66–9,
    341; British intervention, 25, 31,
    43–4, 63; truce and ELAS
    withdrawal, 44, 61, 62; evidence of
    ELAS atrocities, 62–4, 66–9;
    Varkiza agreement, 69, 341;
    British casualties, 341
Greenwood, Arthur, 128, 193, 199, 277
Grenfell, Captain Russell, RN, 319
Grese, Irma, hanged, 348
Grew, Joseph, 142–3, 144, 318
Griffiths, James, 270
Grigg, Sir James, 288
Gringoire, anti-British paper, 160, 162,
    163
Grol, Dr. Milan, 339–40
Gromyko, A. A., 295
Groza, Dr., Rumanian Communist
    leader, 337
Guadalcanal, 136

Hamburg, devastation in, 232
Hancock, Alexander, 285 and n., 309
Hanover, 209, 212, 251
Harmon, General Millard F., 138
Harper, Corporal John, awarded
    posthumous VC, 151–2
Harriman, Averell, 294
Harsch, Joseph, 59, 133, 325
Harz mountains, fighting in, 216
Hastings, Sir Patrick, 40
Hata, Field Marshal Shunroku, 334
Hayek, Friedrich August von, 265
Headlam, Sir Cuthbert, 196
Heine, Major General, 234, 235
Heroism, tales of, 149–53
Hess, Rudolf, 348
Het Parool, Dutch Resistance paper, 173
Hewitt, Gerald, 157–8
High, Stanley, 256
Himmler, Heinrich, 92, 208, 236, 238;
    prominence of, 86, 88; meetings
    with Count Bernadotte, 225, 227;
    offer of unconditional surrender,
    225; suicide, 249
Hirohito, Emperor of Japan, and the
    Japanese surrender, 326–8, 334;
    broadcast to his peoples, 333–4
Hiroshima, atom bomb on, 321–5, 331;
    casualties, 335

Hitler, Adolf, 88, 95, 97, 105, 132, 152,
  207, 213–14, 217, 224, 225, 227,
  234–6, 257, 296, 298, 299, 306, 330,
  347; long silence, 86, 88; speeches in
  January, 88–92, 97–9; his physical
  and psychological condition, 91–2,
  212; question of his whereabouts,
  211–12; Order to defend Berlin,
  216; announcement of his death,
  226–7
Hodges, General Courtney, 187, 220
Hogg, Quintin (Lord Hailsham), 200, 260
Holland, 172, 173–4, 212–13;
  German-occupied parts, 172, 173,
  174,212; shortages, 38, 172, 173,
  174; Resistance movement, 173;
  railway system on strike, 173;
  German dismantlement of
  economy, 173; continued German
  resistance, 212, 227, 298;
  punishment of collaborators, 346
Holtz, Karl, Gauleiter of Nuremberg,213
Homma, Japanese General, 139
Hoover, President Herbert C., 122–3
Hoover, J. Edgar, 36
Hopkins, Harry, 100, 103, 116, 297
Hore-Belisha, Leslie, 272
Horizon, 254
Horse-racing banned in USA, 33
Horthy, Admiral Nikolaus, 91
Houffalize, 50, 54
Hungary, 47, 351; seeks to withdraw
  from the war, 91, 92; transfer of
  German population, 310;
  attempted Russian intervention,
  336–7; elections, 337

India: trial of traitors, 345; Congress
  Party, 347
Indian Army, 347; Victoria Cross
  awards, 152
Indian National Army, 347
Indianapolis Star, 10
International Monetary Fund, 342
Iowa, USS, 315, 316
Italy, 57, 94–5, 169–72; Partisans, 16,
  222, 352; campaign, 19; Coalition
  Government, 23; Britain and
  Count Sforza, 23–4, 31;
  government freed from
  dependence on Allied
  Commission, 169; shortages, 169;

black market, 169; Mussolini's
  Fascist Republic, 170, 222;
  military stalemate, 170–1; trial of
  Fascists, 171–2
Allied breakthrough, 222, 225;
  crossing of the Po, 222; rising of
  Partisans, 222; Mussolini put to
  death, 222, 224; German surrender,
  226
Ivanov, General, 292, 294
Iwo Jima, fighting for and US capture
  of, 146, 315, 318

Japan, 6, 10, 12, 60–1, 95, 102, 103,
  132–3, 135, 136, 138–40, 142–4,
  146, 148, 220, 290, 291, 306, 334;
  in Philippines, 19, 136, 139, 140,
  142–4; in Burma, 16, 19, 136, 144;
  gains in China, 136, 138; US air
  attacks, 139, 146; US capture of
  Manila, 143, 146
atrocities in Burma and the
  Philippines, 154–7; prison camps,
  143, 154–5; and the
  Thailand–Burma railway, 155
Russia renounces Neutrality Pact,
  294–5; Potsdam Declaration, 308,
  312, 319, 326, 327, 331, 333; US
  capture of Okinawa and Iwo Jima,
  314, 315, 318; air raids on Tokyo
  and other cities, 314, 316, 318,
  320, 321; bombardment of coast by
  sea, 315–6, 318, 320; lack of
  Japanese resistance, 316; dropping
  of atom bombs, 321–26; Russia
  enters war against her, 325, 326;
  question of surrender, 326–8; the
  Emperor's prerogatives, 326–8;
  unconditional surrender, 328, 330,
  333–4; surrender in different
  theatres of war, 334–5; official
  surrender on *Missouri*, 335–6; joint
  Allied control, 352; casualty
  figures, 18, 354
Japanese Air Force, 316, 325
Japanese Navy, 144, 316
Je Suis Partout, pro-German paper, 162,
  164
Joad, C. E. M., 195; on concentration
  camps, 253–4
Jodl, General Alfred, 232–3, 298; tried
  at Nuremberg, 348

363

Macarthur, General Douglas, 19, 77, 136, 140, 142, 143, 152, 155, 320, 326, 334; landing in Lingayen Gulf, 142; capture of Manila, 143; receives official Japanese surrender, 335
Macarthy, George, 177
McAuliffe, Brigadier-General, 46
McCormac, John, 207, 246
McCormick, Anne O'Hare, 21, 100, 102, 305, 306
MacDermott, Frank, 319
MacIntyre, Dr. R. Scottish Nationalist MP, 200
McIntyre, Vice-Admiral Ross T., 216–17
Mackensen, Field-Marshal August von, 235–6
Mackenzie King, William, Canadian Prime Minister, 328
Macmillan, Harold, 273, 288; President of Allied Commission in Italy, 169
MacNeill, Hector, 341
Madariaga, Bishop Mariano, 156
Magdeburg, 208; German counter-attack, 213, 219
Maidanek concentration camp, 240
Mainz, 187
Malan, D. F., 122
Malaya, Japanese defiance of surrender order, 334
Malmedy, German shooting of US prisoners, 254–5
Malraux, André, 164
Manchester Guardian, 2, 4, 12, 31, 37, 44, 54, 71, 72, 77, 82, 91, 92, 94, 179, 195, 197, 227n., 265n., 266, 270–3, 286–9, 294, 299–300, 323, 324, 328; on Yalta Conference, 122
Manchuria, Red Army in, 327
Mandalay, captured by British, 144
Manila, captured by US, 143, 146, 155, 156
Manteuffel, General, 232
Mao Tse-Tung, 138, 335
Margaret, Princess, 6, 8
Marshall, General George C., 314
Marshall, Howard, 177
Martin, Dr. Clifford, Bishop of Liverpool, 194
Martin, Kingsley, 270, 291
Mauriac, François, 164; and the case of Henri Béraud, 160, 163
Maurras, Charles, charged with collaboration, 160; imprisoned, 164
Matthews, Herbert, 287
Messerschmidt fighters, 48, 210
Metaxas, General Yanni, 24
Meuse, River, 46, 85
Michael, King of Rumania, 337
Middleton, Drew, 203, 206
Midway, naval battle (1942), 136
Mihailovitch, General Drazha, 70
Mikolajczyk, Stanislav, 111, 113, 124, 292, 294, 296, 300, 301, 310
Milan, 222, 224
Millay, Edna St. Vincent, 105
Millington, Wing-Commander, elected for Chelmsford, 200–2
Milwaukee Journal, 10
Mindoro, 136, 139, 140
Minneapolis Star Journal, 256
Missouri, US battleship, scene of Japanese surrender, 335–6
Mohne Dam bombing, 153
Molotov, V. M., 71, 107, 130, 295, 300, 341, 352; and the San Francisco Conference, 295
Molotov, Mrs, 296
Montgomery, Field-Marshal Sir Bernard (Viscount), 177, 181–2, 214, 216; and the Ardennes battle, 48, 50; accepts German surrender, 230, 232
Moorehead, Alan, 48, 228, 254
Morley, Iris, 80–1, 240
Morrison, Herbert, 103–4, 193, 200, 262, 276, 281, 283, 284
Morrow, Lieutenant-Colonel (KRRC), 64
Mortimer, Raymond, 167, 168
Moscow, 122; and the German surrender, 2; in January 1945, 74, 79; Foreign Ministers' meeting, 351
Mosley, Leonard, 188
Mosquito aircraft, 178
Motherwell by-election, 200
Mountbatten, Admiral Lord Louis, 204, 308, 324, 325
München-Gladbach, 183
Munich, 225–6; US entry, 226
Murrow, Ed., 214, 248–9
Muselier, Admiral, 162–3

365

Williams, Francis, 291–2
Wills, Colin, 245
Wilmot, Chester, 232
Wilson, President Woodrow, 29, 98, 305
Wissembourg gap, German attacks in, 48, 54
Witos, Vincenty, 294, 296, 300, 301
Woodford constituency, 1945 Election, 285, 309
Wyceka, Polish politician, 301

Yalta Conference, 104, 105, 109, 110, 114, 117–18, 120–31, 176, 217, 291, 300, 302; conduct of the war, 118; occupation and control of Germany, 118, 120, 299; reparations, 120; the United Nations, 120, 304; liberated Europe, 120; Poland and Polish frontiers, 120–1, 294–7, 301, 308; Yugoslavia, 121; machinery for consultation, 121
reception of decisions, 121–4; House of Commons debate, 125–31;

Roosevelt's statement to Congress, 131–3
Yamashita, General, 140
Yoniuri Hochi, Japanese newspaper, 318
York and Lancaster Regiment, 151
Yorkshire Evening News, 34
Yorkshire Post, 29, 30
Yugoslavia, 70–3, 109, 121, 337–40; the Chetniks and Tito's Communist Partisans, 70; Tito-Subasitch agreement, 70–2, 109, 121, 338–40; reports of tyranny, 338; elections, 339–40; revenge against Chetniks, 346; casualty figures, 354

Zakowski, Julian, 300
Zenkl, Peter, former Mayor of Prague, in Buchenwald, 248
Zhukov, Marshal, 1, 77, 82, 83, 216, 304
Zimmerman, Kapitan-Leutnant Arnim, and surrender of Channel Islands, 234
Zionism, 349